Ordnance Survey

STREET ATLAS
Oxfordshire

Contents

PHILIP'S

First published 1992 by

George Philip Ltd, a division of
Octopus Publishing Group Ltd
2-4 Heron Quays, London E14 4JP

First colour edition 1998
Fourth impression 2001

ISBN 0-540-07512-4 (hardback)
ISBN 0-540-07513-2 (spiral)

© George Philip Ltd 1998

Digital Data

The exceptionally high-quality mapping
found in this book is available as digital
data in TIFF format, which is easily
convertible to other bit-mapped (raster)
image formats.

The index is also available in digital form
as a standard database table. It contains
all the details found in the printed index
together with the National Grid reference
for the map square in which each entry
is named and feature codes for places
of interest in eight categories such as
education and health.

For further information and to discuss
your requirements, please contact
Philip's on 020 7531 8440 or
george.philip@philips-maps.co.uk

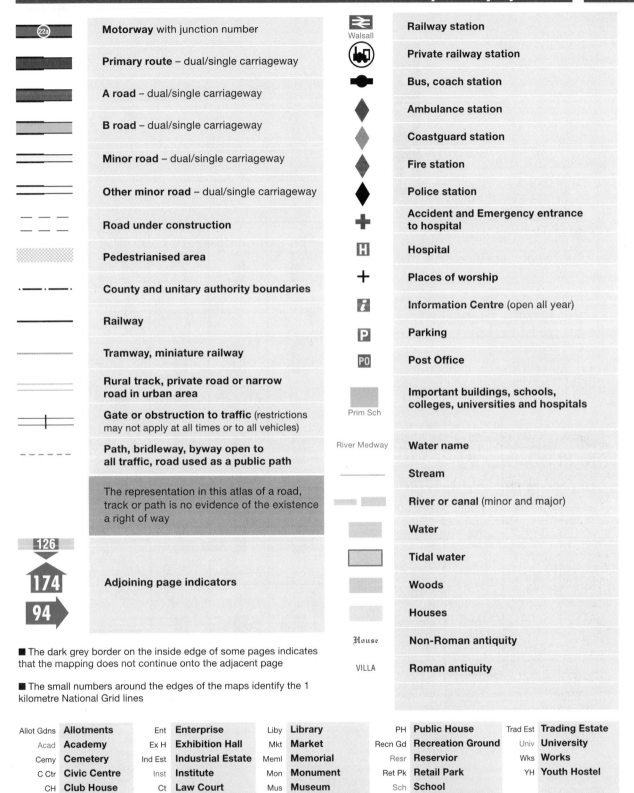

Motorway with junction number	**Railway station** (Walsall)
Primary route – dual/single carriageway	**Private railway station**
A road – dual/single carriageway	**Bus, coach station**
B road – dual/single carriageway	**Ambulance station**
Minor road – dual/single carriageway	**Coastguard station**
Other minor road – dual/single carriageway	**Fire station**
Road under construction	**Police station**
Pedestrianised area	**Accident and Emergency entrance to hospital**
County and unitary authority boundaries	**Hospital**
Railway	**Places of worship**
Tramway, miniature railway	**Information Centre** (open all year)
Rural track, private road or narrow road in urban area	**Parking**
Gate or obstruction to traffic (restrictions may not apply at all times or to all vehicles)	**Post Office**
Path, bridleway, byway open to all traffic, road used as a public path	**Important buildings, schools, colleges, universities and hospitals** (Prim Sch)
The representation in this atlas of a road, track or path is no evidence of the existence a right of way	**Water name** (River Medway)
	Stream
	River or canal (minor and major)
126 / **174** / **94** **Adjoining page indicators**	**Water**
	Tidal water
	Woods
	Houses
	Non-Roman antiquity (House)
	Roman antiquity (VILLA)

■ The dark grey border on the inside edge of some pages indicates that the mapping does not continue onto the adjacent page

■ The small numbers around the edges of the maps identify the 1 kilometre National Grid lines

Allot Gdns	**Allotments**	Ent	**Enterprise**	Liby	**Library**	PH	**Public House**	Trad Est	**Trading Estate**
Acad	**Academy**	Ex H	**Exhibition Hall**	Mkt	**Market**	Recn Gd	**Recreation Ground**	Univ	**University**
Cemy	**Cemetery**	Ind Est	**Industrial Estate**	Meml	**Memorial**	Resr	**Reservoir**	Wks	**Works**
C Ctr	**Civic Centre**	Inst	**Institute**	Mon	**Monument**	Ret Pk	**Retail Park**	YH	**Youth Hostel**
CH	**Club House**	Ct	**Law Court**	Mus	**Museum**	Sch	**School**		
Coll	**College**	L Ctr	**Leisure Centre**	Obsy	**Observatory**	Sh Ctr	**Shopping Centre**		
Crem	**Crematorium**	LC	**Level Crossing**	Pal	**Royal Palace**	TH	**Town Hall/House**		

The scale of the maps is 5.52 cm to 1 km (3½ inches to 1 mile) 1: 18103

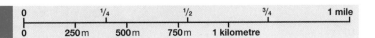

0 — ¼ — ½ — ¾ — 1 mile

0 — 250m — 500m — 750m — 1 kilometre

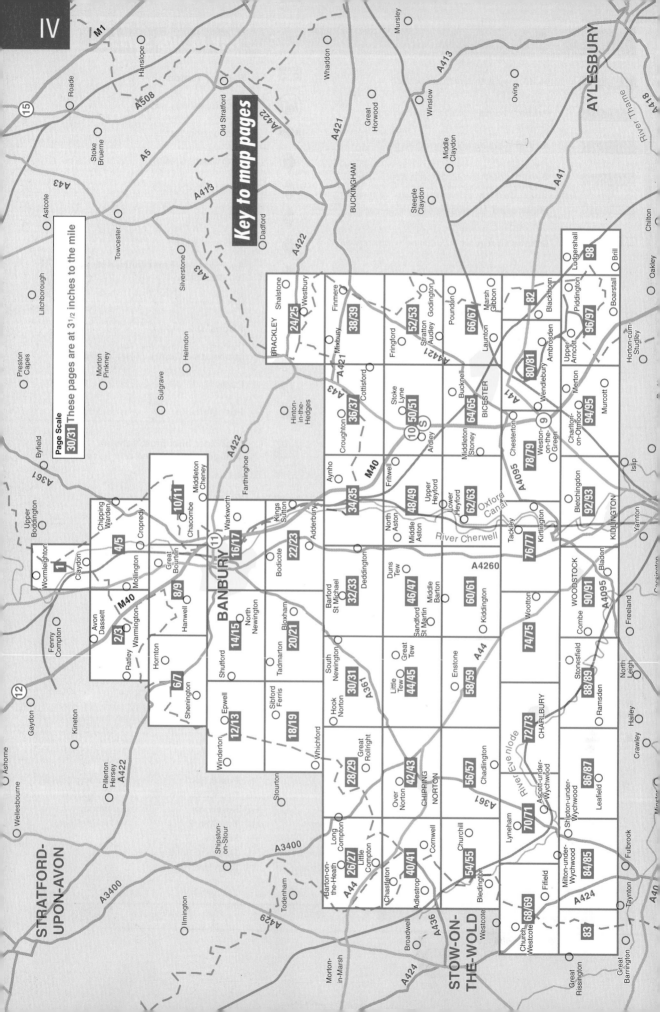

IV

Key to map pages

Page Scale

30/31 These pages are at 3½ inches to the mile

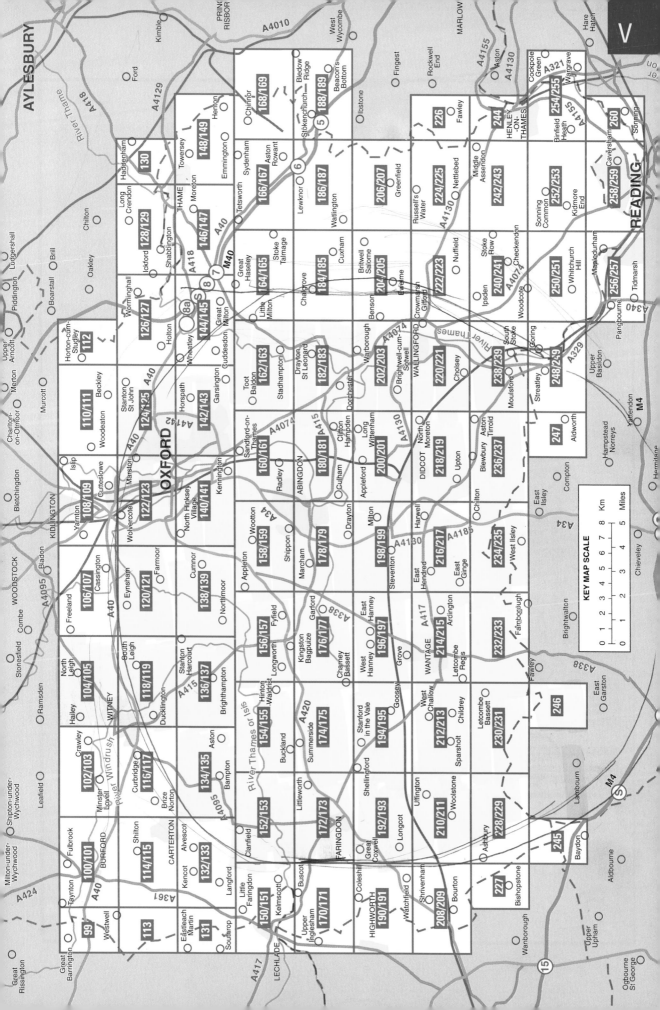

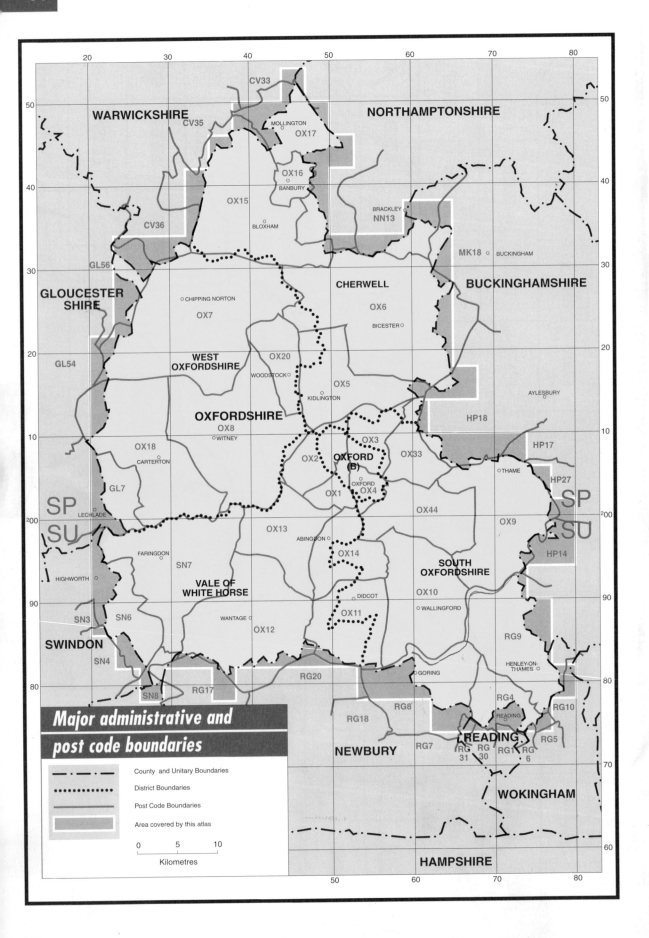

Major administrative and post code boundaries

County and Unitary Boundaries

District Boundaries

Post Code Boundaries

Area covered by this atlas

0   5   10
Kilometres

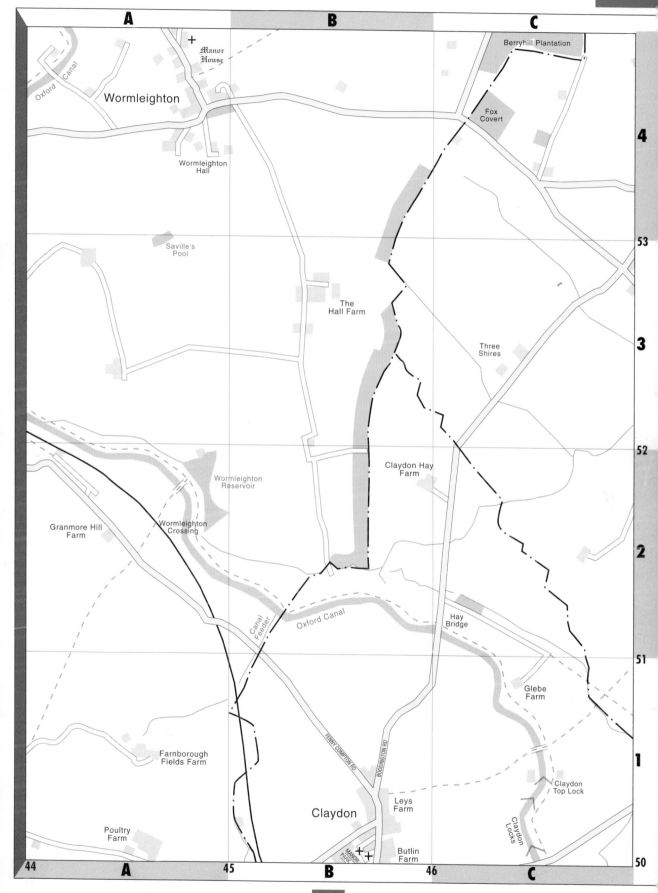

A B C

Berryhill Plantation

Manor
House

Oxford Canal

Wormleighton

Fox
Covert

4

Wormleighton
Hall

Saville's
Pool

53

The
Hall Farm

Three
Shires

3

Wormleighton
Reservoir

Claydon Hay
Farm

52

Granmore Hill
Farm

Wormleighton
Crossing

2

Canal Feeder

Oxford Canal

Hay
Bridge

51

Glebe
Farm

Farnborough
Fields Farm

FENNY COMPTON RD

BODDINGTON RD

1

Claydon
Top Lock

Claydon

Leys
Farm

Claydon Locks

Poultry
Farm

MANOR PARK

Butlin
Farm

44 A 45 B 46 C 50

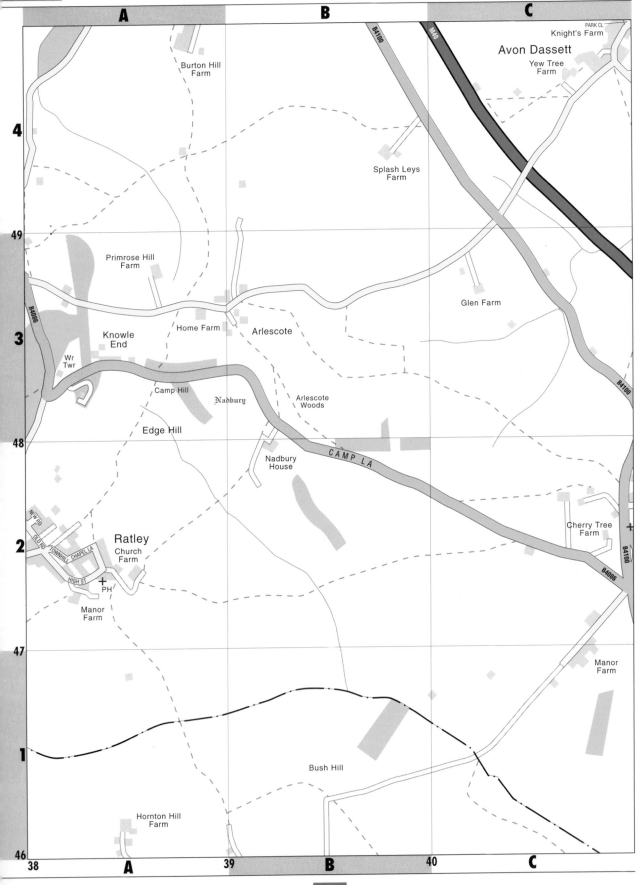

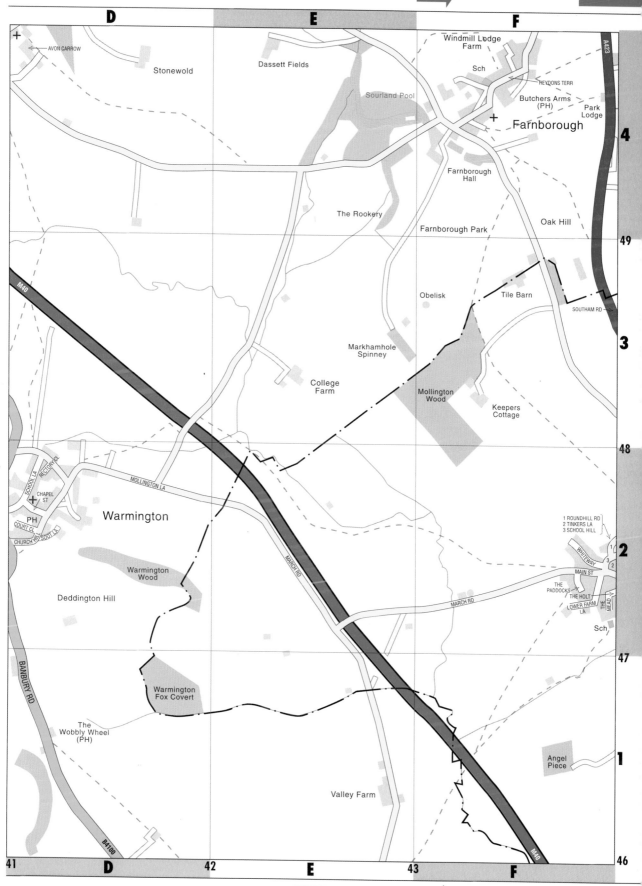

A **B** **C**

Farnborough Hill Farm

Claydon Crossing

Manor Park

BIGNOLDS CL

Filter Bed

Claydon Locks

Manor Farm

4

Farnborough Hill

Lawn Hill

Firs Farm

Priory (remains of)

Clattercote

49

Oxford Canal

Towing Path

Oathill Farm

3

A423

Clattercote Reservoir

Cropredy Lawn

Lambert's Barn

48

Beecham's Cottages

SOUTHAM RD

Mollington

2

ROUNDHILL RD

ROUNDHILL RD

CHURCH LA

CHURCH LA

BLACKSMITHS LA

THE HOLLOWAY

MAIN ST

OXHEY HILL

CHESTNUT RD

ORCHARD PIECE

IVY LA

Manor Farm

Mill Farm

Cropredy Hill

Oxhay Farm

Cemy

CLAYDON RD

CREAMPOT CRES

KYETTS CNR

47

CHEAMPOT LA

PO

ORCHARD VIEW

HIGH ST

CHAPEL LA

RED LION ST

ORCHARD LA

1

CUP AND SAUCER PH

Cropredy

VICARAGE GDNS

THE PLANTATION

STATION RD

Thickthorn Farm

A423

Oxford Canal

River Cherwell

Sch

46

44   **A**   **45**   **B**   **46**   **C**

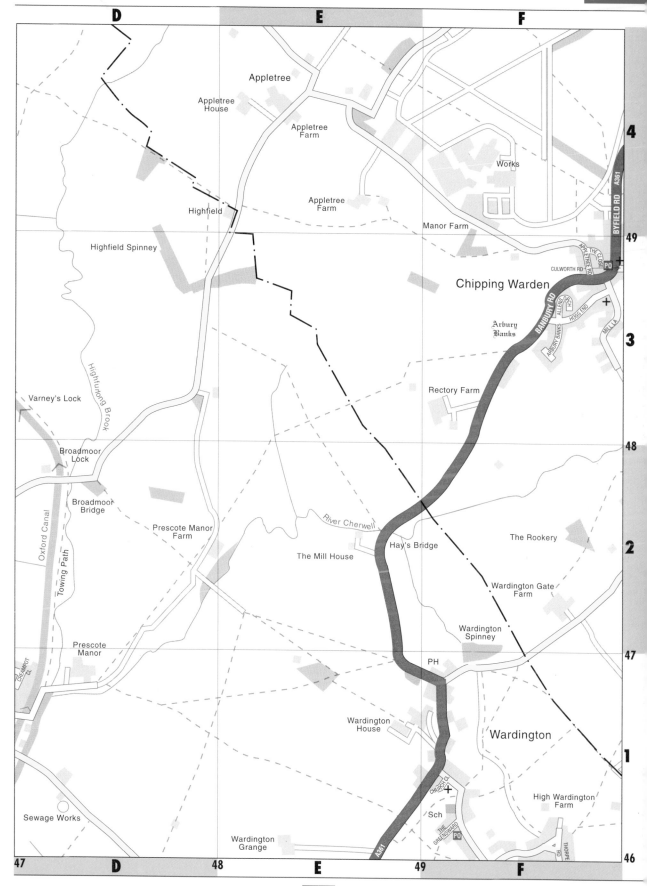

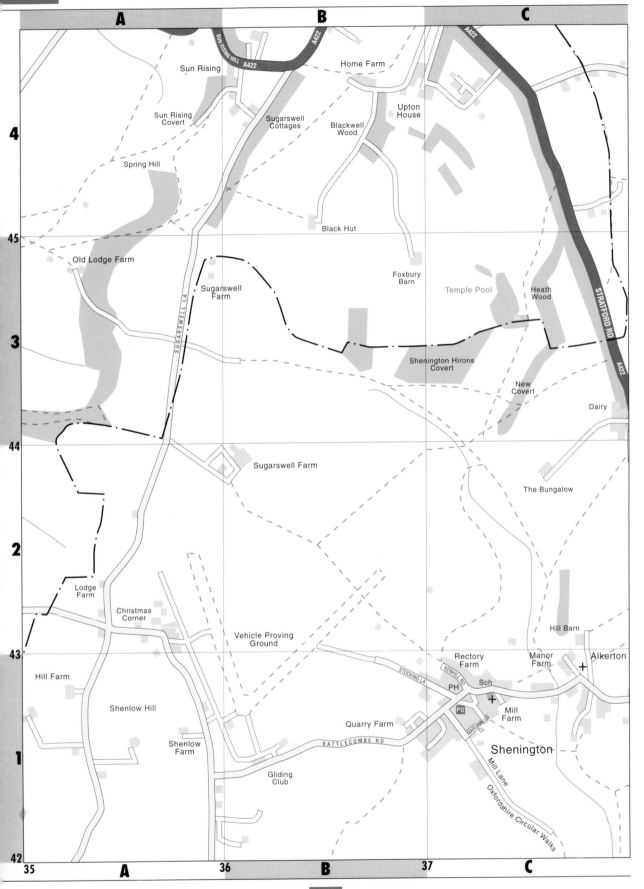

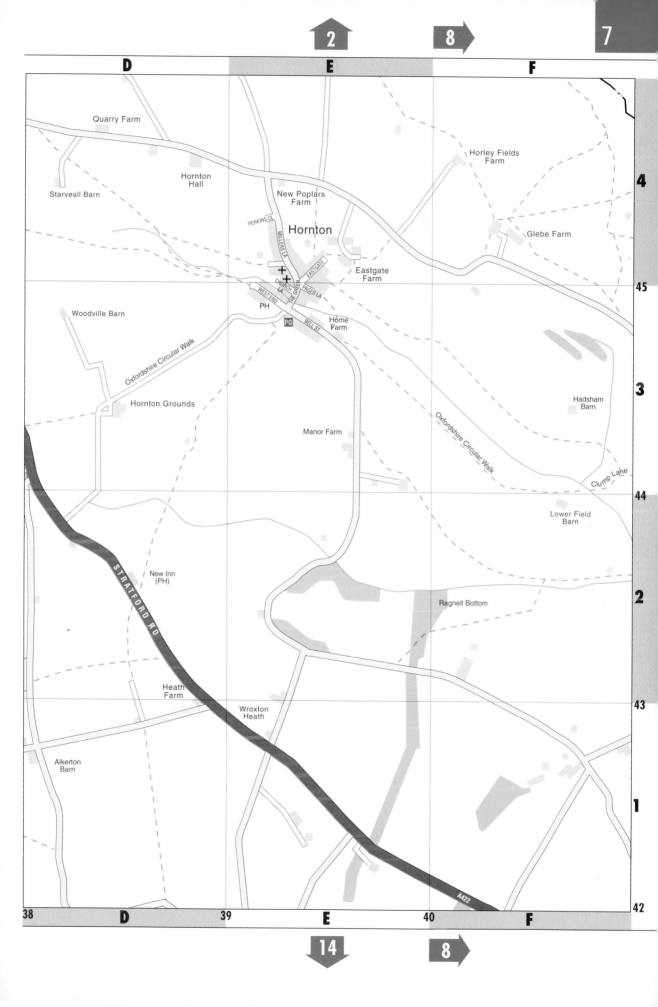

A **B** **C**

B4100

Slated
Barn

Slade
Barn

Laurel
Farm

MOLLINGTON RD

SNUFF LA

BAKEHOUSE LA

MIDDLE LA

NEW

Bury Court
Farm

+

Shotteswell

4

Sor Brook

45

Hadsham House
Manor Farm

Water
Tower

3

Horley
House

Clump Lane

44

+

MANOR ORCH

LANE CL

PH

PO

GULLIVER'S CL

Hanwell

SPRINGFIELD

HANWELL CT

MAIN ST

PARK CL

CHURCH LA

Bramhill
Park
Farm

SACKVILLE CL

+

Hanwell
Castle

Horley

GULLICOTE LA

Park
Farm

2

WARWICK RD

43

Oxfordshire Circular Walk

Drayton
Lodge

1

Cemy

HORLEY PATH RD

Lord's
Spinney

Golf
Course

B4100

HARDWICK PARK

EYE CT

WINCHELSEA CL

HIGHLANDS

BARCOMBE CL

CHEVIOT WAY

HORSHAM CL

CHELSEA CT

RYE CL

ROMNEY RD

42

A422

41 **A** **42** **B** **43** **C**

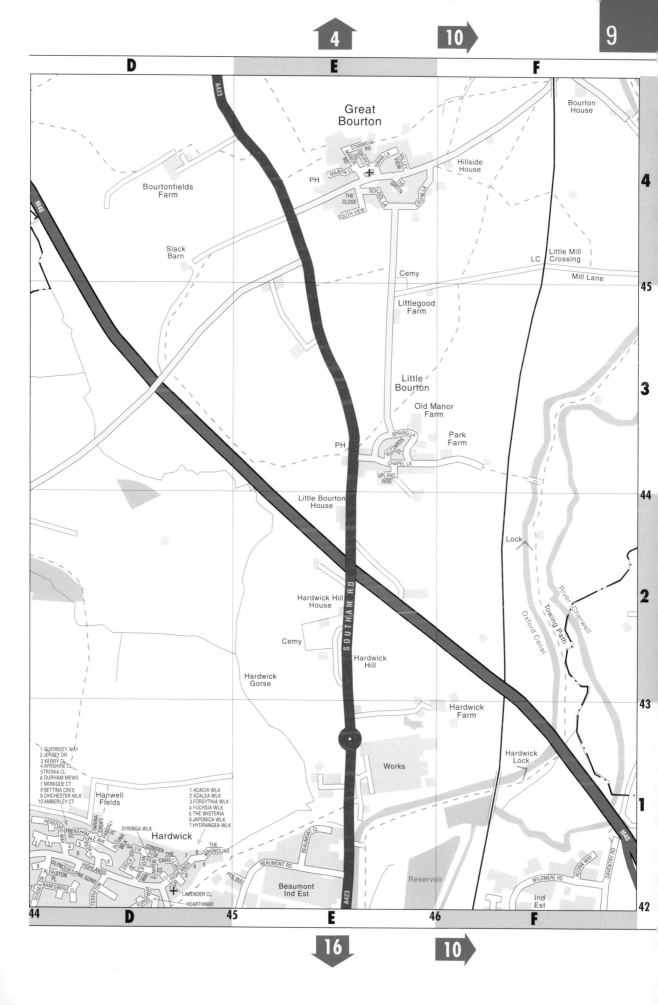

| | A | B | C |

Lower Lodge

Williamscot House

Williamscot
Village Spinney

Weir

4

Oxford Canal

Mount Pleasant
Bennetts Farm
Trent Farm
Barn Farm
Upper Wardington
CHELMSCOT ROW
THORPE RD

Dawkins's Barn

Peewit Farm

45

Bell Land

WARDINGTON RD

Williamscot Hill Farm

3

River Cherwell

WILLIAMSCOT HILL

Coton Farm

Bridge Lake Fisheries

Redlunch Barn

Marsh Barn Farm

Works

44

The Priory

SILVER ST NORTH
SILVER ST
BEAN FURLONG
POPLARS RD
BENNETTS CL
Chacombe
Sch

CHURCH LA
WESLEY PL
THORPE RD
PH
BANBURY RD
SMH
PO
THORNHILL
MIDDLETON RD

BANBURY RD

Chacombe House

2

Golf Course
CH

43

Castle Farm

Seale's Farm

1

Yew Tree Cottage

BANBURY LA
CHENEY GDNS
CHACOMBE RD
STILE
MEWS
STANWELL LEA 1
STANWELL DR 2

Huscote Farm

M40
A361

Windmill Farm

GLOVERS LA
CHURCH LA
HIGH ST
RECTORY LA

B4525

42
| 47 | A | 48 | B | 49 | C |

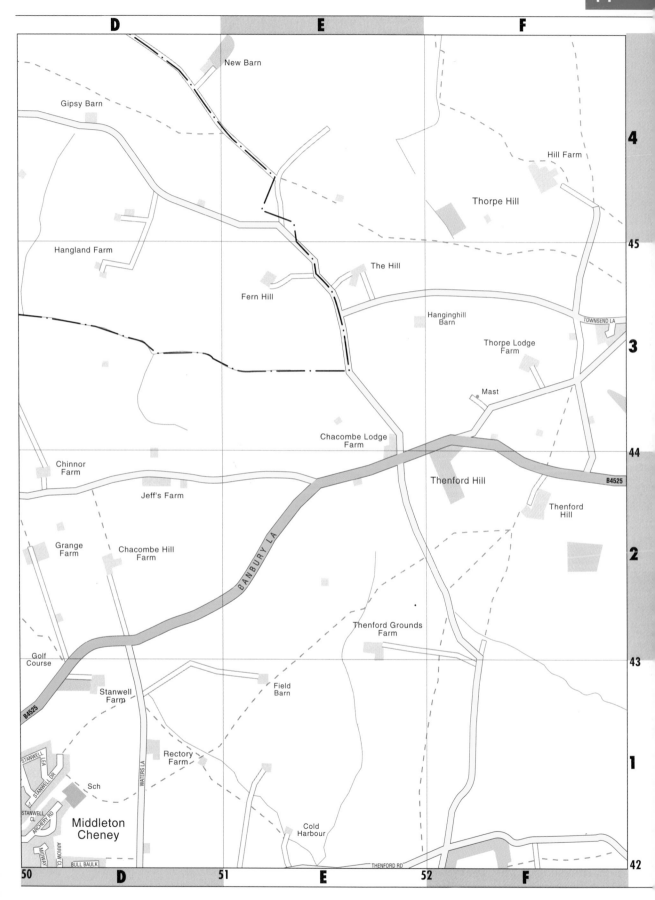

New Barn

Gipsy Barn

Hill Farm

Thorpe Hill

4

Hangland Farm

45

The Hill

Fern Hill

Hanginghill
Barn

TOWNSEND LA

Thorpe Lodge
Farm

3

Mast

Chacombe Lodge
Farm

44

Chinnor
Farm

Thenford Hill

B4525

Jeff's Farm

Thenford
Hill

Grange
Farm

Chacombe Hill
Farm

BANBURY LA

2

Thenford Grounds
Farm

Golf
Course

43

Stanwell
Farm

Field
Barn

B4525

Rectory
Farm

STANWELL LEA

STANWELL DR

WATERS LA

1

Sch

STANWELL CL

ARCHERY RD

Middleton
Cheney

Cold
Harbour

MIDWAY

ARROW CL

BULL BAULK

THENFORD RD

42

50   D   51   E   52   F

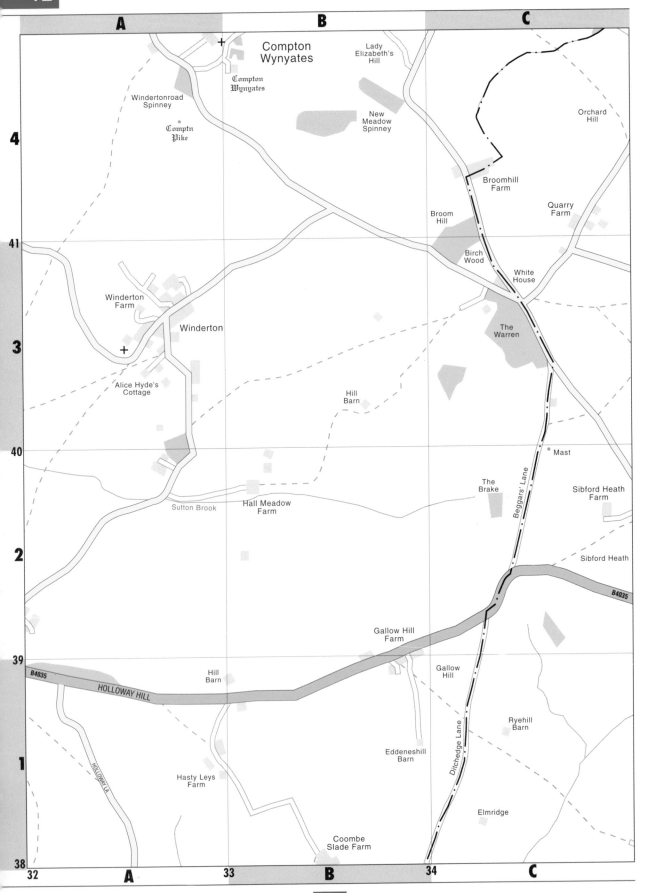

A **B** **C**

Compton Wynyates

Lady Elizabeth's Hill

Compton Wynyates

Windertonroad Spinney

New Meadow Spinney

Orchard Hill

Compton Pike

4

Broomhill Farm

Broom Hill

Quarry Farm

41

Birch Wood

White House

Winderton Farm

The Warren

Winderton

3

Alice Hyde's Cottage

Hill Barn

40

Mast

The Brake

Sibford Heath Farm

Sutton Brook

Hall Meadow Farm

Beggars' Lane

Sibford Heath

2

B4035

Gallow Hill Farm

39

Gallow Hill

B4035

HOLLOWAY HILL

Hill Barn

Ditchedge Lane

Ryehill Barn

1

HOLLOWAY LA

Hasty Leys Farm

Eddeneshill Barn

Elmridge

38

32 **A** **33** **B** **34** **C**

D
E
F

Rough Hill

Rough Hill Farm

OC Walks

Epwell Hill

Yarn Hill Farm

Field Barn

4

Yarn Hill

Epwell Grounds Farm

Lower Barn

Rectory Farm

41

Shutford Grounds Farm

Epwell

EPWELL RD

Long Hill

3

BIRDS LA

THE CLOSE

PO

THATCHERS CL

Epwell Mill

Slatters Barn

Cemy

Cranes Farm

Gage Farm

PH

Woodington Spinney

Bottle Barn

Heath Plantation

40

Woodington Barn

Chillaway Barn

Barton Hill

Farmington Farm

2

Heathnell Spinney

Lake Spinney

SIBFORD RD

Blenheim Farm

39

Handywater Farm

Redland Barn

POUND LA

Brakelands Farm

1

Tyne Hill

Tyne Hill Farm

B4035

BACKSIDE LA

HIGH MEADOW

35
D
36
E
37
F
38

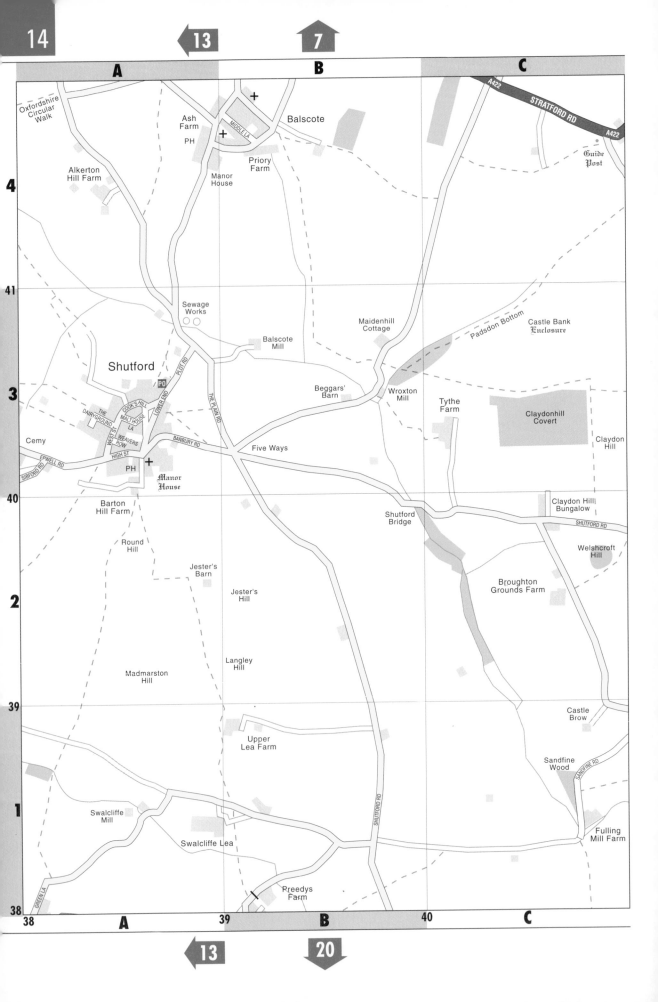

A

B

C

Oxfordshire Circular Walk

Ash Farm
PH

Balscote

MIDDLE LA

Priory Farm

Manor House

STRATFORD RD
A422
A422

Guide Post

Alkerton Hill Farm

4

41

Sewage Works

Balscote Mill

Maidenhill Cottage

Padsdon Bottom

Castle Bank Enclosure

Shutford

PLOT RD

THE PLAIN RD

Beggars' Barn

Wroxton Mill

Tythe Farm

Claydonhill Covert

Claydon Hill

3

COOK'S HILL
THE DAIRYGROUND
MALT HOUSE LA
WEST ST
WEAVERS ROW
LOWER END

BANBURY RD

Five Ways

Cemy

EPWELL RD
SIBFORD RD

HIGH ST

PH

Manor House

40

Shutford Bridge

Claydon Hill Bungalow

SHUTFORD RD

Barton Hill Farm

Round Hill

Jester's Barn

Welshcroft Hill

Broughton Grounds Farm

2

Jester's Hill

Langley Hill

Madmarston Hill

39

Castle Brow

Upper Lea Farm

Sandfine Wood

SANDFINE RD

1

Swalcliffe Mill

SHUTFORD RD

Fulling Mill Farm

Swalcliffe Lea

GREEN LA

38

Preedys Farm

38

A

39

B

40

C

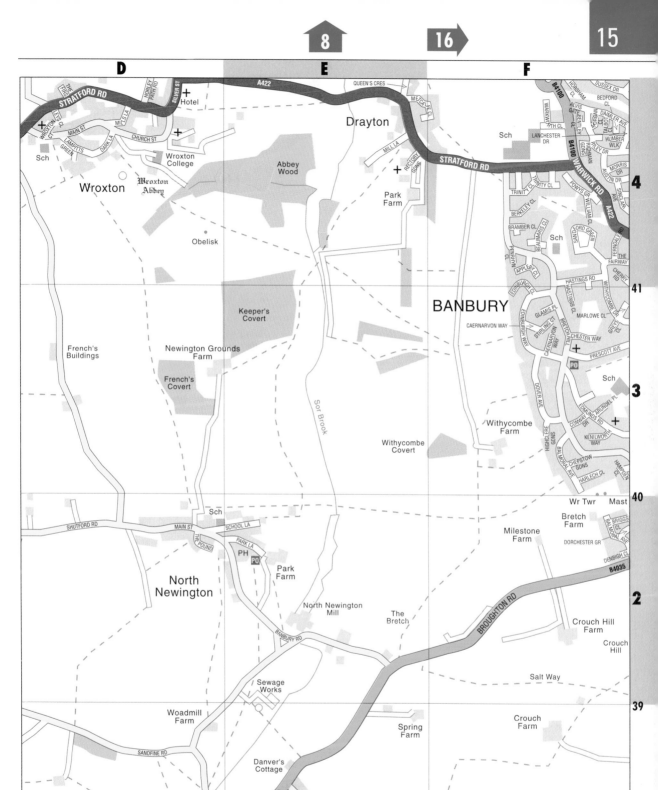

D · E · F

A422
STRATFORD RD
Hotel
Wroxton
Sch
Wroxton College
Wroxton Abbey
Drayton
Abbey Wood
Park Farm
Queen's Cres
Stratford Rd
B4100
WARWICK RD
Sch
Lanchester Dr
Sch
BANBURY
4

Obelisk
Keeper's Covert
Newington Grounds Farm
French's Buildings
French's Covert
Sor Brook
Withycombe Covert
Withycombe Farm
Caernarvon Way
PO
Sch
41
3

Shutford Rd
Sch
Main St
School La
Park La
The Pound
PH
PO
North Newington
Park Farm
North Newington Mill
The Bretch
BROUGHTON RD
Milestone Farm
Bretch Farm
Dorchester Gr
Denbigh Cl
B4035
Crouch Hill Farm
Crouch Hill
Wr Twr   Mast
Briggs Cl
40
2

Woadmill Farm
Sewage Works
Sandfine Rd
Danver's Cottage
Broughton Park
Broughton Castle
Weir
B4035
PH
Broughton
Main Rd
Danvers Rd
Danvers Cl
Spring Farm
Salt Way
Crouch Farm
Rectory Farm
Wykham La
A361 BLOXHAM RD
Cross Road Cottages
39
1
38

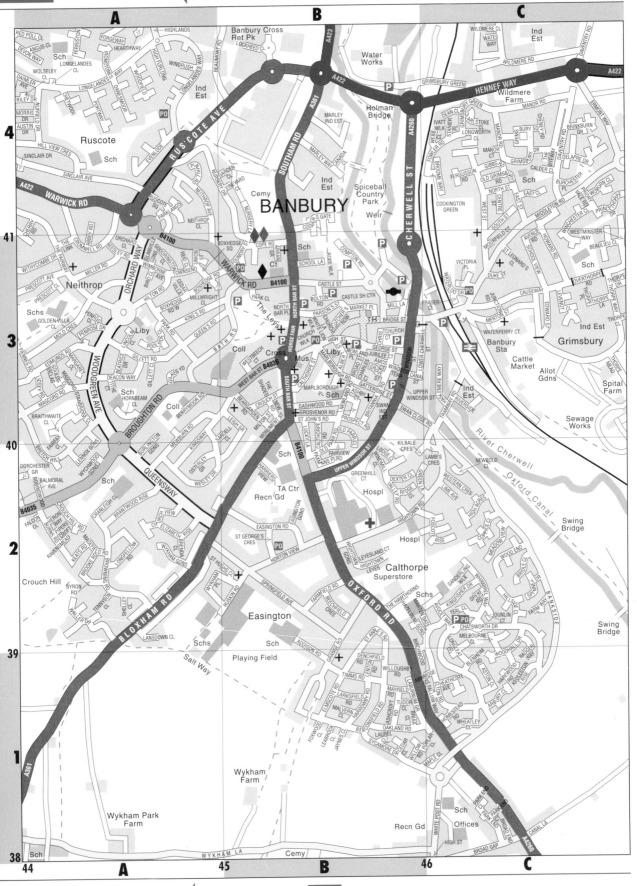

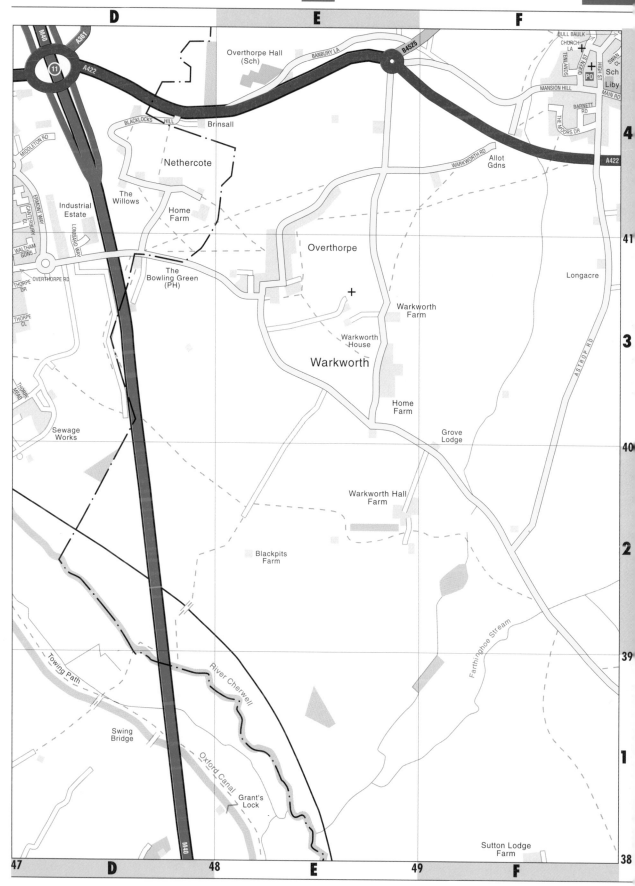

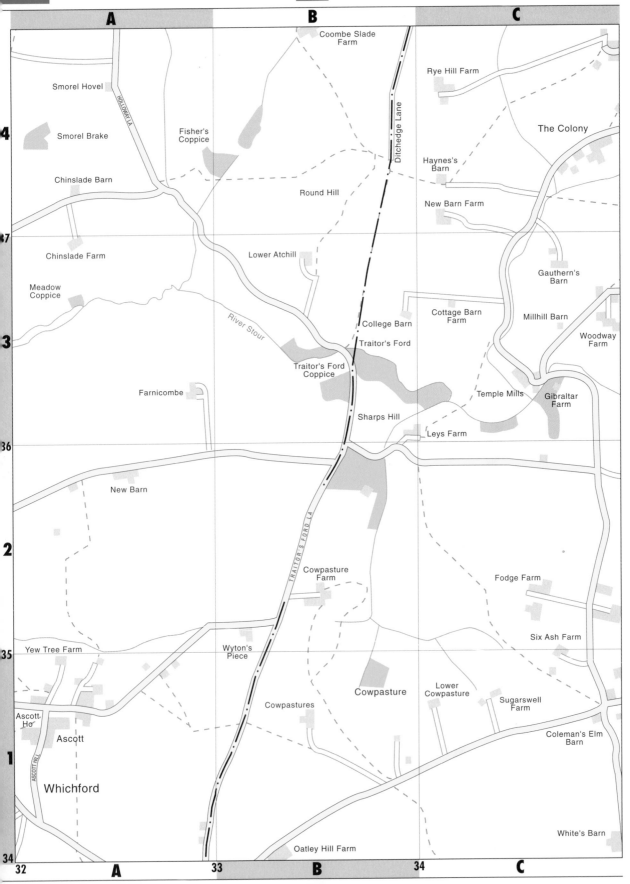

A B C

4

Smorel Hovel

Smorel Brake

Fisher's Coppice

Coombe Slade Farm

Rye Hill Farm

The Colony

HOLLOWAY LA

Ditchedge Lane

Haynes's Barn

Round Hill

New Barn Farm

Chinslade Barn

37

Chinslade Farm

Lower Atchill

Gauthern's Barn

Meadow Coppice

Cottage Barn Farm

Millhill Barn

Woodway Farm

River Stour

College Barn

3

Traitor's Ford

Traitor's Ford Coppice

Temple Mills

Gibraltar Farm

Farnicombe

Sharps Hill

36

Leys Farm

New Barn

TRAITOR'S FORD LA

2

Cowpasture Farm

Fodge Farm

Six Ash Farm

35

Yew Tree Farm

Wyton's Piece

Cowpasture

Lower Cowpasture

Sugarswell Farm

Ascott Ho

Cowpastures

Coleman's Elm Barn

Ascott

1

ASCOTT HILL

Whichford

White's Barn

34

Oatley Hill Farm

32 A 33 B 34 C

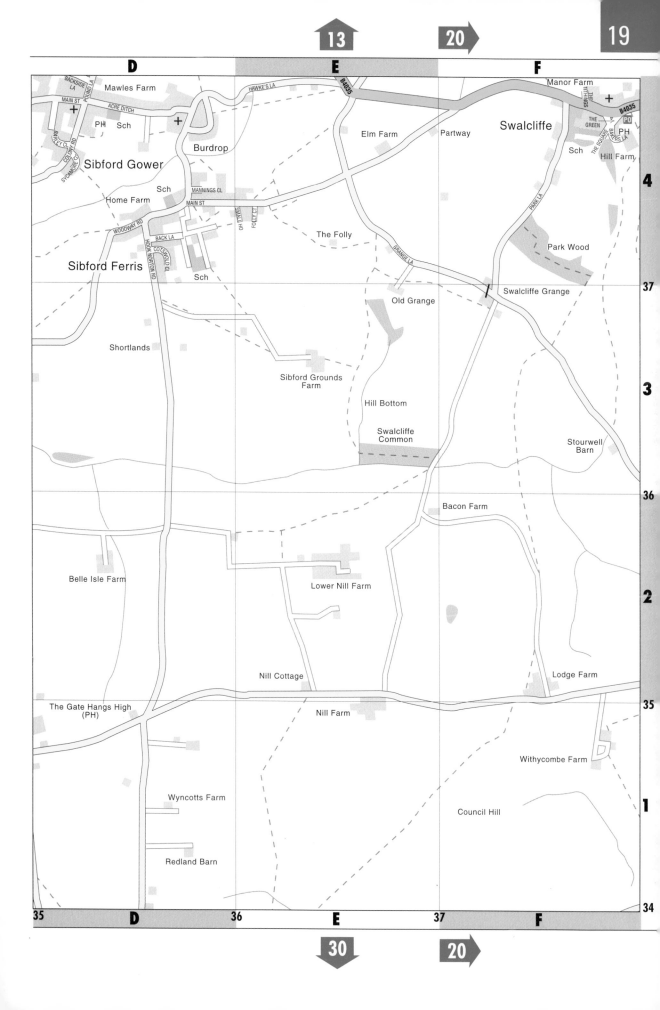

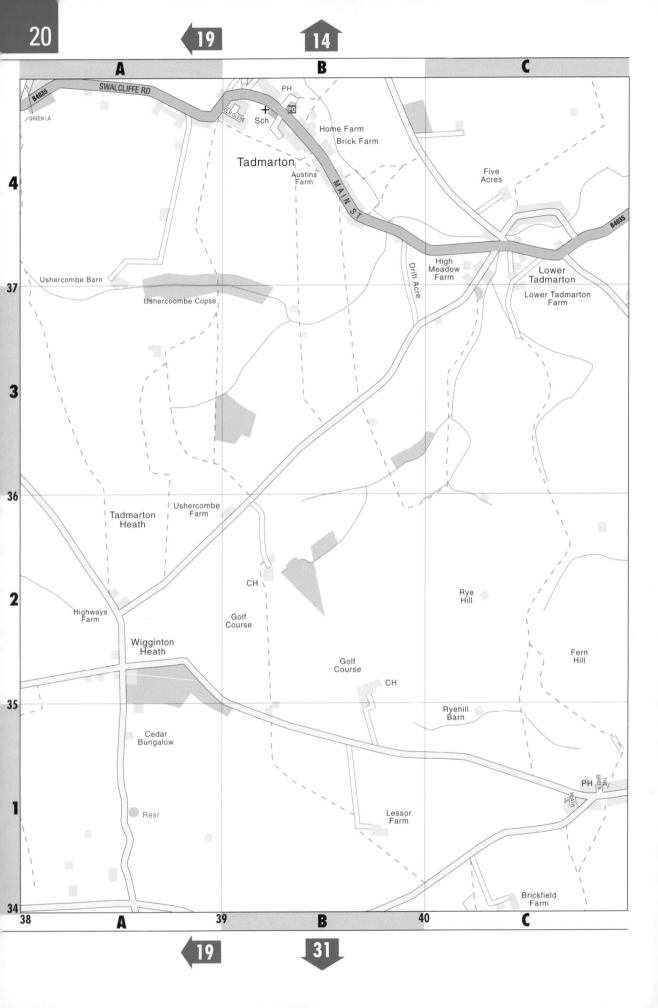

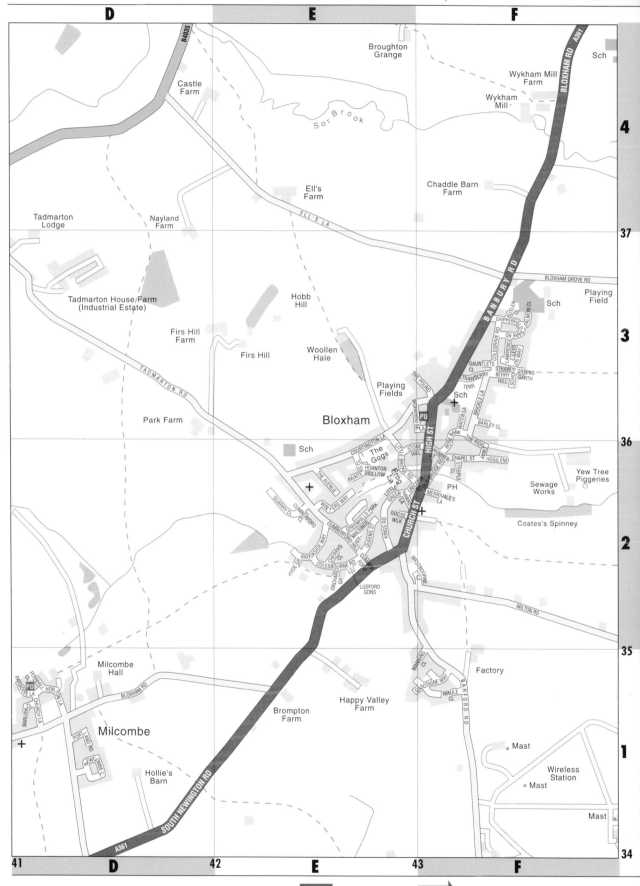

D   E   F

Broughton
Grange

B4035

Castle
Farm

Wykham Mill
Farm

Wykham
Mill

BLOXHAM RD   A361

Sch

4

Sor Brook

Ell's
Farm

Chaddle Barn
Farm

Tadmarton
Lodge

Nayland
Farm

ELL'S LA

BLOXHAM GROVE RD

37

Tadmarton House Farm
(Industrial Estate)

Hobb
Hill

BANBURY RD

Sch

Playing
Field

Firs Hill
Farm

Woollen
Hale

CHIPPERFIELD
COLEGRAVE RD
LAWRENCE LEYS
SALMON CL
SCHOFIELDS WAY
BUTLER CL

3

TADMARTON RD

Firs Hill

Playing
Fields

THE POUND
WORKHOUSE LA

GAUNTLETS
CL
STRAW
BERRY
TERR
STRAWBERRY
HILL
BRICKLE LA
GREENS
GARTH

Park Farm

Bloxham

Sch
PO
WATER LA

Sch

BARLEY CL

36

Sch

The
Gogs

COURTINGTON LA
CL
PAINTER'S
HORNTON
HOLLOW

LITTLE BRIDGE RD
STONE
HILL

HIGH ST

RISE BANK

THE RIDGE

CHAPEL ST
AVE
HOGG END

QUARRY CL

THE AVENUE

FROG LA

UNION ST
OLD BRIDGE WAY
STEEPLE
CL

CUMBERFORD

WINTERS WAY

GREENHILLS PARK
MALTINGS

LITTLE
GREEN LA
GOOSE
WLK

CHURCH ST

MERRIVALE'S
LA

PH

Coates's Spinney

Sewage
Works

Yew Tree
Piggeries

2

HYDE GR

BROOKSIDE WAY

CUMBERFORD RD

CHERRYS CL

COLESBOURNE RD

ORCHARD GR

KINGS RD

QUEENS ST

CHAMBERS

WESTBOURNE
CL

MILTON RD

LUDFORD
GDNS

35

Milcombe
Hall

BLOXHAM RD

Factory

FERNHILL
PARADISE
PO
HORNTON LA

CHURCH LA

BARLEY HILL

Brompton
Farm

Happy Valley
Farm

MANNING
CL
GASCOIGNE WAY

MAULE
CL

BARFORD RD

Milcombe

PORTLAND RD

LEWCOMBE C.

Mast

Wireless
Station

1

Hollie's
Barn

SOUTH NEWINGTON RD

Mast

Mast

34

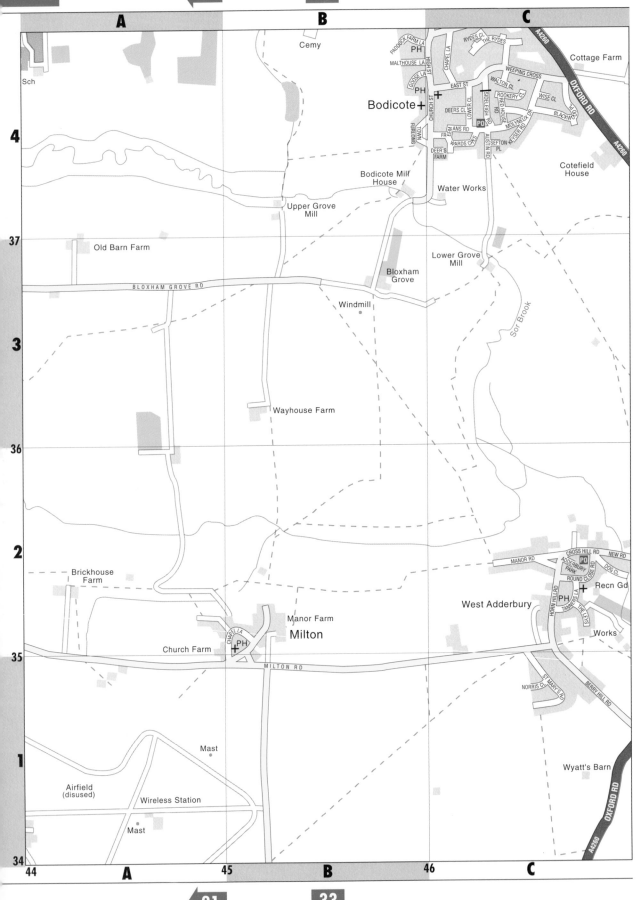

Cemy

Sch

Bodicote

PADDOCK FARM LA

PH

MALTHOUSE LA

GOOSE LA

HIGH ST

CHAPEL LA

RYDES CL

THE RYDES

Cottage Farm

WEEPING CROSS

EAST ST

WALTON CL

WISE CL

A4260

OXFORD RD

PH

DEERS CL

LOWER CL

ROOKERY CL

RED HOUSE

BLACKWO

SIDELEIGH RD

PO

MOLYNEUX DR

KEYSER RD

Cotefield House

TOWN FURLONG

FR

EM

ANS RD

WARDS CRS

AUSTIN RD

SEFTON PL

DEER'S FARM

Bodicote Mill House

Water Works

37

Old Barn Farm

Upper Grove Mill

Lower Grove Mill

Sor Brook

BLOXHAM GROVE RD

Bloxham Grove

4

Windmill

3

Wayhouse Farm

36

2

Brickhouse Farm

MANOR RD

CROSS HILL RD

NEW RD

ADDERBURY PARK

PO

DOG CL

ROUND CLOSE RD

West Adderbury

PH

Recn Gd

HORN HILL RD

TANNER'S LA

THE LEYS

Manor Farm

Milton

Works

Church Farm

CHAPEL LA

PH

MILTON RD

35

NORRIS CL

ST MARY'S RD

BERRY HILL RD

1

Mast

Wyatt's Barn

Airfield (disused)

Wireless Station

Mast

OXFORD RD

A4260

34

44

45

46

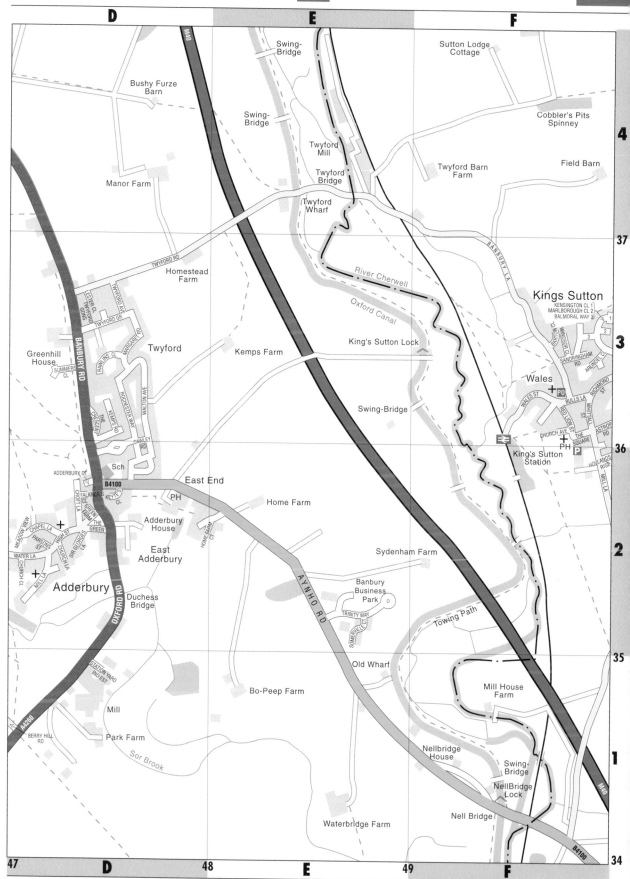

Swing-Bridge

Sutton Lodge
Cottage

Bushy Furze
Barn

Swing-
Bridge

Cobbler's Pits
Spinney

4

Twyford
Mill

Twyford Barn
Farm

Field Barn

Manor Farm

Twyford
Bridge

Twyford
Wharf

37

TWYFORD RD

BANBURY LA

Homestead
Farm

River Cherwell

Kings Sutton

KENSINGTON CL 1
MARLBOROUGH CL 2
BALMORAL WAY 3

LESTER CL
TWYFORD GDNS

TWYFORD AVE

Oxford Canal

Greenhill
House

BANBURY RD

MARGARET RD

RAWLINS CL

TWYFORD GR

Twyford

Kemps Farm

King's Sutton Lock

3

SUMMERS CL

ROCHESTER WAY

KEMPS RD

WALTON AVE

THE CRESCENT

Wales

PO

WALES ST

BULLS LA

WHITTALL ST

ASTROP RD

CAWLEY RD

Swing-Bridge

CHURCH AVE
PH

RICHMOND ST

36

Sch

B4100

East End

PH

Home Farm

King's Sutton
Station

P

HOLLANDS RISE

MILL LA

ADDERBURY DT

FALKNER'S
CROFT LA FARM

CROFT LA
KEYTE'S CL
GREEN

THE
GREEN

Adderbury
House

MEADOW VIEW

CHAPEL LA

HIGH ST

PARSONS ST

SIR GEORGES LA

CHURCH LA

East
Adderbury

Sydenham Farm

Banbury
Business
Park

2

WATER LA

CHURCH CL

MILL LA

Adderbury

OXFORD RD

Duchess
Bridge

AYNHO RD

TRINITY WAY

SOMERVILLE CT

Towing Path

A4260

STATION YARD
IND EST

Old Wharf

35

BERRY HILL
RD

Mill

Bo-Peep Farm

Mill House
Farm

Park Farm

Sor Brook

Nellbridge
House

Swing-
Bridge

1

NellBridge
Lock

M40

Waterbridge Farm

Nell Bridge

B4100

34

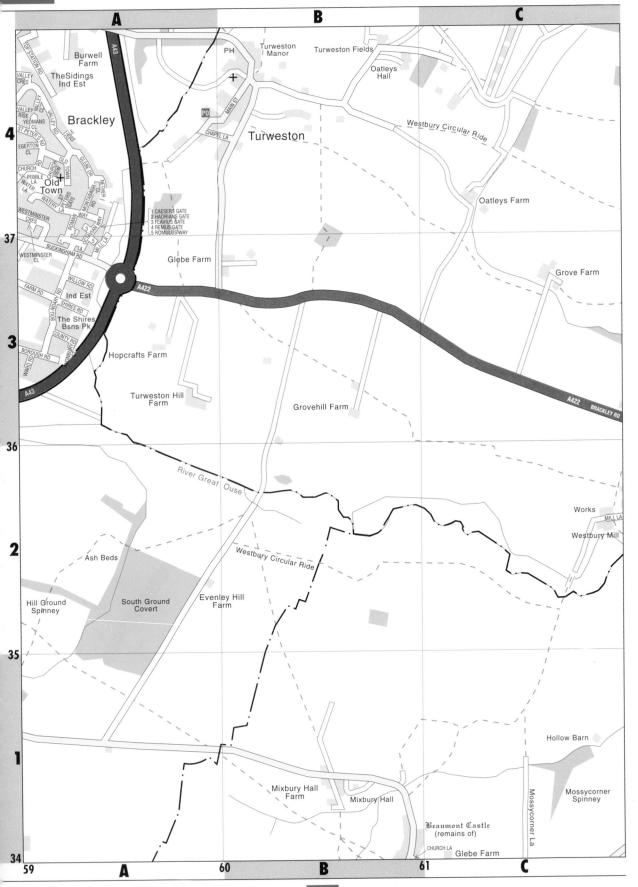

Burwell
Farm
TheSidings
Ind Est

TOP STATION RD
VALLEY
CRES
VALLEY
RISE
YEOMANS
CL
ST PETERS RD
EGERTON
CL

Brackley

VALLEY WALK
YATES CL
VALLEY RD

GLEBE DR
NETHER RD
OLD TOWN

CHURCH
PEBBLE
LA
WATER
LA
WALK

Old
Town

CHURCH RD
WESTMINSTER
CRES
WESTMINSTER
CL

FARM RD
BOUNDARY RD
WILLOW RD
SHIRES RD
COUNTY RD
BOROUGH RD
WARD RD
NOMBARD RD

PO
CHAPEL LA
MAIN ST

PH

Turweston
Manor

Turweston Fields

Turweston

Oatleys
Hall

Westbury Circular Ride

1 CAESERS GATE
2 HADRIANS GATE
3 FLAVIUS GATE
4 REMUS GATE
5 ROMULUS WAY

ROMAN WAY
OCTAVIAN WAY
MV LA

BUCKINGHAM RD

Glebe Farm

A43

A422

Ind Est

The Shires
Bsns Pk

Hopcrafts Farm

Turweston Hill
Farm

Oatleys Farm

Grove Farm

Grovehill Farm

A422 BRACKLEY RD

River Great Ouse

Works

Westbury Mill
MILL LA

Westbury Circular Ride

Ash Beds

South Ground
Covert

Evenley Hill
Farm

Hill Ground
Spinney

Hollow Barn

Mixbury Hall
Farm

Mixbury Hall

Mossycorner
Spinney

Mossycorner La

Beaumont Castle
(remains of)

CHURCH LA
Glebe Farm

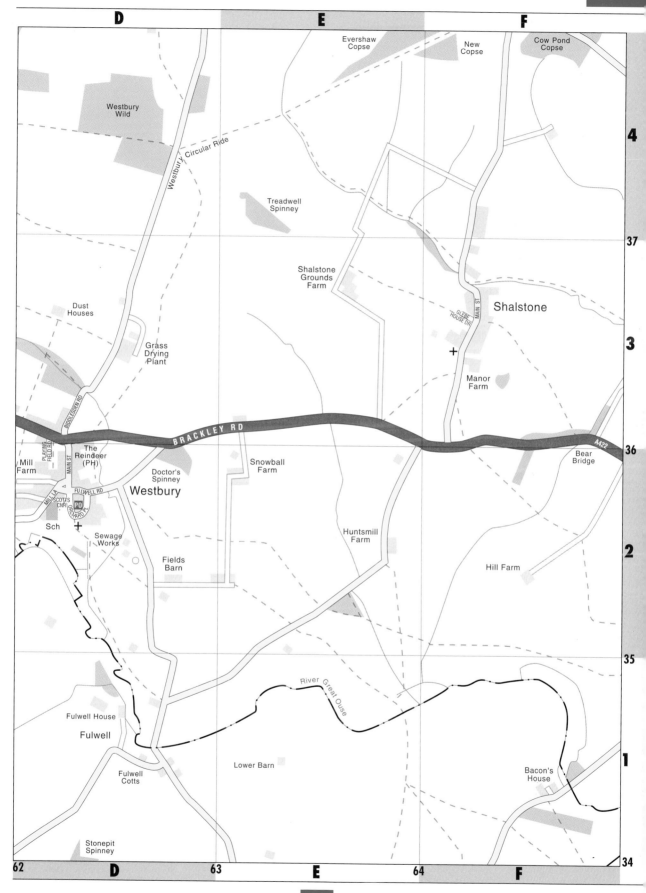

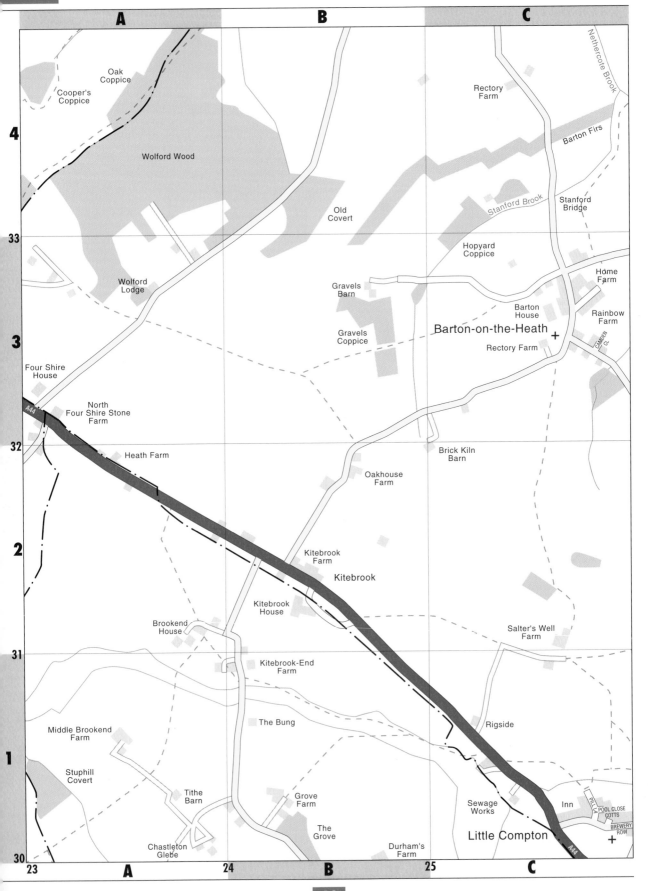

A
B
C

4

Oak
Coppice

Cooper's
Coppice

Wolford Wood

Rectory
Farm

Barton Firs

Nethercote Brook

Old
Covert

Stanford Brook

Stanford
Bridge

33

Hopyard
Coppice

Wolford
Lodge

Gravels
Barn

Home
Farm

3

Four Shire
House

Gravels
Coppice

Barton
House

Barton-on-the-Heath

Rectory Farm

Rainbow
Farm

CAMDEN CL

A44

North
Four Shire Stone
Farm

Brick Kiln
Barn

32

Heath Farm

Oakhouse
Farm

2

Kitebrook
Farm

Kitebrook

Kitebrook
House

Brookend
House

Salter's Well
Farm

31

Kitebrook-End
Farm

The Bung

Rigside

1

Middle Brookend
Farm

Stuphill
Covert

Tithe
Barn

Grove
Farm

Sewage
Works

Inn

POOL CLOSE
COTTS

PILL C

BREWERY
ROW

The
Grove

Little Compton

30

Chastleton
Glebe

Durham's
Farm

A44

23
A
24
B
25
C

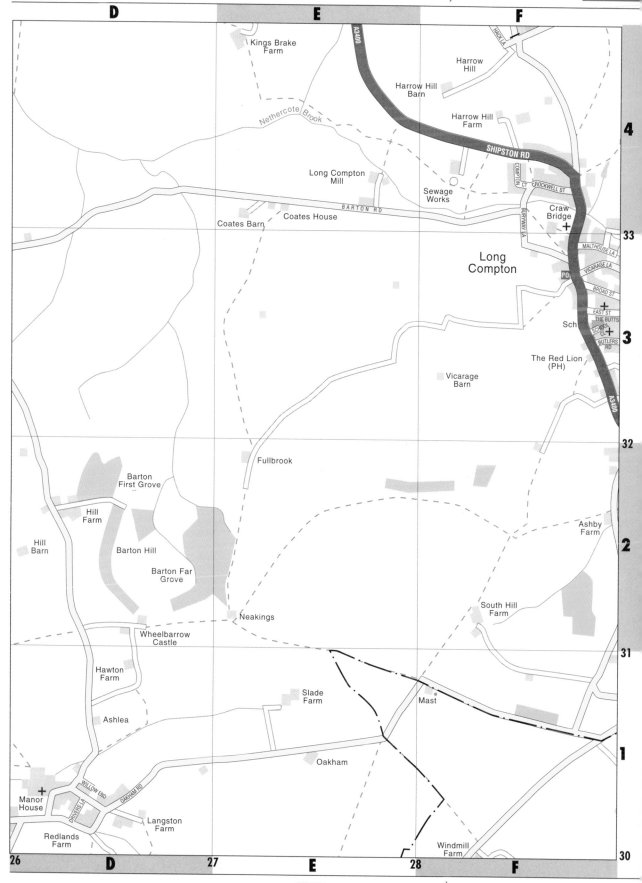

D · E · F

Kings Brake Farm

Harrow Hill

Harrow Hill Barn

Harrow Hill Farm

A3400

SHIPSTON RD

HACK LA

Nethercote Brook

Long Compton Mill

Sewage Works

COMPTON CT

CROCKWELL ST

Craw Bridge

BURWAY LA

BARTON RD

Coates House

Coates Barn

Long Compton

MALTHOUSE LA

VICARAGE LA

PO

BROAD ST

EAST ST

THE BUTTS

Sch

SCHOOL CL

BUTLERS RD

The Red Lion (PH)

Vicarage Barn

A3400

Fullbrook

Barton First Grove

Hill Farm

Ashby Farm

Hill Barn

Barton Hill

Barton Far Grove

South Hill Farm

Neakings

Wheelbarrow Castle

Hawton Farm

Slade Farm

Mast

Ashlea

Oakham

Manor House

WILLOW END

DRIVERS LA

OAKHAM RD

Langston Farm

Redlands Farm

Windmill Farm

4
33
3
32
2
31
1
30

27

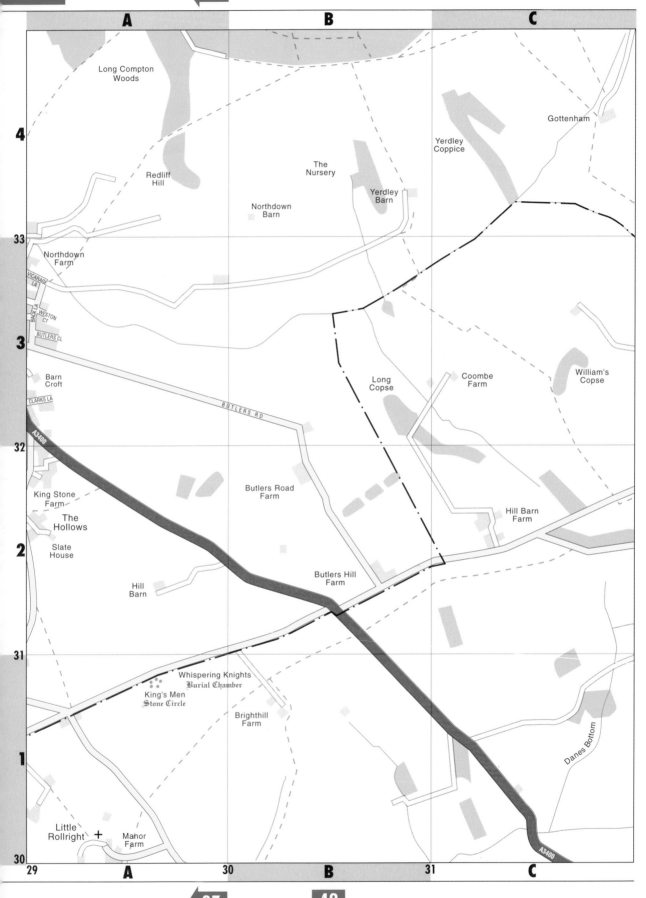

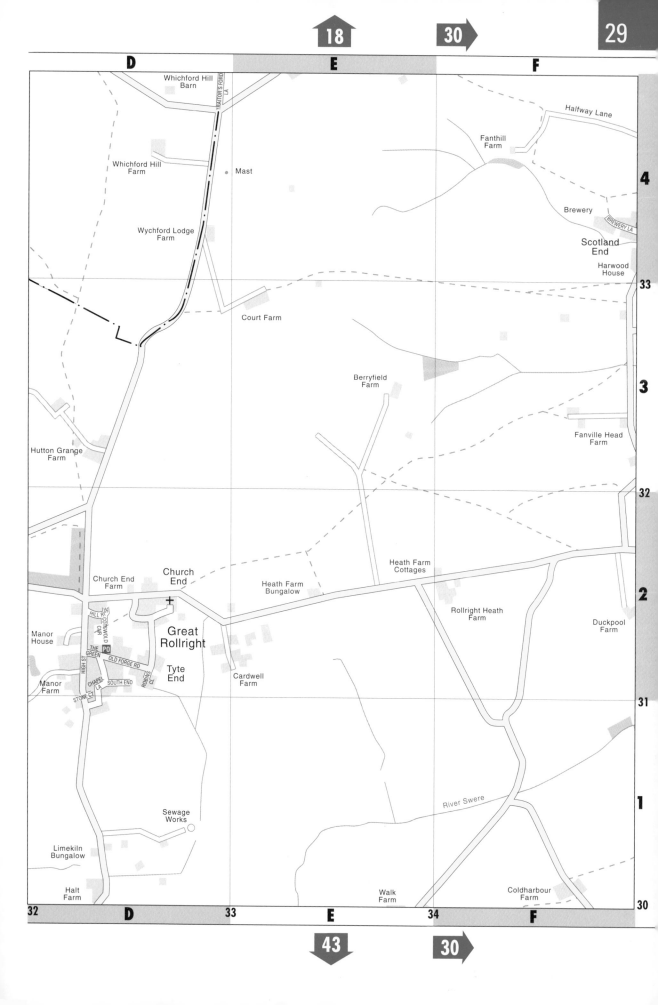

D
E
F

Whichford Hill Barn

TRAITOR'S FORD LA

Halfway Lane

Fanthill Farm

4

Whichford Hill Farm

Mast

Brewery

BREWERY LA

Wychford Lodge Farm

Scotland End

Harwood House

33

Court Farm

Berryfield Farm

3

Fanville Head Farm

Hutton Grange Farm

32

Heath Farm Cottages

Church End Farm

Church End

Heath Farm Bungalow

2

Rollright Heath Farm

Duckpool Farm

Manor House

HILL RISE

COTSWOLD CNR

Great Rollright

PO

THE GREEN

OLD FORGE RD

HIGH ST

CHAPEL LA

Tyte End

Cardwell Farm

ROBINS CL

SOUTH END

Manor Farm

STONE CT

31

Sewage Works

River Swere

1

Limekiln Bungalow

Halt Farm

Walk Farm

Coldharbour Farm

30

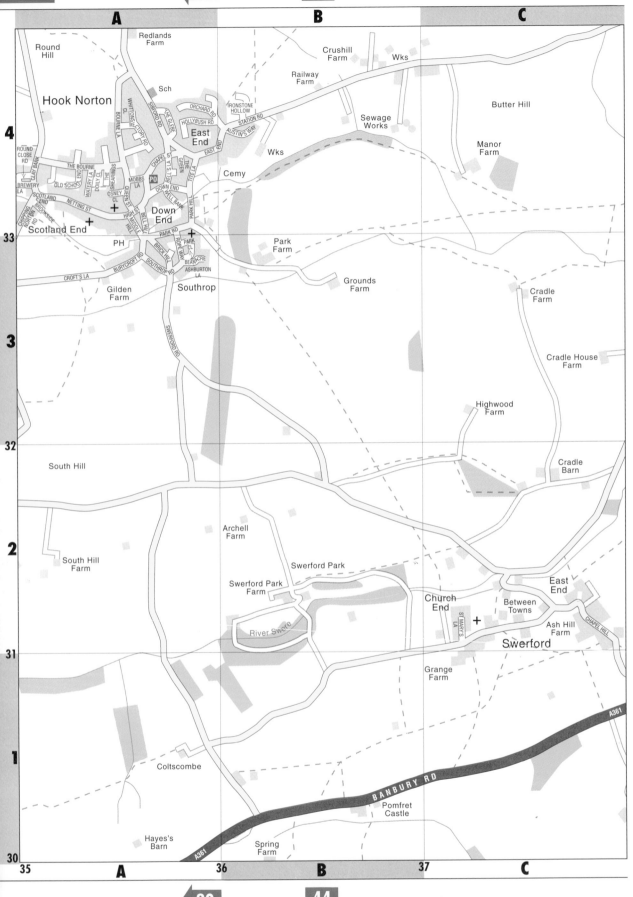

A   B   C

Round Hill
Redlands Farm
Crushill Farm
Wks
Railway Farm
Butter Hill
Hook Norton
Sch
ORCHARD RD
IRONSTONE HOLLOW
STATION RD
Sewage Works
Manor Farm

4

WHITTONS RD
THE GLEBE
BOURNE LA
HOLLYBUSH RD
AUSTIN'S WAY
East End
Wks
THE BOURNE
CHAPEL ST
BELL'S LA
GREEN
TITLE LA
EAST END
Cemy

ROUND CLOSE RD
CLAY BANK
OLD SCHO'
DOWN END
PARK RD
BREWERY LA
SCOTLAND END
WATERY LA
DOILY CL
THE SHEARINGS
MOBBS LA
WELL BANK
Down End
Park Farm

33

CHIPPING NORTON RD
BROOKSIDE
NETTING ST
QUEEN ST
HIGH ST
MIDDLE HILL
BELL HILL
OSNEY CL
PARK HILL
Scotland End
PH
PARK
ROPE WAY
Grounds Farm
Cradle Farm

BURYCROFT RD
SOUTHROP RD
BRICK HILL
ACRE
BEAN
ASHBURTON LA
Southrop
CROFT'S LA
Gilden Farm

Cradle House Farm

3

SWERFORD RD

Highwood Farm

32

South Hill

Cradle Barn

Archell Farm

2

South Hill Farm
Swerford Park
East End
Swerford Park Farm
Church End
Between Towns
Ash Hill Farm
CHAPEL HILL

River Swere
ST MARY'S LA
Swerford

31

Grange Farm

A361

1

Coltscombe
BANBURY RD

Pomfret Castle

Hayes's Barn
A361
Spring Farm

30

35   A   36   B   37   C

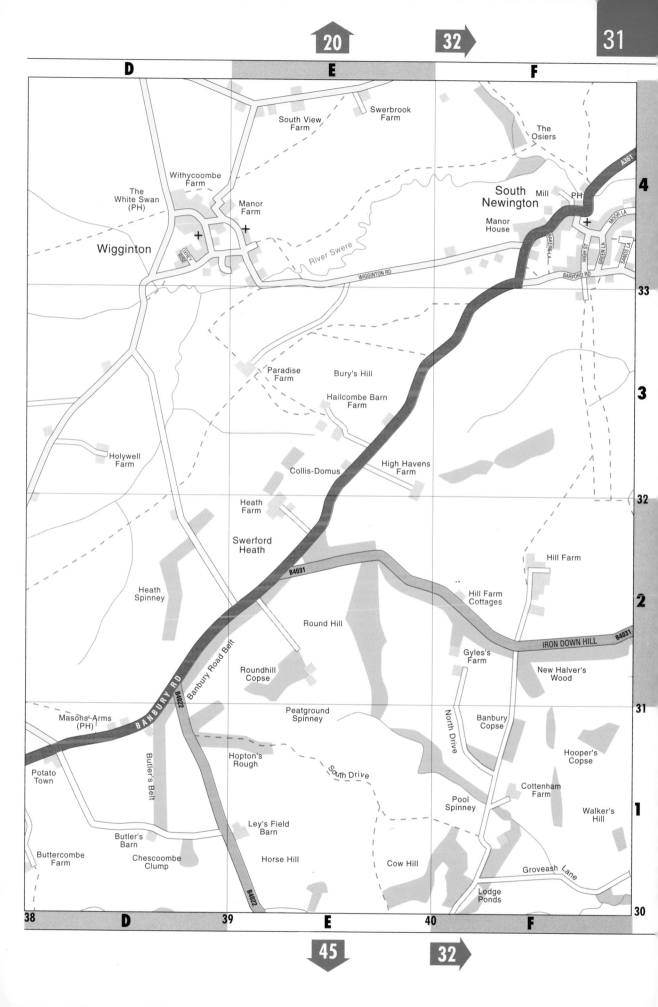

D E F

South View
Farm

Swerbrook
Farm

The
Osiers

Withycoombe
Farm

4

The
White Swan
(PH)

Manor
Farm

South
Newington

Mill

PH

A361

Manor
House

Wigginton

River Swere

WIGGINTON RD

BAKER LA

HIGH ST

GREEN LA

MOOR LA

SANDS LA

BARFORD RD

33

Paradise
Farm

Bury's Hill

Hailcombe Barn
Farm

3

Holywell
Farm

Collis-Domus

High Havens
Farm

32

Heath
Farm

Swerford
Heath

B4031

Hill Farm

Heath
Spinney

Round Hill

Hill Farm
Cottages

2

IRON DOWN HILL

B4031

Banbury Road Belt

Roundhill
Copse

Gyles's
Farm

New Halver's
Wood

Masons' Arms
(PH)

BANBURY RD

B4022

Peatground
Spinney

North Drive

Banbury
Copse

31

Potato
Town

Butler's Belt

Hopton's
Rough

South Drive

Hooper's
Copse

Cottenham
Farm

Ley's Field
Barn

Pool
Spinney

Walker's
Hill

1

Buttercombe
Farm

Butler's
Barn

Chescoombe
Clump

Horse Hill

Cow Hill

Groveash Lane

B4022

Lodge
Ponds

30

38 D 39 E 40 F

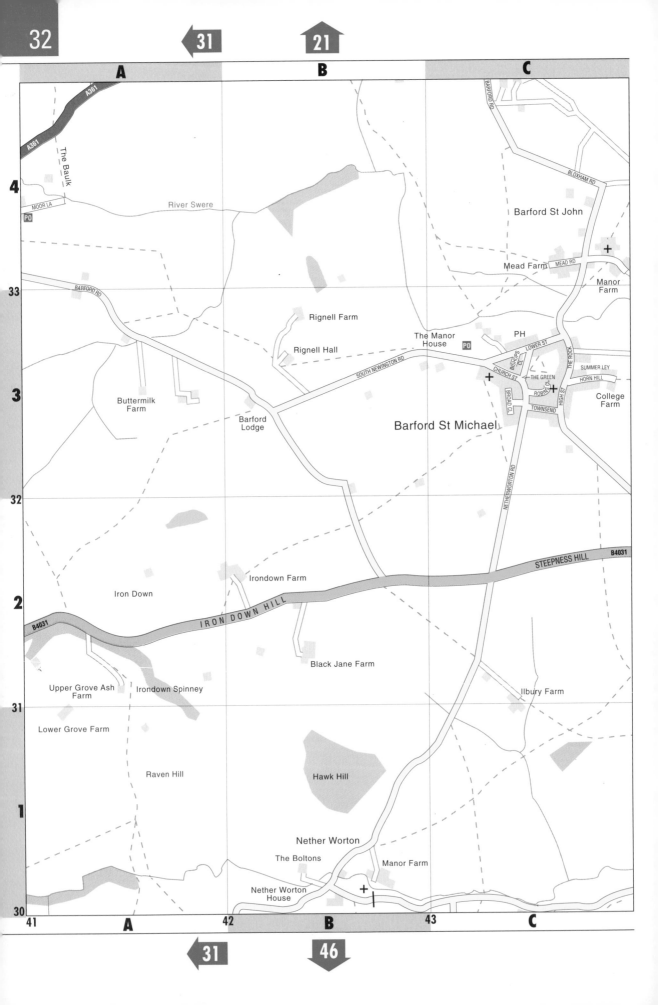

A   B   C

4

A361

The Baulk

MOOR LA

PO

River Swere

BARFORD RD

Barford Rd

BLOXHAM RD

BARFORD RD

Barford St John

Mead Farm   MEAD RD

Manor Farm

33

Rignell Farm

Rignell Hall

The Manor House

PO

PH

Lower St

BISHOPS CL

CHURCH ST

THE GREEN

THE ROCK

SUMMER LEY

HORN HILL

3

Buttermilk Farm

Barford Lodge

SOUTH NEWINGTON RD

Barford St Michael

BROAD CL

RORY

HIGH ST

TOWNSEND

College Farm

32

NETHER WORTON RD

STEEPNESS HILL   B4031

2

Iron Down

Irondown Farm

IRON DOWN HILL

B4031

Black Jane Farm

Ilbury Farm

31

Upper Grove Ash Farm

Irondown Spinney

Lower Grove Farm

Raven Hill

Hawk Hill

1

Nether Worton

The Boltons

Manor Farm

Nether Worton House

30

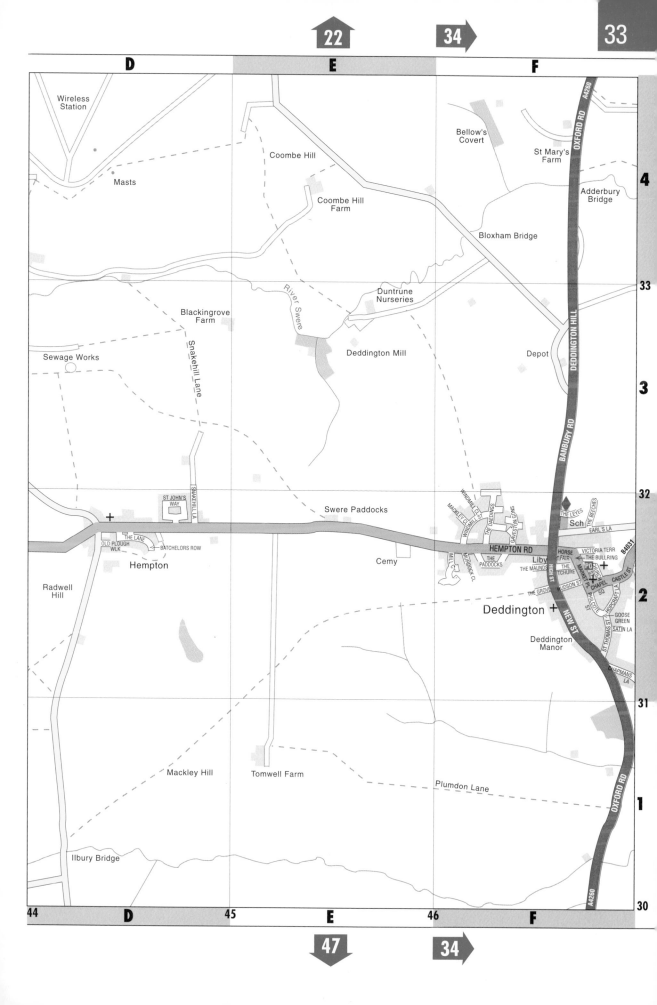

Wireless Station

Coombe Hill

Bellow's Covert

St Mary's Farm

OXFORD RD

A4260

Masts

Coombe Hill Farm

Adderbury Bridge

4

Bloxham Bridge

DEDDINGTON HILL

33

River Swere

Duntrune Nurseries

Blackingrove Farm

Snakehill Lane

Depot

Sewage Works

Deddington Mill

BANBURY RD

3

St John's Way

SNAKEHILL LA

Swere Paddocks

32

THE LEYES

THE BEECHES

WINDMILL CL'ST

THE DAEDINGS

GAVESTON GDNS

MACKLEY CL

Sch

EARL'S LA

THE LANE

OLD PLOUGH WLK

BATCHELORS ROW

HEMPTON RD

HORSE FAIR

Lib

VICTORIA TERR

THE BULLRING

B4031

Cemy

MILL CL

MURDOCK CL

THE PADDOCKS

HIGH ST

THE MAUNDS

POST

CHURCH

CHAPEL SQ

MARKET PL

HUDSON ST

PHILCOTE ST

CASTLE ST

Hempton

THE GROVE

Deddington

NEW ST

ST THOMAS ST

HOPCRAFT LA

SATIN LA

GOOSE GREEN

2

Radwell Hill

Deddington Manor

CHAPMANS LA

31

Mackley Hill

Tomwell Farm

Plumdon Lane

OXFORD RD

1

Ilbury Bridge

A4260

30

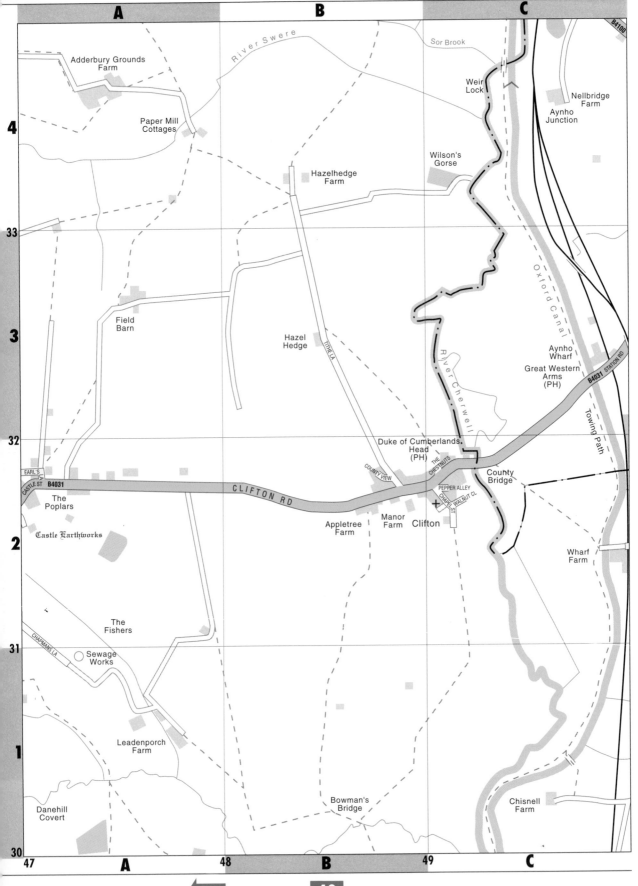

A B C

Adderbury Grounds Farm

River Swere

Sor Brook

Weir Lock

Nellbridge Farm

Aynho Junction

4

Paper Mill Cottages

Hazelhedge Farm

Wilson's Gorse

Oxford Canal

33

Field Barn

Hazel Hedge

TIME LA

River Cherwell

Aynho Wharf

Great Western Arms (PH)

B4031 STATION RD

3

32

Duke of Cumberlands Head (PH)

Towing Path

EARL'S

CASTLE ST

B4031

CLIFTON RD

COUNTY VIEW

THE CHESTNUTS

County Bridge

The Poplars

Castle Earthworks

Appletree Farm

Manor Farm

Clifton

PEPPER ALLEY

CHAPEL ST

WALNUT CL

Wharf Farm

2

The Fishers

CHAPMANS LA

Sewage Works

31

Leadenporch Farm

Bowman's Bridge

Chisnell Farm

1

Danehill Covert

30

47 A 48 B 49 C

Pesthouse Wood

Ox House

Bricklands Farm

Aynho

CHARLTON RD

HE BUTTS

B4100 BANBURY RD

PO

PORTWAY

PORTWAY GDNS

4

B4100

B4031

B4031

BLACKSMITHS

BUTTS

SCHOOL

BOWMEN'S

THE GLEBE

ILEA

HILLS

LITTLE LA

SKITTLE ALLEY 1
HOLLOW WAY 2
THE HILL 3

CROUGHTON RD

THE SQUARE

THE BOTHY

CARTWRIGHT

SMITH

Inn

B4031

ROUNDTOWN

Aynho Fields

33

Friar's Well

Aynhoe Park House

Ryeland Hill

Northcotehill Covert

Aynho Park

Ash Grove

Puckwell

The Mill House

Keeper's Hill

3

The Firs

Lower Aynho Grounds

Park Flat

Holloway's Flat

STATION RD

The Oaks

32

Viaduct

Sewage Works

Risley's Corner

Souldern

Souldern Mill

Old Shaws

WHARF LA

2

Souldern Manor

BATES LA

THE PADDOCKS

FOX LA

HIGH ST

BOVEWELL

FOXHILL LA

The Bear (PH)

Ploughley Hill

31

Viaduct

Holtage Lane

Foxhill Lane

Fox Hill

B4100

1

Souldern Grounds

Souldern Grounds Farm

Foxhill Barn

Inkerman Farm

M40

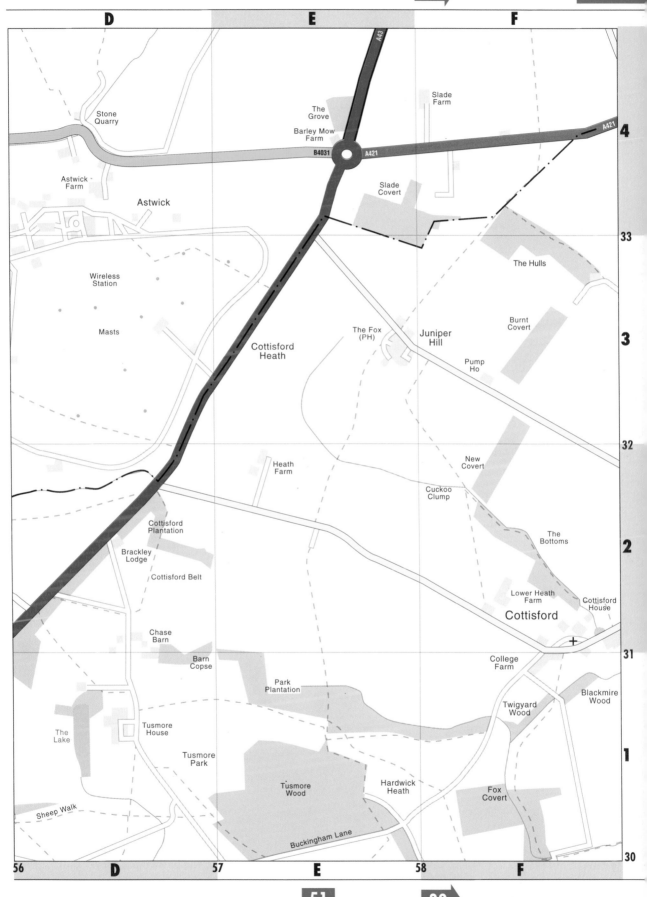

D
E
F

Stone
Quarry

The
Grove

A43

Slade
Farm

A421

Barley Mow
Farm

B4031

A421

4

Astwick
Farm

Slade
Covert

Astwick

33

The Hulls

Wireless
Station

Burnt
Covert

Masts

The Fox
(PH)

Juniper
Hill

3

Cottisford
Heath

Pump
Ho

32

Heath
Farm

New
Covert

Cuckoo
Clump

Cottisford
Plantation

The
Bottoms

2

Brackley
Lodge

Cottisford Belt

Lower Heath
Farm

Cottisford
House

Chase
Barn

Cottisford

Barn
Copse

College
Farm

31

Park
Plantation

Twigyard
Wood

Blackmire
Wood

The
Lake

Tusmore
House

Tusmore
Park

1

Sheep Walk

Tusmore
Wood

Hardwick
Heath

Fox
Covert

Buckingham Lane

30

56
D
57
E
58
F

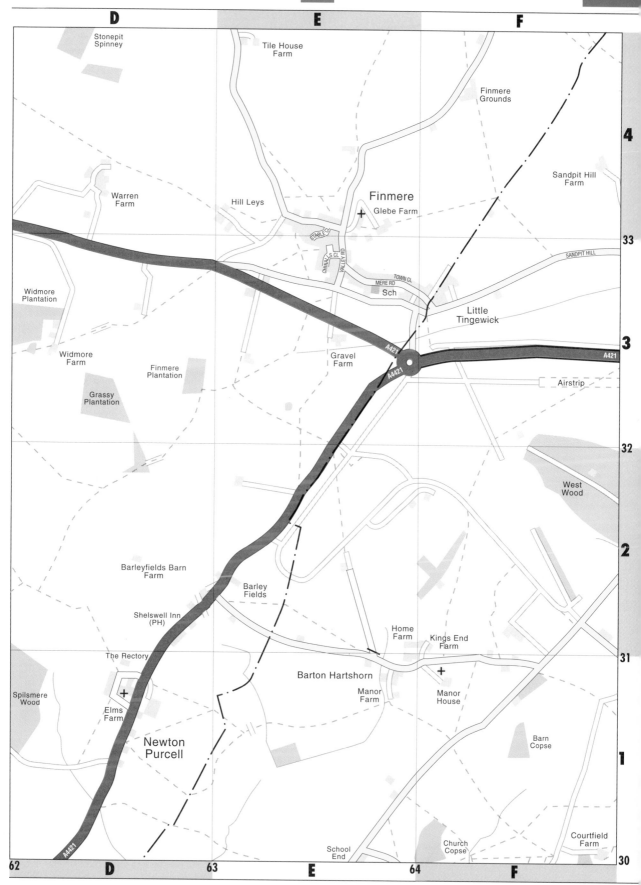

D E F

4

33

3

32

2

31

1

30

Stonepit Spinney

Tile House Farm

Finmere Grounds

Sandpit Hill Farm

Warren Farm

Hill Leys

Finmere

Glebe Farm

STABLE CL

CHINALS CL

VALLEY RD

Sandpit Hill

Widmore Plantation

TOWN CL

MERE RD

Sch

Little Tingewick

Widmore Farm

Finmere Plantation

Gravel Farm

A421

A4421

A421

Airstrip

Grassy Plantation

West Wood

Barleyfields Barn Farm

Barley Fields

Shelswell Inn (PH)

Home Farm

Kings End Farm

The Rectory

Barton Hartshorn

Manor Farm

Manor House

Spilsmere Wood

Elms Farm

Newton Purcell

Barn Copse

School End

Church Copse

Courtfield Farm

A4421

62 D 63 E 64 F

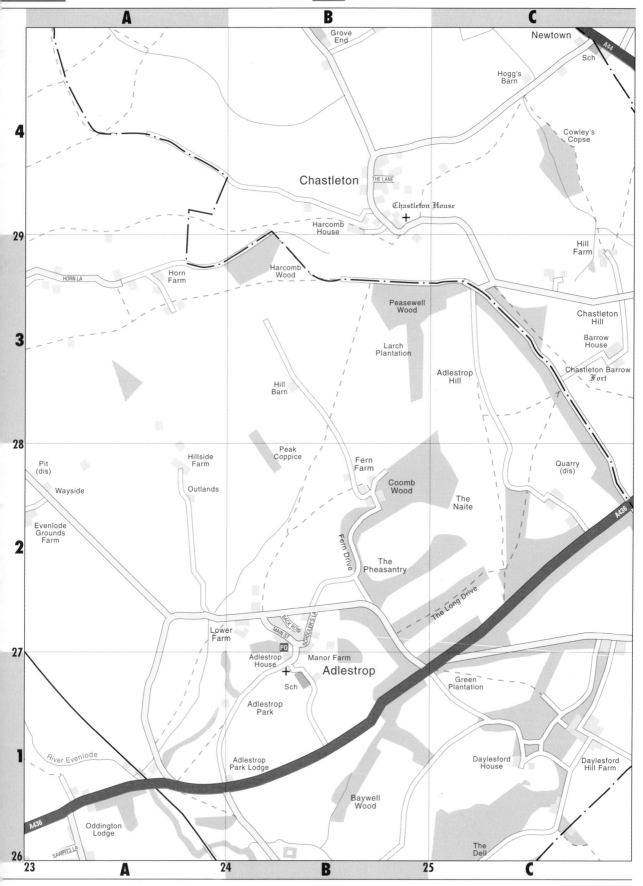

A **B** **C**

Newtown

A44

Grove
End

Hogg's
Barn

Cowley's
Copse

4

Chastleton

THE LANE

Chastleton House

Hill
Farm

Harcomb
House

29

HORN LA

Horn
Farm

Harcomb
Wood

Chastleton
Hill

Peasewell
Wood

Barrow
House

Larch
Plantation

Chastleton Barrow
Fort

3

Adlestrop
Hill

Hill
Barn

28

Peak
Coppice

Fern
Farm

Quarry
(dis)

Pit
(dis)

Hillside
Farm

Coomb
Wood

The
Naite

A436

Wayside

Outlands

Evenlode
Grounds
Farm

Fern Drive

The
Pheasantry

2

The Long Drive

Lower
Farm

BACK ROW

SCHOOL LA

MAIN ST

PO

Green
Plantation

27

Adlestrop
House

Manor Farm

Adlestrop

Sch

Adlestrop
Park

River Evenlode

Daylesford
House

Daylesford
Hill Farm

1

Adlestrop
Park Lodge

A436

Baywell
Wood

Oddington
Lodge

SAWPITS LA

The
Dell

26

23 **A** **24** **B** **25** **C**

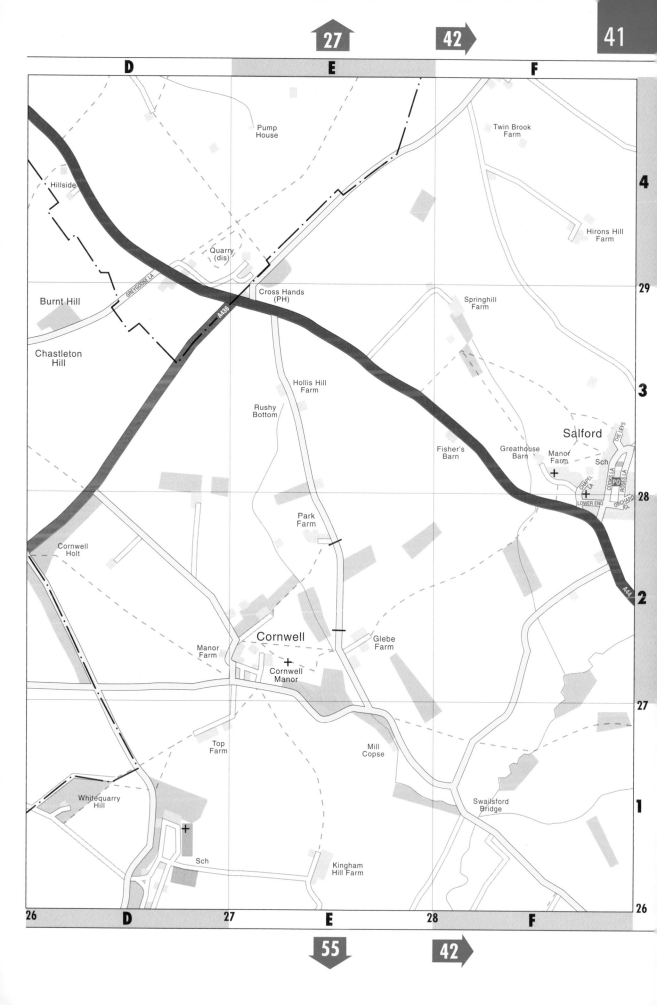

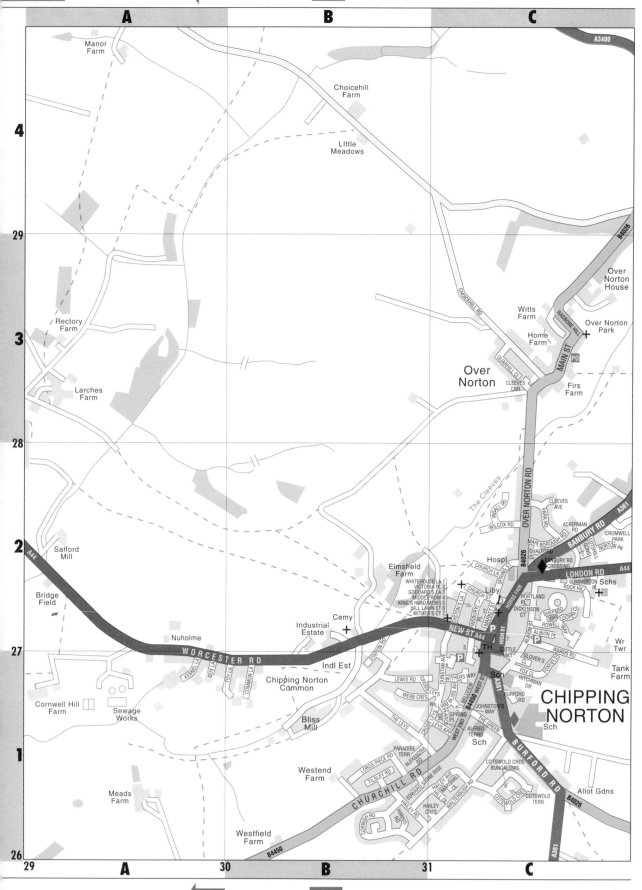

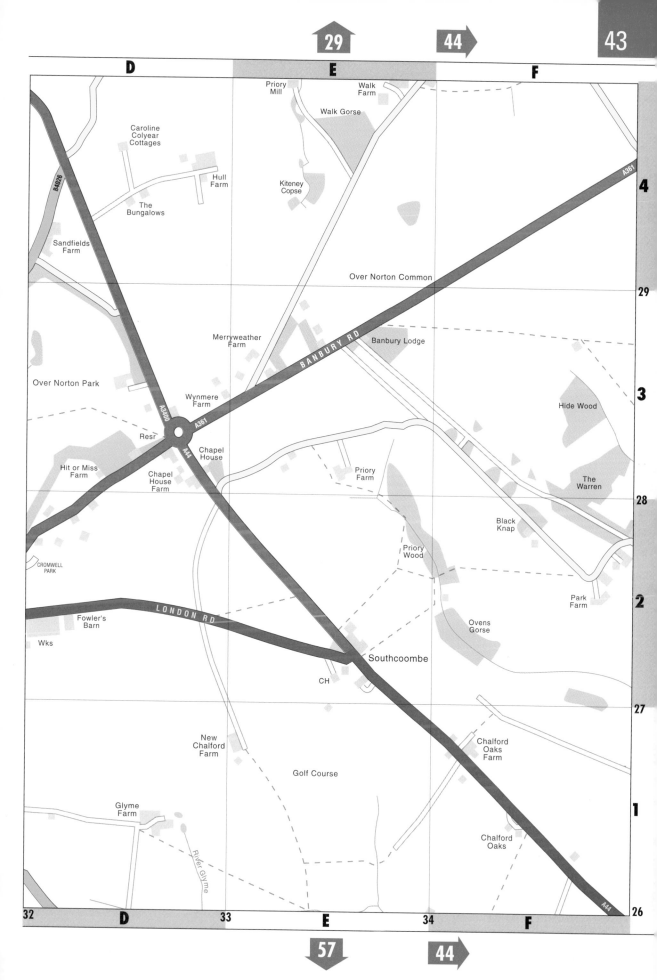

D E F

Priory Mill

Walk Farm

Walk Gorse

Caroline Colyear Cottages

B4026

Hull Farm

Kiteney Copse

4

The Bungalows

Sandfields Farm

A3361

Over Norton Common

29

Merryweather Farm

BANBURY RD

Banbury Lodge

Over Norton Park

Wynmere Farm

A3400

Hide Wood

3

Resr

A361

A44

Chapel House

Priory Farm

The Warren

Hit or Miss Farm

Chapel House Farm

28

Black Knap

CROMWELL PARK

Priory Wood

LONDON RD

Fowler's Barn

Ovens Gorse

Park Farm

2

Wks

Southcoombe

CH

27

New Chalford Farm

Chalford Oaks Farm

Golf Course

Glyme Farm

1

Chalford Oaks

River Glyme

A44

32 D 33 E 34 F 26

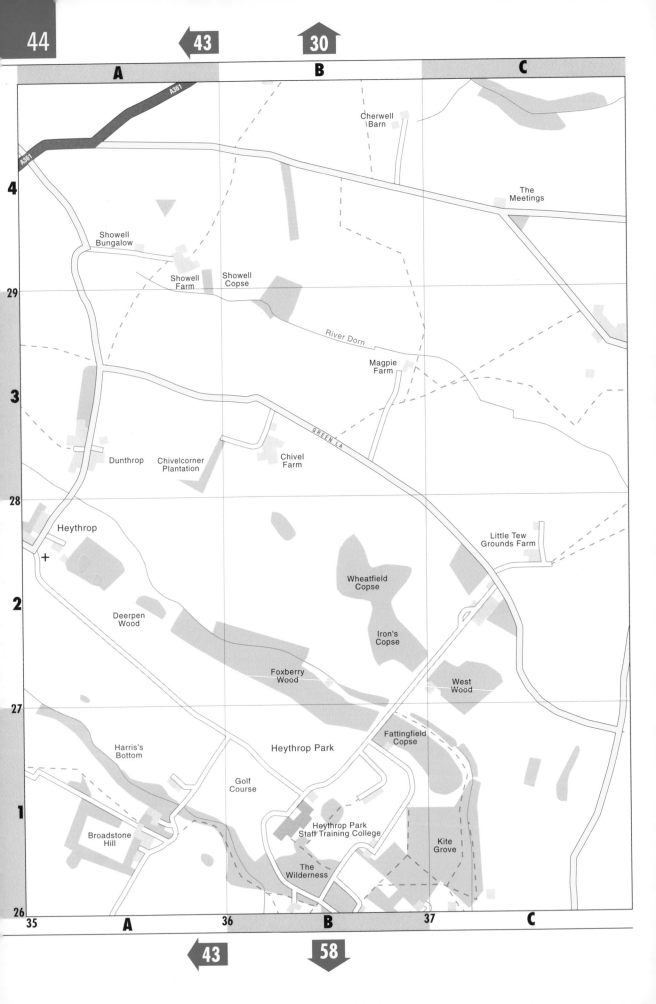

A361

A **B** **C**

Cherwell Barn

The Meetings

4

Showell Bungalow

Showell Farm

Showell Copse

29

River Dorn

Magpie Farm

3

GREEN LA

Dunthrop

Chivelcorner Plantation

Chivel Farm

28

Heythrop

+

Little Tew Grounds Farm

Wheatfield Copse

2

Deerpen Wood

Iron's Copse

Foxberry Wood

West Wood

27

Harris's Bottom

Heythrop Park

Fattingfield Copse

Golf Course

1

Broadstone Hill

Heythrop Park Staff Training College

Kite Grove

The Wilderness

26

35 **A** 36 **B** 37 **C**

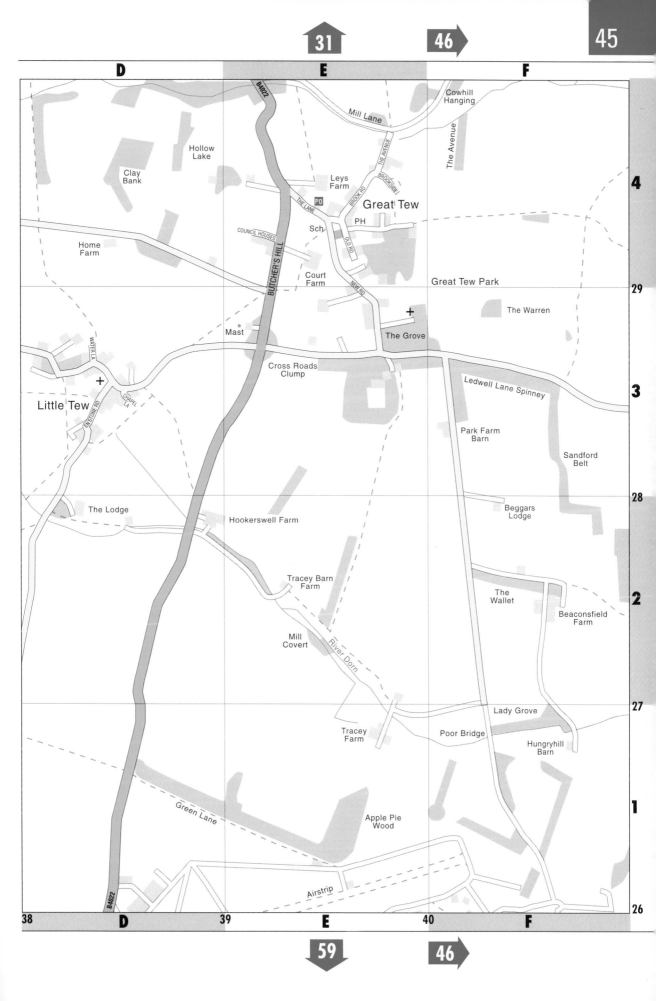

D
E
F

B4022

Cowhill
Hanging

Mill Lane

The Avenue

Hollow
Lake

Clay
Bank

Leys
Farm

THE LANE

THE AVENUE

BROOKSIDE

Great Tew

4

PO

Sch

PH

BROOK RD

COUNCIL HOUSES

BUTCHER'S HILL

Home
Farm

Court
Farm

OLD RD

Great Tew Park

29

NEW RD

The Warren

Mast

The Grove

WATER LA

Ledwell Lane Spinney

3

Cross Roads
Clump

Little Tew

CHAPEL LA

ENSTONE RD

Park Farm
Barn

Sandford
Belt

The Lodge

28

Hookerswell Farm

Beggars
Lodge

Tracey Barn
Farm

The
Wallet

2

Beaconsfield
Farm

Mill
Covert

River Dorn

Lady Grove

27

Tracey
Farm

Poor Bridge

Hungryhill
Barn

Green Lane

Apple Pie
Wood

1

B4022

Airstrip

26

38
D
39
E
40
F

45
32

A **B** **C**

4

Newhouse
Farm

Flighthill
Farm

Over Worton

Worton
House

Rest Hill Farm

Grange
Farm

+

Flighthill
Cottage

Hobbshole
Farm

Lark
Rise

29

The Bungalow

Brae

3

Hangman's Hill

Cockley Brook

Heath Farm

Ledwell

Close
Farm

28

Worton Wood

Conygree
Wood

2

Parkend
Cottages

Heath Cottage
Farm

Cricket
Ground

High
Ley

27

Down Hill
Farm

Park Farm

Sandford Park

River Dorn

Sandford
St Martin

+

Mill

Brandon
Farm

Manor
House

ORCHARD WAY

Middle
Barton

Manor
Farm

HILLSIDE RD

WORTON RD

1

MANOR RD

HOLLIERS CRES

Manor
House

BALLARD CL

26

41   **A**   42   **B**   43   **C**

45
60

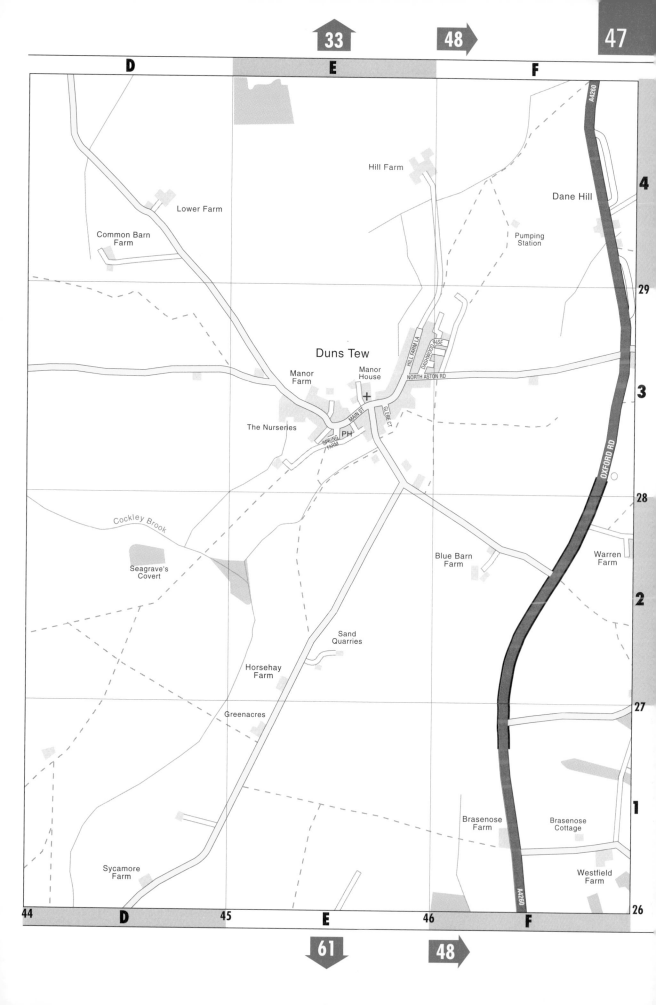

Hill Farm

Dane Hill

Lower Farm

Common Barn
Farm

Pumping
Station

4

29

Duns Tew

HILL FARM LA

DASHWOOD RISE

NORTH ASTON RD

Manor
Farm

Manor
House

The Nurseries

MAIN ST

GLEBE CT

PH

SPRING
FARM

3

Cockley Brook

28

Seagrave's
Covert

Blue Barn
Farm

Warren
Farm

OXFORD RD

A4260

2

Sand
Quarries

Horsehay
Farm

Greenacres

27

Sycamore
Farm

Brasenose
Farm

Brasenose
Cottage

Westfield
Farm

1

A4260

26

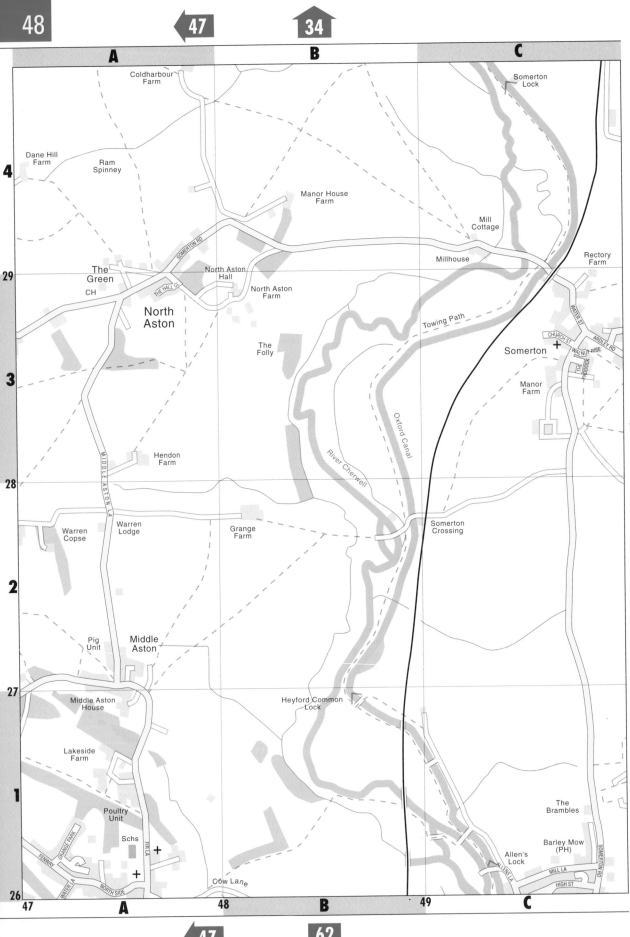

A B C

Somerton Lock

Coldharbour Farm

Dane Hill Farm

Ram Spinney

4

Manor House Farm

Mill Cottage

29

SOMERTON RD

The Green

CH

North Aston Hall

North Aston Farm

THE WALL CL

Millhouse

Rectory Farm

North Aston

WATER ST

Towing Path

Somerton

CHURCH ST

WALNUT-RISE

ARDLEY RD

THE PADDOCK

The Folly

3

Manor Farm

MIDDLE ASTON LA

Hendon Farm

Oxford Canal

River Cherwell

28

Warren Copse

Warren Lodge

Grange Farm

Somerton Crossing

2

Pig Unit

Middle Aston

27

Middle Aston House

Heyford Common Lock

Lakeside Farm

1

The Brambles

Poultry Unit

FIR LA

Barley Mow (PH)

SOMERTON RD

Schs

Allen's Lock

ALLENS LA

MILL LA

GRANGE PARK

FENWAY

WATER LA

NORTH SIDE

Cow Lane

HIGH ST

26

47 A 48 B 49 C

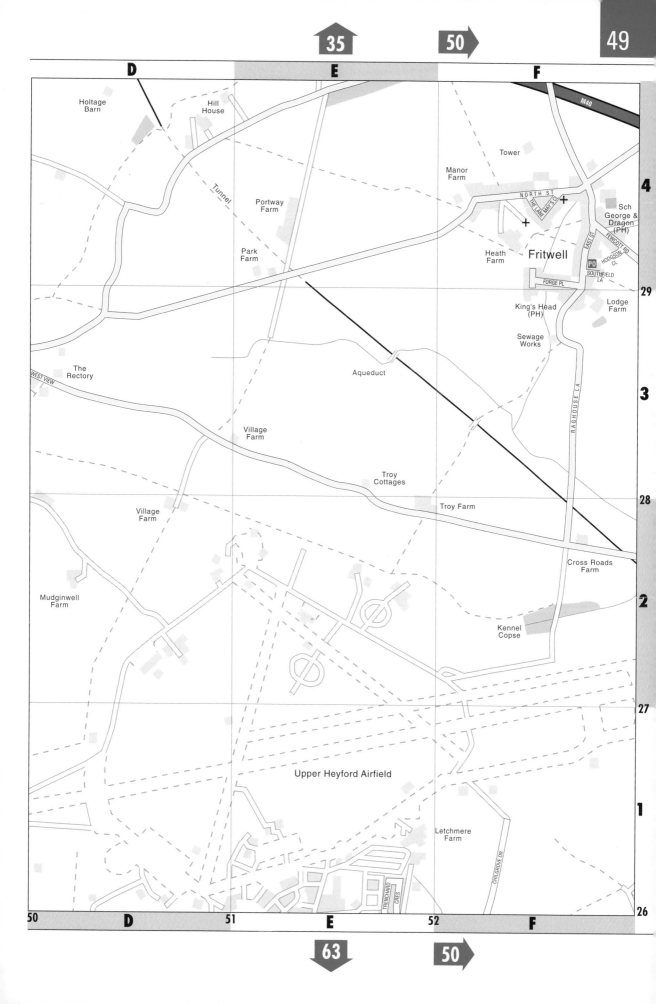

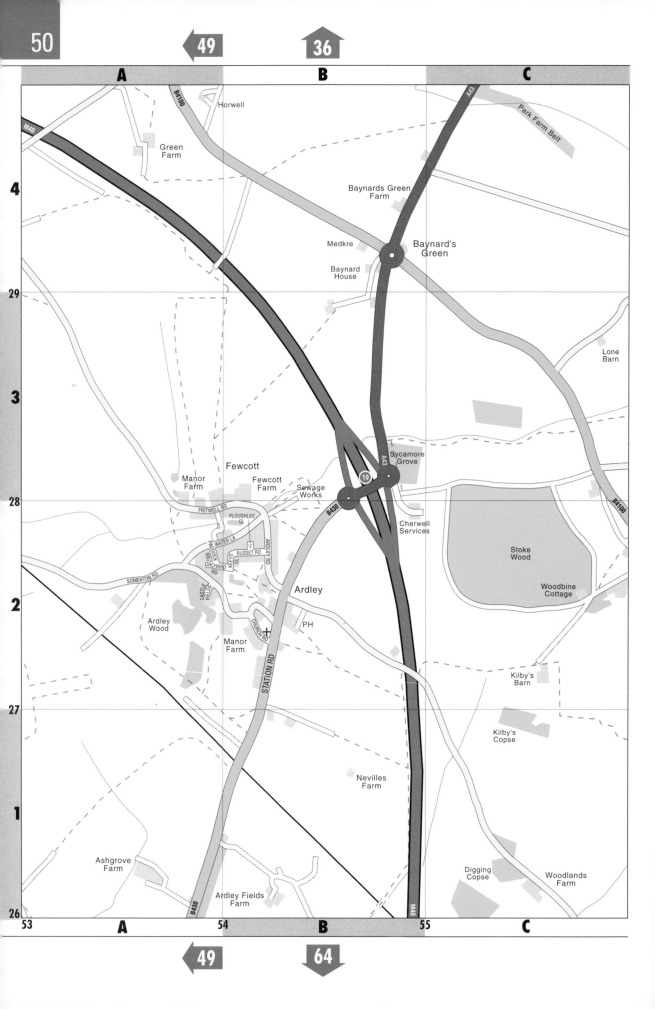

A

B

C

4

Horwell

Green
Farm

Baynards Green
Farm

Medkre

Baynard's
Green

29

Baynard
House

Lone
Barn

3

Fewcott

Sycamore
Grove

Manor
Farm

Fewcott
Farm

Sewage
Works

10

28

FRITWELL RD

PLOUGHLEY
CL

Cherwell
Services

WATER LA

Stoke
Wood

RUSSET RD

PADDOCK RD

ORCHARD RD

KEYS CL

ARDLEY RD

SOMERTON RD

CASTLE
FIELDS

Ardley

Woodbine
Cottage

2

Ardley
Wood

PH

Manor
Farm

CHURCH RD

Kilby's
Barn

27

STATION RD

Kilby's
Copse

1

Nevilles
Farm

Ashgrove
Farm

Digging
Copse

Woodlands
Farm

26

53

A

54

B

55

C

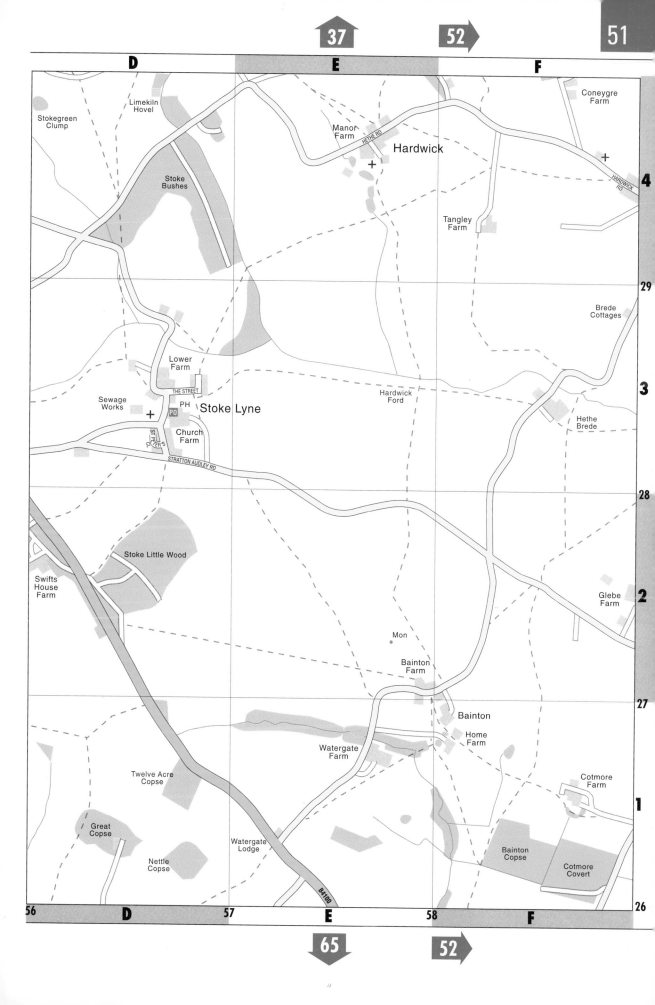

D
E
F

Stokegreen
Clump

Limekiln
Hovel

Coneygre
Farm

Manor
Farm

HETHE RD

Hardwick

+

HARDWICK RD

4

Stoke
Bushes

Tangley
Farm

29

Brede
Cottages

Lower
Farm

THE STREET

Hardwick
Ford

3

Sewage
Works

PH

+

PO

Stoke Lyne

ST PETER'S CL

Church
Farm

Hethe
Brede

STRATTON AUDLEY RD

28

Stoke Little Wood

Swifts
House
Farm

Glebe
Farm

2

Mon

Bainton
Farm

27

Bainton

Watergate
Farm

Home
Farm

Twelve Acre
Copse

Cotmore
Farm

1

Great
Copse

Watergate
Lodge

Bainton
Copse

Cotmore
Covert

Nettle
Copse

B4100

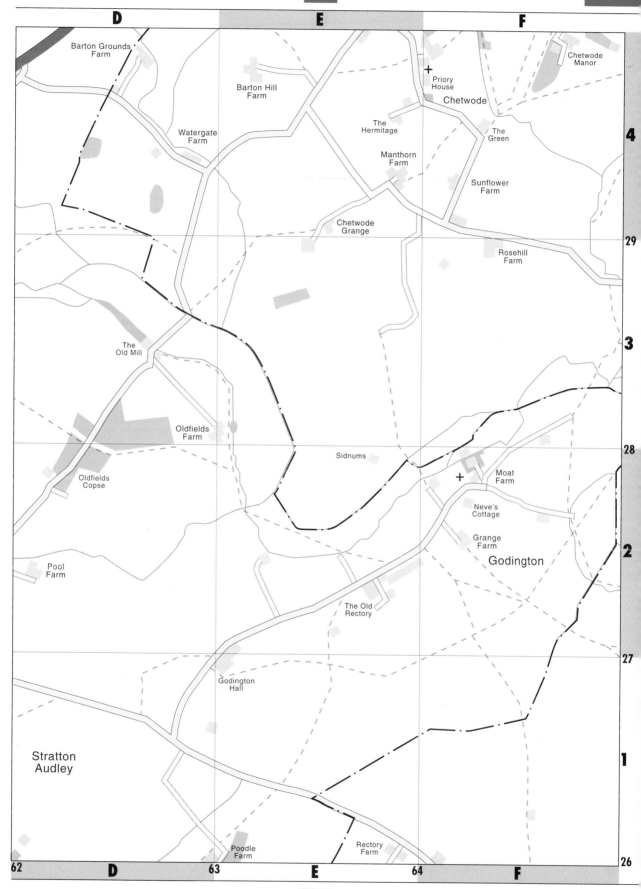

Barton Grounds Farm

Barton Hill Farm

Watergate Farm

Chetwode Manor

Priory House

Chetwode

The Hermitage

The Green

Manthorn Farm

Sunflower Farm

Chetwode Grange

Rosehill Farm

The Old Mill

Oldfields Farm

Sidnums

Moat Farm

Neve's Cottage

Oldfields Copse

Grange Farm

Godington

Pool Farm

The Old Rectory

Godington Hall

Stratton Audley

Poodle Farm

Rectory Farm

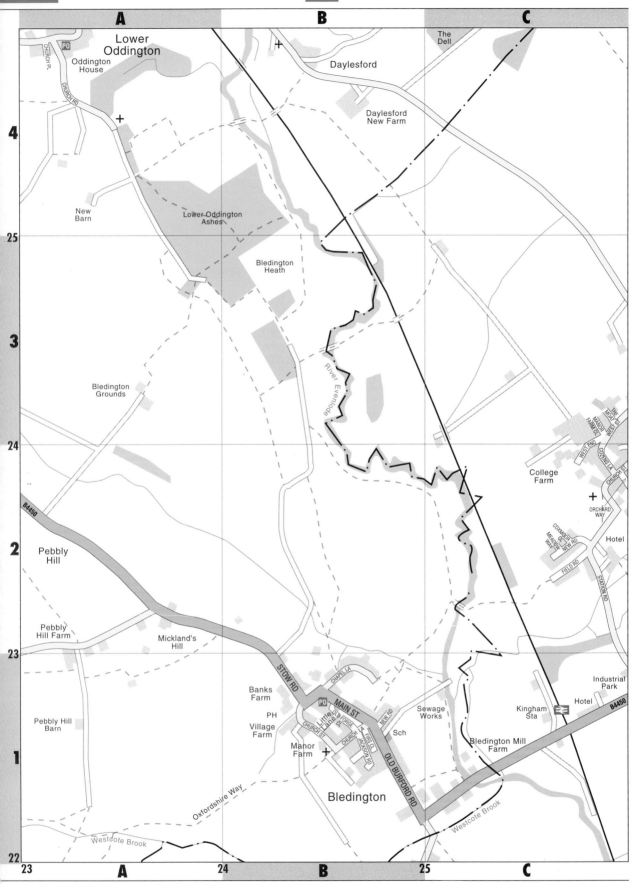

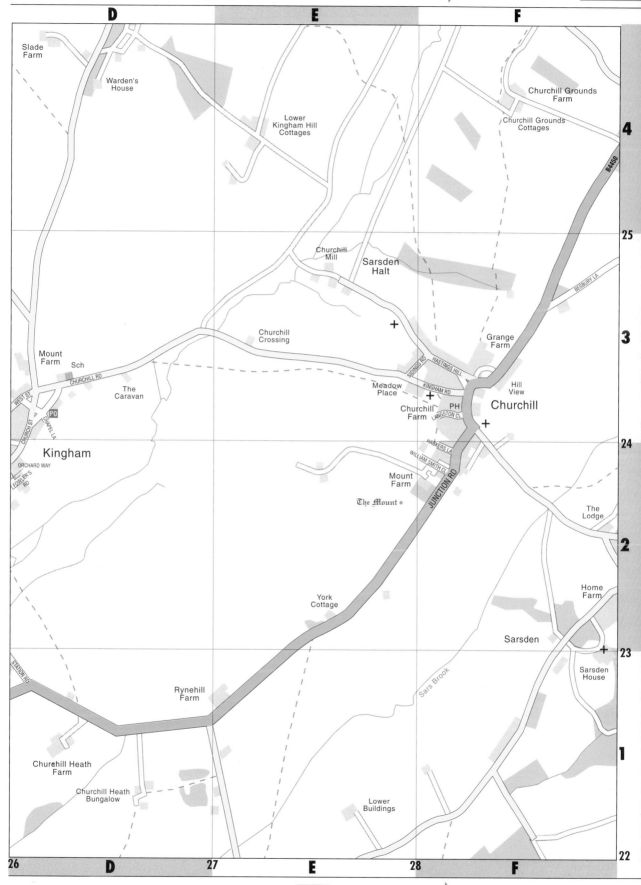

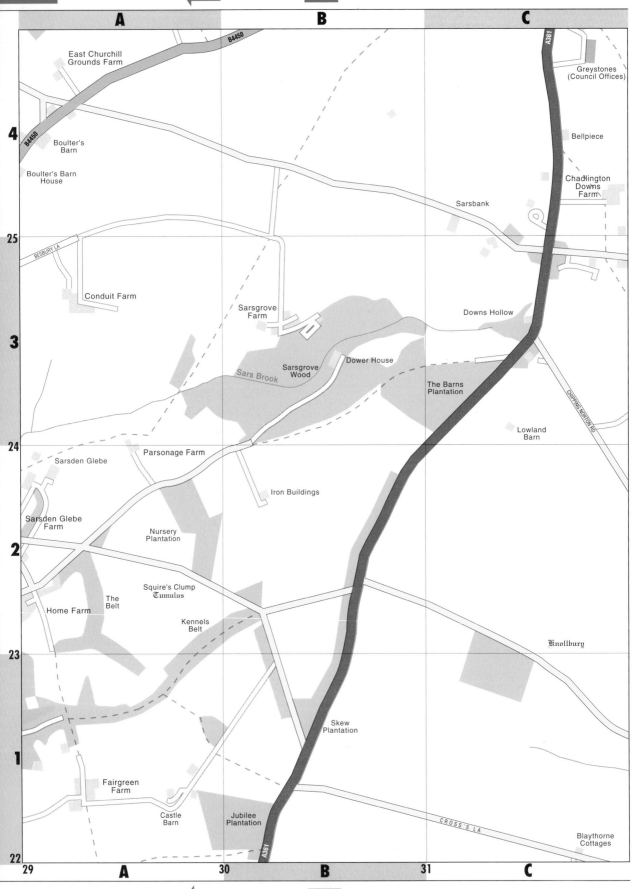

A
B
C

East Churchill
Grounds Farm

B4450

A361

Greystones
(Council Offices)

B4450

4

Boulter's
Barn

Bellpiece

Boulter's Barn
House

Chadlington
Downs
Farm

Sarsbank

25

BESBURY LA

Conduit Farm

Sarsgrove
Farm

Downs Hollow

3

Sars Brook

Sarsgrove
Wood

Dower House

The Barns
Plantation

CHIPPING NORTON RD

24

Parsonage Farm

Lowland
Barn

Sarsden Glebe

Iron Buildings

Sarsden Glebe
Farm

Nursery
Plantation

2

Squire's Clump
Tumulus

Home Farm

The
Belt

Kennels
Belt

Knollbury

23

Skew
Plantation

1

Fairgreen
Farm

Castle
Barn

Jubilee
Plantation

CROSS'S LA

Blaythorne
Cottages

A361

22

29
A
30
B
31
C

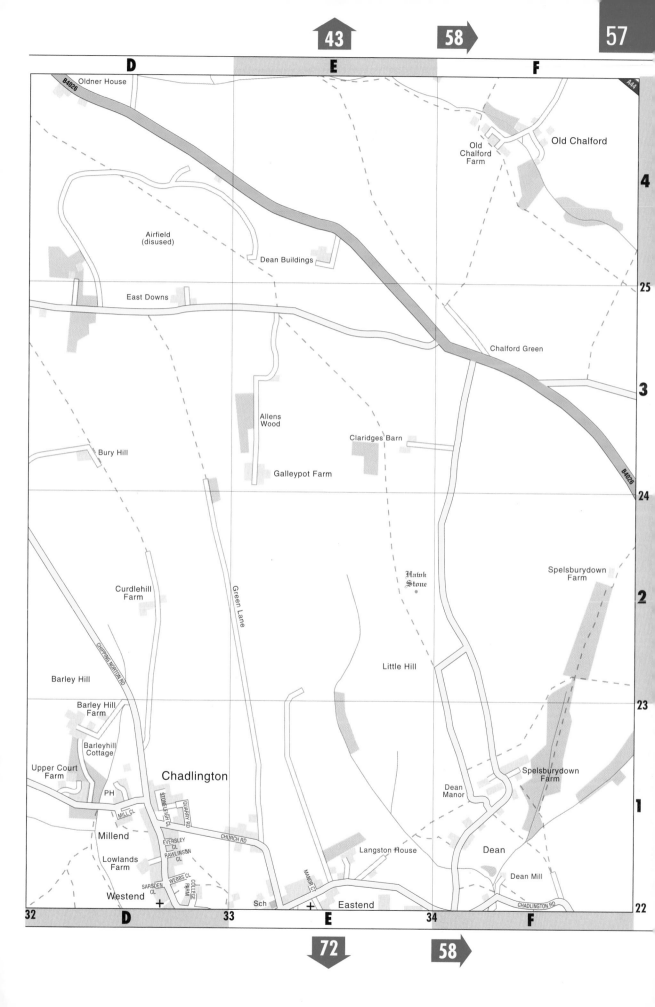

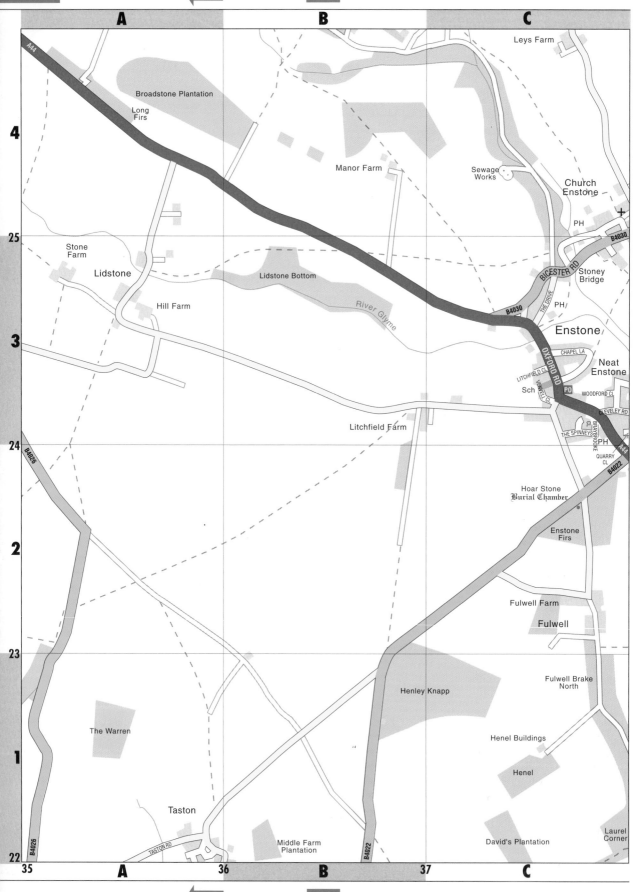

A B C

A44

Broadstone Plantation

Long
Firs

4

Manor Farm

Sewage
Works

Church
Enstone

PH

B4030

25

Stone
Farm

Lidstone

Bicester Rd

Stoney
Bridge

Hill Farm

Lidstone Bottom

River Glyme

B4030

PH

THE DRIVE

Enstone

3

CHAPEL LA

Neat
Enstone

OXFORD RD

LITCHFIELD CL

VENNEL CL

Sch

PO

WOODFORD CL

CLEVELEY RD

Litchfield Farm

THE SPINNEYS

BRAYBROOKE CL

PH

24

B4026

QUARRY CL

A44

B4022

Hoar Stone
Burial Chamber

Enstone
Firs

2

Fulwell Farm

Fulwell

23

Fulwell Brake
North

Henley Knapp

The Warren

Henel Buildings

1

Henel

Laurel
Corner

Taston

B4022

B4026

Middle Farm
Plantation

David's Plantation

22

35 A 36 B 37 C

TASTON RD

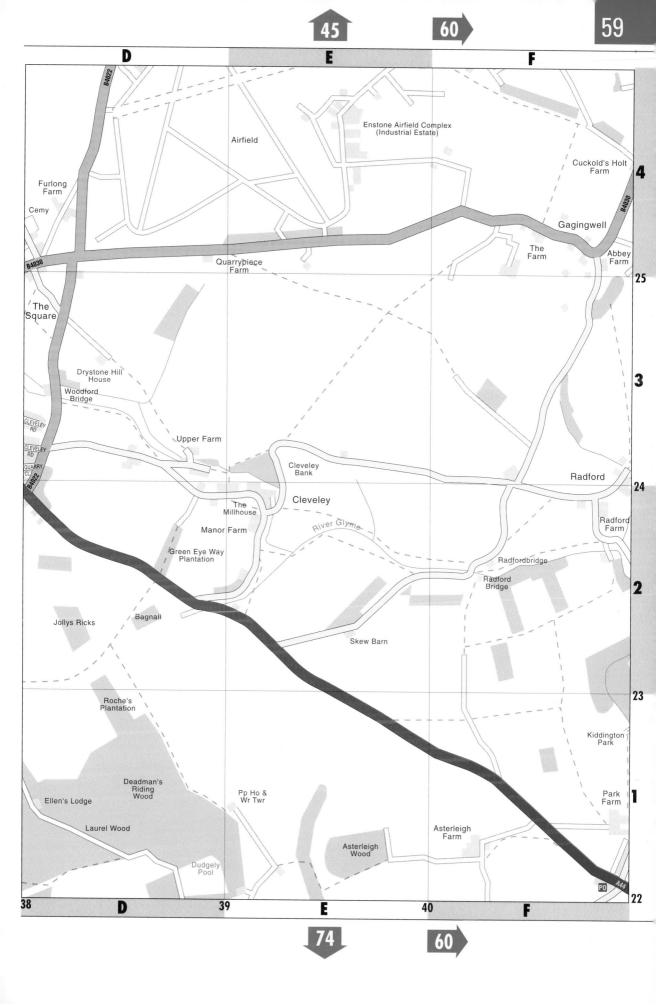

59
46

59
75

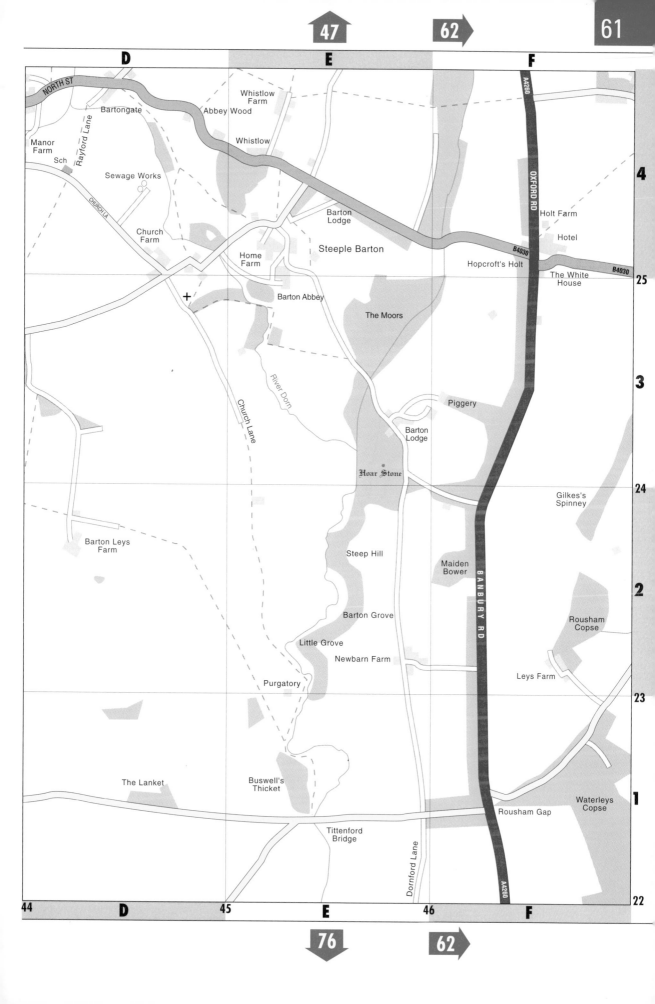

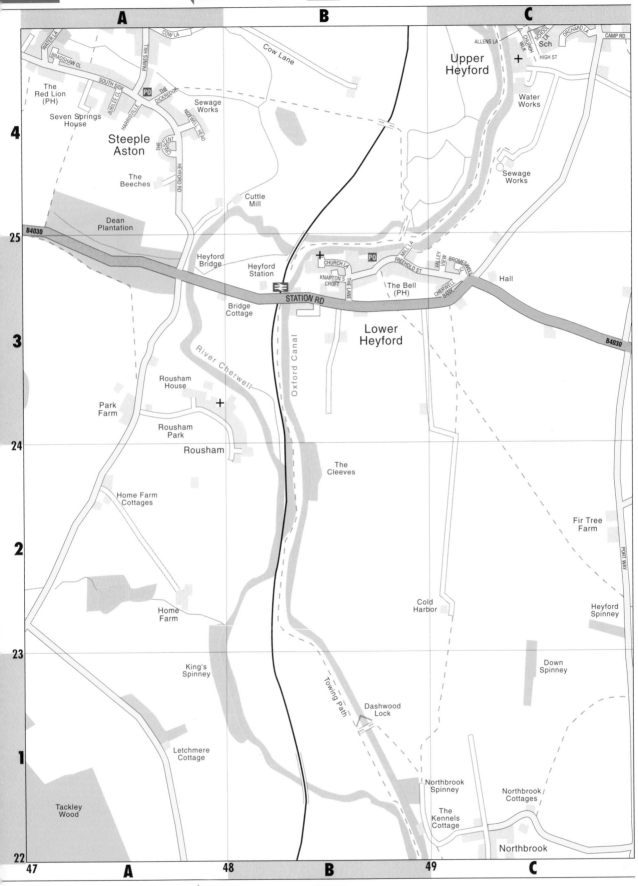

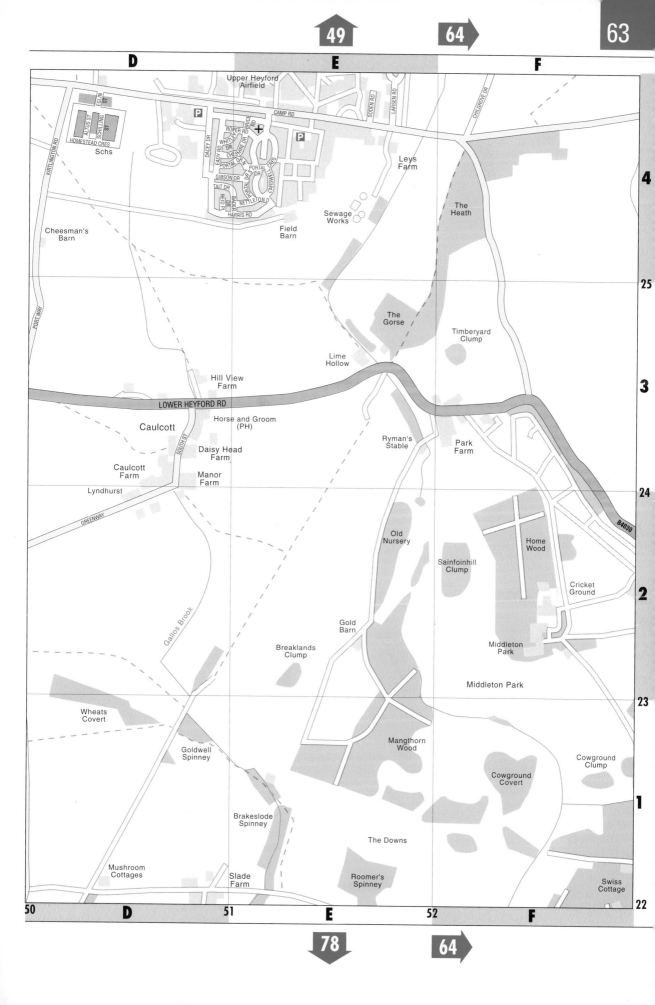

D
E
F

Upper Heyford Airfield

CAMP RD

Schs
HOMESTEAD CRES
ALTUS ST
EGLIN ST
SCHILLING ST

P

DACEY DR
EAVY RD
ROPER RD
WHITLEY DR
CHESHIRE DR
BRIDGE RD

P

PORTAL DR
PORTAL DR
GIBSON DR
TAIT DR
BAKER DR
REID PL
NETTLETON D
HARRIS RD
PORTAL CRES
CARSWELL CRES

KIRTLINGTON RD

SODEN RD
LARSEN RD

CHILGROVE DR

Leys Farm

The Heath

4

Cheesman's Barn

Field Barn

Sewage Works

PORT WAY

25

The Gorse

Timberyard Clump

Lime Hollow

Hill View Farm

LOWER HEYFORD RD

3

Caulcott

Horse and Groom (PH)

Ryman's Stable

Park Farm

SOUTH ST

Daisy Head Farm

Caulcott Farm

Manor Farm

Lyndhurst

GREENWAY

24

Old Nursery

Home Wood

B4030

Sainfoinhill Clump

Cricket Ground

2

Gallos Brook

Gold Barn

Middleton Park

Breaklands Clump

Middleton Park

23

Wheats Covert

Mangthorn Wood

Goldwell Spinney

Cowground Clump

Cowground Covert

1

Brakeslode Spinney

The Downs

Mushroom Cottages

Slade Farm

Roomer's Spinney

Swiss Cottage

22

50
D
51
E
52
F

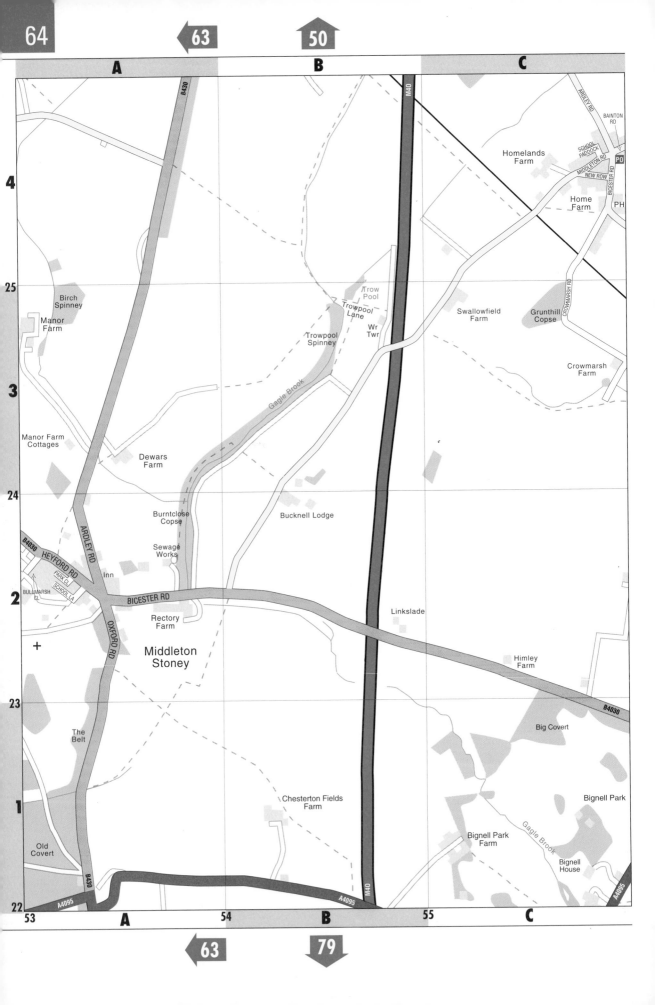

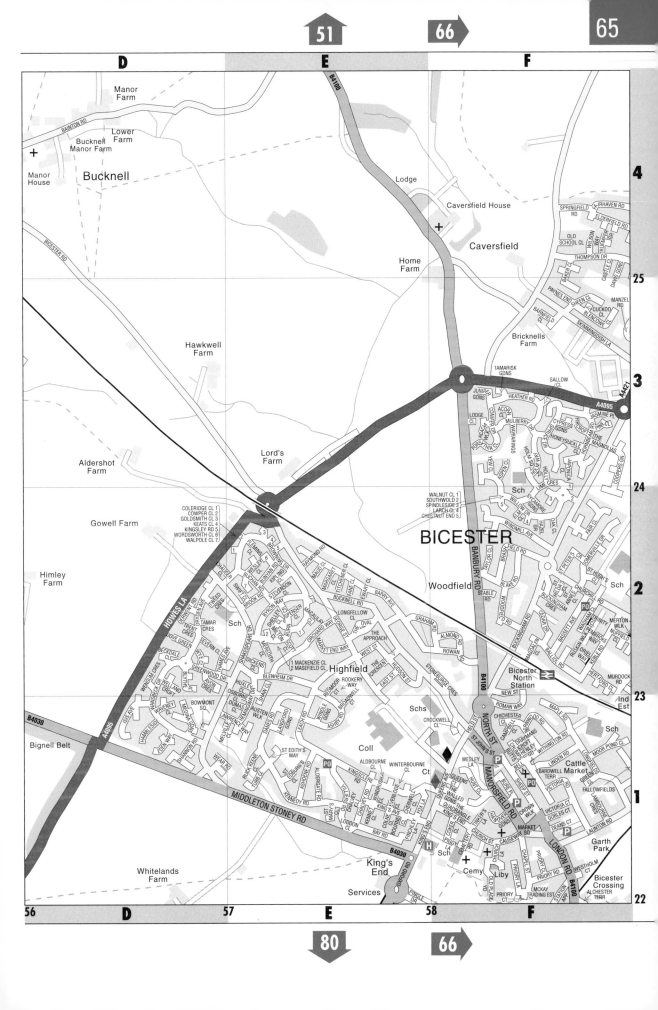

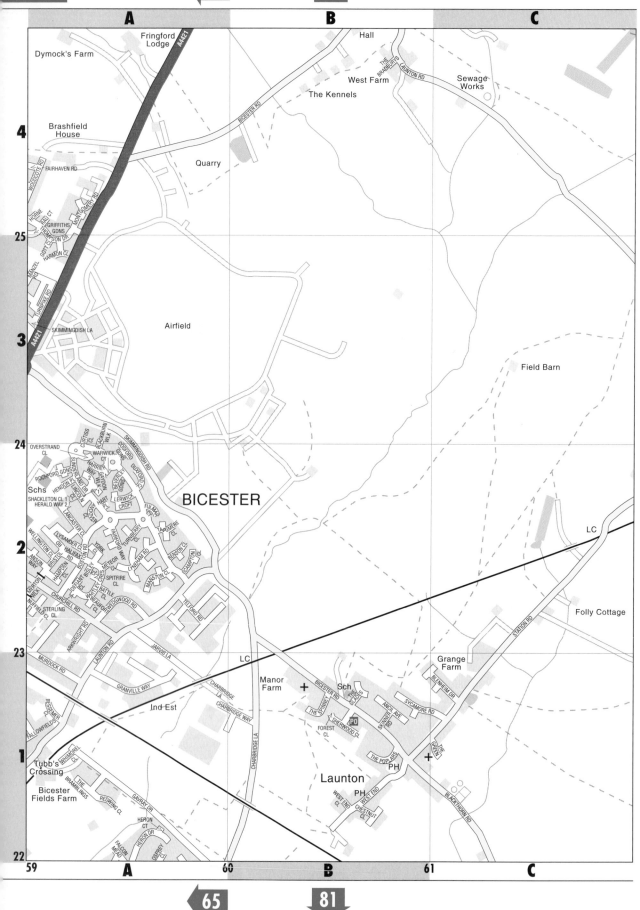

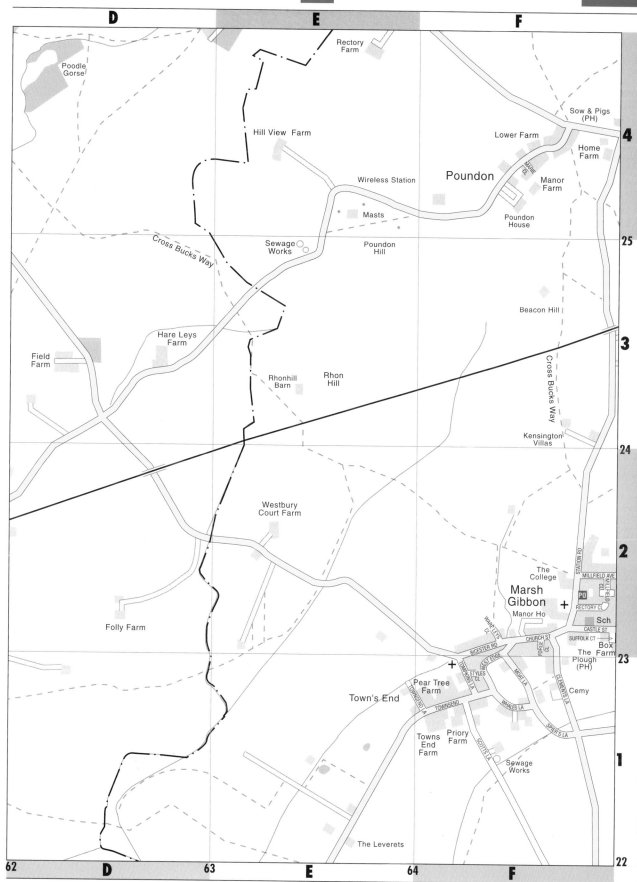

Poodle Gorse

Rectory Farm

Hill View Farm

Wireless Station

Sow & Pigs (PH)

Lower Farm

Home Farm

Poundon

Manor Farm

Masts

Poundon House

Cross Bucks Way

Sewage Works

Poundon Hill

Beacon Hill

Hare Leys Farm

Field Farm

Cross Bucks Way

Rhonhill Barn

Rhon Hill

Kensington Villas

Westbury Court Farm

The College

Folly Farm

STATION RD

MILLFIELD AVE

MILLFIELD CL

Marsh Gibbon

P.O

RECTORY CL

Manor Ho

Sch

CASTLE ST

SUFFOLK CT

WARE LEYS CL

CHURCH ST

FORGE CL

Box Farm

The Plough (PH)

BICESTER RD

WEST EDGE

MOAT LA

CLEMENTS LA

Cemy

Town's End

Pear Tree Farm

STYLES CL

TOMPKINS LA

TOWNSEND LA

TOWNSEND

WHALES LA

SCOTTS LA

SPER'S LA

Towns End Farm

Priory Farm

Sewage Works

The Leverets

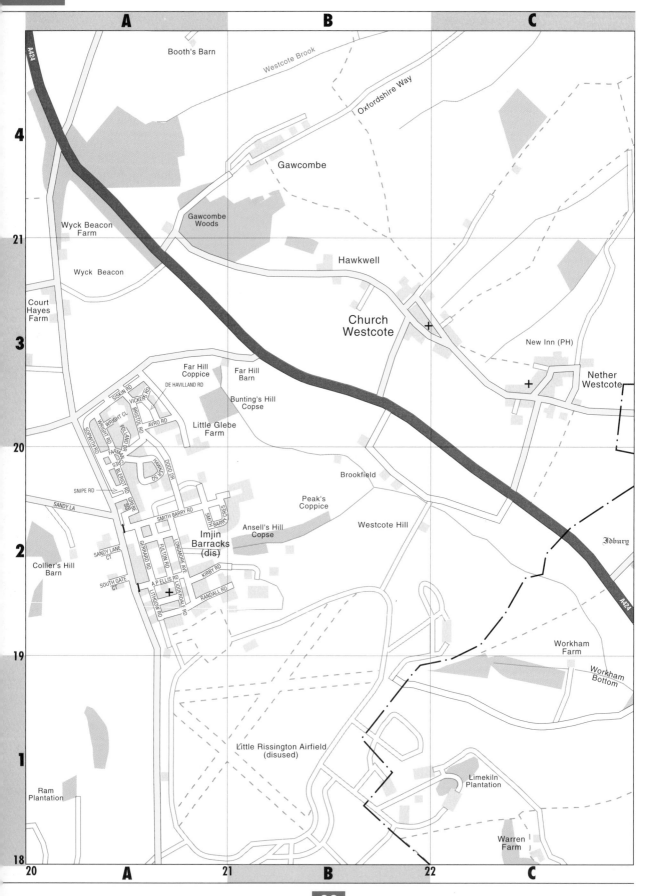

Booth's Barn

Westcote Brook

Oxfordshire Way

Gawcombe

Gawcombe Woods

Wyck Beacon Farm

4

21

Wyck Beacon

Hawkwell

Court Hayes Farm

Church Westcote

New Inn (PH)

3

Nether Westcote

Far Hill Coppice

Far Hill Barn

DE HAVILLAND RD

SISKIN RD

VICKERS RD

BRISTOL RD

WRIGHT CL

Bunting's Hill Copse

POLLAND DR

AVRO RD

Little Glebe Farm

FARMAN CRES

BLERIOT RD

HAWKER RD

SOPWITH RD

WRIGHT RD

20

SNIPE RD

DODD DR

Brookfield

SANDY LA

GREBE RD

SMITH BARRY RD

SMITH BARRY CL

Peak's Coppice

Westcote Hill

Ansell's Hill Copse

Imjin Barracks (dis)

LONGMORE AVE

FULTON RD

GERRARD RD

KIRBY RD

Idbury

2

SANDY LANE CT

Collier's Hill Barn

SOUTH GATE CT

A P ELLIS RD

LIDDERDALE RD

LITHGOW RD

RANDALL RD

Workham Farm

Workham Bottom

19

Little Rissington Airfield (disused)

1

Limekiln Plantation

Ram Plantation

Warren Farm

18

20 A 21 B 22 C

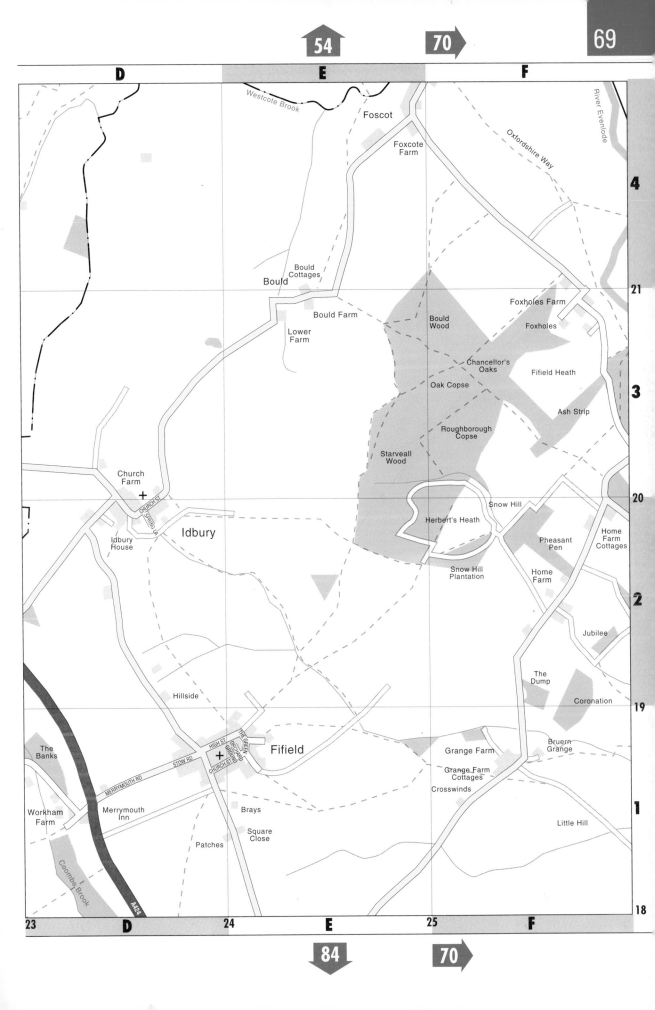

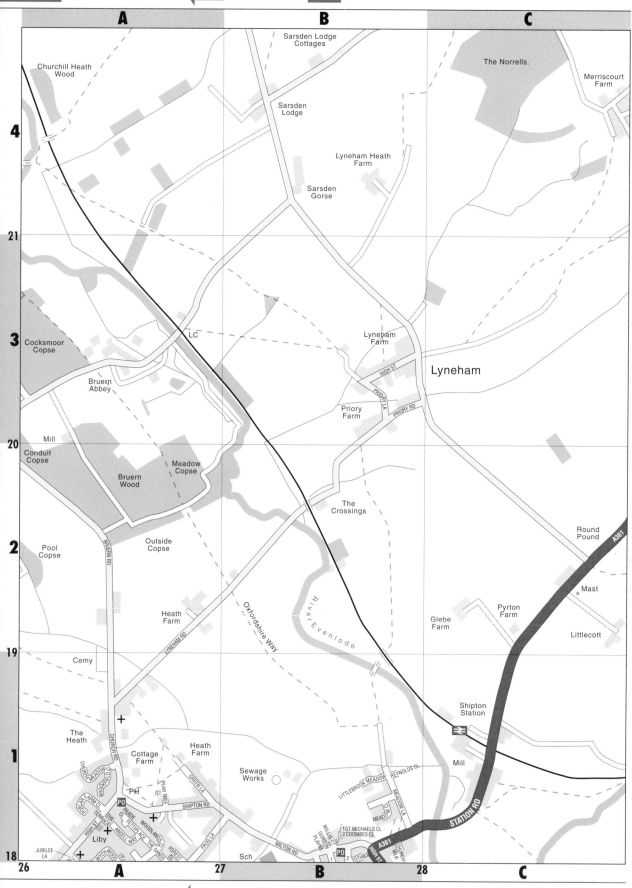

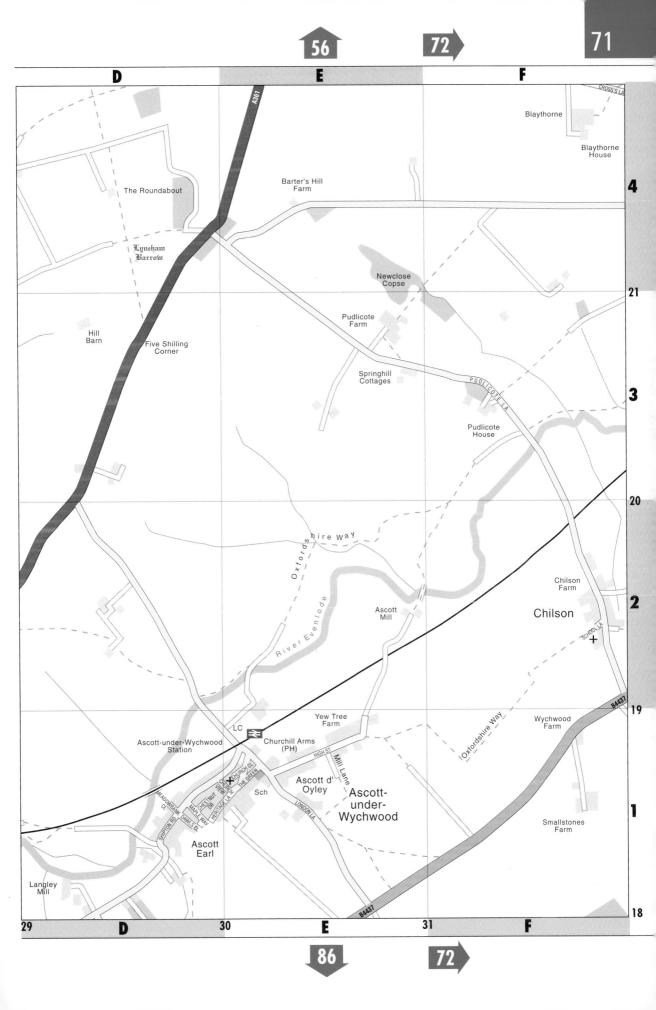

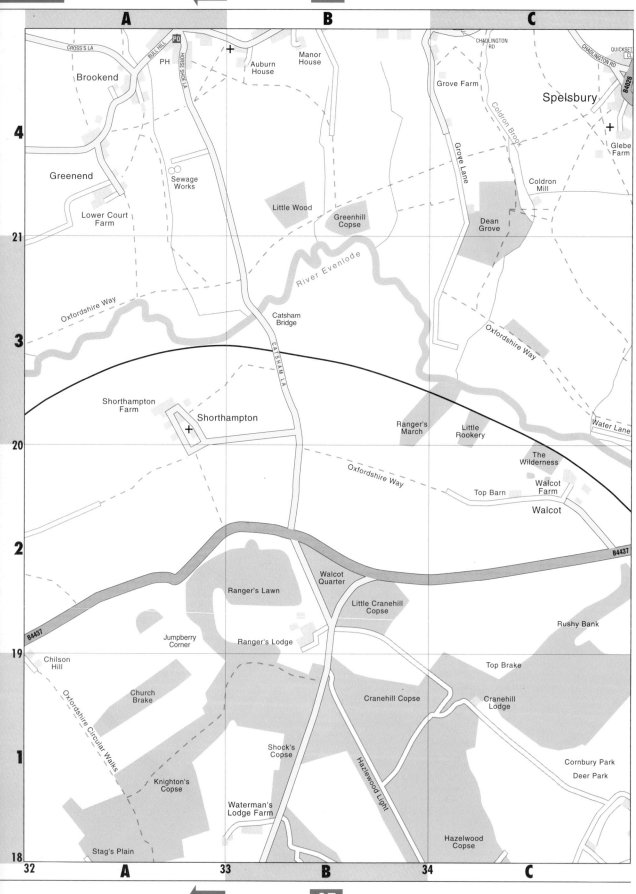

A   **B**   **C**

CROSS'S LA
Brookend
BULL HILL
PO
PH
HORSE SHOE LA
Auburn House
Manor House
Greenend
Sewage Works
Lower Court Farm
Little Wood
Greenhill Copse
CHADLINGTON RD
Grove Farm
Spelsbury
CHADLINGTON RD
QUICKSET CL
B4026
Glebe Farm
Coldron Brook
Grove Lane
Dean Grove
Coldron Mill

4

21

River Evenlode

Oxfordshire Way
Catsham Bridge
CATSHAM LA
Oxfordshire Way

3

Shorthampton Farm
Shorthampton
Ranger's March
Little Rookery
The Wilderness
Walcot Farm
Walcot
Water Lane

20

Oxfordshire Way
Top Barn

2

B4437
Ranger's Lawn
Walcot Quarter
Little Cranehill Copse
Rushy Bank
B4437
Jumpberry Corner
Ranger's Lodge
Chilson Hill
Top Brake

19

Church Brake
Oxfordshire Circular Walks
Cranehill Copse
Cranehill Lodge
Shock's Copse
Hazlewood Light

1

Knighton's Copse
Cornbury Park Deer Park
Waterman's Lodge Farm
Hazelwood Copse
Stag's Plain

18

32   **A**   33   **B**   34   **C**

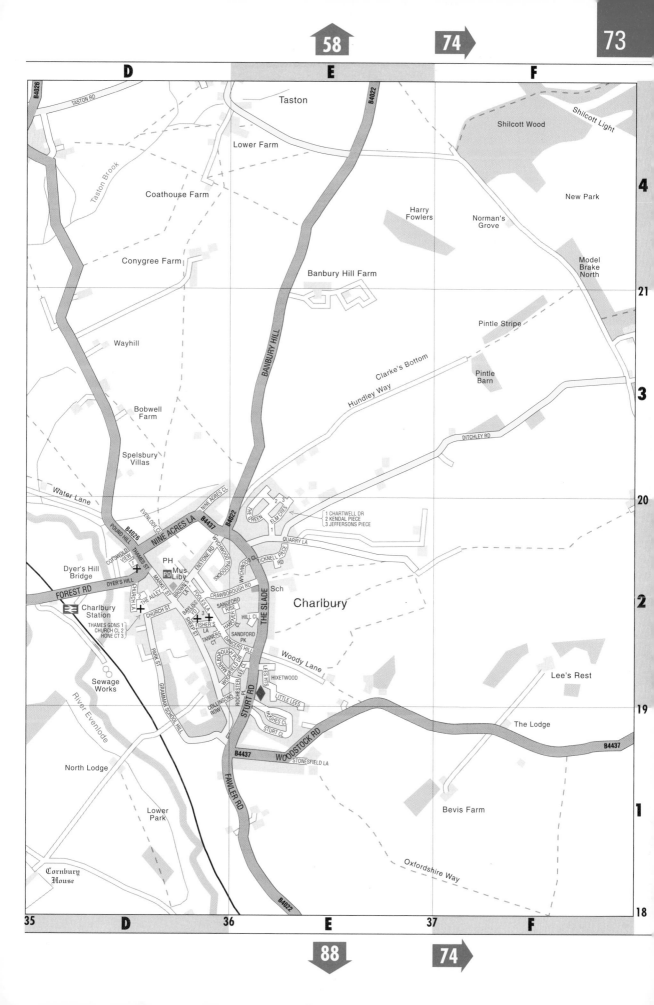

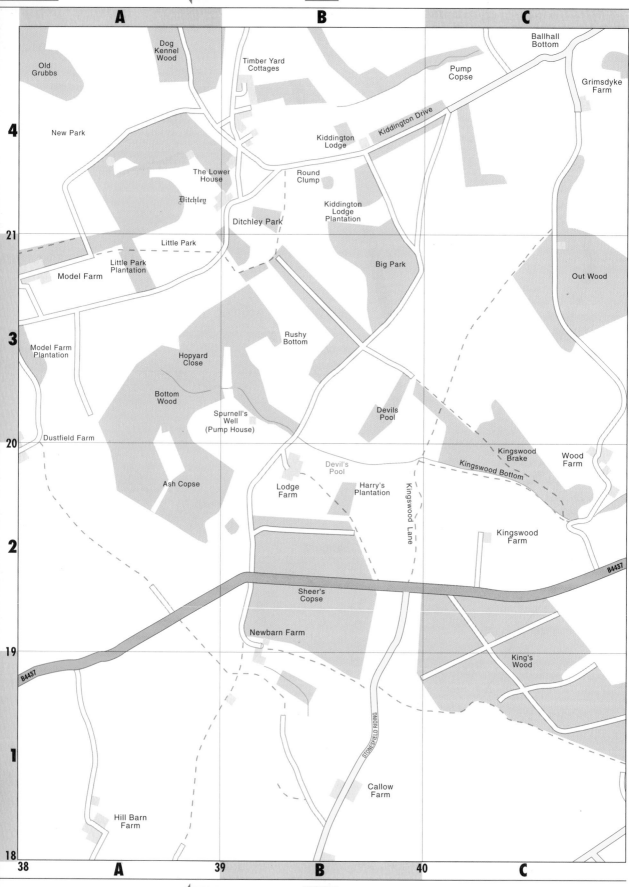

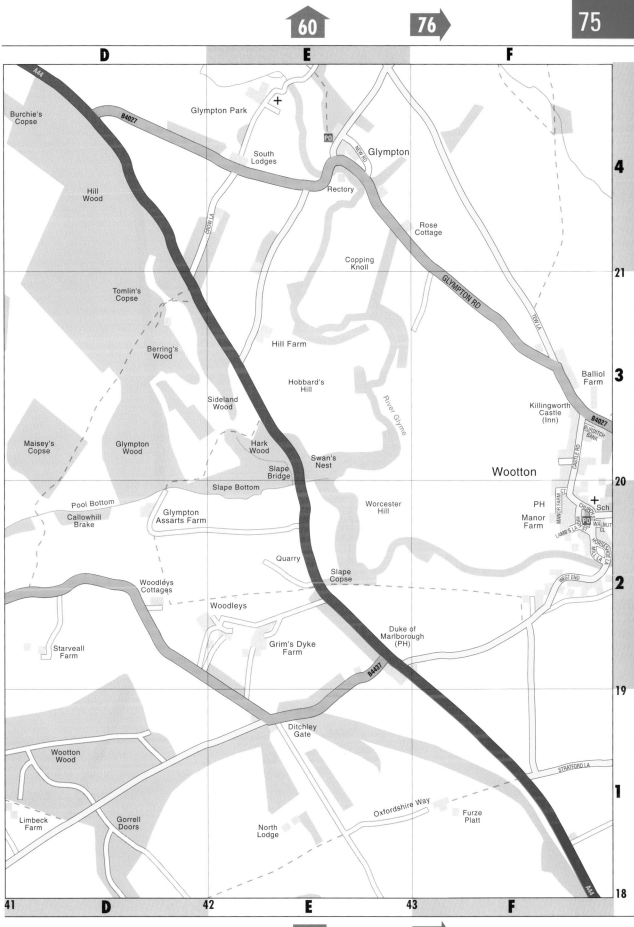

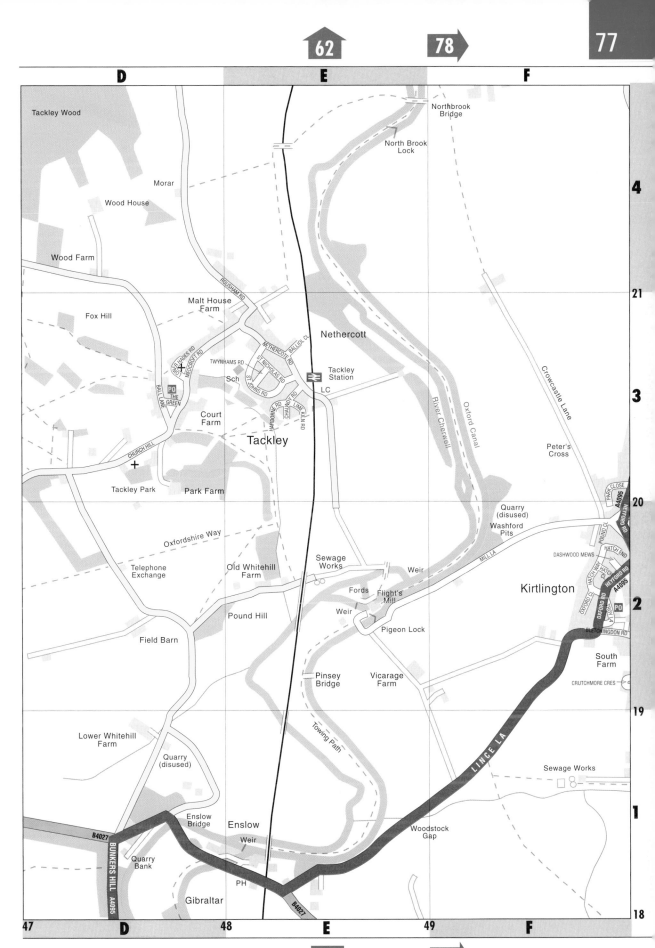

D

Tackley Wood

Morar

Wood House

Wood Farm

Fox Hill

ROUSHAM RD

Malt House Farm

FORGE HABRS RD

NETCROFT RD

TWYNHAMS RD

ST NICHOLAS RD

NETHERCOTT RD

BALLIOL CL

Sch

ST JOHNS RD

BALL LANE

PO
THE GREEN

HARBORNE RD

CHAUNDY RD

LIME KILN RD

Tackley Station

LC

Nethercott

Tackley

CHURCH HILL

Court Farm

Tackley Park

Park Farm

E

North Brook Lock

Northbrook Bridge

River Cherwell

Oxford Canal

Crowcastle Lane

Peter's Cross

F

4

21

3

Oxfordshire Way

Telephone Exchange

Old Whitehill Farm

Pound Hill

Field Barn

Sewage Works

Fords

Weir

Flight's Mill

Weir

Pigeon Lock

Pinsey Bridge

Vicarage Farm

MILL LA

Quarry (disused)
Washford Pits

DASHWOOD MEWS

HATCH END

PARK CLOSE

A4095

HEYFORD RD

Kirtlington

POUND CL

HATCH WAY

HATCH CL

HEYFORD RD

A4095

OXFORD CL

OXFORD RD

PO

BLETCHINGDON RD

South Farm

CRUTCHMORE CRES

20

2

19

Lower Whitehill Farm

Quarry (disused)

Towing Path

LINCE LA

Sewage Works

Enslow Bridge

Quarry Bank

B4027

BUNKERS HILL A4095

PH

Gibraltar

Enslow

Weir

Woodstock Gap

B4027

1

18

47

D

48

E

49

F

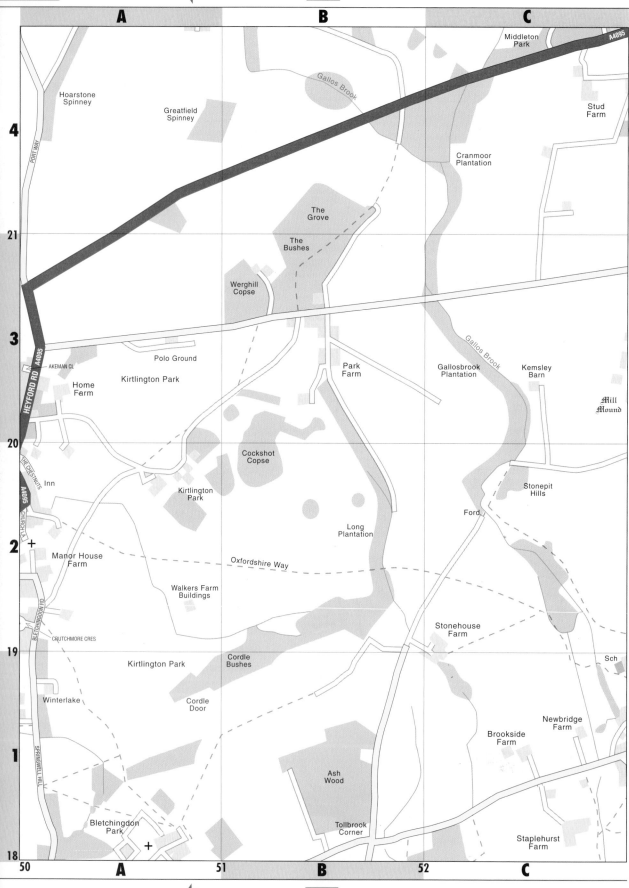

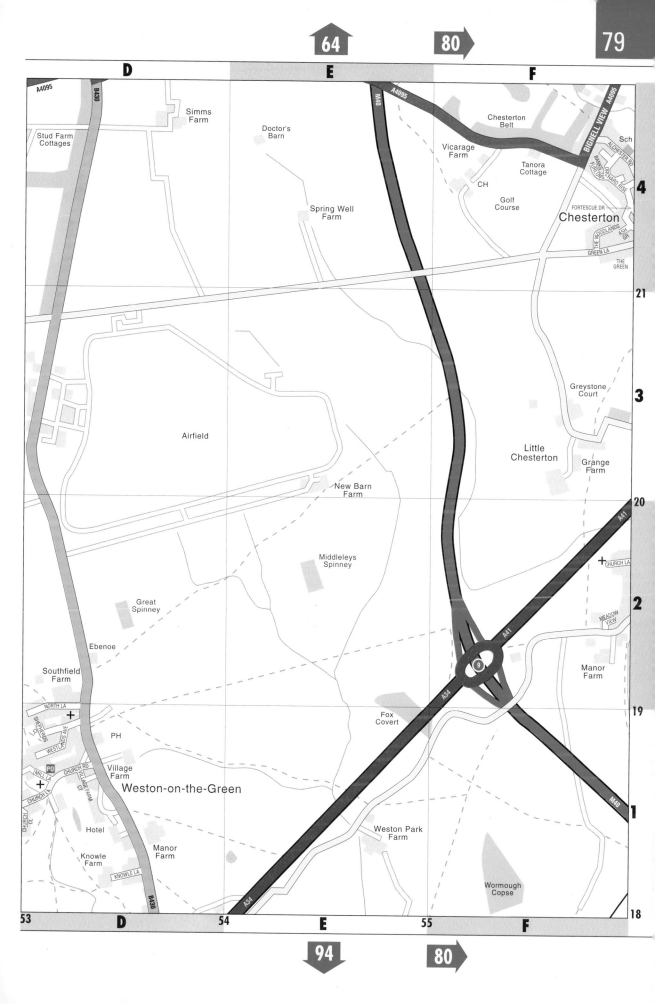

D E F

A4095
B430

Stud Farm Cottages

Simms Farm

Doctor's Barn

Spring Well Farm

M40

A4095

BIGNELL VIEW

Chesterton Belt

Sch

Vicarage Farm

Tanora Cottage

ALCHESTER RD

BANBURY FURLONG

ORCHARD RISE

CH

Golf Course

FORTESCUE DR

Chesterton

THE WOODLANDS

ASH GR

GREEN LA

THE GREEN

4

21

Airfield

New Barn Farm

Greystone Court

3

Little Chesterton

Grange Farm

20

Middleleys Spinney

A41

CHURCH LA

Great Spinney

A41

MEADOW VIEW

Ebenoe

Manor Farm

2

Southfield Farm

9

NORTH LA

SHEPHERDS

WESTLANDS AVE

PH

Fox Covert

A34

19

PO

MILL LA

Village Farm

CHURCH RD

VILLAGE FARM CT

CHURCH LA

Weston-on-the-Green

M40

Hotel

Knowle Farm

Manor Farm

Weston Park Farm

1

CHURCH RD

KNOWLE LA

B430

A34

Wormough Copse

18

53 D 54 E 55 F 18

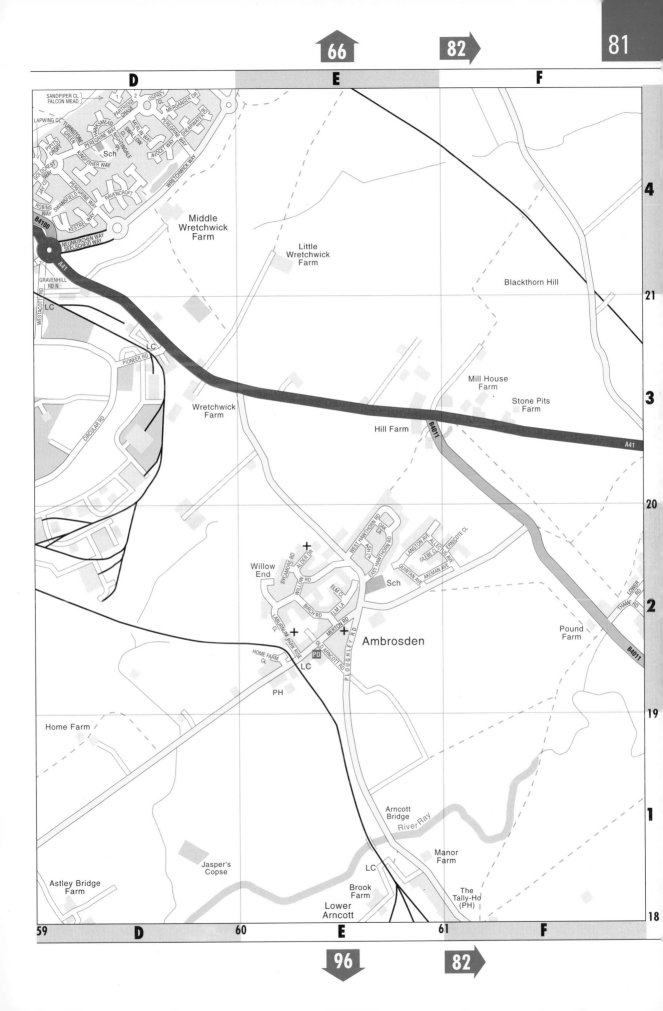

D   E   F

SANDPIPER CL
FALCON MEAD
LAPWING CL
TURNSTONE
PIPIT CL
GREEN
HAWKSMEAD
OSPREY CL
PARTRIDGE CHASE
MERGANSER DR
MERLIN WAY
SWALLOW
PEREGRINE WAY
NIGHTINGALE
SHEARWATER RD
AVOCET WAY
PEREGRINE WAY
Sch
KINGFISHER WAY
GOLDCREST WAY
JAY CL
SWANSFIELD WAY
PEREGRINE WAY
RAVENCROFT
WRETCHWICK WAY
ROBINS WAY
KESTREL WAY
B4100
GRAVENHILL RD N
NEUNKIRCHEN WAY
SEELSCHEID WAY
A41
WESTACOTT RD
LC
PIONEER RD
LC
CIRCULAR RD

Middle Wretchwick Farm

Little Wretchwick Farm

Blackthorn Hill

Wretchwick Farm

Mill House Farm

Stone Pits Farm

Hill Farm

B4011

A41

4

21

3

20

WEST HAWTHORN RD
OAK
ASH
EAST HAWTHORN RD
LANGTON AVE
ALLEN CL
FENNICOTE CL
GLEBE CL
CHAUCER AVE
SYCAMORE RD
ALDER DR
WILLOW RD
QUINTAN AVE
AKEMAN AVE
Willow End
Sch
ELM CL
ELM LA
BIRCH RD
LABURNUM CL
PARK RISE
MERTON RD
OLD ARNCOTT RD
PLOUGHLEY RD
HOME FARM CL
PO
LC
PH

Ambrosden

Pound Farm

LOWER RD

THAME RD

B4011

2

19

Home Farm

Arncott Bridge

River Ray

Manor Farm

Jasper's Copse

LC

Astley Bridge Farm

Brook Farm

Lower Arncott

The Tally-Ho (PH)

1

18

59   D   60   E   61   F

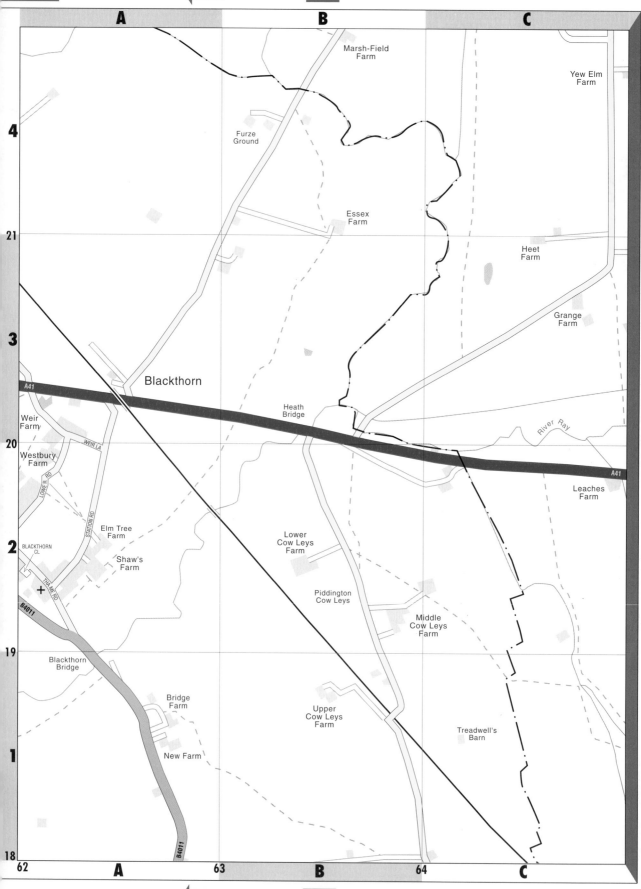

D
E
F

4
17
3
16
2
15
1
14

Great Rissington Farm
North Lodge
Great Rissington Hill
Resr
Sch
The Follies

Airfield (disused)

Littlehill Bank
Choake's Brake
Choake's Barn
Ell Brake
Washpool Copse

Barrington Bushes
Downs Cottages
Hazelford · Brook
Mill Hill
Taynton Bushes
Hill Barn

Bromham Plantation

Miletree Clump

Comb Hill Plantation
Grosvenor Plantation
Barrington Park

Mortar Pits

20
21
22

D
E
F

83
69

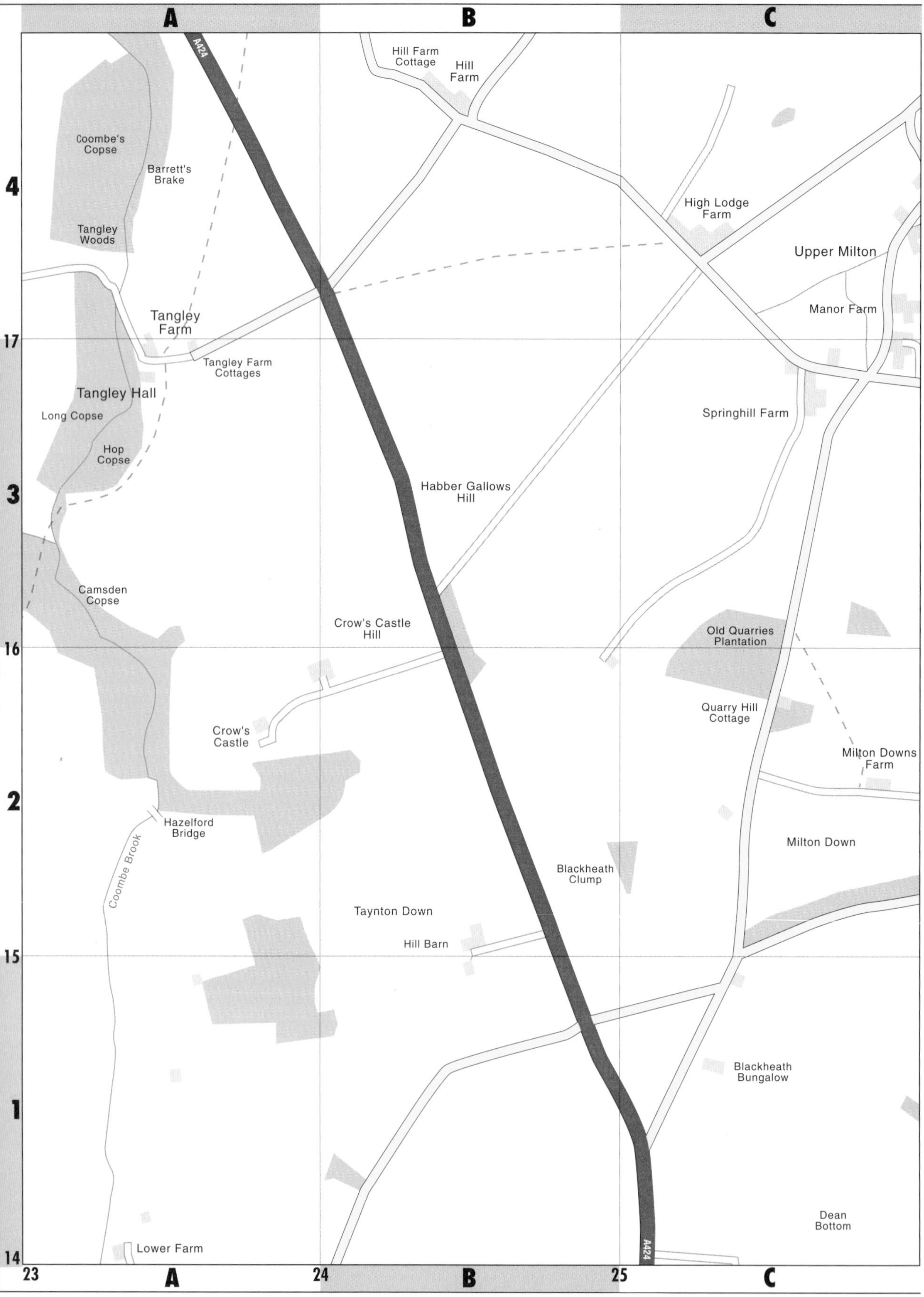

A   **B**   **C**

A424

Coombe's Copse

Barrett's Brake

4

Tangley Woods

Hill Farm Cottage

Hill Farm

High Lodge Farm

Upper Milton

Tangley Farm

Manor Farm

17

Tangley Farm Cottages

Tangley Hall

Long Copse

Springhill Farm

Hop Copse

Habber Gallows Hill

3

Camsden Copse

Crow's Castle Hill

Old Quarries Plantation

16

Quarry Hill Cottage

Crow's Castle

Milton Downs Farm

Hazelford Bridge

2

Coombe Brook

Milton Down

Blackheath Clump

Taynton Down

Hill Barn

15

Blackheath Bungalow

1

Dean Bottom

A424

Lower Farm

14

23   **A**   24   **B**   25   **C**

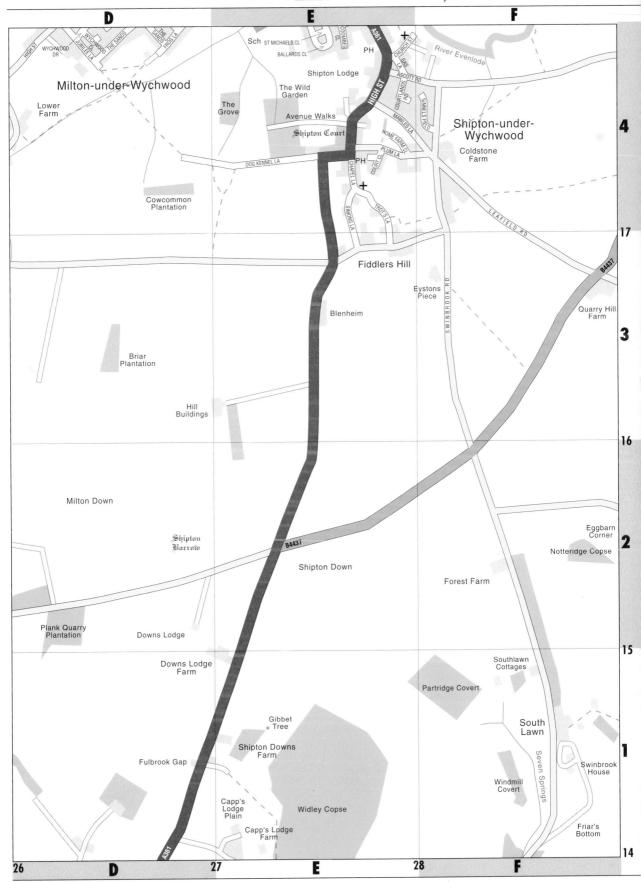

Milton-under-Wychwood

Lower Farm

WYCHWOOD DR
HIGH ST
WYCHWOOD THE SANDS
THE SANDS
FROG LA
JUBILEE LA

Sch
St Michaels Cl
ST MICHAELS CL
BALLARDS CL
COOMBES CL
A361
PH
CHURCH ST
GAS
River Evenlode

Shipton Lodge
ASCOTT RD
COURT LANDS RD

The Wild Garden
HIGH ST
MAWLES LA
SINNELS FIELD

The Grove

Avenue Walks
HOME FARM CL
Shipton-under-Wychwood

Shipton Court
PH
PLUM LA
COURT CL
Coldstone Farm

DOG KENNEL LA
CHAPEL LA
LEAFIELD RD

Cowcommon Plantation
SIMONS LA
TROT'S LA

Fiddlers Hill
B4437

Eystons Piece
SWINBROOK RD
Quarry Hill Farm

Blenheim

Briar Plantation

Hill Buildings

Milton Down

Shipton Barrow

Eggbarn Corner
Notteridge Copse

B4437
Shipton Down
Forest Farm

Plank Quarry Plantation

Downs Lodge

Downs Lodge Farm

Southlawn Cottages

Partridge Covert

Gibbet Tree

South Lawn

Shipton Downs Farm

Fulbrook Gap

Seven Springs
Swinbrook House

Windmill Covert

Capp's Lodge Plain

Widley Copse

Friar's Bottom

Capp's Lodge Farm

A361

85 **71**

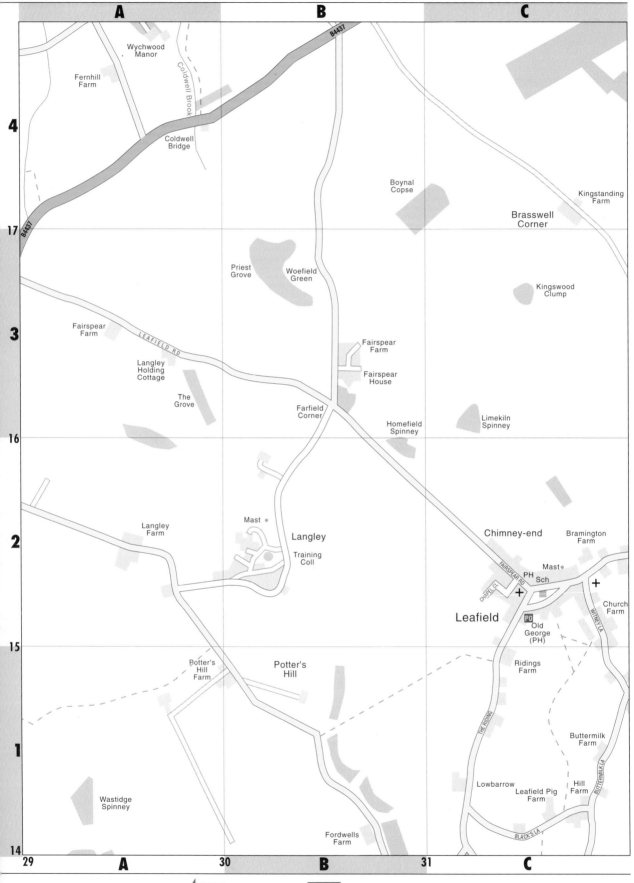

85 **102**

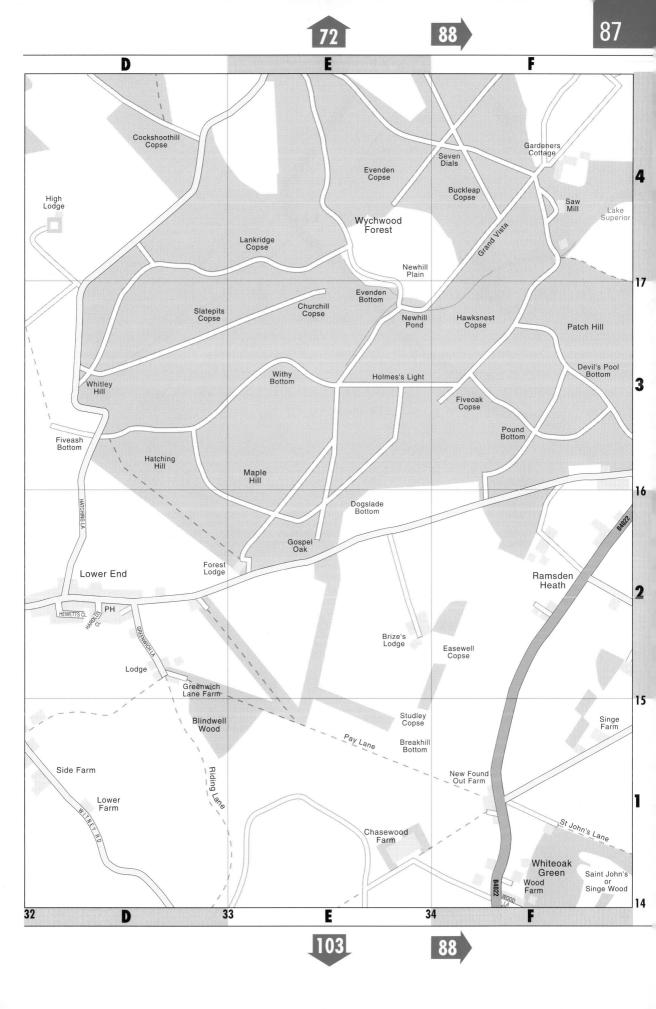

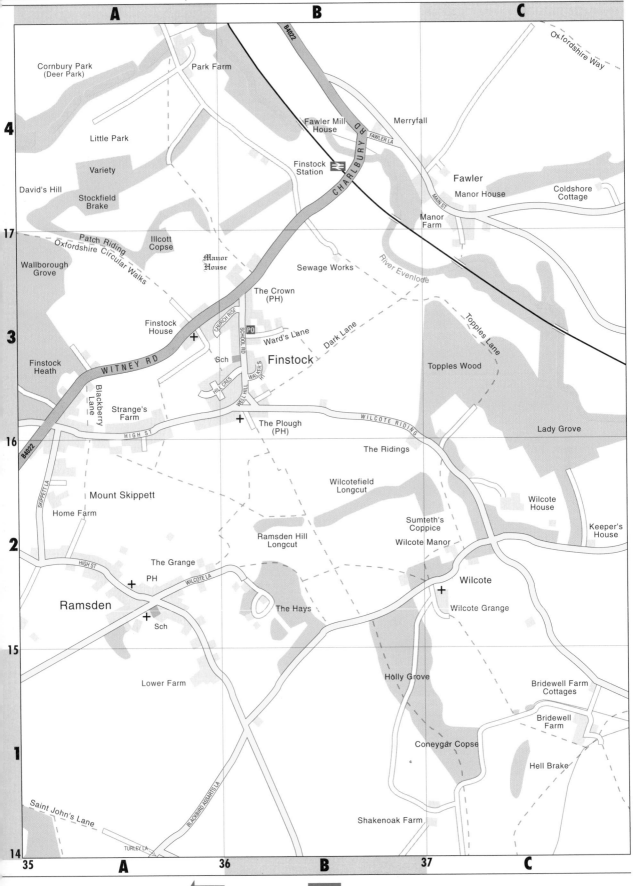

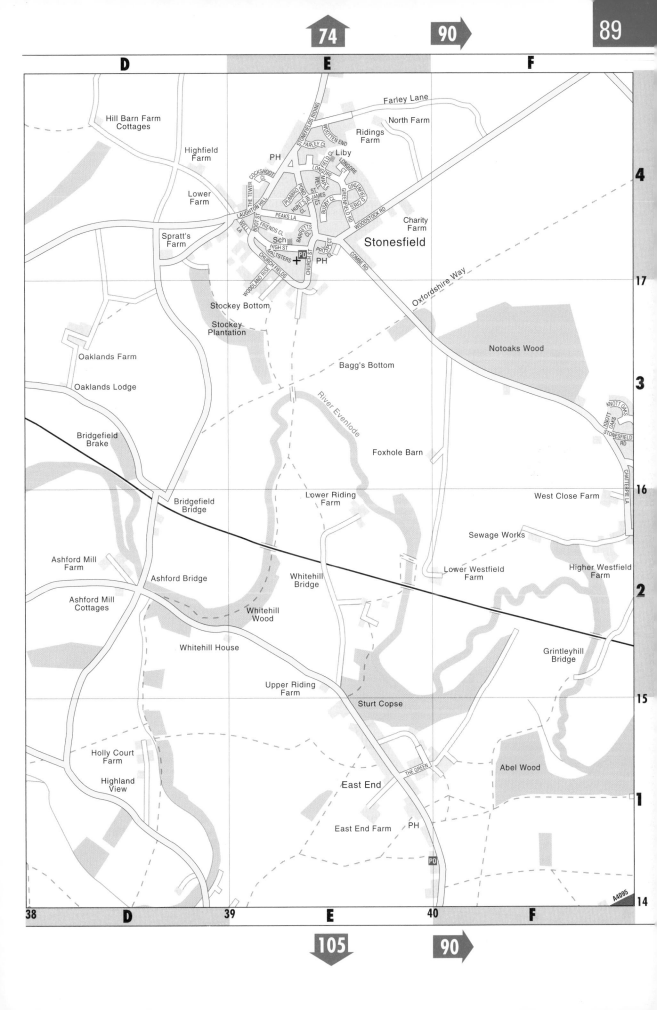

D
E
F

Farley Lane
Hill Barn Farm
Cottages
North Farm
Highfield
Farm
PH
Ridings
Farm
Liby
STONEFIELDS RIDING
WOOTTEN END
FARLEY CL
Lower
Farm
LONGORE
LONGORE CT
GREENFIELD
Spratt's
Farm
COCKSHOOT CL
THE TOWER
LAUGHTON HILL
PEAKS LA
POND ST
PLANBRO CL
HUNTS CL
ST JAMES CT
BUSBY CL
GREENFIELD RD
GREENFIELD CRES
WOODSTOCK RD
Charity
Farm
WELL LA
BOOT ST
FRIENDS CL
BARRETTS CL
Sch
PROSP CT
Stonesfield
4
HIGH ST
MALTSTERS
PO
PH
CHURCH FIELDS
WOODLAND RISE
CHURCH ST
PROSP CL
COMBE RD
17
Stockey Bottom
Stockey
Plantation
Oxfordshire Way
Oaklands Farm
Bagg's Bottom
Notoaks Wood
Oaklands Lodge
3
River Evenlode
KNOTT OAKS LANE
STONESFIELD RD
Bridgefield
Brake
Foxhole Barn
Bridgefield
Bridge
Lower Riding
Farm
West Close Farm
16
CHATTERPIE LA
Sewage Works
Ashford Mill
Farm
Ashford Bridge
Whitehill
Bridge
Lower Westfield
Farm
Higher Westfield
Farm
2
Ashford Mill
Cottages
Whitehill
Wood
Whitehill House
Grintleyhill
Bridge
Upper Riding
Farm
Sturt Copse
15
Holly Court
Farm
THE GREEN
Abel Wood
Highland
View
East End
1
East End Farm
PH
PO
A4095
14

38
D
39
E
40
F

← **89**
↑ **75**

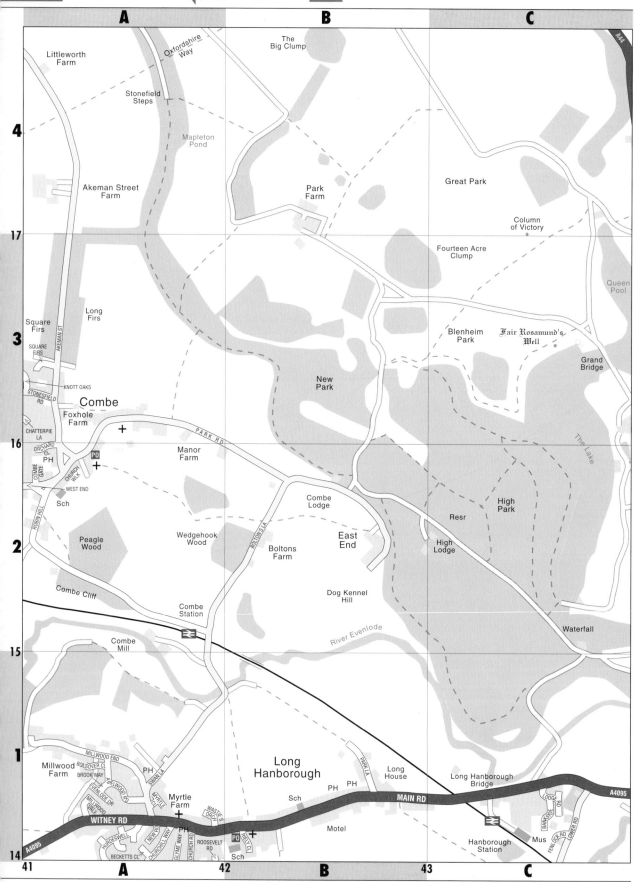

A **B** **C**

Littleworth Farm

Oxfordshire Way

The Big Clump

Stonefield Steps

Mapleton Pond

4

Park Farm

Great Park

Akeman Street Farm

Column of Victory

17

Fourteen Acre Clump

Long Firs

Blenheim Park

Fair Rosamund's Well

Queen Pool

Square Firs

3

SQUARE FIRS

AKEMAN ST

New Park

Grand Bridge

KNOTT OAKS

STONESFIELD RD

Combe

Foxhole Farm

The Lake

CHATTERPIE LA

PARK RD

16

ORCHARD CL

PH

PO

COMBE GATE

CHURCH WLK

Manor Farm

Combe Lodge

High Park

WEST END

Sch

Resr

ROBIN HILL

Wedgehook Wood

BOLTONS LA

Combe Station

Boltons Farm

East End

High Lodge

2

Peagle Wood

Combe Cliff

Dog Kennel Hill

Waterfall

15

Combe Mill

River Evenlode

1

MILLWOOD END

Millwood Farm

BOLSOVER CL

PH

SWAN LA

Long Hanborough

PARK LA

Long House

Long Hanborough Bridge

LODGE DR

A4095

BROOK WAY

EVENLODE DR

MYRTLE

Myrtle Farm

WASTIE'S ORCH

Sch

PH

PH

MAIN RD

BANKSIDE

FENNOCK RD

LOWER RD

MILLWOOD VALE

A PELWOOD RD

PH

GLYME WAY

CHURCH RD

ROOSEVELT RD

PO

RILEY CL

Motel

Mus

WITNEY RD

HURDESWELL

NEW RD

Sch

Hanborough Station

14

A4095

BECKETTS CL

GLYME RD

41   **A**   **42**   **B**   **43**   **C**

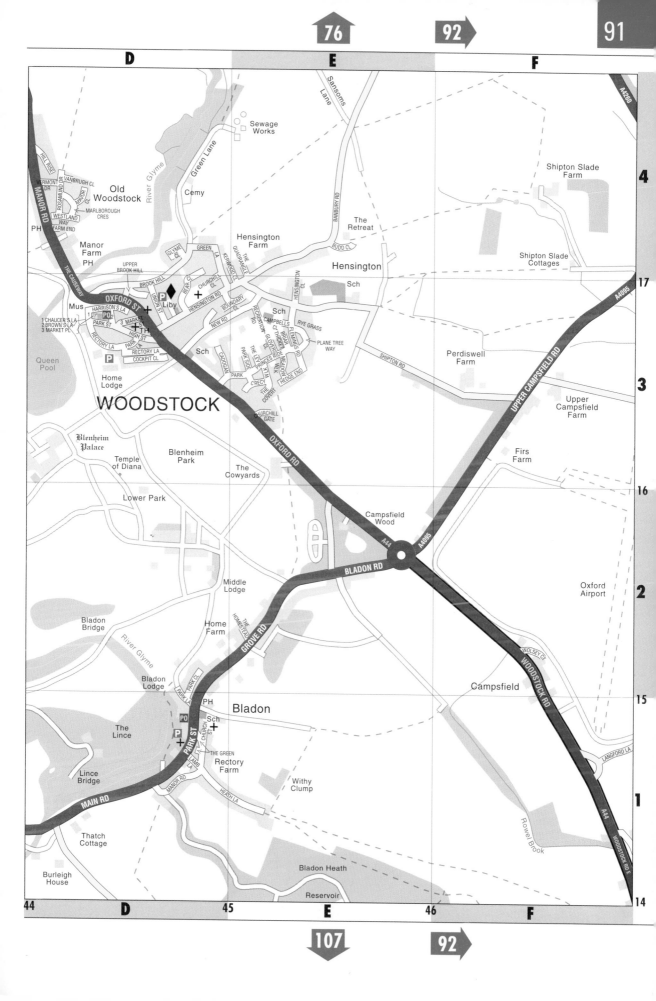

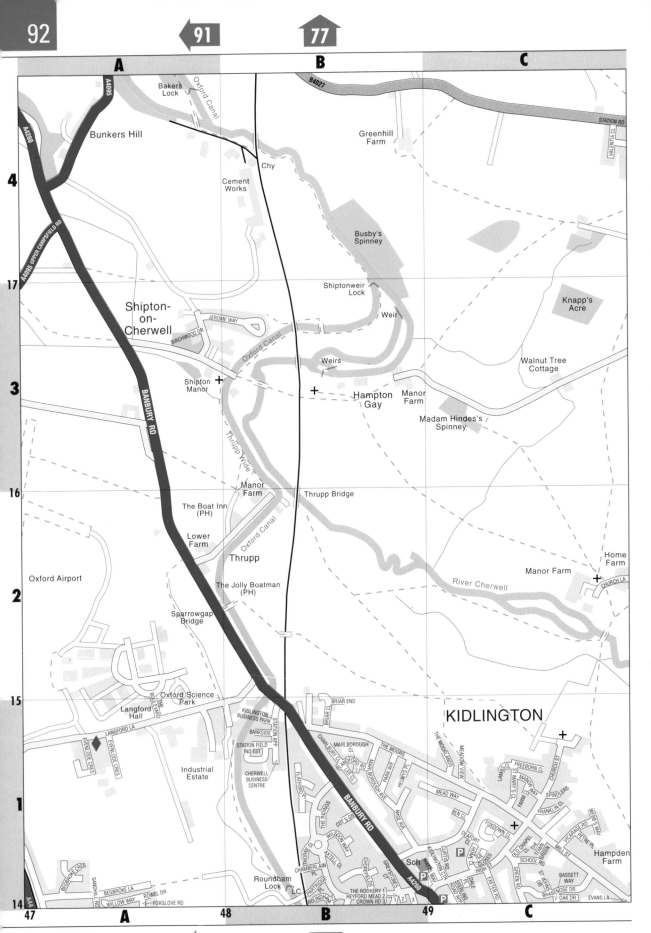

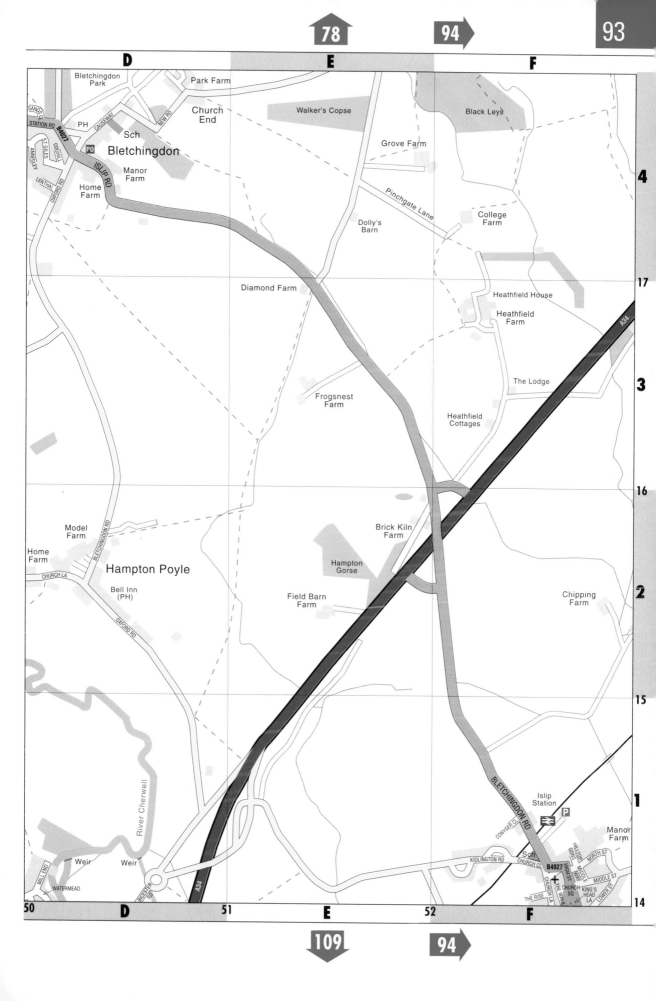

D

Bletchingdon Park

Park Farm

Church End

Walker's Copse

Black Leys

Grove Farm

SANDY LA
STATION RD
B4027
PH
ST GILES
COGHILL
ANNESLEY
LENTHAL
OXFORD RD
Sch
PO
Bletchingdon

E

F

NEW RD
CAUSEWAY
ISLIP RD

Manor Farm

Home Farm

Pinchgate Lane

College Farm

4

Dolly's Barn

Diamond Farm

Heathfield House

17

Heathfield Farm

Frogsnest Farm

The Lodge

A34

3

Heathfield Cottages

16

Model Farm

Brick Kiln Farm

BLETCHINGDON RD

Home Farm

CHURCH LA

Hampton Poyle

Hampton Gorse

Chipping Farm

2

Bell Inn (PH)

OXFORD RD

Field Barn Farm

15

River Cherwell

Islip Station

BLETCHINGDON RD

1

CONYGER CL

Manor Farm

Weir

Weir

MILL END
WATERMEAD

BICESTER RD

A34

KIDLINGTON RD

Sch

CHURCH CL

HILLTOP GDNS
NEW WAY
NORTH ST
MIDDLE ST
B4027
CHURCH
KING'S HEAD LA
LOWER ST
THE RISE
CHURCH LA
THE WALK
KING'S SQ
MIDDLE ST

50

D

51

E

52

F

14

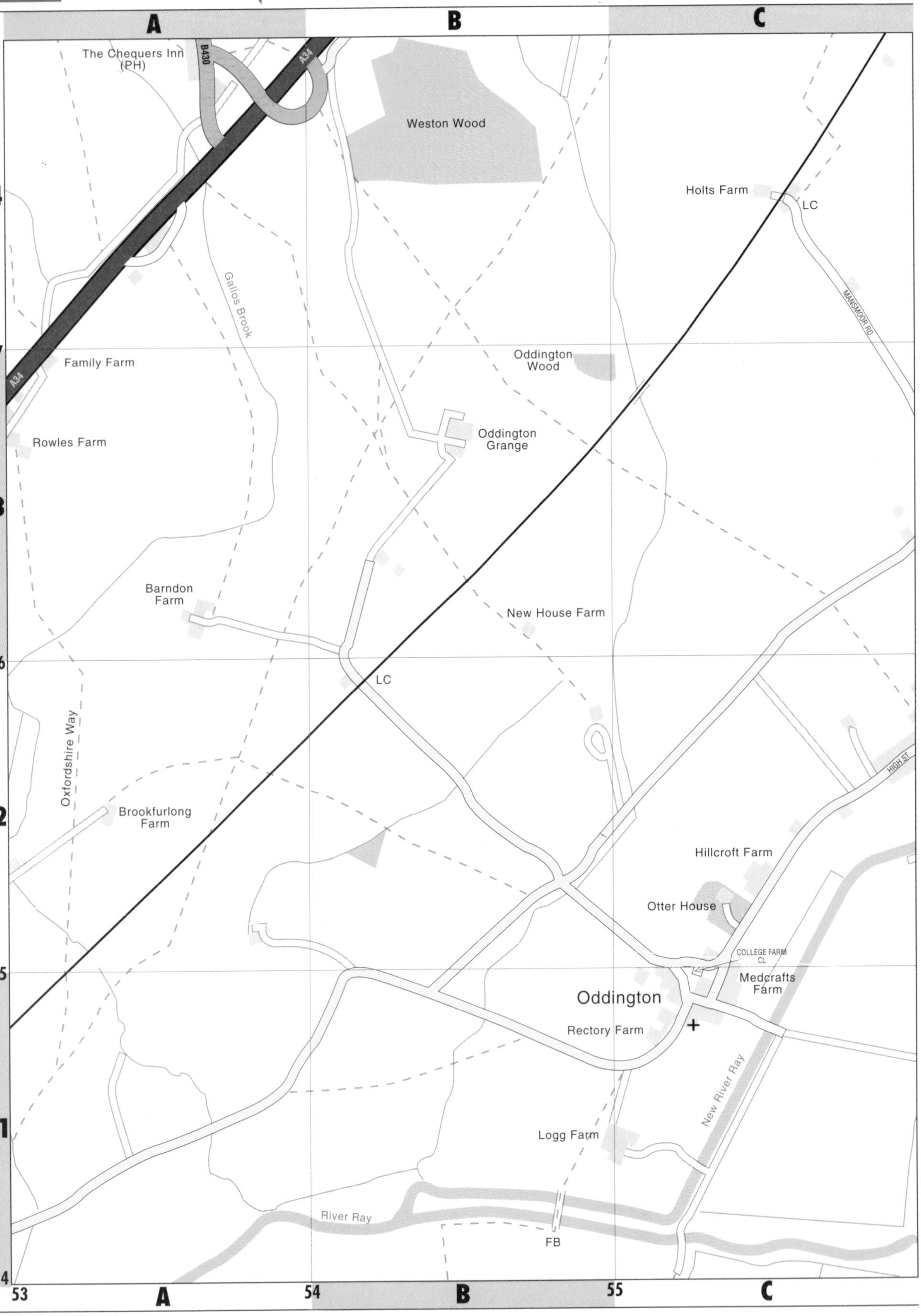

A **B** **C**

The Chequers Inn (PH)

B430

A34

Weston Wood

Holts Farm

LC

MANSMOOR RD

4

Gallos Brook

17

Family Farm

Oddington Wood

A34

Rowles Farm

Oddington Grange

3

Barndon Farm

New House Farm

16

LC

Oxfordshire Way

HIGH ST

2

Brookfurlong Farm

Hillcroft Farm

Otter House

COLLEGE FARM CL

15

Medcrafts Farm

Oddington

Rectory Farm

+

New River Ray

1

Logg Farm

River Ray

FB

14

53 **A** 54 **B** 55 **C**

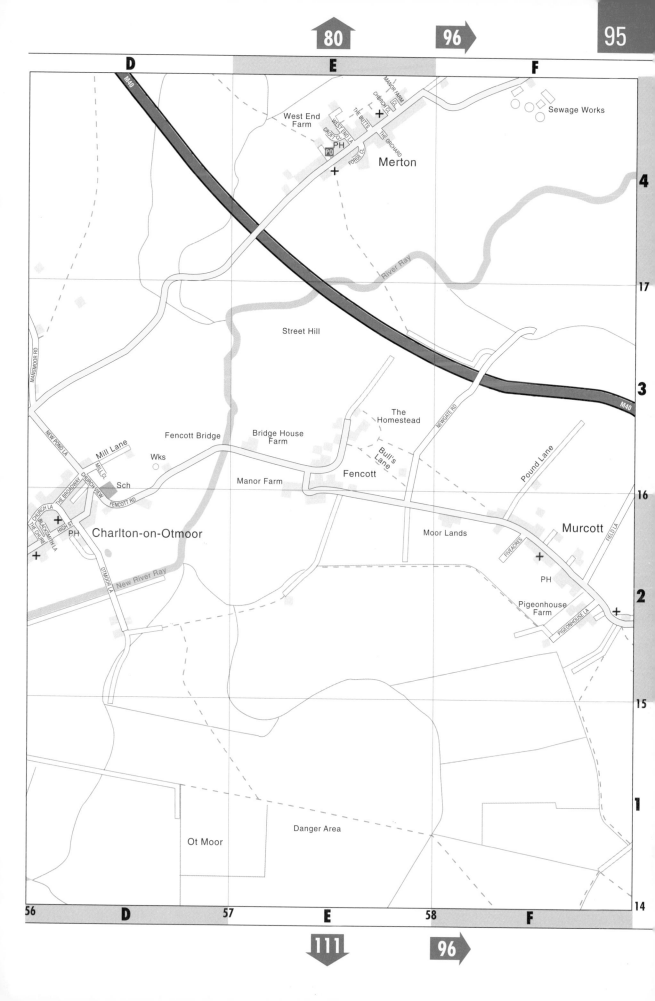

D

E

F

4

Sewage Works

West End Farm

MANOR FARM

THE BUTTS

CHURCH CL

WEST END LA

CROFT CL

PO

PH

FORGE CL

THE ORCHARD

Merton

17

River Ray

Street Hill

3

M40

NEWGATE RD

The Homestead

Bridge House Farm

Fencott Bridge

Bull's Lane

Pound Lane

Mill Lane

MILL CL

Wks

Fencott

Manor Farm

NEW POND LA

THE BROADWAY

CHURCH VIEW

Sch

FENCOTT RD

16

Murcott

FIVE ACRES

FIELD LA

CHURCH LA

BLACKSMITH LA

HIGH ST

Charlton-on-Otmoor

THE CHURC

PH

Moor Lands

PH

OTMOOR LA

New River Ray

Pigeonhouse Farm

PIGEONHOUSE LA

2

15

1

Ot Moor

Danger Area

A **B** **C**

4

River Ray

Astley Bridge Farm

LC

The Plough (PH)

Bridge Farm

PALMER AVE

LC

LC

PLOUGHLEY RD

NORRIS RD

PATRICK HAUGH RD

Upper Arncott

Depot

LC

GREEN LA

TEALE CL

HOPCRAFT CL

MILL LA

HILLSIDE CL

BUCHANAN RD

CH

CONSTABLE'S CROFT

HARPER CL DS

GREEN FIELDS

WOODPIECE RD

Arncott Hill

17

LGs

MURCOTT RD

Arncott Hill Farm

Arncott Wood

LC

LC

Depot

3

M40

FIELD RD

LC

ARNCOTT WOOD RD

LC

LC

16

Boarstall Lane

New Park Farm

Red House Farm

Murcott

Marlake House

Latchmeads

Four Winds Farm

Oldhouse Spinney

2

Whitecross Green

Panshill Farms

Pans Hill

15

Manor Farm

Upper Panshill Farm

Whitecross Green Wood

Nature Reserve

1

M40

Upper Wood

Oriel Wood

14

59 **A** **60** **B** **61** **C**

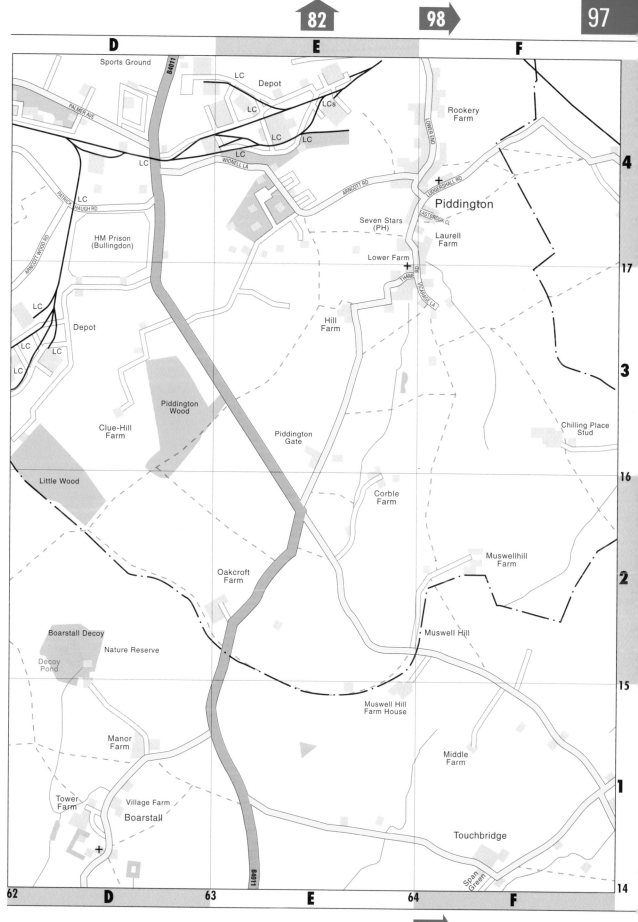

D   E   F

Sports Ground

B4011

PALMER AVE

LC   Depot   LCs

LC

Rookery
Farm

LC   LC

LC   LC

WIDNELL LA

ARNCOTT RD

LUDGERSHALL RD

LC

PATRICK HAUGH RD

LC

ARNCOTT WOOD RD

HM Prison
(Bullingdon)

Piddington

EASTBROOK CL

Seven Stars
(PH)

Laurell
Farm

Lower Farm

THAME RD

VICARAGE LA

4

17

LC

Depot

Hill
Farm

LC

LC   LC

LC

Piddington
Wood

Clue-Hill
Farm

Piddington
Gate

Chilling Place
Stud

3

Little Wood

16

Corble
Farm

Muswellhill
Farm

Oakcroft
Farm

2

Muswell Hill

Boarstall Decoy

Nature Reserve

Decoy
Pond

15

Muswell Hill
Farm House

Manor
Farm

Middle
Farm

1

Tower
Farm

Village Farm

Boarstall

Touchbridge

B4011

Span Green

62   D   63   E   64   F   14

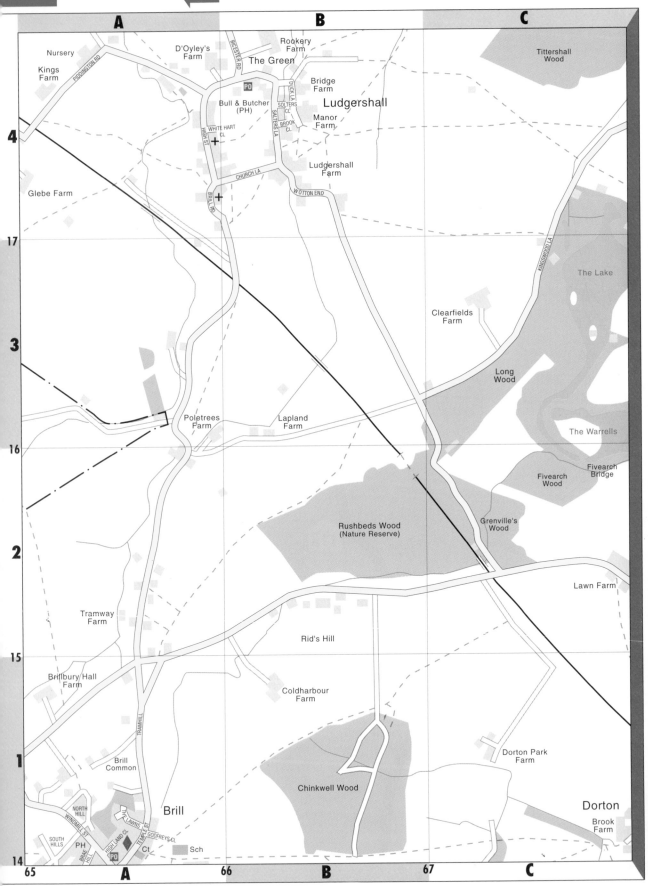

A B C

Nursery

Kings
Farm

PIDDINGTON RD

D'Oyley's
Farm

Rookery
Farm

The Green

BICESTER RD

PO

DUCK LA

Bridge
Farm

Ludgershall

Bull & Butcher
(PH)

SOLTERS
CL

SALTERS LA

BROOK CL

Manor
Farm

WHITE HART
CL

HIGH ST

4

Glebe Farm

BRILL RD

CHURCH LA

Ludgershall
Farm

WOTTON END

Tittershall
Wood

KINGSWOOD LA

17

The Lake

Clearfields
Farm

3

Long
Wood

Poletrees
Farm

Lapland
Farm

The Warrells

16

Fivearch
Wood

Fivearch
Bridge

Rushbeds Wood
(Nature Reserve)

Grenville's
Wood

2

Lawn Farm

Tramway
Farm

Rid's Hill

15

Brillbury Hall
Farm

Coldharbour
Farm

TRAMHILL

Dorton Park
Farm

1

Brill
Common

Chinkwell Wood

Dorton

NORTH
HILL

THE LAWNS

TEMPLE ST

GODFREYS CL

Brook
Farm

WINDMILL ST

BRAKE HILL

SOUTH
HILLS

PH

HIGH LAND CL

PO

Ct

Sch

Brill

14

65 A 66 B 67 C

Barrington Park

Park Farm

Sch

Barrington Farm

Great
Barrington

4

+

Barrington Park

Waterloo
Copse

The Fox Inn
(PH)

Barrington
Mill

River Windrush

13

Green Drive
Farm

PO

Church
Farm

+

MINNOW LA

MIDDLE RD

Barrington
Grove

Paper Mill
Cottages

Sanctuary
Wood

Guggle
Wood

Little
Barrington

Home Farm

Drive
Covert

Boundary
Covert

3

A40

Allotment
Plantation

The Lodge

The Inn for
all Seasons
(PH)

Brindles

12

A40

Ell
Plantation

Upton Downs
Farm

B4425

Hurst Barn
Farm

2

Upton Down

Leys Farm

Cat's Abbey
Barn

11

Poverty

Freeland
Plantation

1

Handpost
Covert

Hollowbarn
Farm

B4425

Pig Unit

Westwell

+

Freelands
Farm

10

99
84

A **B** **C**

Upper Farm
Lower Farm

Taynton

Garnes Farm

Manor Farm

4

Fernhill Copse

Taynton Mill

Cobbler's Bottom

Fulbrook Manor

Fulbrook

Field House

BEECH GR

DOLPHIN LA

GARNE'S LA

CHURCH LA

MEADOW LA

A361

UPPER END

ORCHARD ROW

13

Westhall Hill

Manor Farm

PH

THE RICKYARD

A24

River Windrush

Tadpole Farm

A361

Lower Upton Farm

The Belt

Market Plantation

Upton

Staytes Farm

Priory

Sch

BEAR CT

Sch

LAWRENCE LA

Sewage Works

3

A40

Kitt's Quarry

Cemy

CHURCH LA

PRIORY LA

HIGH ST

P

CHURCH LA

H

OLD GEORGE YD

SHEEP ST

PO

GUILDENFORD

PETHER'S PIECE

SWEET'S LA

SWAN LA

ST. SYLVESTER

WITNEY ST

PITT'S

Mus

CHAPMANS PIECE

TANNERY CL

BURFORD

TANNER'S LA

BARN LA

WHITE MEWS

SWAN LANE CL

WINDRUSH CL

12

B4425

A40

HUNTS CL

THE HILL

BARNS LA

WINDRUSH CT

Sch

FRETHERN CL

WYSDOM WAY

Upton Down

Sch

A361

CHEATLE CL

OXFORD RD

2

CH

Signet End

B4020 SHILTON RD

A40

Golf Course

Mount Pleasant

Signet Hill

11

Signethill Farm

Whitehills Farm

1

Druvas

Barley Park

B4020

Signet

JOB's Lane

Signet Farm

A361

10

23 **A** 24 **B** 25 **C**

99
114

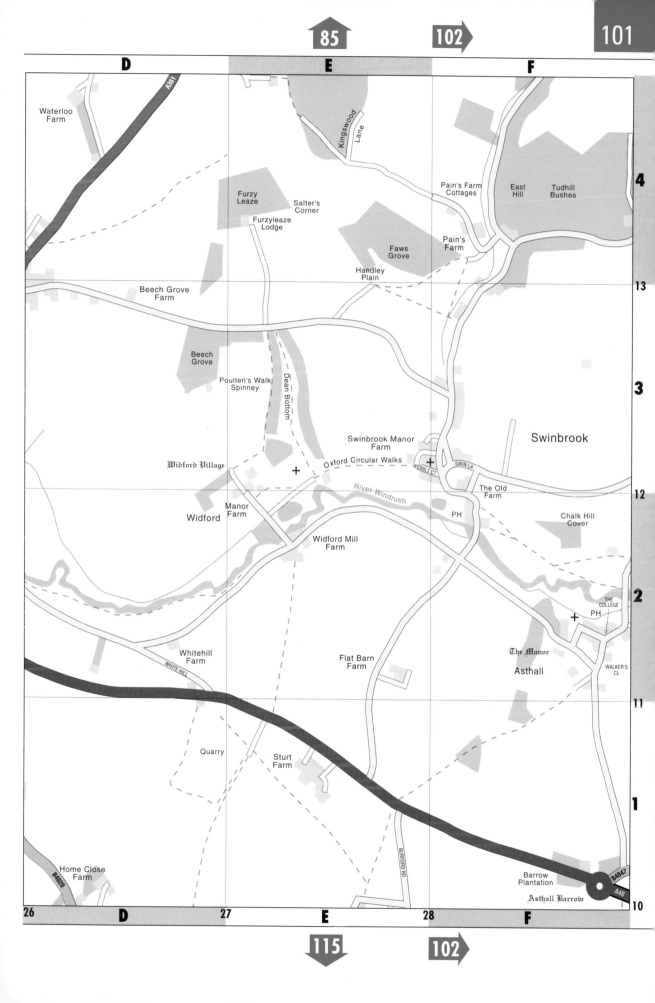

D
E
F

Waterloo Farm

Kingswood Lane

Pain's Farm Cottages

East Hill

Tudhill Bushes

4

Furzy Leaze

Salter's Corner

Furzyleaze Lodge

Faws Grove

Pain's Farm

Handley Plain

Beech Grove Farm

13

Beech Grove

Poulten's Walk Spinney

Dean Bottom

3

Swinbrook Manor Farm

Swinbrook

Widford Village

Oxford Circular Walks

PEBBLE CT

SWIN LA

The Old Farm

12

Manor Farm

Widford

River Windrush

PH

Chalk Hill Cover

Widford Mill Farm

THE COLLEGE

PH

2

Whitehill Farm

WHITE HILL

Flat Barn Farm

The Manor

Asthall

WALKER'S CL

11

Quarry

Sturt Farm

1

BURFORD RD

Home Close Farm

B4020

Barrow Plantation

B4047

Asthall Barrow

A40

26
D
27
E
28
F
10

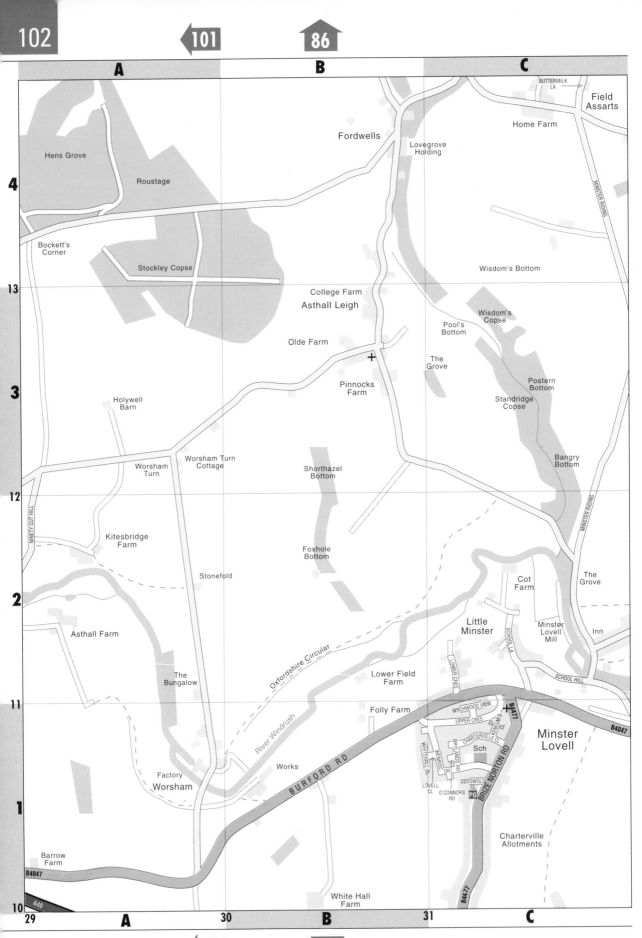

A

B

C

BUTTERMILK LA

Field Assarts

Home Farm

Fordwells

Lovegrove Holding

Hens Grove

Roustage

MINSTER RIDING

4

Bockett's Corner

Stockley Copse

Wisdom's Bottom

13

College Farm

Asthall Leigh

Wisdom's Copse

Pool's Bottom

Olde Farm

The Grove

Postern Bottom

Holywell Barn

Pinnocks Farm

Standridge Copse

3

Worsham Turn Cottage

Shorthazel Bottom

Bangry Bottom

Worsham Turn

NINETY CUT HILL

12

Kitesbridge Farm

Foxhole Bottom

Stonefold

MINSTER RIDING

Cot Farm

The Grove

2

Asthall Farm

Little Minster

SCHOOL LA

Minster Lovell Mill

Inn

Oxfordshire Circular

Lower Field Farm

LOWER CRES

SCHOOL HILL

The Bungalow

River Windrush

Folly Farm

WYCHWOOD VIEW

B4477

11

UPPER CRES

B4047

CHARTERVILLE CL

KERELM S

Minster Lovell

DRYLANDS RD

WENRISC DR

WHITEHALL CL

Sch

BRIZE NORTON RD

Factory

Worsham

Works

LOVELL CL

COTSWOLD CL

O'CONNORS RD

PO

1

Charterville Allotments

Barrow Farm

B4047

B4477

A40

White Hall Farm

10

29

A

30

B

31

C

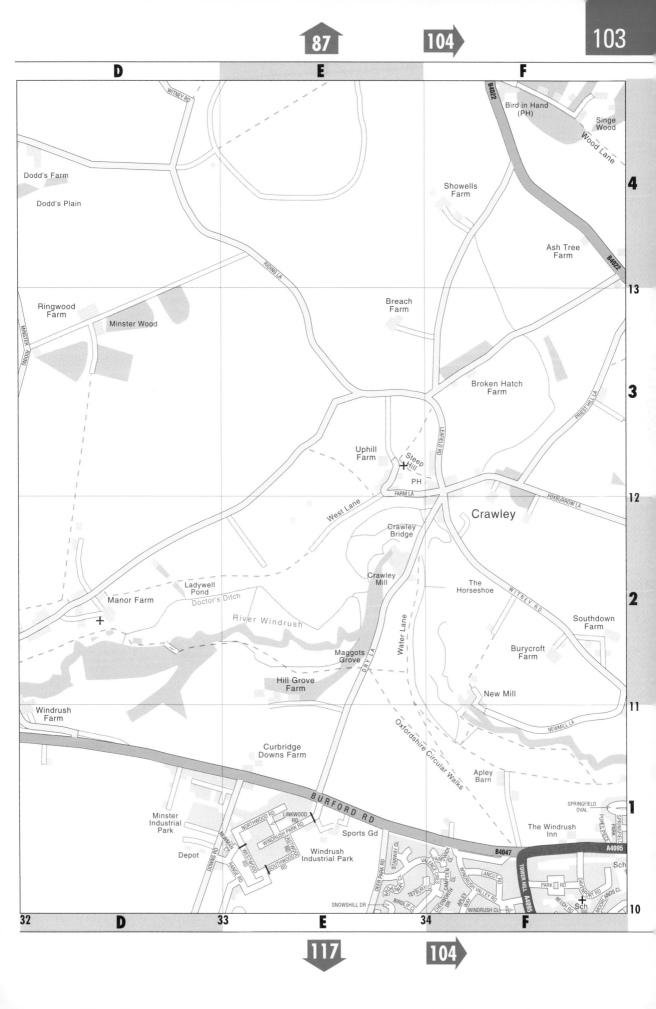

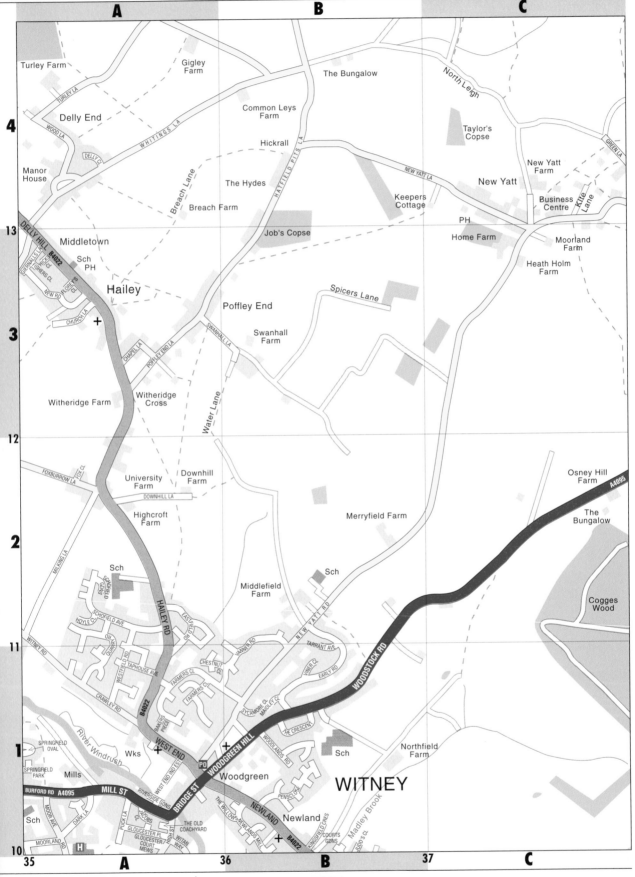

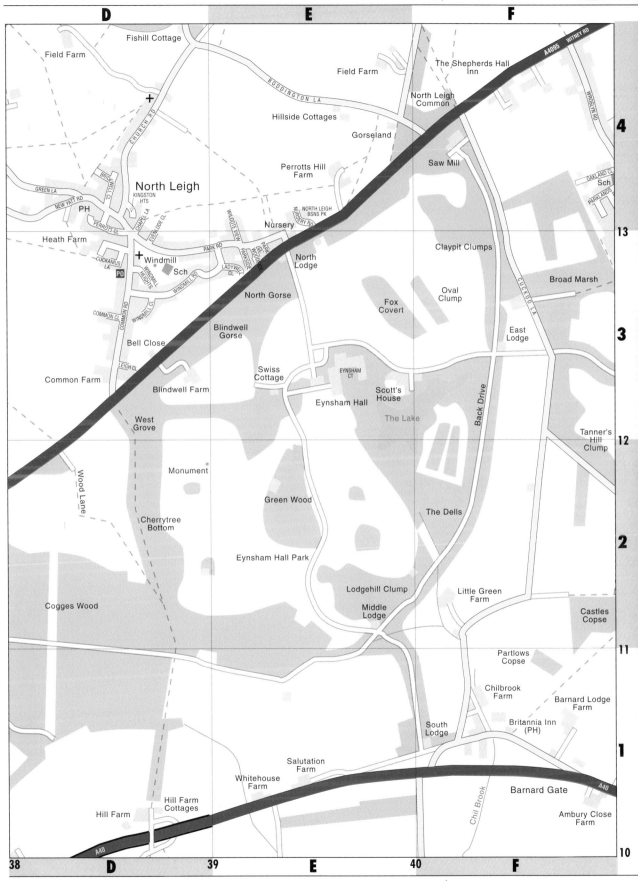

D

Field Farm

Fishill Cottage

CHURCH RD

BODDINGTON LA

Field Farm

The Shepherds Hall Inn

A4095 WITNEY RD

WROSLYN RD

E

F

Hillside Cottages

North Leigh Common

4

Gorseland

Saw Mill

Perrotts Hill Farm

BRIDWELL CL

GREEN LA

NEW YATT RD

North Leigh

KINGSTON HTS

PH

CHAPEL LA

EVENLODE CL

PERROTT CL

WILCOTE VIEW

PARK RD

PARKSIDE

NURSERY RD

NORTH LEIGH BSNS PK

Nursery

OAKLAND CL

Sch

PARKLANDS

13

Heath Farm

Claypit Clumps

CUCKOO LA

Broad Marsh

CUCKAMUS LA

PO

Windmill

WINDMILL HEIGHTS

WINDMILL RD

LADYWELL CL

Sch

North Lodge

Fox Covert

Oval Clump

East Lodge

3

Common CL

COMMON RD

WINDMILL CL

North Gorse

LEIGH CL

Blindwell Gorse

Bell Close

Swiss Cottage

EYNSHAM CT

Scott's House

Back Drive

Blindwell Farm

Eynsham Hall

The Lake

Common Farm

West Grove

Tanner's Hill Clump

12

Wood Lane

Monument

Green Wood

The Dells

2

Cherrytree Bottom

Eynsham Hall Park

Little Green Farm

Castles Copse

Cogges Wood

Lodgehill Clump

Middle Lodge

Partlows Copse

11

Chilbrook Farm

Barnard Lodge Farm

South Lodge

Britannia Inn (PH)

1

Salutation Farm

Whitehouse Farm

Barnard Gate

A40

Chill Brook

Ambury Close Farm

Hill Farm Cottages

Hill Farm

A40

10

38

D

39

E

40

F

105
90

A   B   C

HURDSWELL
GLYME WAY
BOROUGH CR
CHURCHILL WAY
SISSS
ROOSEVELT RD
PINSLEY RD
Allot Gdns

Mill Farm

4

Cook's Corner Farm

Pinsley Wood

Cemy

CHURCH RD

OAKLAND CL
Sch
PARKLANDS
PO

Freeland

MASH LA
WROSLYN RD
WOODLANDS THE
THE GREEN
CHURCH WALKERS
Little Blenheim

Sewage Works

13

MANSELL CL

Church Hanborough

PH

College Farm

MARSH LA
WEBSTER'S CL
BLENHEIM LA

PH

Whitehouse Farm

PIGEON HOUSE LA

Dreydon House

3

Freeland House

Elm Farm

The Thrift

Goose Eye Farm

The Green

12

Lady Grove

Oxfordshire Circular Walks

New Barn Farm

River Evenlode

Vincents Wood

2

CUCKOO LA

Bowles Farm

CUCKOO LA

Oxfordshire Circular Walks

City Farm

11

Eynsham Mill

Acre Hill Farm

New Wintles Farm

1

Mill Lane

A40

Chil Brook

Evenlode Farm

Acre Hill House

A40

10

41   A   42   B   43   C

LOWER RD

D
E
F

4

Burleigh
Lodge

Bladon Heath

Hall
Farm

ST MICHAEL'S LA
Priory

SPRING HILL RD

Burleigh
Wood

Worton Heath

Dolton Lane

Begbroke
Wood

13

Burleigh
Farm

River Evenlode

Spring
Hill

3

Frogwelldown Lane

Works

12

Purwell
Farm

CASSINGTON RD

Jericho
Farm

2

YARNTON RD

Rectory
Farm

Worton

The
Elms

11

ELMS RD

THE
TENNIS

BELL CL

LYNTON LA

BELL LA

Cassington

ORCHARD
CL

ST PETER'S
CL

Sch

HORSEMERE LA

A40

Manor
Farm

THE GREEN

HOLTON
SPRING

CHURCH
LA

1

EYNSHAM RD

MANOR CL

POUND LA

MARLBOROUGH
DR

Wharf
Farm

CASSINGTON RD

Works

Durham Lane

Marlborough
Pool

River Thames or Isis

Oxfordshire Circular
Walk

10

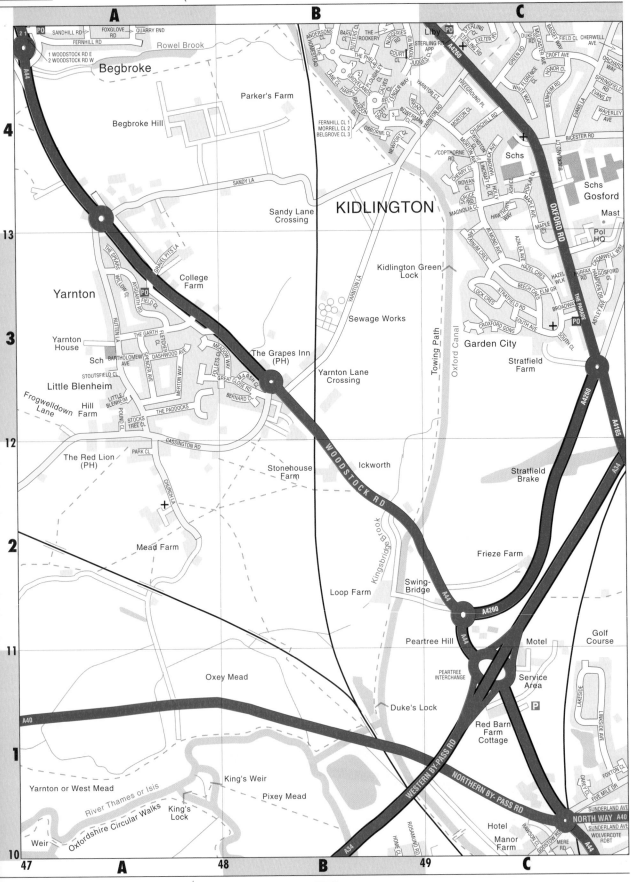

A B C

PO
SANDHILL RD
FOXGLOVE RD
QUARRY END
FERNHILL RD
Rowel Brook

1 WOODSTOCK RD E
2 WOODSTOCK RD W

Begbroke

Parker's Farm

Begbroke Hill

4

SANDY LA

FERNHILL CL 1
MORRELL CL 2
BELGROVE CL 3

Sandy Lane Crossing

KIDLINGTON

13

Yarnton

College Farm

Kidlington Green Lock

Sewage Works

3

Yarnton House

Little Blenheim

The Grapes Inn (PH)

Yarnton Lane Crossing

Garden City

Stratfield Farm

Frogwelldown Lane

Hill Farm

Towing Path

Oxford Canal

12

The Red Lion (PH)

Stonehouse Farm

Ickworth

Stratfield Brake

Mead Farm

Kingsbridge Brook

Frieze Farm

2

Loop Farm

Swing-Bridge

Peartree Hill

Golf Course

11

Oxey Mead

Duke's Lock

Peartree Interchange

Service Area

A40

Red Barn Farm Cottage

WESTERN BY-PASS RD
NORTHERN BY-PASS RD

1

King's Weir

Pixey Mead

Hotel

Manor Farm

NORTH WAY A40

Yarnton or West Mead

River Thames or Isis

King's Lock

Oxfordshire Circular Walks

Weir

10

47 A 48 B 49 C

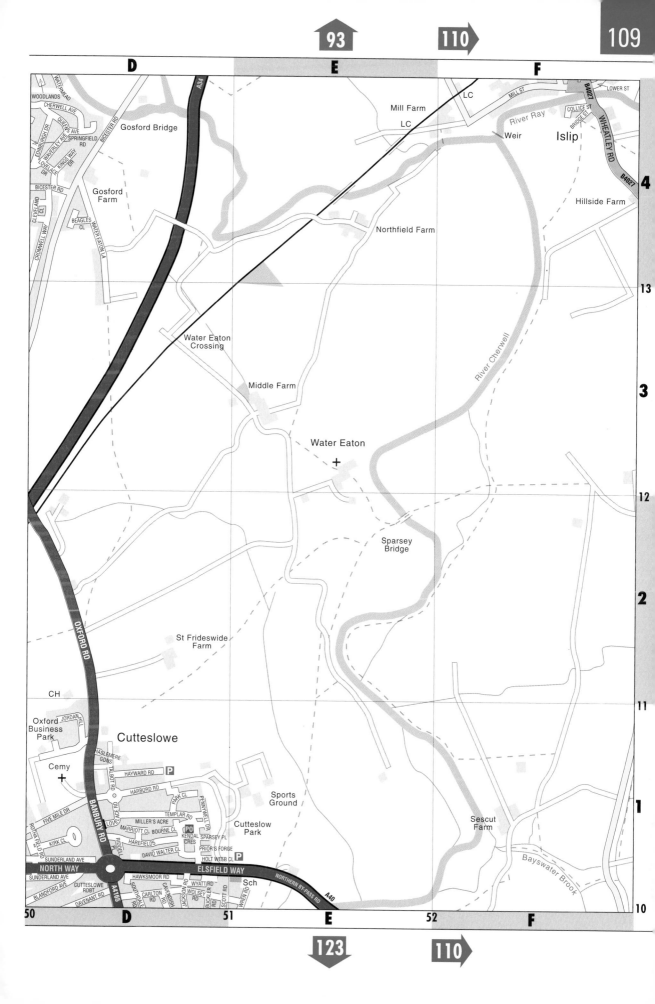

109
94

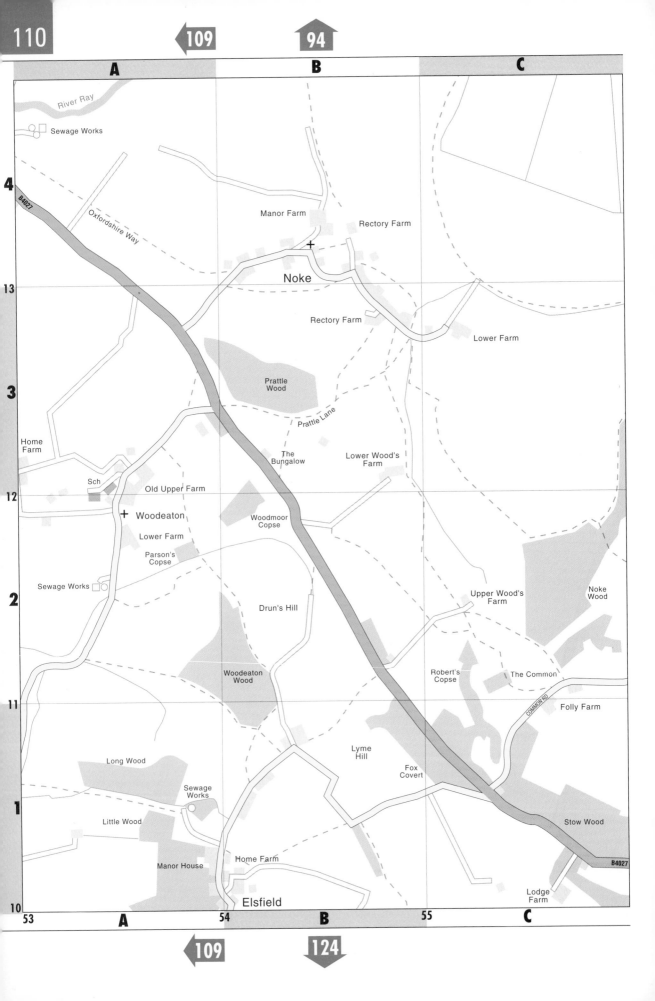

A　　**B**　　**C**

4

River Ray

Sewage Works

B4027

Oxfordshire Way

Manor Farm

Rectory Farm

+

Noke

13

Rectory Farm

Lower Farm

Prattle Wood

3

Prattle Lane

Home Farm

The Bungalow

Lower Wood's Farm

Sch

Old Upper Farm

12

+ Woodeaton

Woodmoor Copse

Lower Farm

Parson's Copse

Sewage Works

Drun's Hill

Upper Wood's Farm

Noke Wood

2

Woodeaton Wood

Robert's Copse

The Common

COMMON RD

11

Folly Farm

Long Wood

Lyme Hill

Fox Covert

Sewage Works

Little Wood

1

Stow Wood

Manor House

Home Farm

B4027

Elsfield

Lodge Farm

10

53　　**A**　　54　　**B**　　55　　**C**

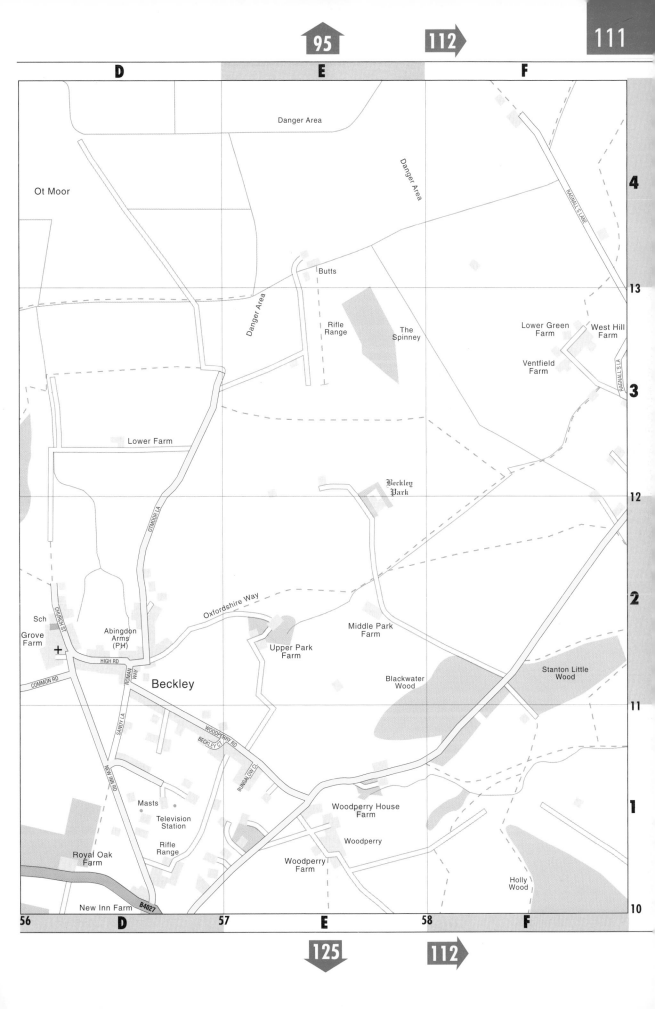

111
96

A
B
C
4
13
3
12
2
11
1
10
59
60
61
Old Arngrove
New Arngrove Farm
M40
Warren Farm
Gardner's Barn
Tippens Copse
Nursery
Sermin's Copse
RAGNALL'S LA
Studley Farm
Pasture Farm
Horton-cum-Studley
MILL LA
PO
CHURCH LA
VENTFIELD CL
THE GREEN
FORGE CL
Danes Brook
Manor Far
New Farm
PRIORY CL
Studley Priory
Hotel
Moors Farm
Sewage Works
Studley Wood
P
Oakley Wood
Corner Farm
Nature Trail
The Moat
Nature Reserve
Bernwood Forest (Nature Reserve)
York's Wood
Danesbrook Farm
Danes Brook
Moorbirge Brook
Oxfordshire Way
Hell Coppice
Beckley
Menmarsh Guide Post
Moorbirge Bridge

111
126

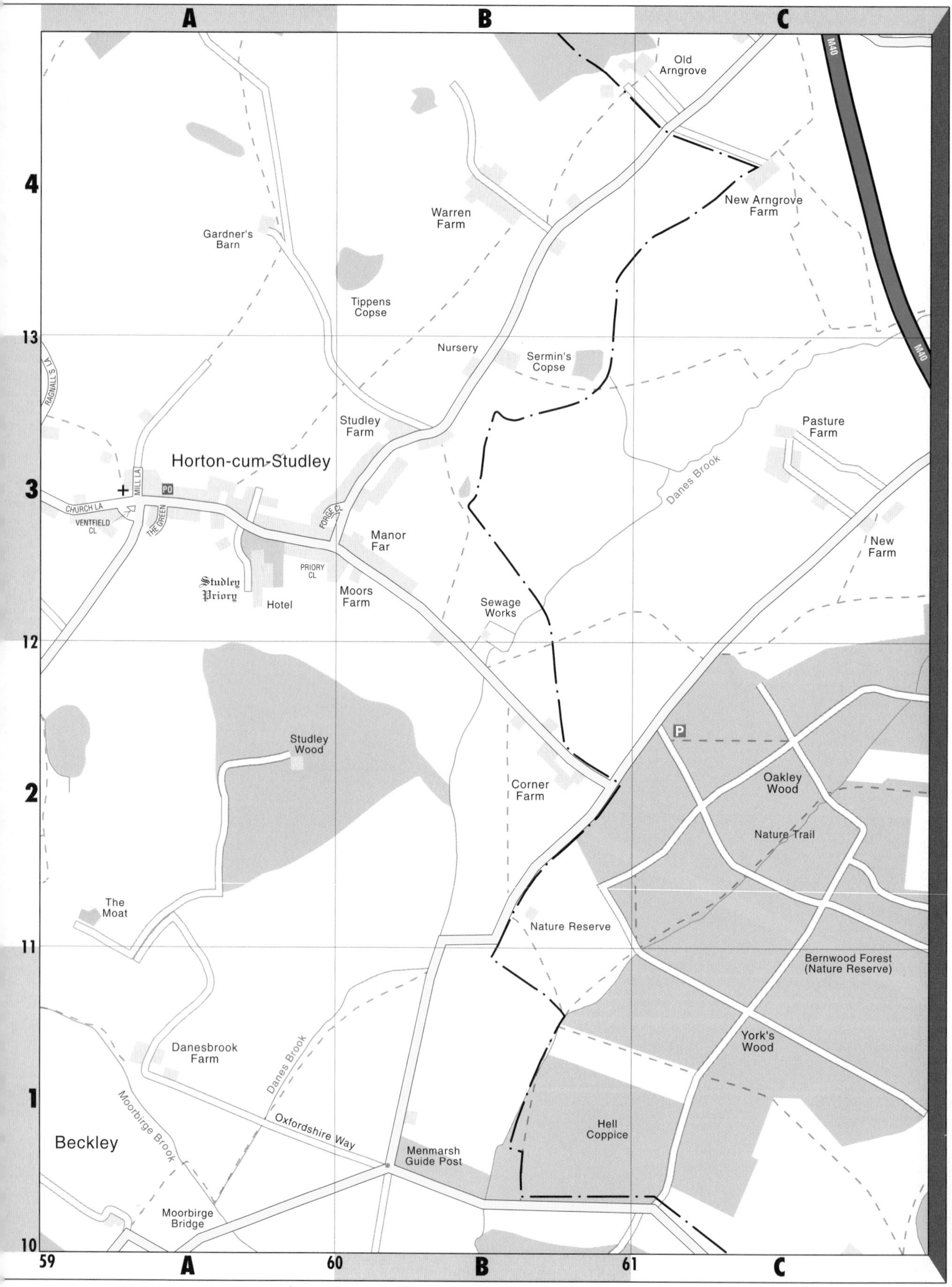

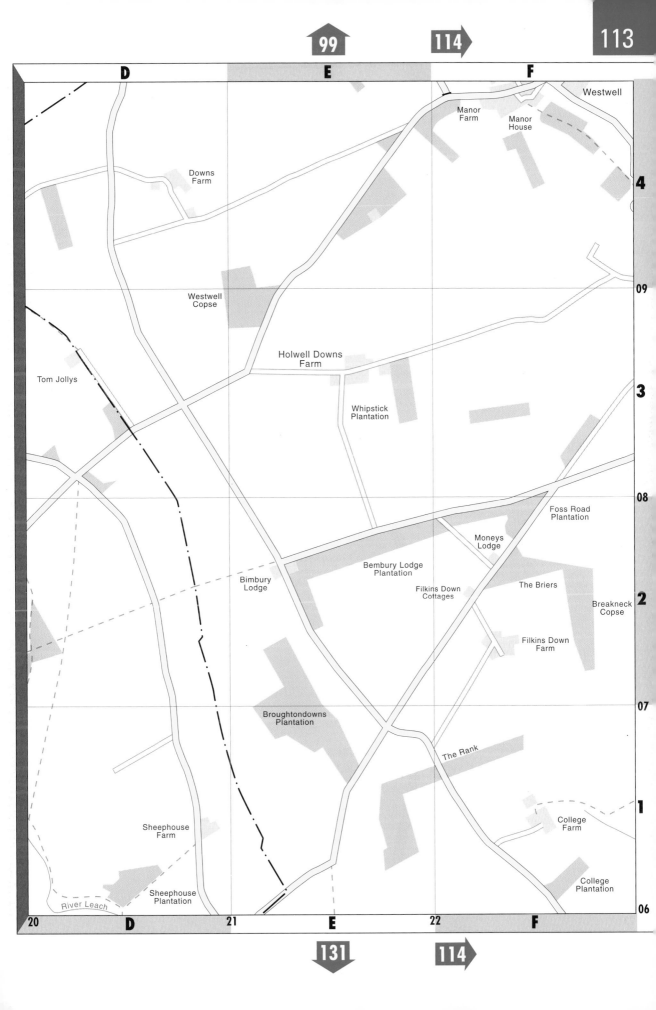

D
E
F

Westwell

Manor
Farm

Manor
House

Downs
Farm

4

09

Westwell
Copse

Holwell Downs
Farm

Tom Jollys

3

Whipstick
Plantation

08

Foss Road
Plantation

Moneys
Lodge

Bembury Lodge
Plantation

Bimbury
Lodge

Filkins Down
Cottages

The Briers

2

Breakneck
Copse

Filkins Down
Farm

07

Broughtondowns
Plantation

The Rank

1

College
Farm

Sheephouse
Farm

Sheephouse
Plantation

College
Plantation

River Leach

06

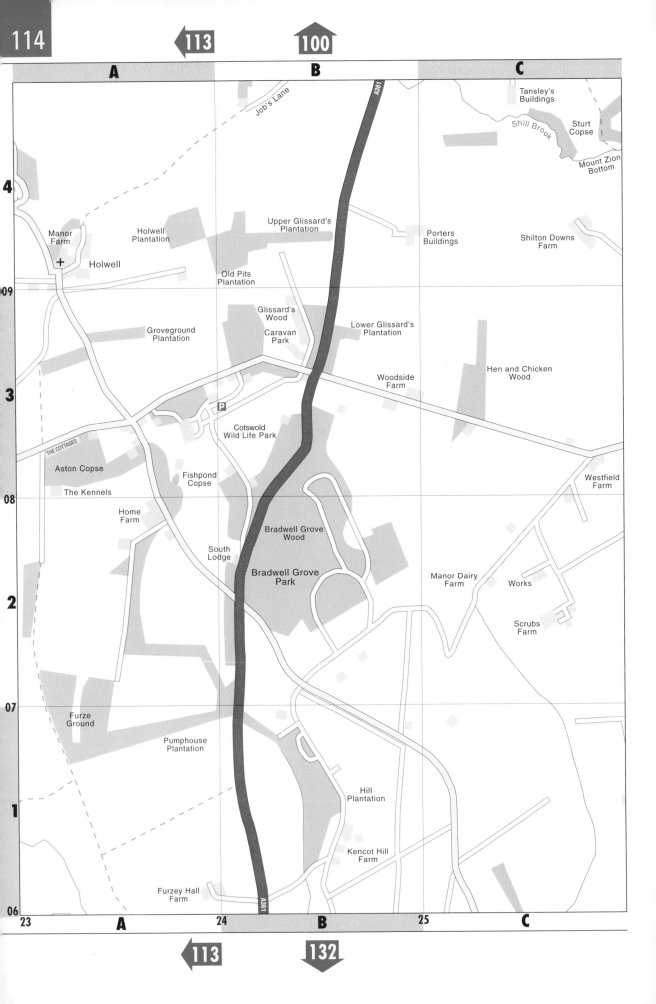

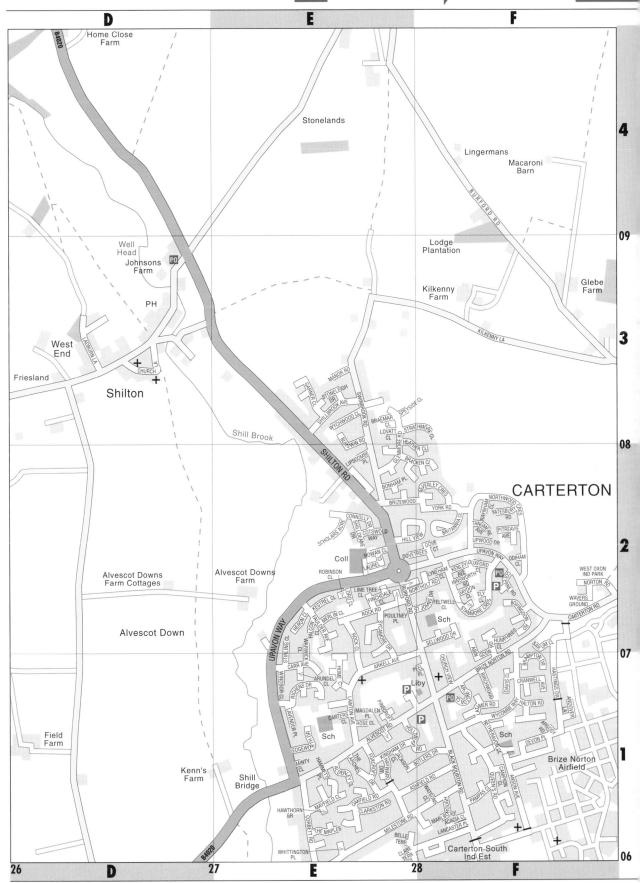

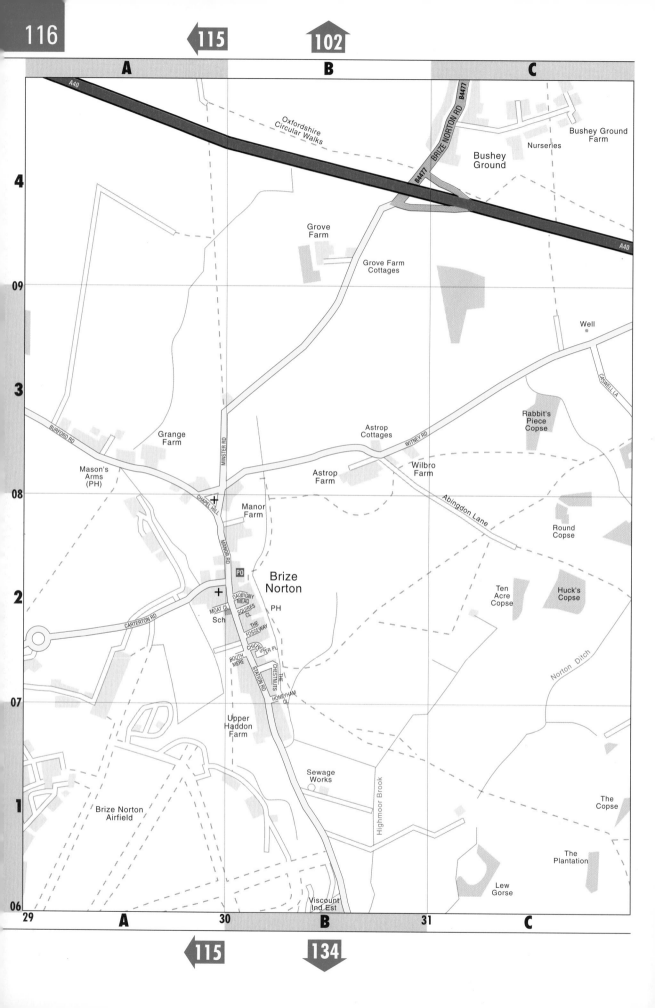

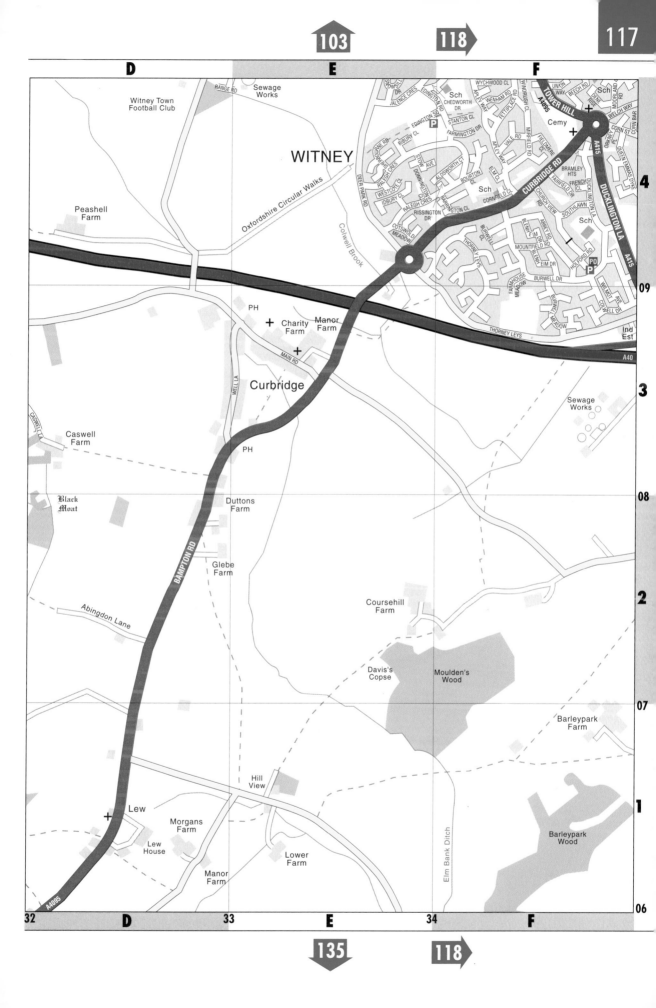

D   E   F

RANGE RD

Sewage
Works

Witney Town
Football Club

WITNEY

WYCHWOOD CL

Sch
CHEDWORTH
DR

TOWER HILL

A4095

Cemy

Sch

A415

CURBRIDGE RD

DUCKLINGTON LA

BRAMLEY
HTS

4

Peashell
Farm

Oxfordshire Circular Walks

Colwell Brook

FARMINGTON DR

Sch

RISSINGTON
DR

COTSWOLD
MEADOW

CORNFIELD CL

Sch

FARMHOUSE
MEADOW

BURWELL DR

P
PO

09

THORNEY LEYS

Ind
Est

A40

PH

Charity
Farm

Manor
Farm

Sewage
Works

3

WELL LA

MAIN RD

Curbridge

PH

Caswell
Farm

Black
Moat

Duttons
Farm

08

BAMPTON RD

Glebe
Farm

Abingdon Lane

Coursehill
Farm

2

Davis's
Copse

Moulden's
Wood

07

Barleypark
Farm

Hill
View

1

Lew

Morgans
Farm

Elm Bank Ditch

Barleypark
Wood

Lew
House

Lower
Farm

Manor
Farm

A4095

06

32   D   33   E   34   F

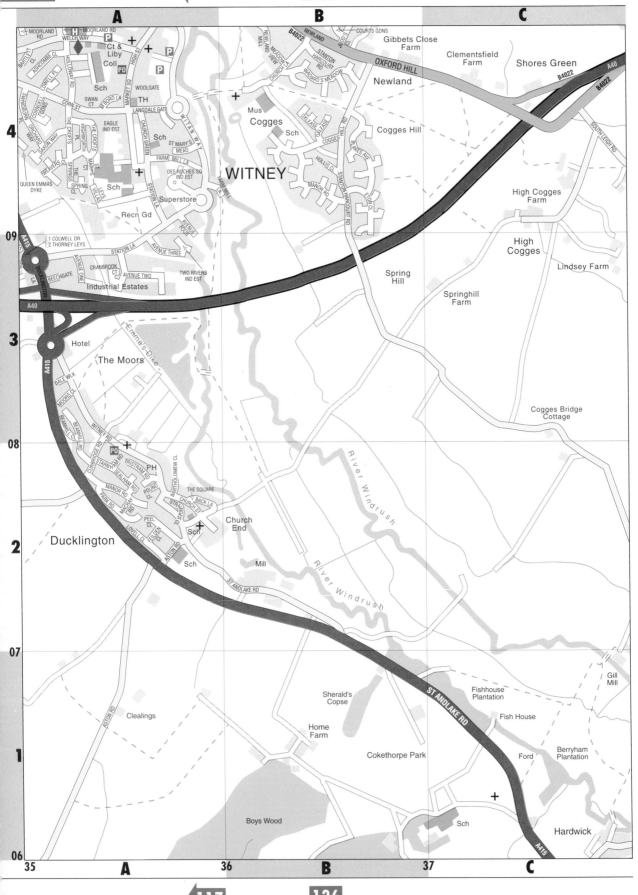

A   **B**   **C**

Chil Brook

4

Twelve Acre Farm

Paddock Close

PH

A40

TILGARSLEY RD

OLD WITNEY RD

TRUTLANDS

BARTHOLOMEW CL

WITNEY RD

WILLOWS EDGE

THORNBURY RD

SHAKESPEARE RD

DUNCAN CL

STRATFORD DR

FALSTAFF CL

Sch

CLOVER PL

GREEN'S RD

HANBOROUGH CL

MARLBOROUGH PL

MARLBOROUGH RD

SPAREACRE LA

PELICAN

CL

EVANS CL

OLD SWAN LA

JOHN LOPES RD

BACK LA

MILL ST

WYTHAM VIEW

WYNHAM CL

ENSLOW CL

B4449

Sch

HAWTHORN RD

BEECH RD

MILLWOOD

HANBOROUGH RD

MILL ST MEWS

NEWLAND ST

NEWLAND

QUEEN'S CL

QUEEN'S LA

TANNERS LA

ORCHARD CL

BITTERELL

CASSINGTON RD

PO

Liby

THAMES

HIGH ST

Litchfield Farm

CHILBRIDGE RD

Chil Brook

MERTON CL

BLAINSTONE CL

STATION RD

ACRE END ST

LOMBARD ST

ABBEY PL

HEDNALL CL

SWAN ST

ABBEY

ST

1 THE TUER
2 THE SQUARE
3 CHURCH ST

OXFORD RD

Eynsham

Abbey Farm

09

B4044

Oxfordshire Circular Walks

OASIS PARK

Southfield Cottages

PINKHILL LA

OAKFIELDS IND EST

Oxfordshire Circular Walks

The Nunnery

3

Southfield Barn

Foxley Farm

08

Limb Brook

Bell Bridge

The Bungalow

Pinkhill Farm

Weir

2

University Cottages

07

Nicholls' Farm

Sutton Farm

Sutton Green

River Thames or Isis

Towing Path

1

B4448

Beaumont House

Sutton

SUTTON LA

FOXBURROW CL

BURR CL

DUCK END LA

Cox's Farm

Lower Farm

The Fox (PH)

Sewage Works

06

41   **A**   42   **B**   43   **C**

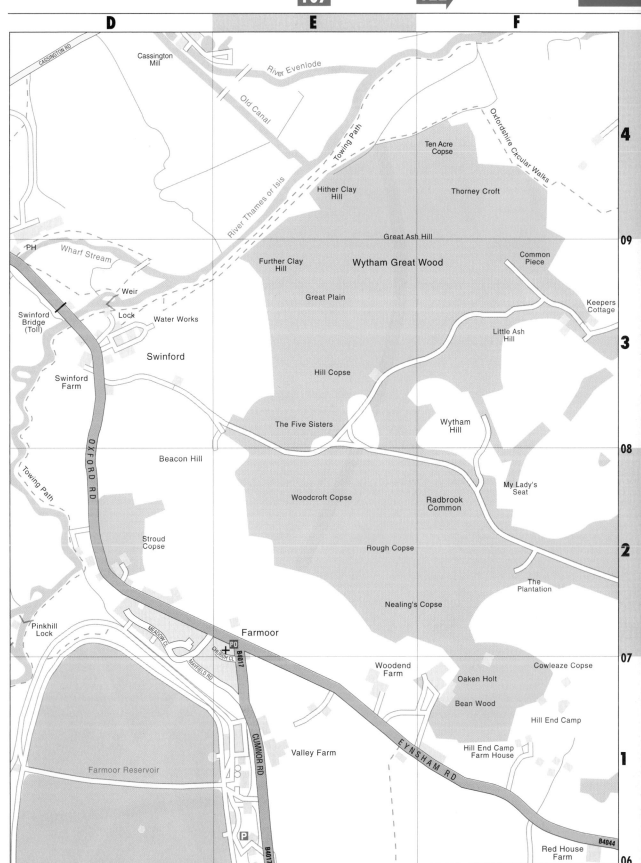

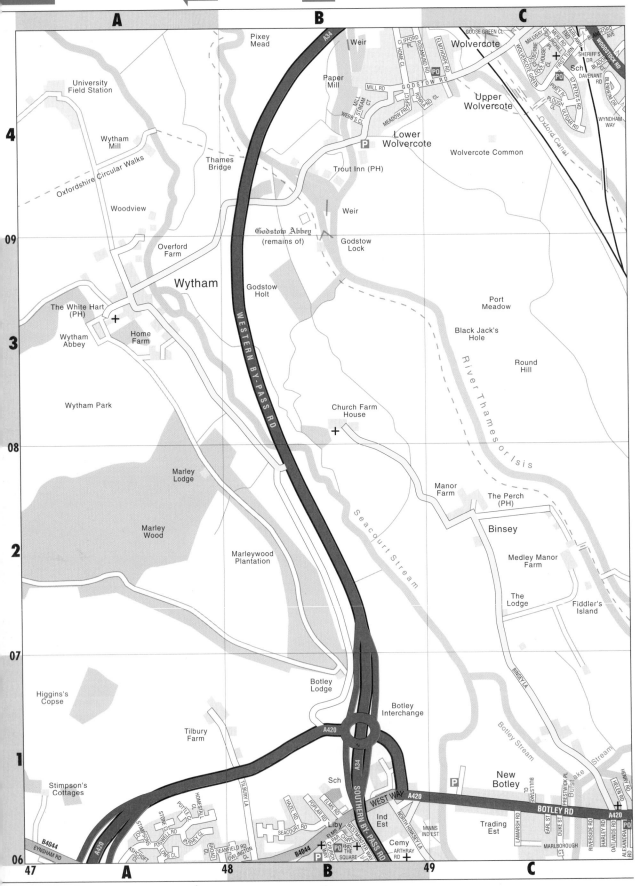

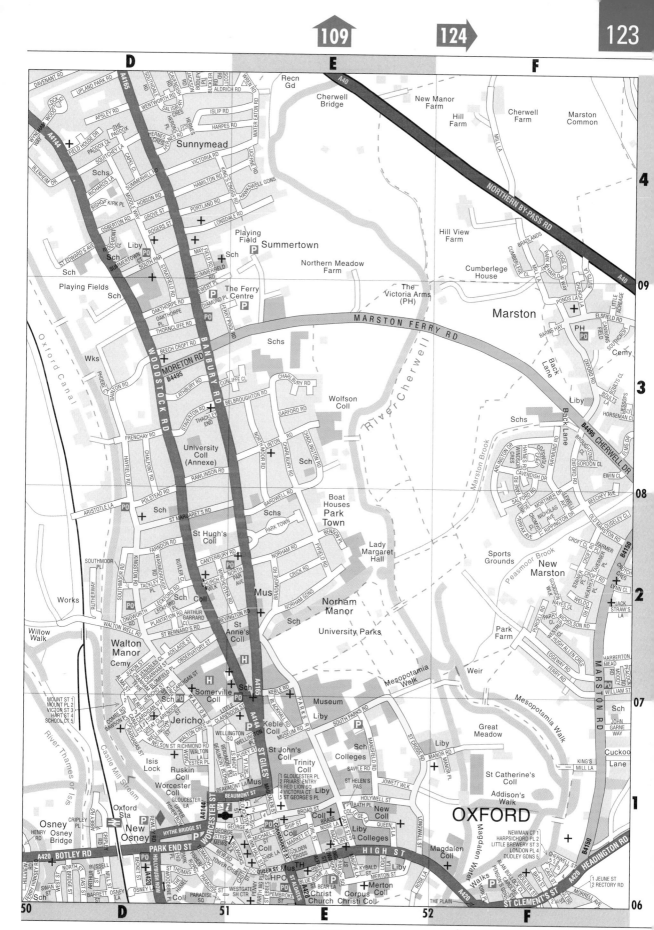

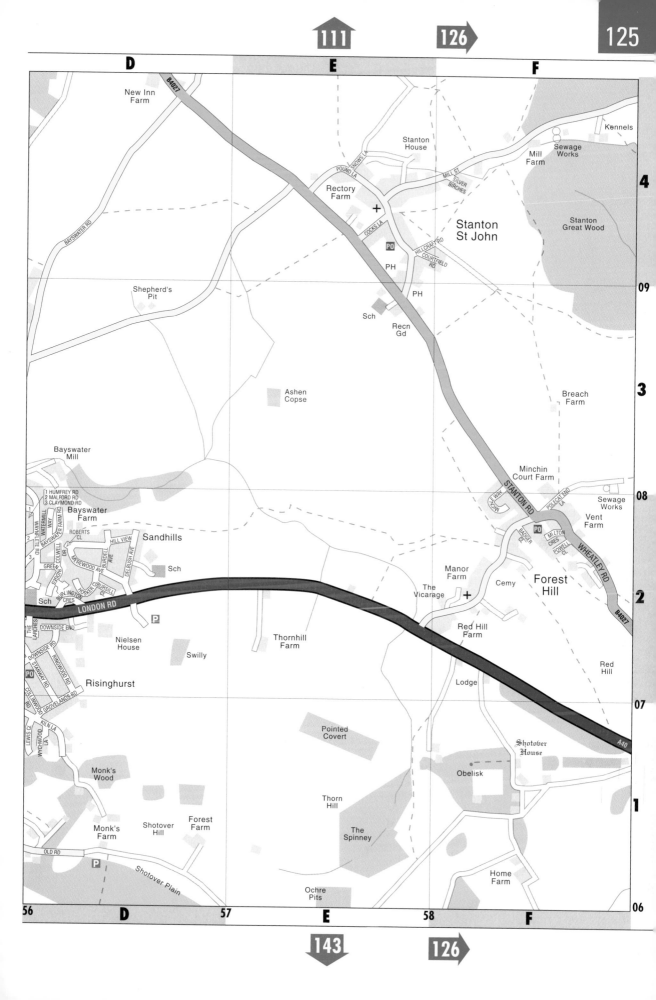

D
E
F

B4027

New Inn
Farm

Kennels

Stanton
House

Mill
Farm

Sewage
Works

SNOWS LA

POUND LA

MILL ST

SILVER
BIRCHES

Rectory
Farm

4

COCKS LA

Stanton
St John

Stanton
Great Wood

Shepherd's
Pit

HILLCRAFT RD

09

PO

PH

COURTFIELD RD

Sch

PH

Recn
Gd

Breach
Farm

3

Ashen
Copse

Bayswater
Mill

Minchin
Court Farm

08

1 HUMFREY RD
2 MALFORD RD
3 CLAYMOND RD

Bayswater
Farm

STANTON RD

POLECAT END LA

Sewage
Works

MACK LA WAY

Vent
Farm

WATERMILL
WAY

BAYSWATER FARM RD

WAYFLETE RD

Sandhills

ROBERTS
CL

HILL VIEW

BADGER
CL

PO

MILTON
CRES

WHEATLEY RD

COLWELL
DR

MEREWOOD AVE

BURDELL
AVE

DELBUSH AVE

Sch

POWELL
CL

GREEN
CL

SPODY

CL

BURLINGTON
CRES

HONOR
CL

BURSILL
CL

Manor
Farm

Cemy

Forest
Hill

Sch

LONDON RD

The
Vicarage

2

THE
LARCHES

P

Red Hill
Farm

B4027

DOWNSIDE END

Nielsen
House

Thornhill
Farm

Swilly

Red
Hill

DOWNSIDE END

STANWAY RD

RINGWOOD RD

GROVELANDS RD

Lodge

07

PO

Risinghurst

COLLINWOOD
RD

A40

LEWIS CL

KILN LA

WYCHWOOD
LA

Pointed
Covert

Shotover
House

Monk's
Wood

Obelisk

Thorn
Hill

1

OLD RD

Monk's
Farm

Shotover
Hill

Forest
Farm

The
Spinney

Home
Farm

P

Shotover Plain

Ochre
Pits

56
D
57
E
58
F
06

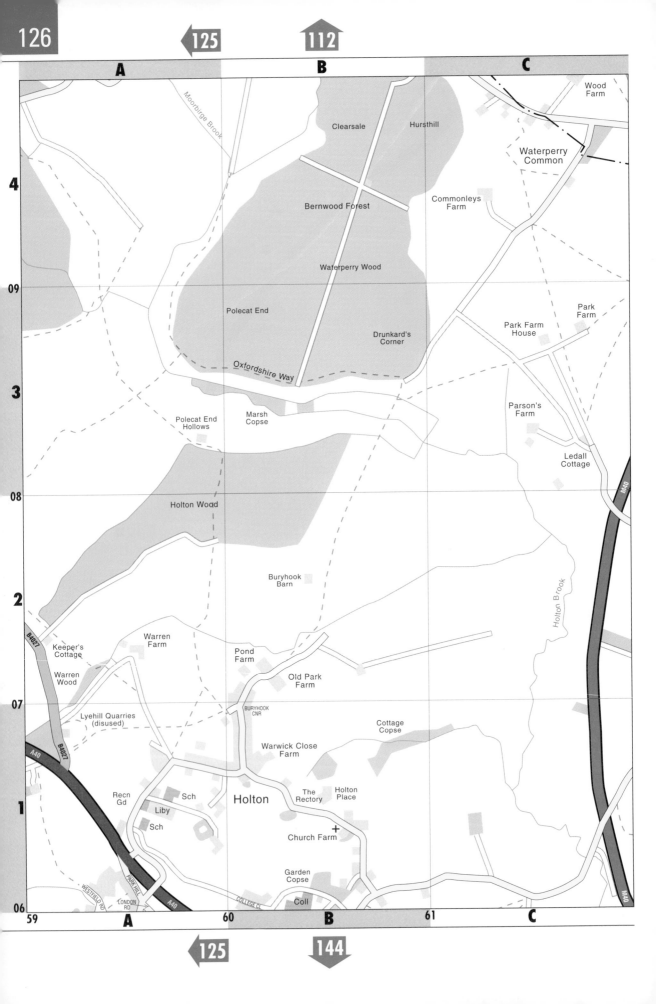

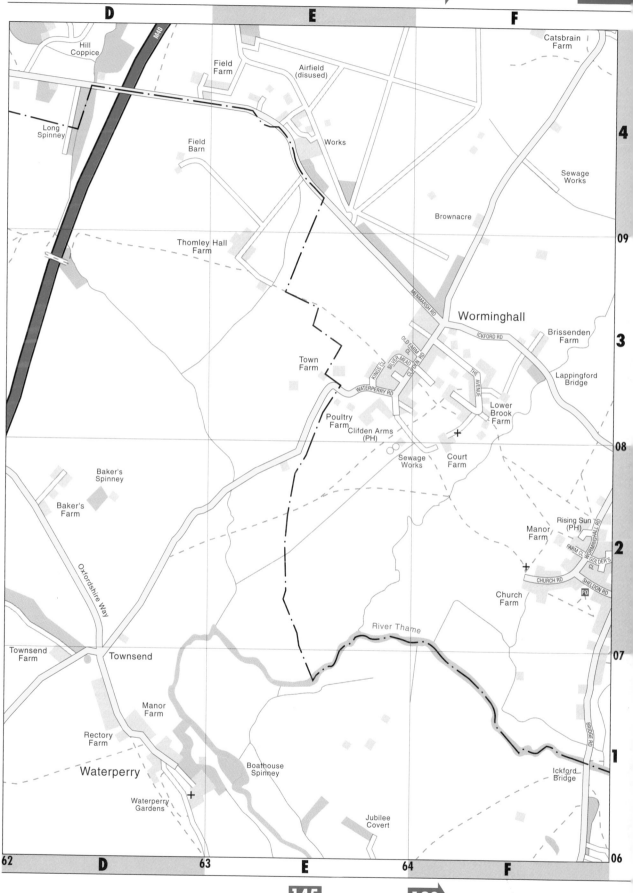

D **E** **F**

Hill Coppice

M40

Long Spinney

Field Farm

Airfield (disused)

Field Barn

Works

Catsbrain Farm

Sewage Works

Brownacre

4

Thomley Hall Farm

09

MENMARSH RD

Worminghall

ICKFORD RD

Brissenden Farm

OLD FARM CL

3

Town Farm

SILVER MEAD CL

KINGS CL

WATERPERRY RD

THE AVENUE

Lappingford Bridge

Poultry Farm

Clifden Arms (PH)

Lower Brook Farm

✛

Baker's Spinney

Sewage Works

Court Farm

08

Baker's Farm

Rising Sun (PH)

Manor Farm

FARM CL

GOLDER'S CL

WORMINGHALL RD

2

Oxfordshire Way

✛

CHURCH RD

SHELDON RD

PO

Church Farm

Townsend Farm

Townsend

River Thame

07

Manor Farm

Rectory Farm

BRIDGE RD

1

Waterperry

Boathouse Spinney

Ickford Bridge

✛

Waterperry Gardens

Jubilee Covert

06

62 **D** **63** **E** **64** **F**

127

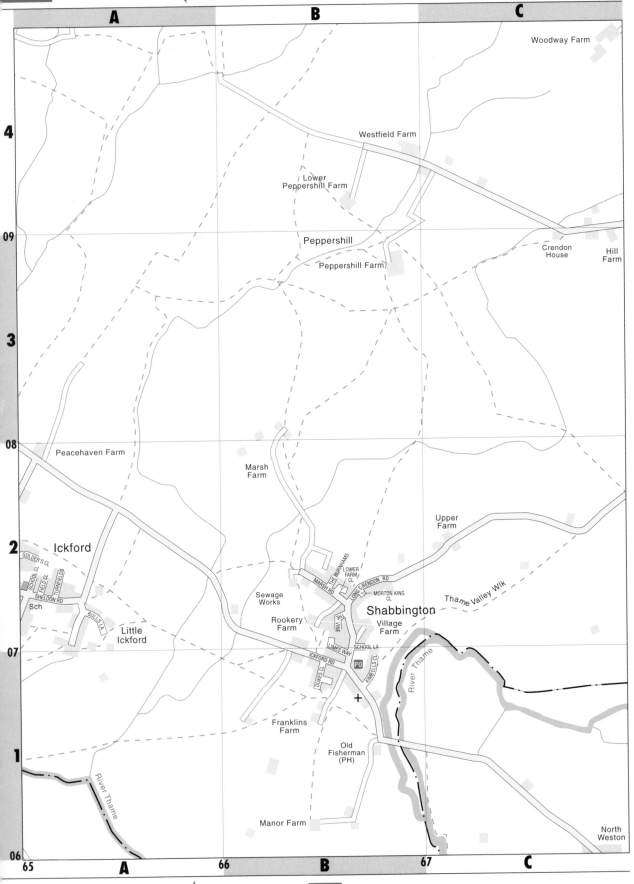

A B C

Woodway Farm

4

Westfield Farm

Lower
Peppershill Farm

09 Peppershill

Crendon
House

Hill
Farm

Peppershill Farm

3

08 Peacehaven Farm

Marsh
Farm

Upper
Farm

2 Ickford

GOLDER'S CL
SCHOOL CL
FIELD CL
TURNFIELDS

SHELDON RD

Sch

BULL'S LA

Little
Ickford

Sewage
Works

MARSH RD
THE BURNHAMS
LOWER
FARM
CL
LONG C.RENDON RD

MORTON KING
CL

Thame Valley Wlk

Rookery
Farm

THE VINE

Shabbington

Village
Farm

River Thame

07

LIMES WAY

ICKFORD RD

PO

SCHOOL LA

KIMBELLS CL

DUKES CL

Franklins
Farm

Old
Fisherman
(PH)

1

River Thame

Manor Farm

North
Weston

06

65 A 66 B 67 C

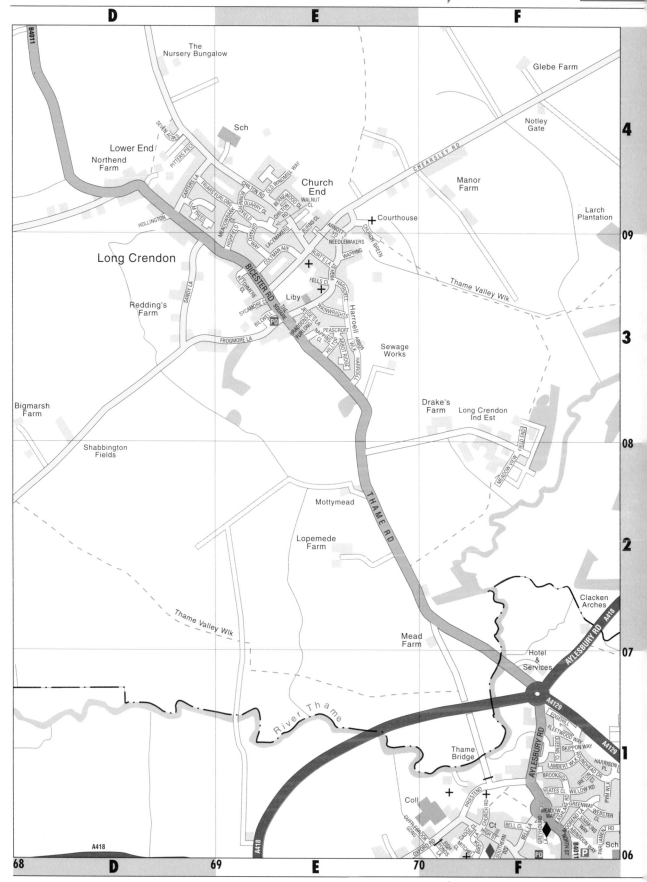

129

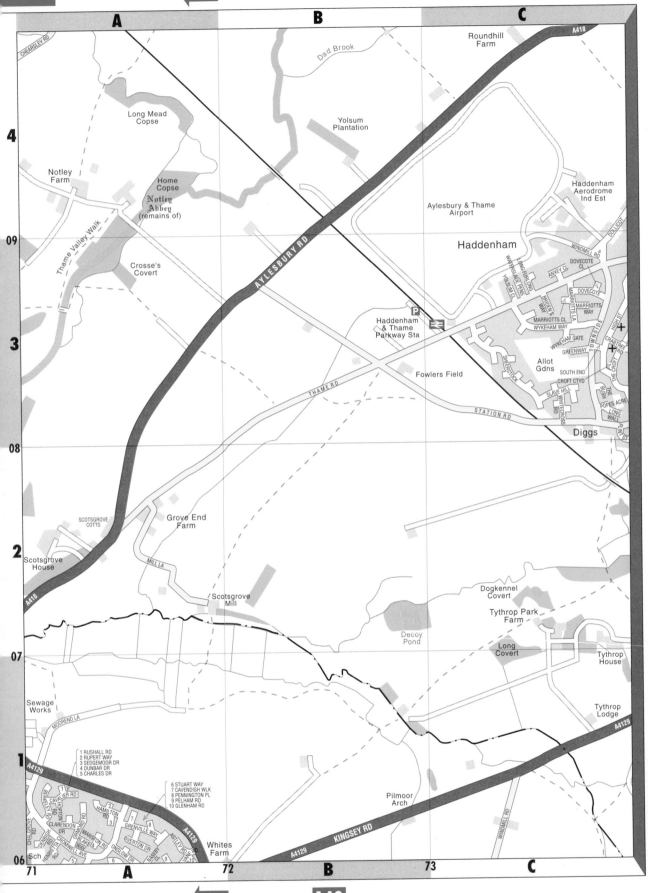

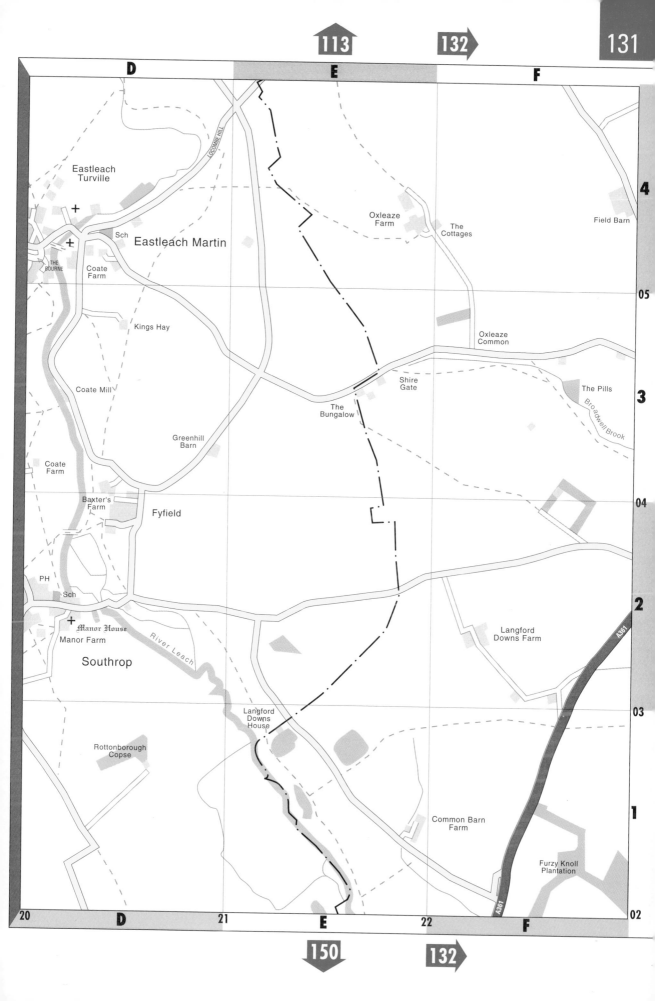

D
E
F

4

Eastleach
Turville

Oxleaze
Farm

The
Cottages

Field Barn

Sch
Eastleach Martin

THE
BOURNE

Coate
Farm

05

Oxleaze
Common

Kings Hay

The Pills

3

Coate Mill

Shire
Gate

Broadwell Brook

The
Bungalow

Greenhill
Barn

Coate
Farm

04

Baxter's
Farm

Fyfield

2

Langford
Downs Farm

A361

PH

Sch

Manor House

River Leach

Manor Farm

Southrop

03

Langford
Downs
House

Rottonborough
Copse

1

Common Barn
Farm

Furzy Knoll
Plantation

A361

20
D
21
E
22
F
02

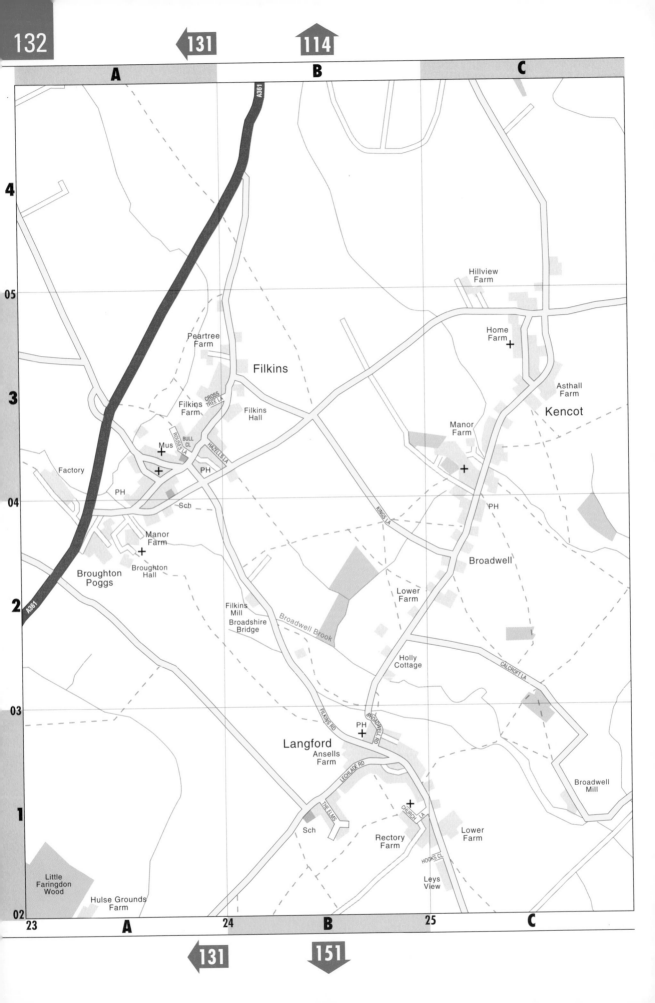

A B C

131

151

A361

4

05

Peartree
Farm

Filkins

3

CROSS
TREE LA

Filkins
Farm

Filkins
Hall

Hillview
Farm

Home
Farm

Asthall
Farm

Kencot

Manor
Farm

Mus

BULL
CL

HAXELLS LA

ROUSES LA

Factory

PH

PH

Scb

04

Manor
Farm

Broughton
Poggs

Broughton
Hall

Filkins
Mill
Broadshire
Bridge

Broadwell Brook

KINGS LA

Lower
Farm

Broadwell

PH

Holly
Cottage

CALCROFT LA

03

FILKINS RD

PH

BROADWELL RD

Broadwell
Mill

Langford

Ansells
Farm

LECHLADE RD

2

A361

1

THE ELMS

Sch

CHURCH LA

Rectory
Farm

HOOKS CL

Lower
Farm

Little
Faringdon
Wood

Leys
View

Hulse Grounds
Farm

02

23 A 24 B 25 C

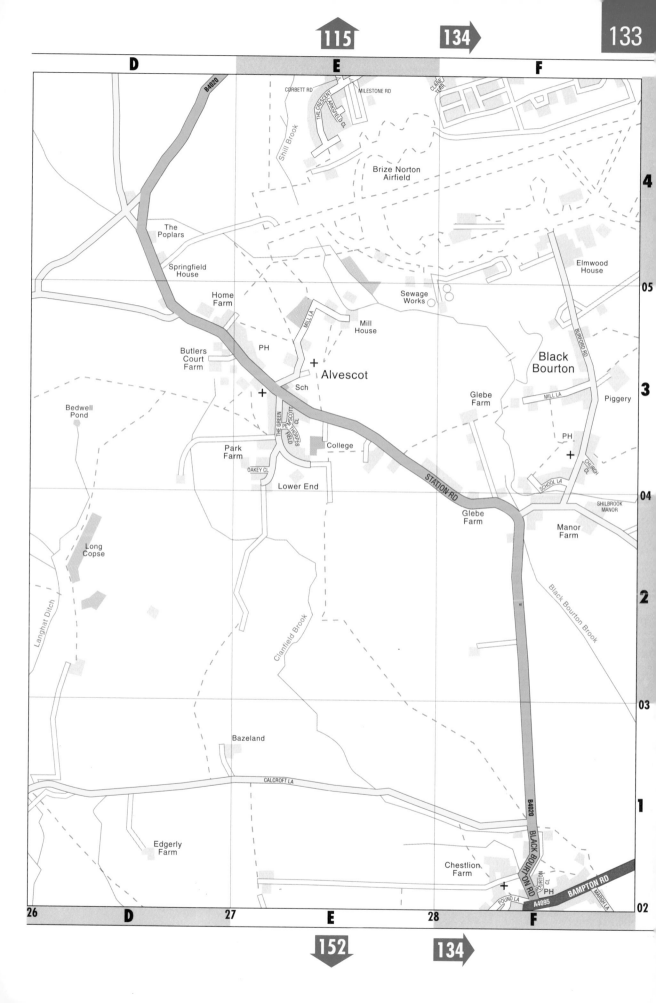

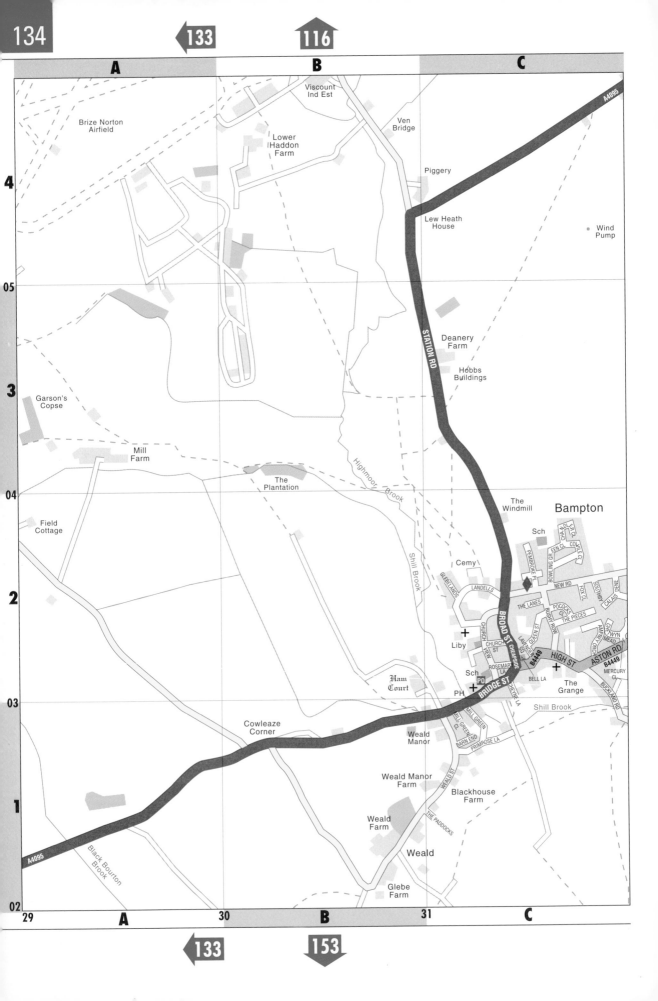

133
116

A B C

4

05

3

04

2

03

1

02

29 30 31

133
153

Brize Norton
Airfield

Viscount
Ind Est

Lower
Haddon
Farm

Ven
Bridge

Piggery

A4095

Lew Heath
House

Wind
Pump

Deanery
Farm

STATION RD

Hobbs
Buildings

Garson's
Copse

Mill
Farm

Highmoor Brook

The
Plantation

Shill Brook

The
Windmill

Bampton

Sch

Field
Cottage

Cemy

GLEBELANDS

LANDELLS

THE LANES

PEMBROKE PL

NEW RD

EEN CL

BOW GR

CHEQ

LRCL

COLE CL

SOUTHBY

CALAIS DENE

FOX CL

POCOCKS CL

THE PIECES

BUSBY ROW

CHERWYN

AMPLE MEAD

CHK

BROAD ST

Liby

CHEAPSIDE

Church
View

CHURCH
ST

LANDELLS RD

GREEN ST

ROSEMARY
LA

THE NE LA

BELL LA

HIGH ST

ASTON RD

B4449

B4449

B4449

MERCURY
CL

The
Grange

BUCKLAND RD

Ham
Court

Sch

PO

PH

BRIDGE ST

MILL GREEN
CL

Shill Brook

Cowleaze
Corner

Weald
Manor

BARN END

WEALD ST

PRIMROSE LA

Weald Manor
Farm

Blackhouse
Farm

Weald
Farm

THE PADDOCKS

Weald

A4095

Black Bourton
Brook

Glebe
Farm

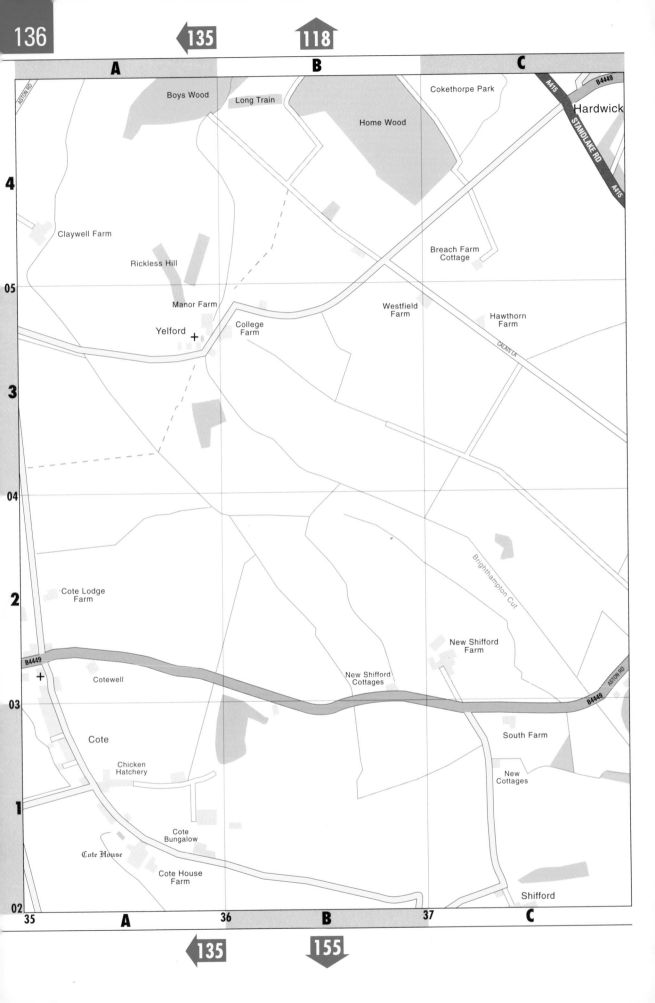

135
118

A
B
C

Boys Wood

Long Train

Home Wood

Cokethorpe Park

A415

B4449

STANDLAKE RD

Hardwick

A415

4

Claywell Farm

Rickless Hill

Breach Farm
Cottage

05

Manor Farm

Yelford

College
Farm

Westfield
Farm

Hawthorn
Farm

CALAIS LA

3

04

Brighthampton Cut

Cote Lodge
Farm

2

New Shifford
Farm

B4449

Cotewell

New Shifford
Cottages

ASTON RD

03

B4449

Cote

South Farm

Chicken
Hatchery

New
Cottages

1

Cote
Bungalow

Cote House

Cote House
Farm

Shifford

02

35

ASTON RD

A
36
B
37
C

135
155

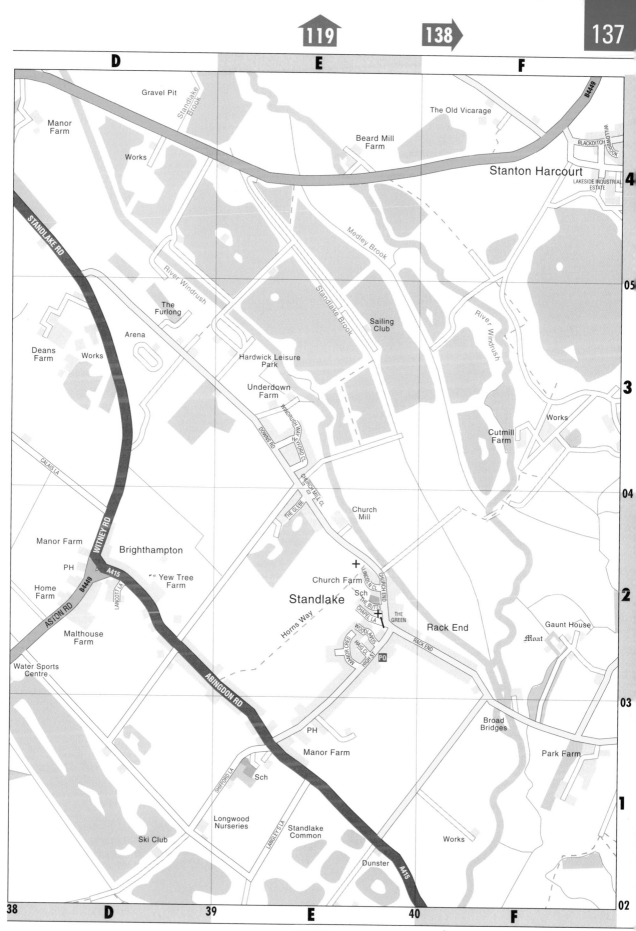

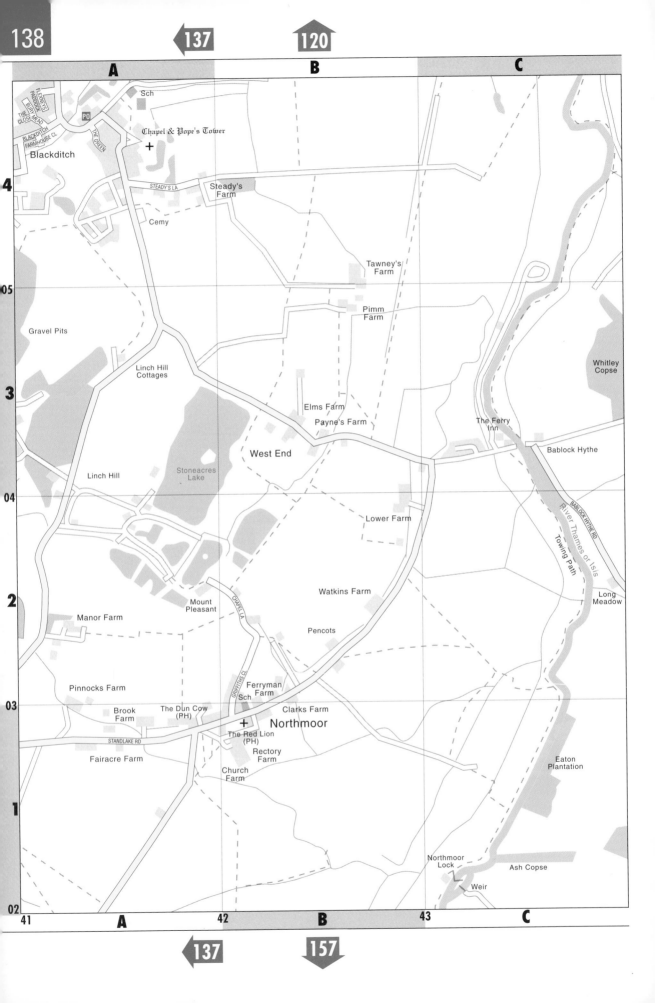

A **B** **C**

4

05

3

04

2

03

1

02

Sch

Chapel & Pope's Tower

Steady's Farm

STEADY'S LA

Cemy

FLEXNEY'S PADDOCK
THE BURY
CLOSE END
BLACKDITCH FARMHOUSE CL
PO
Blackditch
THE GREEN

Tawney's Farm

Pimm Farm

Gravel Pits

Whitley Copse

Linch Hill Cottages

Elms Farm

Payne's Farm

The Ferry Inn

West End

Linch Hill

Stoneacres Lake

Bablock Hythe

Lower Farm

BABLOCK HYTHE RD

River Thames or Isis

Towing Path

Manor Farm

Mount Pleasant

CHAPEL LA

Watkins Farm

Pencots

Long Meadow

Pinnocks Farm

GRIFFITHS CL

Ferryman Farm
Sch

Clarks Farm

Brook Farm

The Dun Cow (PH)

Northmoor

The Red Lion (PH)

STANDLAKE RD

Rectory Farm

Eaton Plantation

Fairacre Farm

Church Farm

Northmoor Lock

Ash Copse

Weir

A **B** **C**

41 42 43

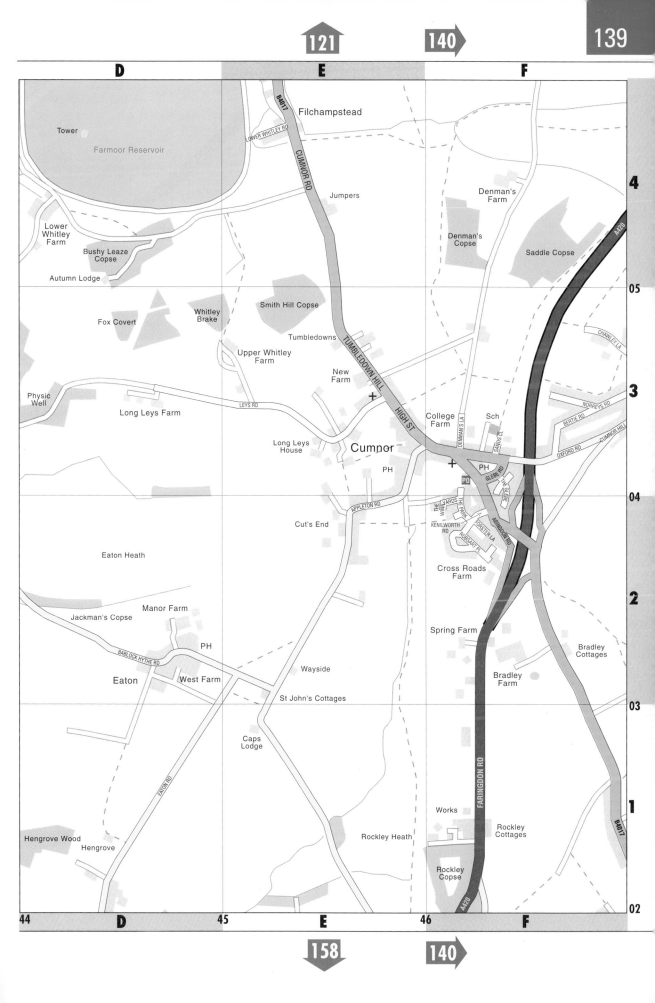

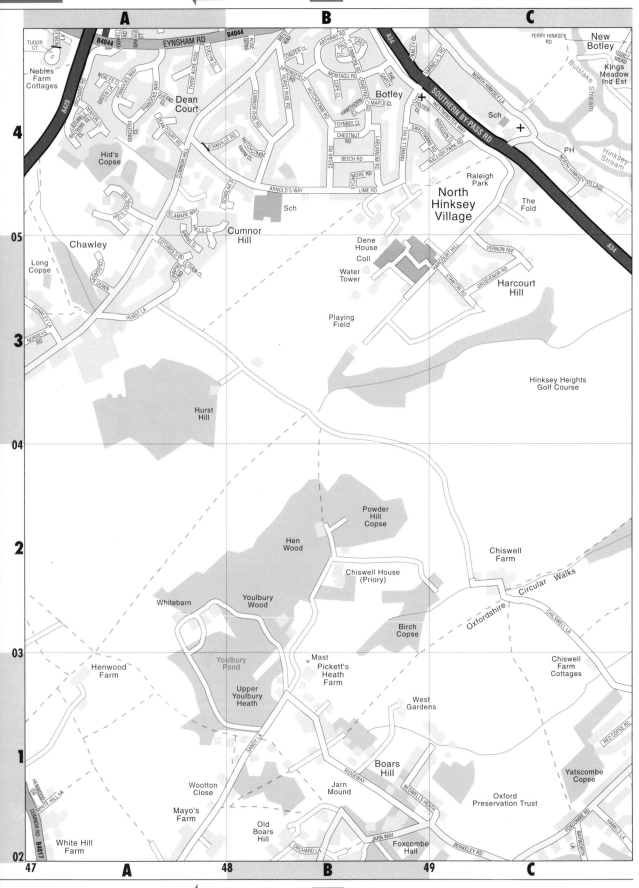

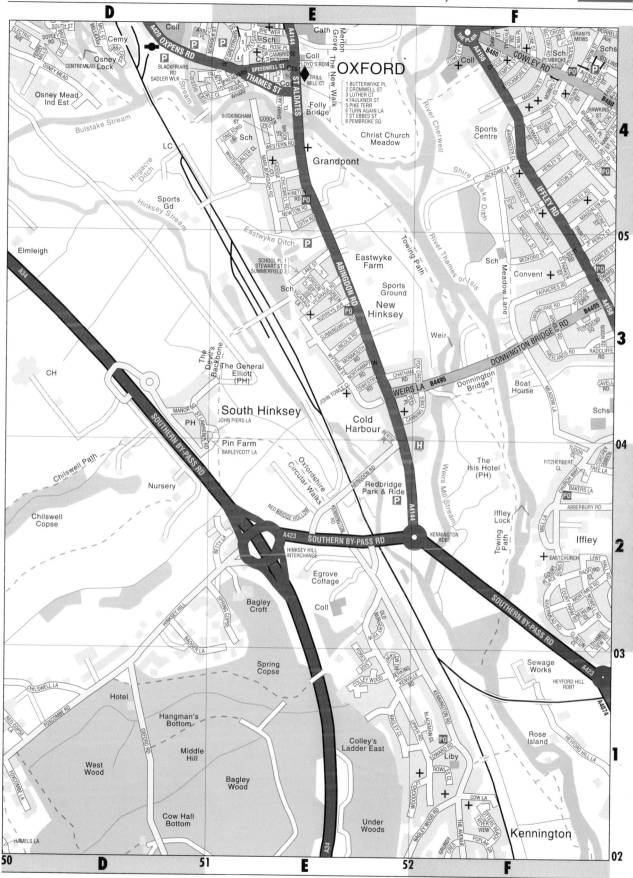

OXFORD

1 BUTTERWYKE PL
2 CROMWELL ST
3 LUTHER CT
4 FAULKNER ST
5 PIKE TERR
6 TURN AGAIN LA
7 ST EBBES ST
8 PEMBROKE SQ

Christ Church Meadow

Grandpont

Eastwyke Farm

Sports Ground

New Hinksey

SCHOOL PL 1
STEWART ST 2
SUMMERFIELD 3

The Devil's Backbone

The General Elliott (PH)

South Hinksey

Cold Harbour

Pin Farm

Oxfordshire Circular Walks

Redbridge Park & Ride

The Isis Hotel (PH)

Iffley Lock

Iffley

Nursery

Chilswell Copse

Bagley Croft

Coll

Egrove Cottage

Hinksey Hill Interchange

SOUTHERN BY-PASS RD

Kennington RDBT

Spring Copse

Colley Wood

Sewage Works

Heyford Hill RDBT

Colley's Ladder East

Rose Island

Hotel

Hangman's Bottom

Middle Hill

West Wood

Bagley Wood

Cow Hall Bottom

Under Woods

Kennington

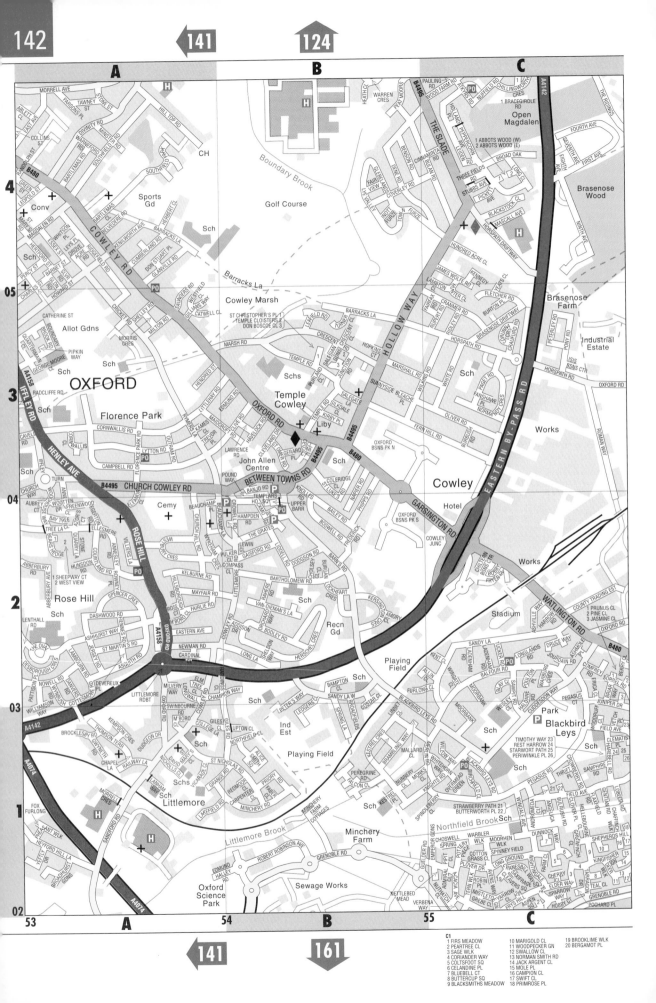

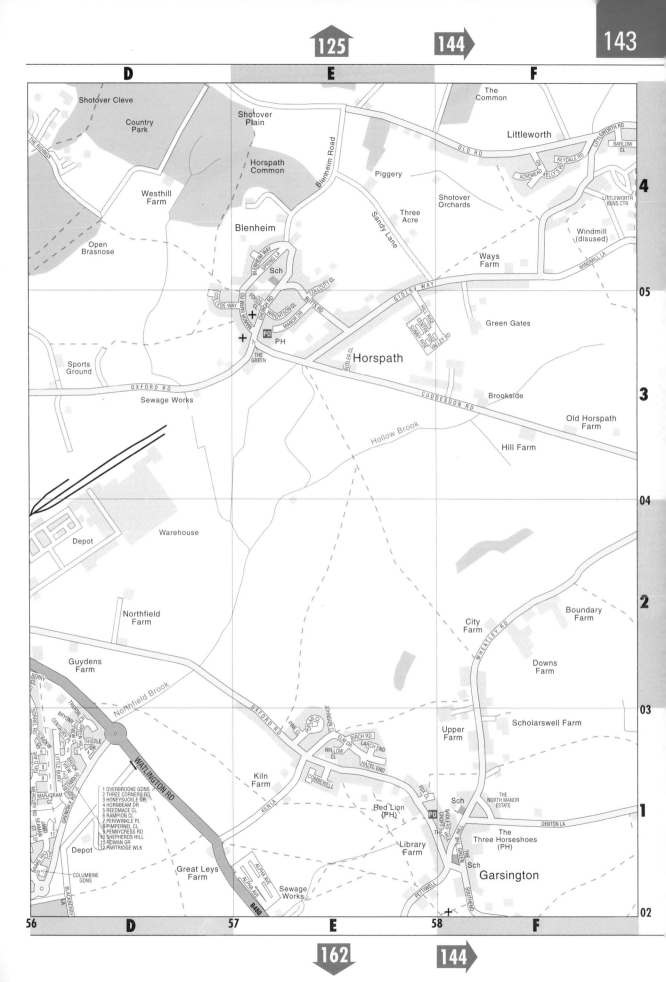

Shotover Cleve
Country Park
Westhill Farm
Open Brasnose

Shotover Plain
Blenheim Road
Horspath Common
Blenheim
BLENHEIM WAY
SPRING LA
Sch
COLLEGE WAY
MANOR FARM RD
FORDS CL
CHURCH RD
WRIGHTSON CL
MANOR DR
BUTTS RD
COLLCUTT CL
PO
PH
THE GREEN
The Common
Littleworth
LITTLEWORTH RD
BARLOW CL
KEYDALE RD
KELLY'S RD
ACREMEAD
LITTLEWORTH BSNS CTR
4
Piggery
Shotover Orchards
Sandy Lane
Three Acre
Ways Farm
Windmill (disused)
WINDMILL LA
GIDLEY WAY
HILL RISE
CENTRE RISE
SUNNY RISE
VALLEY RD
Green Gates
05

Sports Ground
OXFORD RD
Sewage Works
Horspath
BUTLER CL
CUDDESDON RD
Brookside
Old Horspath Farm
Hill Farm
3
Hollow Brook

Warehouse
Depot
04

Northfield Farm
City Farm
WHEATLEY RD
Boundary Farm
Downs Farm
2

Guydens Farm
Northfield Brook
OXFORD RD
Scholarswell Farm
Upper Farm
03

THE RIDINGS
BLACKBERRY CL
SORREL RD
LITTLE BURY
CENTAURY PL
BRYONY CL
THE OIL
GREEN HILL
CLOVER CL
REDWOOD DR
THISTLE DR
BROOK VIEW
OLD DOWNS
1
2
4
MARJORAM CL
SEAMAN
JAMES
MERCURY RD
BAY CL
8
9
11
Depot
COLUMBINE GDNS
GREENORE RD
BOWER HILL
WATLINGTON RD
1 OVERBROOKE GDNS
2 THREE CORNERS RD
3 HONEYSUCKLE GR
4 HORNBEAM DR
5 REEDMACE CL
6 RAMPION CL
7 PERIWINKLE PL
8 PIMPERNEL CL
9 PENNYCRESS RD
10 SHEPHERDS HILL
11 ROWAN GR
12 PARTRIDGE WLK
Kiln Farm
KILN LA
Combewell
Red Lion (PH)
Library Farm
PO
SADLERS CROFT
CROFT HILL
THE HILL
THE GREEN
PETTIWELL
SOUTHEND
DENTON LA
Sch
THE NORTH MANOR ESTATE
The Three Horseshoes (PH)
Sch
Garsington
1

Great Leys Farm
B480
ALPHA AVE
ALPHA AVE
Sewage Works
02

POPLAR CL
PINE CL
JOHNSONS CL
ELM DR
BIRCH RD
LARCH END
WILLOW CL
HAZEL END
FOX CL

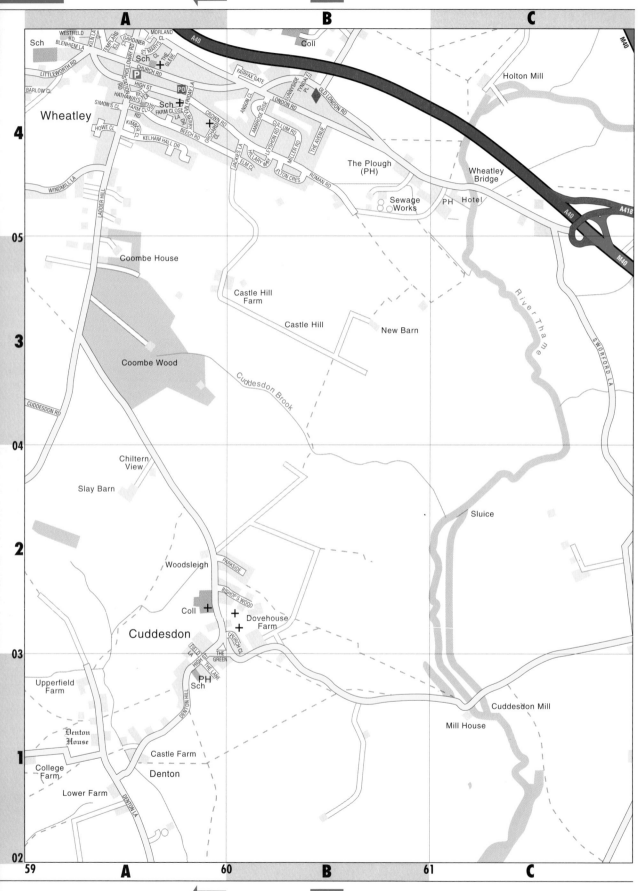

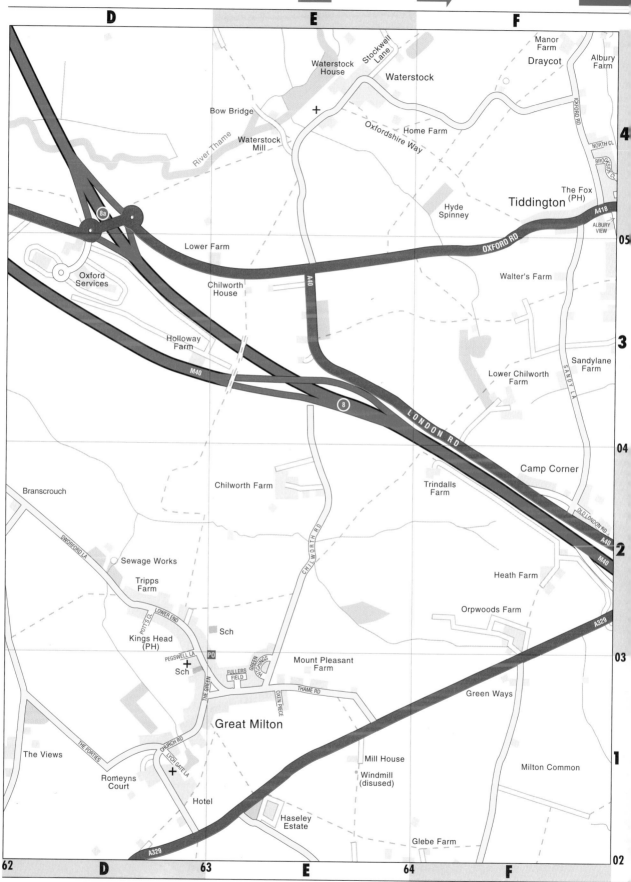

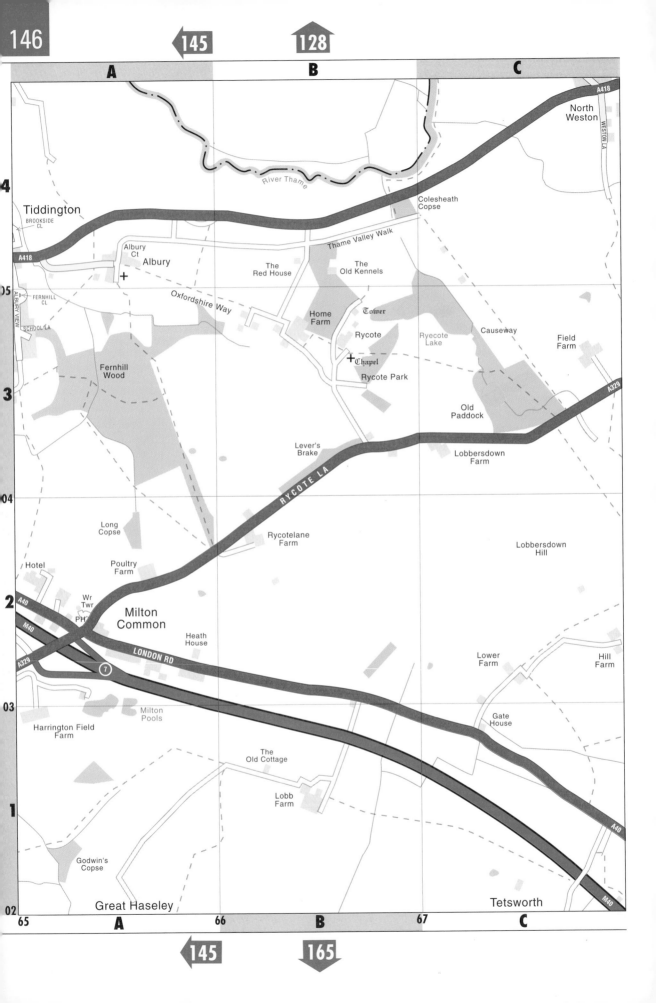

A   B   C

A418
North
Weston

River Thame

WESTON LA

Coglesheath
Copse

4

Tiddington

BROOKSIDE
CL

Thame Valley Walk

A418

Albury
Ct   Albury

The
Red House

The
Old Kennels

FERNHILL
CL

Oxfordshire Way

Home
Farm

Tower

Ryecote
Lake

Causeway

Field
Farm

05

SCHOOL LA

ALBURY VIEW

Rycote

Chapel

Rycote Park

A329

Fernhill
Wood

3

Old
Paddock

Lever's
Brake

Lobbersdown
Farm

RYCOTE LA

04

Long
Copse

Rycotelane
Farm

Lobbersdown
Hill

Hotel

Poultry
Farm

Wr
Twr

Milton
Common

A40

2

M40

Heath
House

Lower
Farm

Hill
Farm

A329

LONDON RD

PH

7

03

Milton
Pools

Gate
House

Harrington Field
Farm

The
Old Cottage

1

Lobb
Farm

A40

Godwin's
Copse

M40

02

Great Haseley

Tetsworth

65   A   66   B   67   C

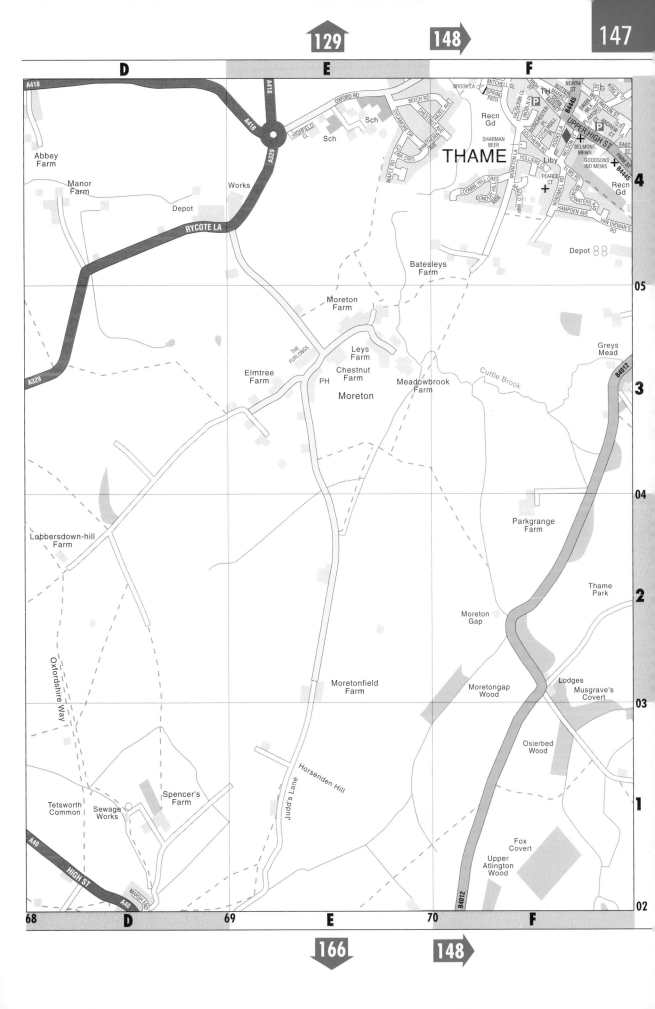

D

A418

Abbey
Farm

Manor
Farm

Depot

A418

A329

Works

RYCOTE LA

A329

Oxford Way

Lobbersdown-hill
Farm

Tetsworth
Common

Sewage
Works

Spencer's
Farm

A40

HIGH ST

A40

MARSH END

E

Oxford Rd

BEECH RD

Sch

Sch

HIGHFIELD CL

MAPLE RD

SYCAMORE DR

CEDAR CRES

CHESTNUT CL

HAZEL AVE

HAWTHORN AVE

BROOK LA

MITCHELL CL

SPRING
PATH

HAZELTON CL

LINCOLN PL

DORCHESTER
PL

ROTHERHILL

MORETON LA

HOLLIERS CL

COOMBE HILL CRES

COOMBE HILL
RISE

COND'S HILL

SOUTHERN RD

PEARCE
CT

ASTON MIL Q'TON WK

NELSON ST

ROOKS LA

WINDMILL RD

HAMPDEN AVE

LMS RD

MS RD

WATERS LA

VAN DIEMAN'S
RD

Batesleys
Farm

Moreton
Farm

THE FURLONGS

Leys
Farm

Chestnut
Farm

PH

Elmtree
Farm

Moreton

Meadowbrook
Farm

Cuttle Brook

THAME

Recn
Gd

SHARMAN
BEER

Liby

BELMONT
MEWS

GOODSONS
IND MEWS

Recn
Gd

Depot 88

Greys
Mead

B4012

Parkgrange
Farm

Thame
Park

Moreton
Gap

Moretonfield
Farm

Moretongap
Wood

Lodges

Musgrave's
Covert

Osierbed
Wood

Judd's Lane

Horsenden Hill

Fox
Covert

Upper
Atlington
Wood

B4012

THAME

TH

UPPER HIGH ST

B4445

B4445

NORTH
ST

HIGH
ST

MARKET

BUTTER
MARKET

SWAN WK

WELLINGTON ST

LEE

KING'S CL

EAST
ST

PARK ST

ANDREW
CT

PLAYFORD

PLAYFORD

05

4

3

04

2

03

1

02

68

D

69

E

70

F

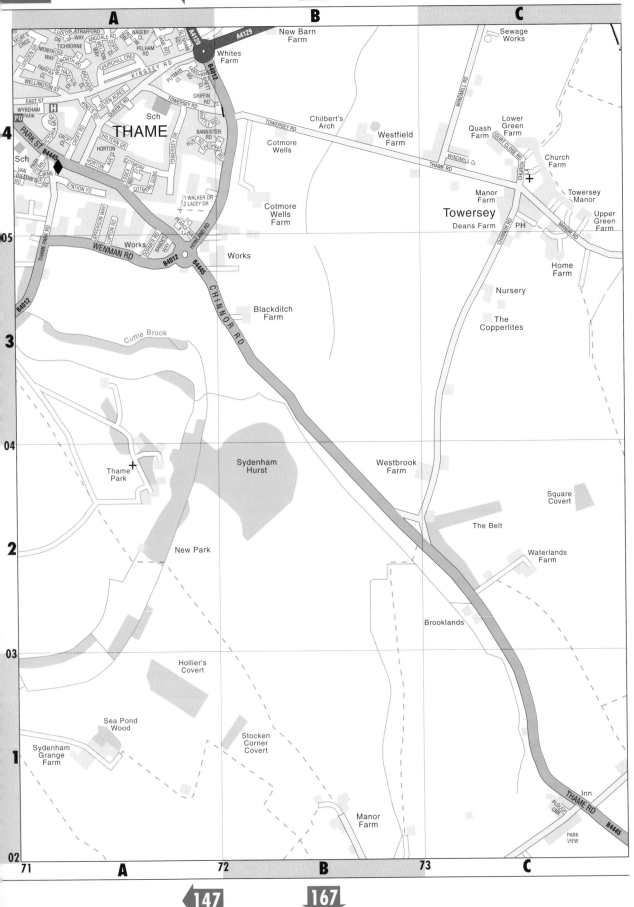

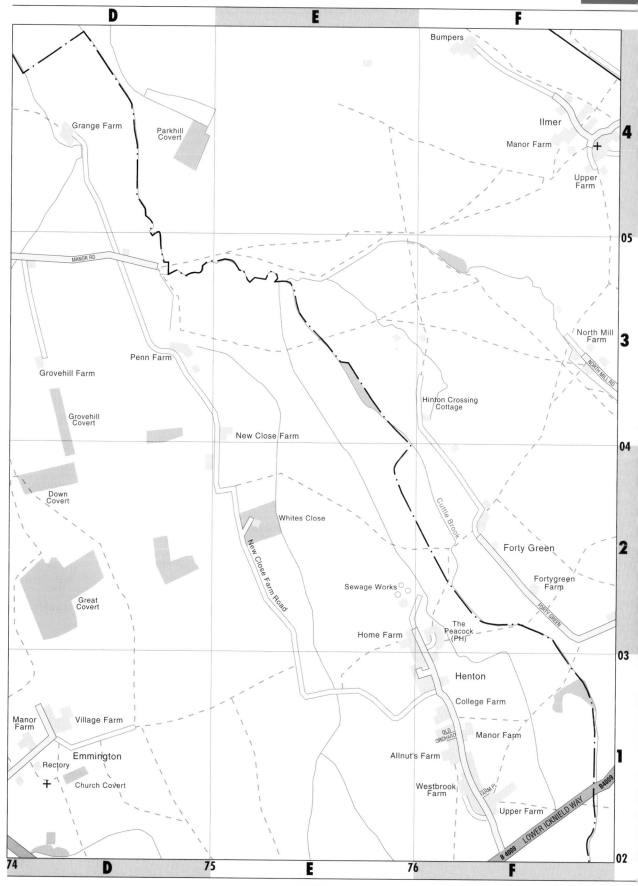

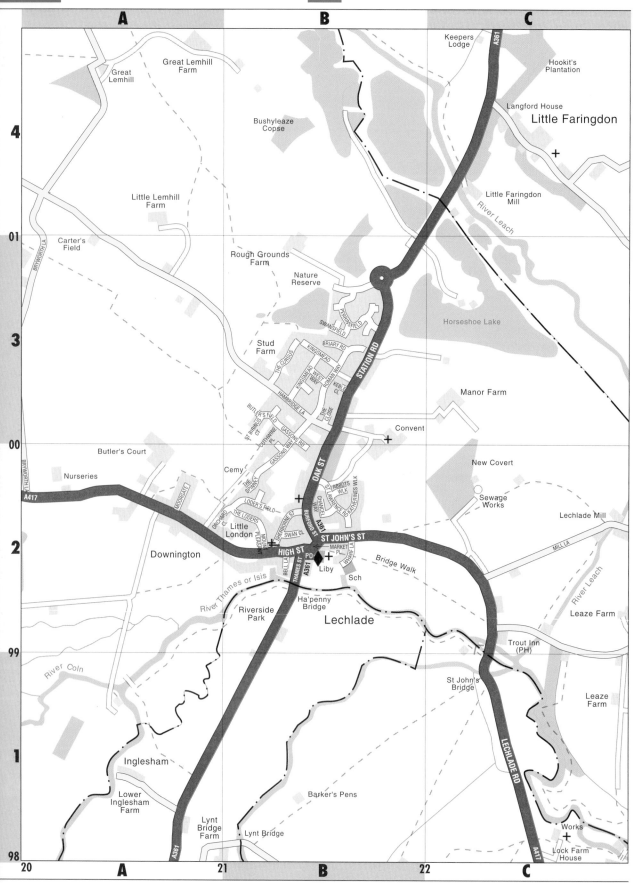

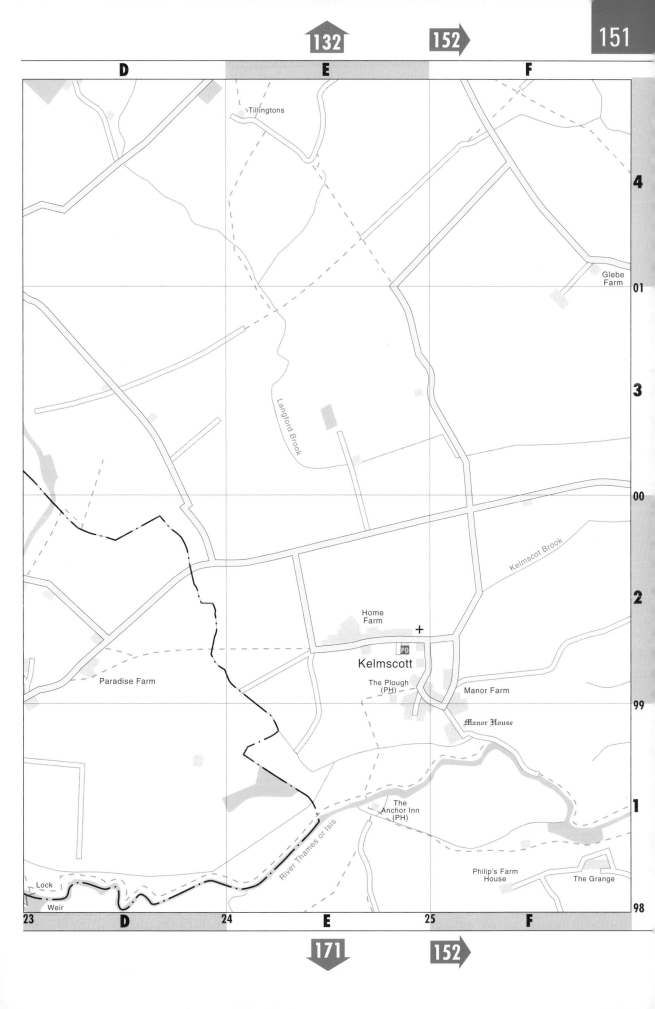

D

E

F

4

01

3

Tillingtons

Glebe
Farm

Langford Brook

00

Kelmscot Brook

2

Home
Farm

+

PO

Kelmscott

99

The Plough
(PH)

Manor Farm

Paradise Farm

Manor House

1

The
Anchor Inn
(PH)

River Thames or Isis

Philip's Farm
House

The Grange

Lock

Weir

98

D

E

F

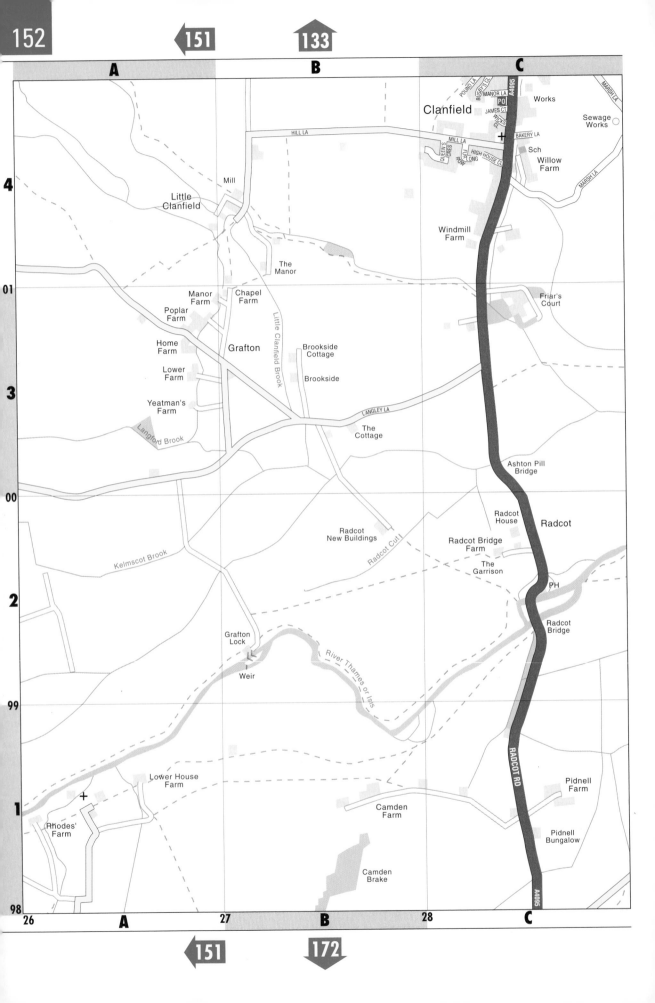

A
B
C

4

01

3

00

2

99

1

98

26
A
27
B
28
C

Clanfield

POUND LA
BUSBY'S CL
MANOR LA
PO
JAMES CT
WICKS CL
A4095
Works

Sewage Works

HILL LA

MILL LA
QUEEN'S CRES
HIGH HOUSE CL
FURLONG ROW
BAKERY LA
Sch
Willow Farm

Mill

Little Clanfield

Windmill Farm

The Manor

Friar's Court

Manor Farm
Chapel Farm

Poplar Farm

Grafton

Home Farm

Brookside Cottage

Lower Farm

Brookside

Little Clanfield Brook

Yeatman's Farm

Langley La

The Cottage

Langford Brook

Ashton Pill Bridge

Radcot House

Radcot

Kelmscot Brook

Radcot New Buildings

Radcot Cut

Radcot Bridge Farm

The Garrison

PH

Grafton Lock

River Thames or Isis

Radcot Bridge

RADCOT RD

Weir

Lower House Farm

Pidnell Farm

Rhodes' Farm

Camden Farm

Pidnell Bungalow

Camden Brake

A4095

D   **E**   **F**

4

Black Bourton Brook

Marsh Lane

White Lodge

Glebe Farm

01

Radcot Cut

Sharney Bridge

Sharney Brook

3

Burroway Bridge

Burroway Brook

Weir

Old Man's Bridge

River Thames or Isis

Radcot Lock

00

2

Wadley Stream

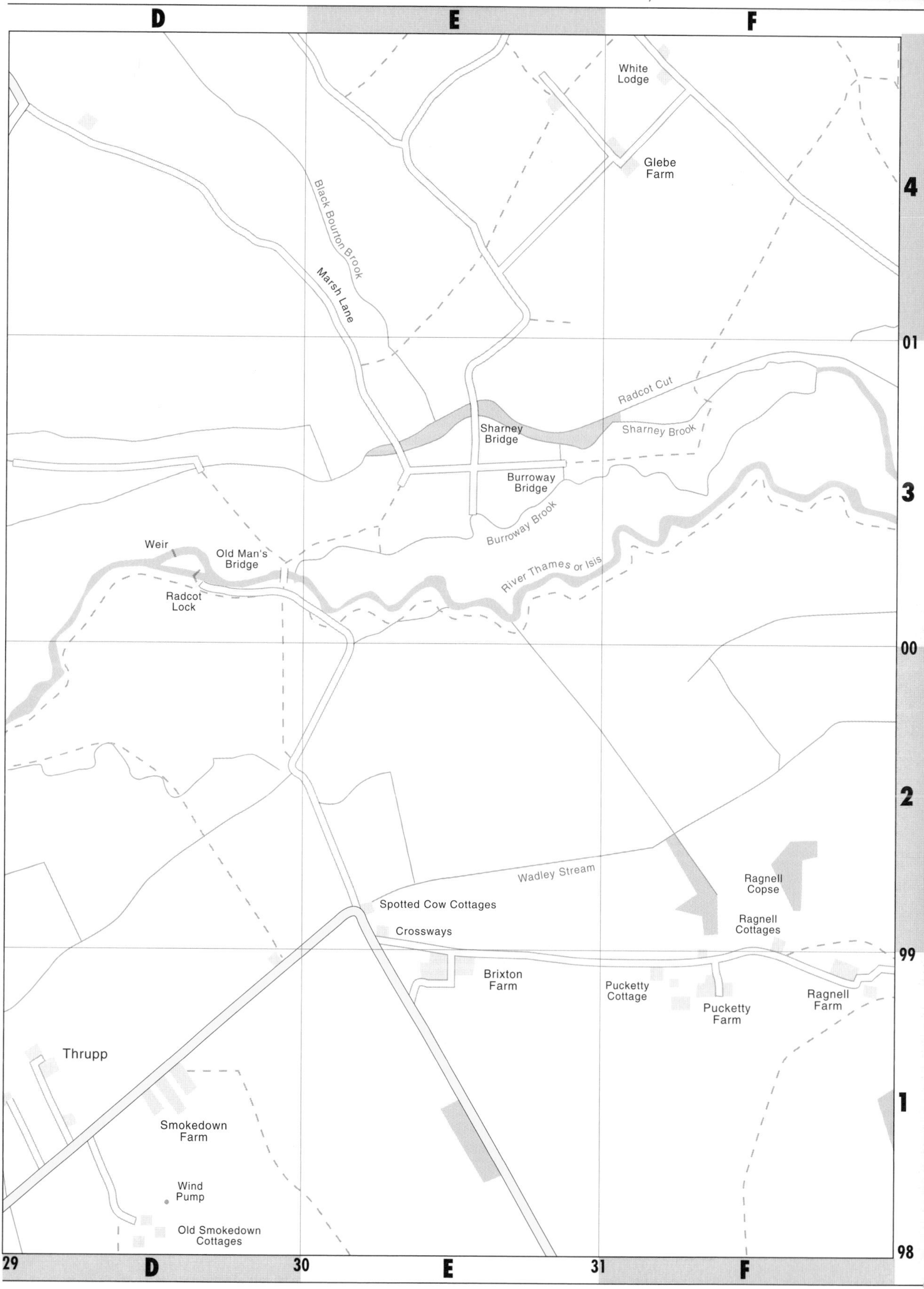

Ragnell Copse

Spotted Cow Cottages

Ragnell Cottages

Crossways

99

Brixton Farm

Pucketty Cottage

Pucketty Farm

Ragnell Farm

Thrupp

1

Smokedown Farm

Wind Pump

Old Smokedown Cottages

98

29   **D**   **30**   **E**   **31**   **F**

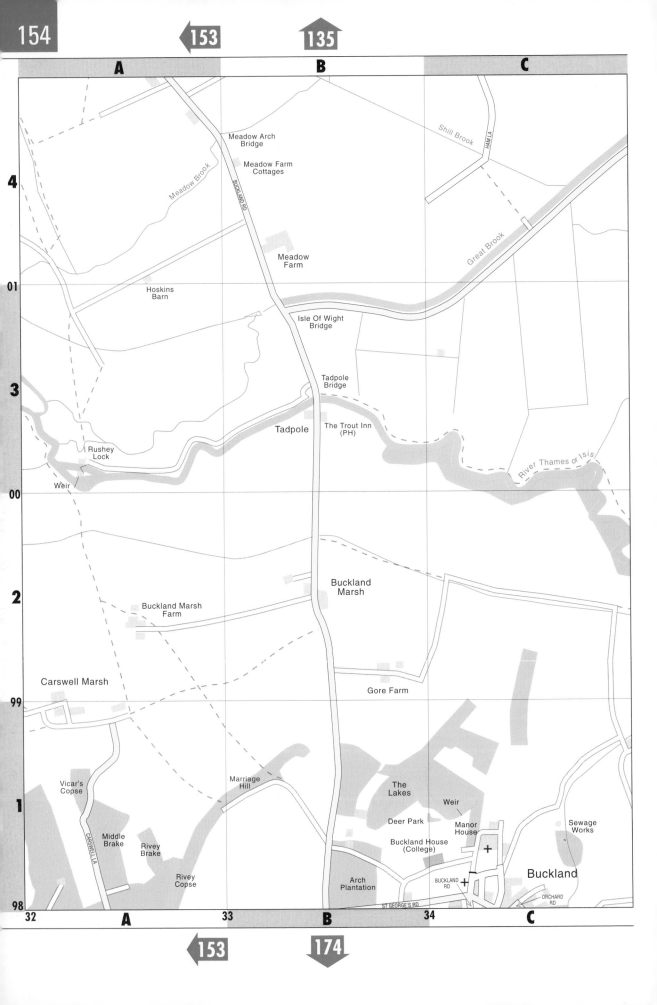

A
B
C

4

01

3

00

2

99

1

98

Meadow Arch
Bridge

Meadow Farm
Cottages

Shill Brook

HAM LA

Meadow Brook

BUCKLAND RD

Meadow
Farm

Great Brook

Hoskins
Barn

Isle Of Wight
Bridge

Tadpole
Bridge

Tadpole

The Trout Inn
(PH)

River Thames or Isis

Rushey
Lock

Weir

Buckland
Marsh

Buckland Marsh
Farm

Carswell Marsh

Gore Farm

Vicar's
Copse

Marriage
Hill

The
Lakes

Weir

Sewage
Works

CARSWELL LA

Middle
Brake

Rivey
Brake

Deer Park

Manor
House

Buckland House
(College)

Rivey
Copse

Arch
Plantation

BUCKLAND
RD

Buckland

ORCHARD
RD

St George's Rd

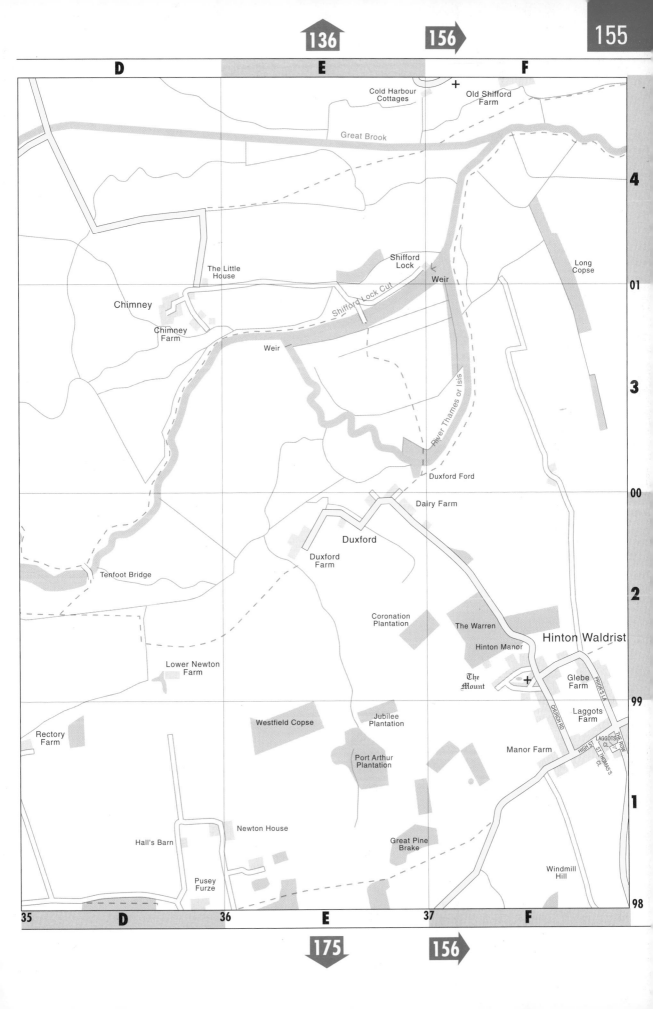

D
E
F

Cold Harbour Cottages

Old Shifford Farm

Great Brook

4

Shifford Lock

Weir

Long Copse

The Little House

01

Chimney

Shifford Lock Cut

Chimney Farm

Weir

River Thames or Isis

3

Duxford Ford

00

Dairy Farm

Duxford

Duxford Farm

Coronation Plantation

2

Tenfoot Bridge

The Warren

Hinton Manor

Hinton Waldrist

Lower Newton Farm

The Mount

Glebe Farm

PRIOR'S LA

99

Laggots Farm

CHURCH RD

Rectory Farm

Westfield Copse

Jubilee Plantation

Manor Farm

HIGH ST

THE ROW

LAGGOTS CL

ST THOMAS'S CL

Port Arthur Plantation

1

Hall's Barn

Newton House

Great Pine Brake

Windmill Hill

Pusey Furze

98

35
D
36
E
37
F

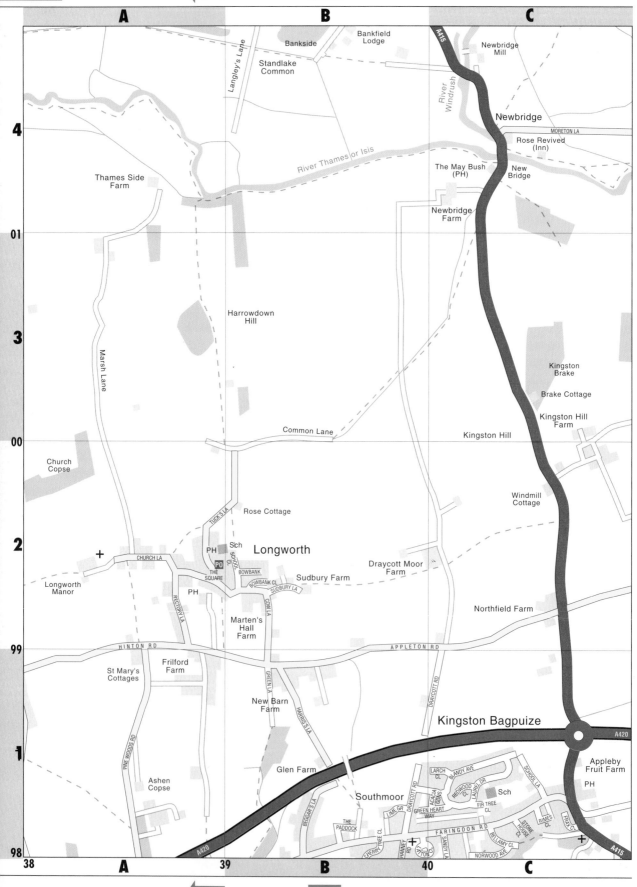

Bankside

Bankfield
Lodge

Langley's Lane

Standlake
Common

A415

Newbridge
Mill

River Windrush

Newbridge

MORETON LA

Rose Revived
(Inn)

4

River Thames or Isis

Thames Side
Farm

The May Bush
(PH)

New
Bridge

01

Newbridge
Farm

Harrowdown
Hill

3

Marsh Lane

Kingston
Brake

Brake Cottage

Kingston Hill
Farm

Common Lane

Kingston Hill

00

Church
Copse

Windmill
Cottage

TUCK'S LA

Rose Cottage

2

PH Sch

Longworth

CHURCH LA

PO

THE
SQUARE

SCHOOL CL

BOWBANK

Draycott Moor
Farm

+

Longworth
Manor

PH

RECTORY LA

BOWBANK CL

SUDBURY LA

Sudbury Farm

Northfield Farm

Marten's
Hall
Farm

COW LA

APPLETON RD

99

HINTON RD

St Mary's
Cottages

Frilford
Farm

DRAYCOTT RD

GREEN LA

New Barn
Farm

HARRIS'S LA

Kingston Bagpuize

A420

PINE WOODS RD

Glen Farm

Ashen
Copse

BEGGAR'S LA

Southmoor

THE
PADDOCK

CHERRY TREE CL

LIME GR

DRAYCOTT RD

GREEN HEART WAY

LARCH
CL

BRANDY AVE

ACACIA GDNS

REDWOOD CL

AUREL DR

FIR TREE
CL

SCHOOL LA

Sch

FARINGDON RD

STONE
HOUSE
CL

RIMES CL

BELLAMY CL

FRAX CL

+

Appleby
Fruit Farm

PH

A420

HANNEY RD

LEYTON

SANDY LA

NORWOOD AVE

+

A415

1

98

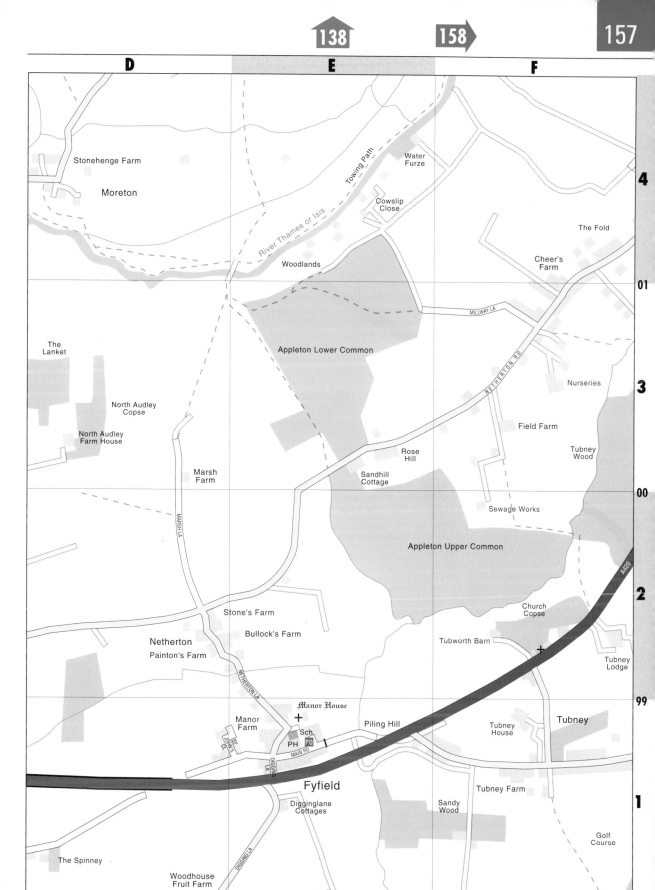

Stonehenge Farm

Moreton

Water Furze

Towing Path

Cowslip Close

River Thames or Isis

Woodlands

The Fold

Cheer's Farm

4

01

The Lanket

North Audley Copse

North Audley Farm House

Appleton Lower Common

MILLWAY LA

NETHERTON RD

Nurseries

Field Farm

Tubney Wood

3

Marsh Farm

MARSH LA

Rose Hill

Sandhill Cottage

Sewage Works

Appleton Upper Common

00

A420

Stone's Farm

Bullock's Farm

Church Copse

Tubworth Barn

Tubney Lodge

2

Netherton

Painton's Farm

NETHERTON LA

Tubney

99

Manor House

Manor Farm

ST JOHN'S CL

Sch
PH PO

DIGGING LA

MAIN RD

Piling Hill

Tubney House

Tubney Farm

Fyfield

Digginglane Cottages

Sandy Wood

1

The Spinney

DIGGING LA

Woodhouse Fruit Farm

Golf Course

98

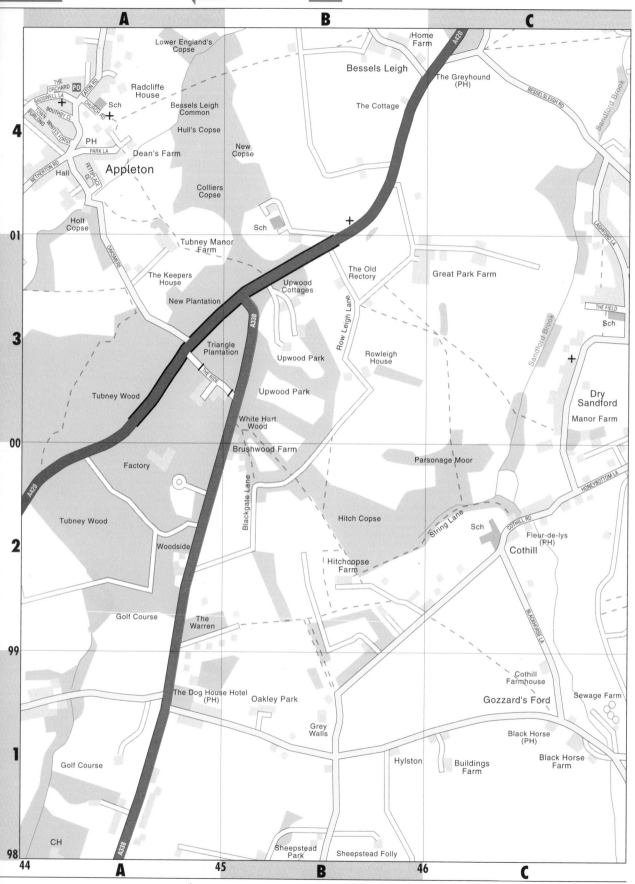

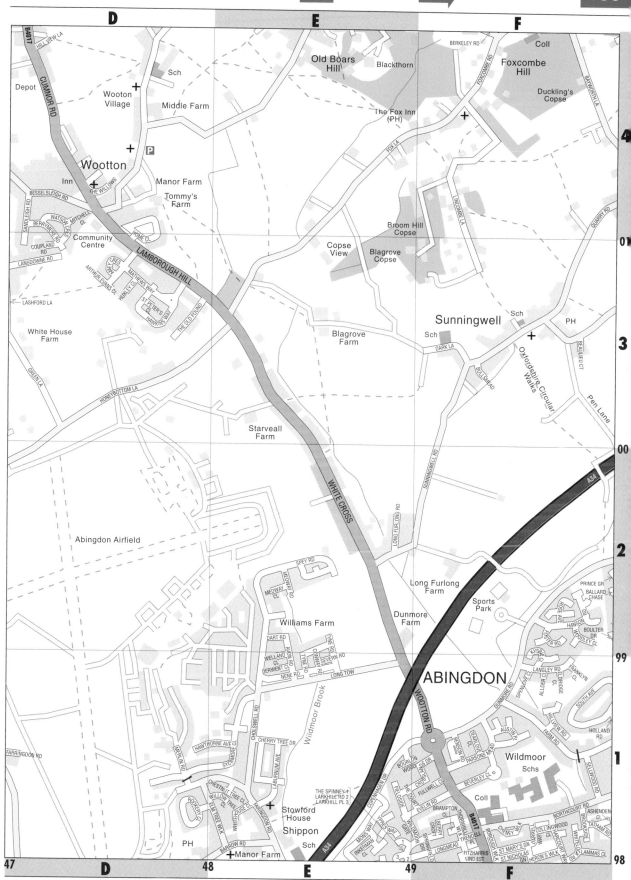

D E F

B4017 HILL VIEW LA
CUMNOR RD
Depot
Wooton Village
Sch
Middle Farm
Old Boars Hill
Blackthorn
BERKELEY RD
Coll
Foxcombe Hill
FOXCOMBE RD
Duckling's Copse
BAYWORTH LA

Wootton
Inn
THE WILLOWS
BESSELSLEIGH RD
SANDLEIGH RD
WATSON CRES
BERRYMER RD
MITCHELL CL
Community Centre
COUPLAND RD
LANSDOWNE RD
Manor Farm
Tommy's Farm
HOME CL
MATHEWS WAY
LAMBOROUGH HILL
ARTHUR EVANS CL
HUXLEY CL
SPEY CRES
ST PETER'S CL
HAWKINS WAY
THE OLD POUND

The Fox Inn (PH)
FOX LA
LINCOMBE LA
Broom Hill Copse
Blagrove Copse
Copse View

Sunningwell
Sch Sch
Sch PH
DARK LA
BILLSMEAD
Oxfordshire Circular Walks
BEAULIEU CT
Pen Lane
QUARRY RD

LASHFORD LA
White House Farm
GREEN LA
HONEYBOTTOM LA
Blagrove Farm
Starveall Farm
WHITE CROSS
SUNNINGWELL RD
LONG FURLONG RD

A34
00

Abingdon Airfield
SPEY RD
MEDWAY RD
MEDWAY CL
Williams Farm
DART RD
WELLAND CL
DERWENT CL
AVON RD
TYNE RD
CONWAY RD
SEVERN RD
LONG TOW
NENE RD
Long Furlong Farm
Dunmore Farm
Sports Park
Prince GR
BALLARD CHASE
ROSE AVE
HANSON RD
WOODLEY CL
BOULTER DR
KYSE CT
LANGLEY RD
SPENLOVE CL
ALLDER CL
ELDRIDGE
FRANKLYN
SOUTH AVE
99

FARRINGDON RD
MERLIN RD
CHOLSWELL RD
HAWTHORNE AVE CL
SYCAMORE CL
CHERRY TREE DR
LABURNUM AVE
Wildmoor Brook
ABINGDON
WOOTTON RD
DUNMORE RD
AUSTIN PL
HILCREST RD
FARM RD
HOLLAND RD
Wildmoor
Schs
SELLWOOD RD
1

CHESTNUT TREE CL
ROKERY CL
WILLOW HOUSE CL
ELM TREE WALK
WHITE HOUSE CL
FARRINGDON RD
BARROW RD
Stowford House
Shippon
Sch
THE SPINNEY
LARKHILL RD 2
LARKHILL PL 3
COPENHAGEN DR
BOURLON
WOODPECKERS DR
BENSON CL
PARSONS MEAD
BEVERLEY CL
Coll
BRAMPTON CL
EVELIN RD
THORNHILL WLK
SPRINGFIELD DR
BERRY CROFT
LONGMEAD
NORTHCOURT RD
BROOKSIDE
ASHENDEN CL
WHITELOCK RD
LAMMAS CL
TATHAM RD

PH
Manor Farm
A34
INKERMAN CL
MONKS WAY
YPRES WAY
WAVENEY DR
THE COURT
FIELDSIDE
PULLWELL CL
WINDRUSH GATE
FITZHARRIS IND EST
ST MARY'S GN
ST NICHOLAS GN
HERON'S WLK
CHEVY WLK
COLLINGWOOD
HARCOURT WAY

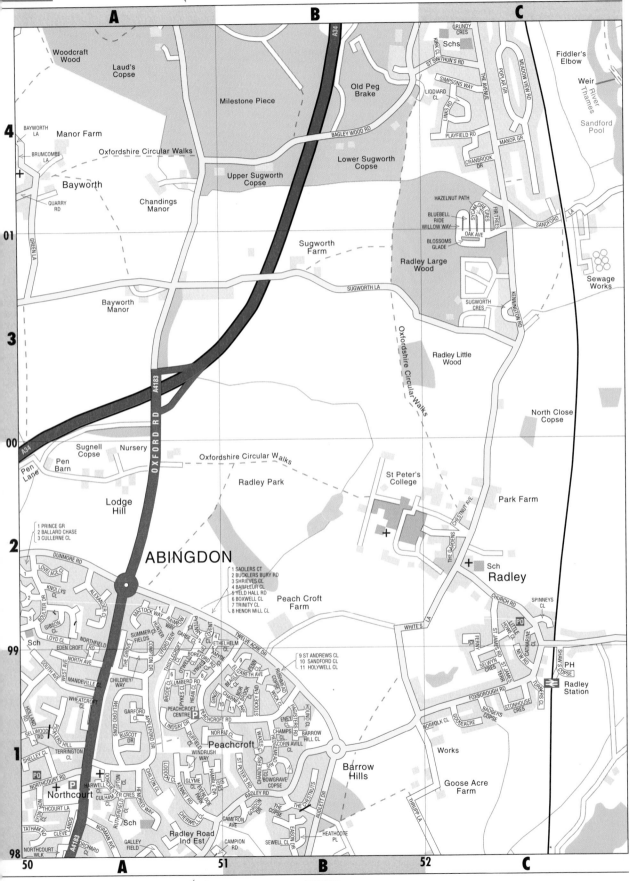

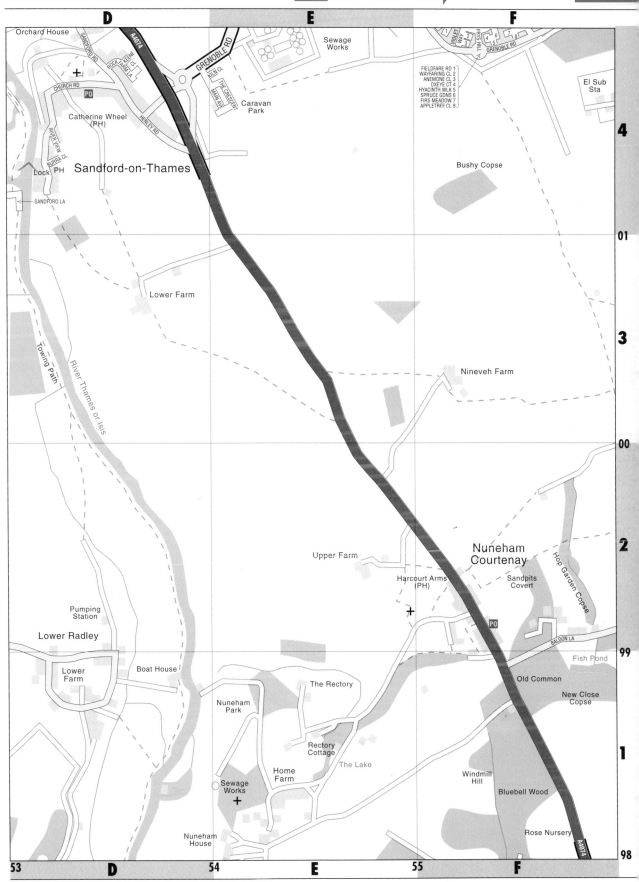

Orchard House

A4074

GRENOBLE RD

Sewage Works

SANDFORD RD

ROCK FARM KEENE CL

KILN CL

VIOLET WAY

FIRS HILL

GRENOBLE RD

El Sub Sta

FIELDFARE RD 1
WAYFARING CL 2
ANEMONE CL 3
OXEYE CT 4
HYACINTH WLK 5
SPRUCE GDNS 6
FIRS MEADOW 7
APPLETREE CL 8

CHURCH RD

PO

THE CRESCENT

MAIN AVE

Caravan Park

HENLEY RD

Catherine Wheel (PH)

4

Bushy Copse

RIVER VIEW

BURRA CL

Lock PH

Sandford-on-Thames

SANDFORD LA

01

Lower Farm

River Thames or Isis

Towing Path

3

Nineveh Farm

00

Upper Farm

Nuneham Courtenay

2

Hop Garden Copse

Harcourt Arms (PH)

Sandpits Covert

Pumping Station

PO

Lower Radley

BALDON LA

Fish Pond

99

Lower Farm

Boat House

The Rectory

Old Common

New Close Copse

Nuneham Park

Rectory Cottage

The Lake

1

Windmill Hill

Home Farm

Sewage Works

Bluebell Wood

Rose Nursery

A4074

Nuneham House

98

A   **B**   **C**

B480

Hillsdown

PETTIWELL

Manor House

WATLINGTON RD

SOUTHEND

Southend

Southend Farm

4

01

College Farm

Manor House

Toot Baldon

PH

Lower Farm

BaldonBrook

3

New Farm

WILMOTS

Court House Farm

Court Leys

+

Baldon Row

00

Gotham Farm

The Croft

Parsonage Farm

Pebble Hill

Sch

2

Marsh Baldon

Richmond Hill

BALDON LA

PH

Durham Leys Farm

+

B480

99

Baldon House

Marylands Farm

B4015

Little Baldon Farm

MARYLANDS GN

1

Sands Corner Copse

Hanginglands Copse

B4015

98

56   57   58

A   **B**   **C**

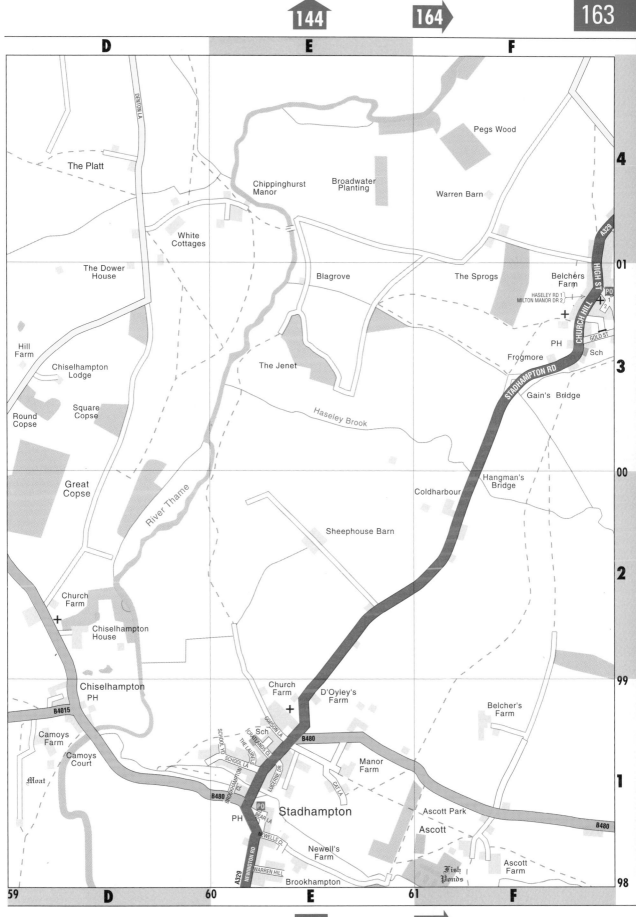

A B C

4

01

3

00

2

99

1

98

The Sands

THAME RD

A329

OLD FIELD

CHILTERN VIEW

Wells Farm

Little Milton

BLENHEIM

Sewage
Works

Ditchend
Farm

Cowleaze
Copse

New
Barn

Rofford
Hall

Rof
Ford

ROFFORD LA

Rofford
Farm

Rofford

Chalgrove Airfield

B480

Back Way

MILL LA

LEWINGTON CL

RECTORY RD

HORSE CLOSE

COTTS

Sands
Farm

The Farm
Sch

PH

Great
Haseley

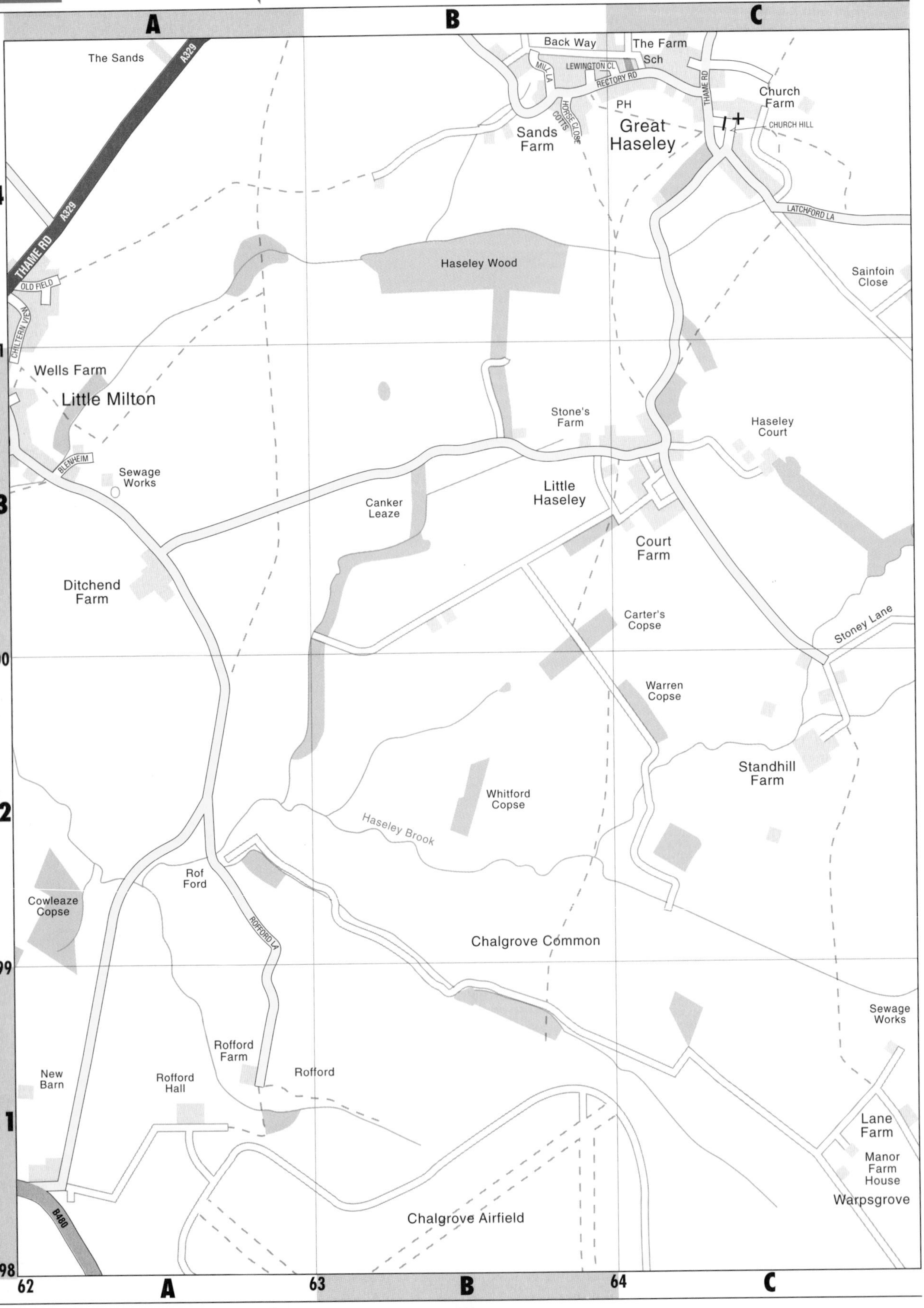

THAME RD

Church
Farm

CHURCH HILL

Church Hill

LATCHFORD LA

Sainfoin
Close

Haseley Wood

Stone's
Farm

Haseley
Court

Canker
Leaze

Little
Haseley

Court
Farm

Carter's
Copse

Stoney Lane

Warren
Copse

Standhill
Farm

Whitford
Copse

Haseley Brook

Chalgrove Common

Sewage
Works

Lane
Farm

Manor
Farm
House

Warpsgrove

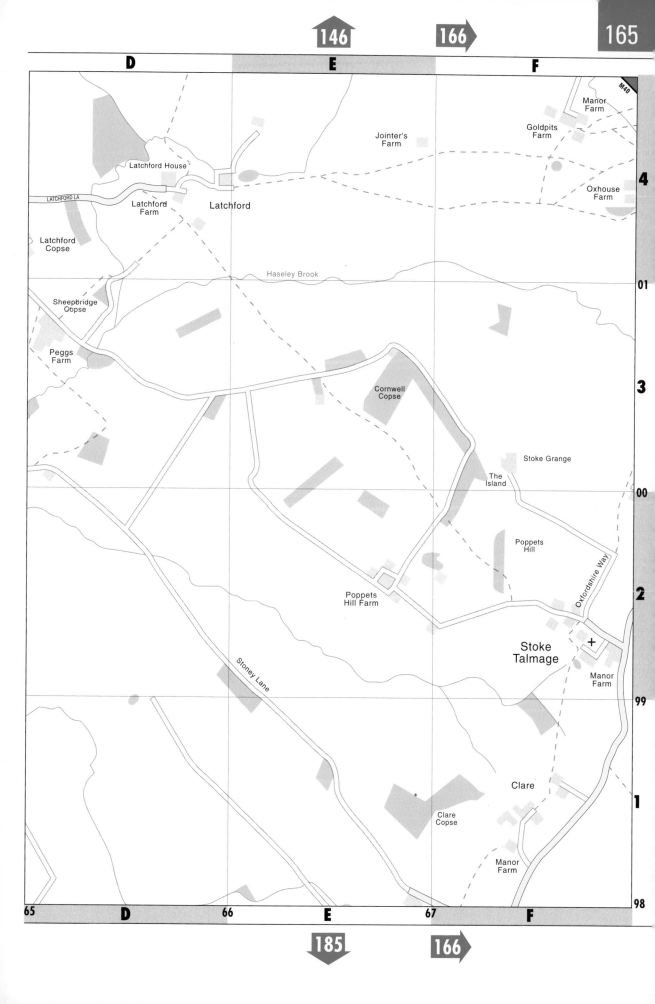

D E F

M40

Manor Farm

Goldpits Farm

Jointer's Farm

Oxhouse Farm

4

Latchford House

LATCHFORD LA

Latchford Farm

Latchford

Latchford Copse

Haseley Brook

01

Sheepbridge Copse

Peggs Farm

Cornwell Copse

3

Stoke Grange

The Island

00

Poppets Hill

Oxfordshire Way

2

Poppets Hill Farm

Stoke Talmage

Manor Farm

99

Stoney Lane

Clare

1

Clare Copse

Manor Farm

98

65 D 66 E 67 F

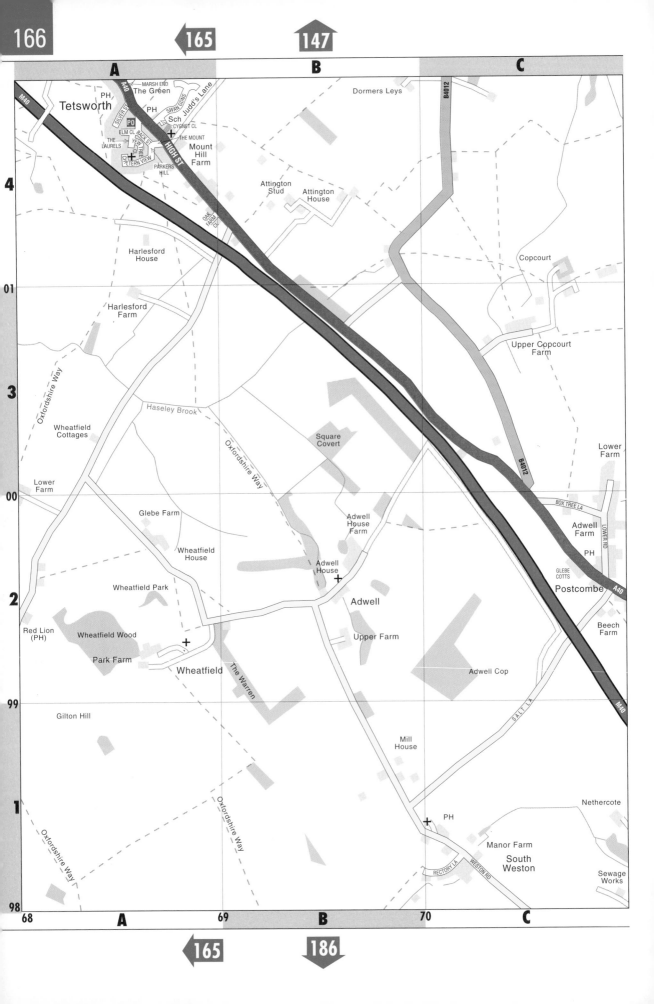

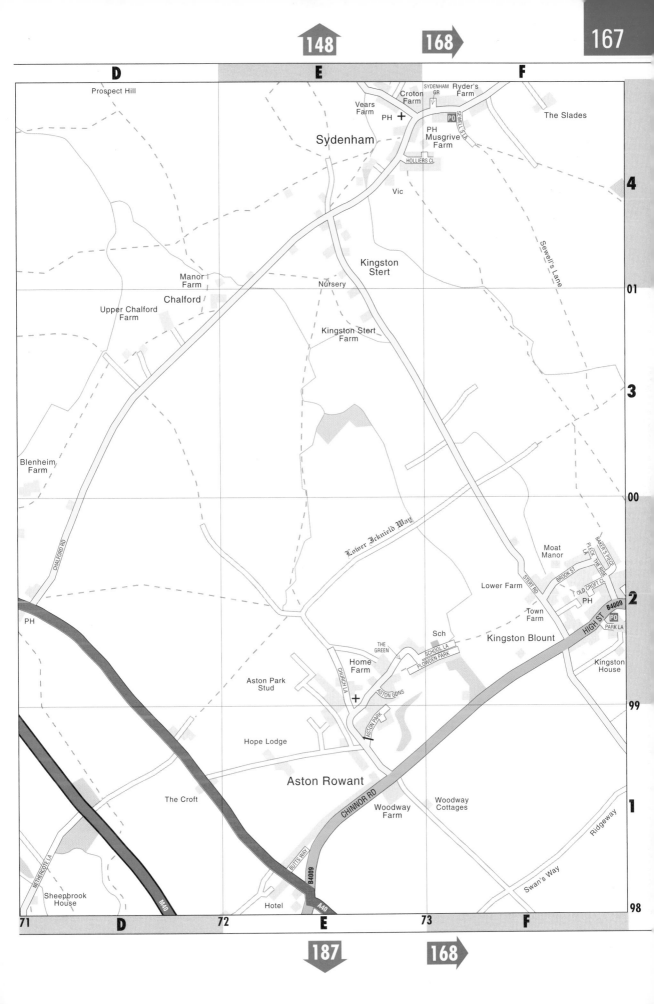

D
E
F

Prospect Hill

Sydenham

Vears Farm

Croton Farm

PH

SYDENHAM GR

Ryder's Farm

The Slades

PO

PH Musgrive Farm

HOLLIERS CL

SEWELL'S LA

Vic

4

Kingston Stert

Manor Farm

Nursery

Chalford

Sewell's Lane

01

Upper Chalford Farm

Kingston Stert Farm

Blenheim Farm

3

CHALFORD RD

00

Lower Icknield Way

Moat Manor

BAKER'S PIECE

PLECK

THE RISE

Lower Farm

STERT RD

BROOK ST

OLD CROFT CL

PH

B4009

2

PH

Town Farm

Kingston Blount

HIGH ST

PO

PARK LA

Sch

Kingston House

THE GREEN

SCHOOL LA

PLOWDEN PARK

Home Farm

Aston Park Stud

CHURCH LA

ASTON GDNS

99

ASTON PARK

Hope Lodge

Aston Rowant

The Croft

Woodway Farm

Woodway Cottages

1

CHINNOR RD

Ridgeway

NETHERCOTE LA

BUTTS WAY

B4009

Swan's Way

Sheepbrook House

M40

Hotel

A40

98

71
D
72
E
73
F

A B C

B4445

THAME RD

B4009

LOWER ICKNIELD WAY

B4009

Lane Farm

HOLLAND CL

ELDERDENE

SPRINGFIELD GDNS

LEYBOURNE GDNS

MALYNS CL

DOVELEAT

New Farm

LOWER RD

BENTON DR

ORCH

HOLLOW

HIGH ST

LC

Lower Wainhill

Hempton Wainhill

P

PH

Sch

Sch

Chinnor

Bledlow Cross

4

MILL LA

Sch

Liby

MUSSGRAVE

RECTORY MEADOW

Sch

DUCK SQ

CHURCH RD

LIME GR

CHURCH LA

HILL FARM

PO

KEENS LA

Icknield Line

LC

01

Middle Farm

DIEMENS

CL

CHERRY TREE RD

BEECH RD

CHARLOTTE

CRAB WILLOW

RAINNAL DR

STATION RD

PH

THE AVENUE

FORESTERS WAY

HEDGERLEY

BENWELLS WAY

HILLWERKE

CLEAVERS

MILLERS TURN

HAILEY CFT

COWLEY

CONIGRE

ESTOVER WAY

LACEMAKERS

DRUIDS WLK

RAVENSMEAD

Saw Mill

ROBINS PLATT

ASHRIDGE

RIDERS WAY

HUNTERS POINT

FOX COVER

GREYSTONE CL

GREENWOOD

WHEEL R

WOODVILLE

TIMBER WAY

GREENWOOD

CLAY MEADOW

WYKEHAM RISE

MEADOW RD

3

OAKLEY LA

PENLEY CL

FLINT CL

HOLLOW CL

OAKLEY RD

ST ANDREW'S RD

GLYMPERS GR

ORCHARD WAY

GREENWOOD AVE

ELM DR

ELM CL

GOLDEN HILLS

HILL RD

Quarry

Chinnor Hill

Oakley

Crowell End Farm

Works

Woodlands Farm

00

Crowell Farm

Ridgeway

HILL TOP LA

RED LA

CHINNOR RD

Crowell

ICKNIELD CL

HIGH ST

B4009

PH

Chalk Quarries

Oakley Hill

CHINNOR HILL

Manor Farm

2

Aston Rowant

Bledlow Circular Ride

Sunley Wood

99

Swan's Way

Venus Wood

Venus Wood

Race Course

Crowellhill Wood

Crowell Hill

Sprig's Alley

1

Grove Farm

KINGSTON HILL

Crowellhill Farm

SPRIGS HOLLY LA

98

Kingston Wood

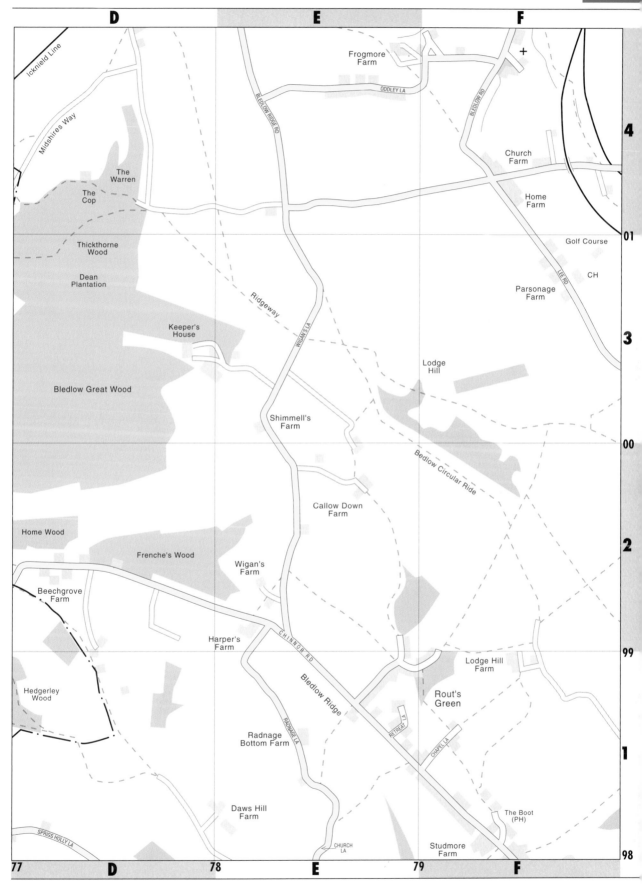

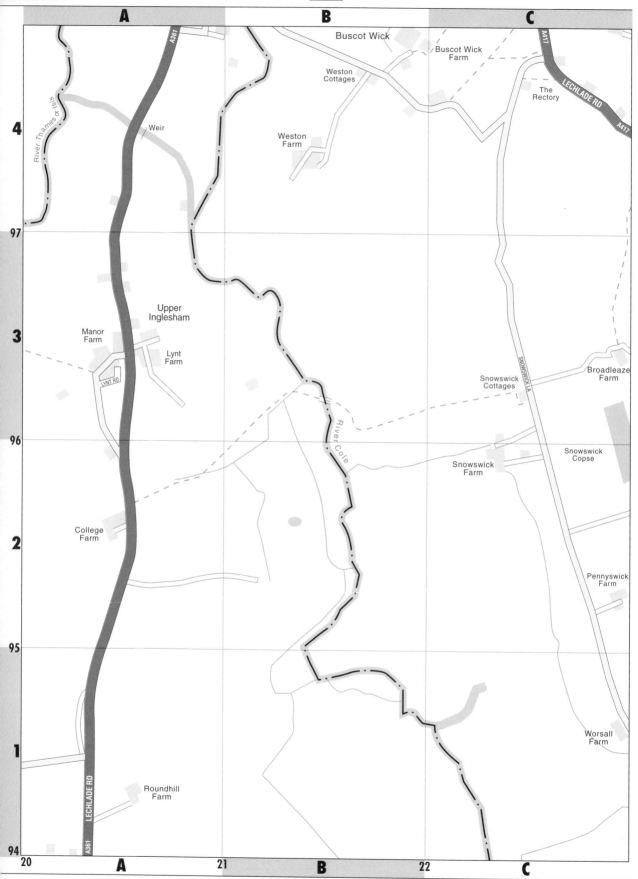

D
E
F

Buscot Wharf

P Buscot

PH
PO

West Lodge

Kilmester Farm

LECHLADE RD

Taylor's Hill

Eaton Hastings

Stud Farm

4

Little Lake

97

A417

Buscot House

The Lake

Roadside Cottages

Resr

Buscot Park

Canada Wood

Bury Hill

Cannon Hill

Old Wood

3

Cannonhill Wood

Black Plantation

Eaton Wood

Bushy Heath

Heath Barn

Resr

Longmead Plantation

Woodacre Wood

96

Oldfield Farm

Rowleaze Wood

Gorse Hill

2

Brimstone Farm

Coxwell Wood

95

Middle Leaze Farm

Fern Copse

1

B4019

Cuckoopen Plantation

B4019

Colleymore Farm

94

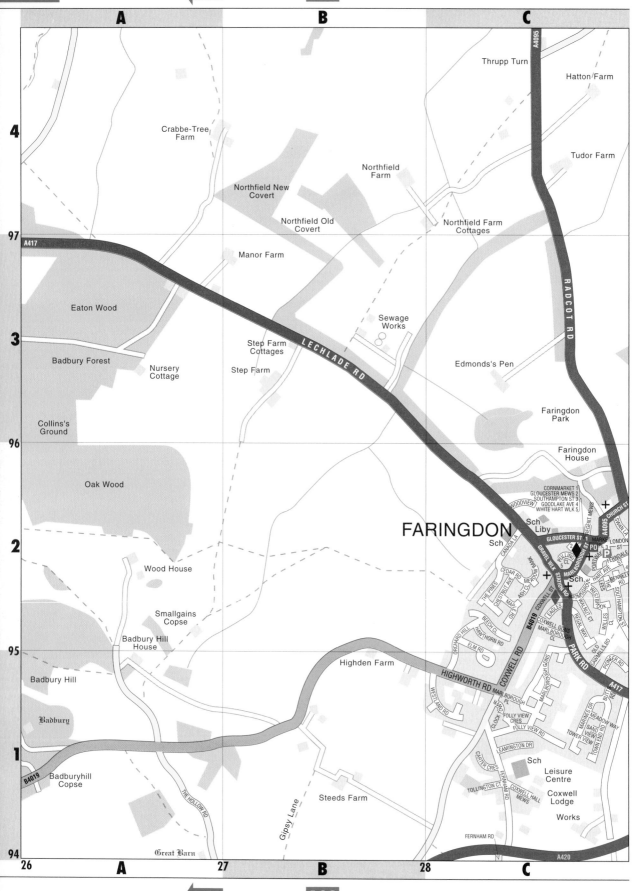

171 152

A   **B**   **C**

A4095

Thrupp Turn

Hatton Farm

4

Crabbe-Tree Farm

Tudor Farm

Northfield Farm

Northfield New Covert

97

Northfield Old Covert

Northfield Farm Cottages

A417

Manor Farm

RADCOT RD

Eaton Wood

Sewage Works

3

Badbury Forest

Step Farm Cottages

LECHLADE RD

Edmonds's Pen

Nursery Cottage

Step Farm

Faringdon Park

Collins's Ground

Faringdon House

96

Oak Wood

CORNMARKET 1
GLOUCESTER MEWS 2
SOUTHAMPTON ST 3
GOODLAKE AVE 4
WHITE HART WLK 5
WOODVIEW

Sch
Liby

FARINGDON

Sch

2

Wood House

GLOUCESTER ST 1
MARKET PL
PO
London

Sch

GRAVEL WLK
STATION RD
PULLING CL
MARLBOROUGH ST
PORTWELL
REGENT MEWS
A4095 CHURCH ST
SWAN LA
FERNDALE

Smallgains Copse

THE PINES
CEDAR RD
CHESTNUT AVE
45H CL
MEWS
WALNUT CT
WEST BROOK
HART AVE
LEES
BENNETT RD
SOUTHAMPTON ST
REGAL WAY

Badbury Hill House

ORCHARD HILL
BEECH CL
HAWTHORN RD
ELM RD
B4019
COXWELL ST
EAGLES
COXWELL GDNS
MARLBOROUGH CL
SAWMILLS RD
PICKET RD

95

Highden Farm

HIGHWORTH RD

COXWELL RD

PARK RD

A417

Badbury Hill

WESTLAND RD

MARLBOROUGH GDNS
MARLBOROUGH PL

MARINES DR
BUTT
MEADOW WAY
TOWN END RD
TOWER VIEW

Badbury

CLOCK
MAY
FOLLY VIEW CRES
FOLLY VIEW RD
LEAMINGTON DR

SAND VIEW

1

B4019

Badburyhill Copse

Sch

Leisure Centre

CARTER CRES
TOLLINGTON CT
FERNHAM RD
COXWELL HALL MEWS

Coxwell Lodge

THE HOLLOW RD

Gipsy Lane

Steeds Farm

Works

FERNHAM RD

94

Great Barn

A420

26   **A**   **27**   **B**   **28**   **C**

171 192

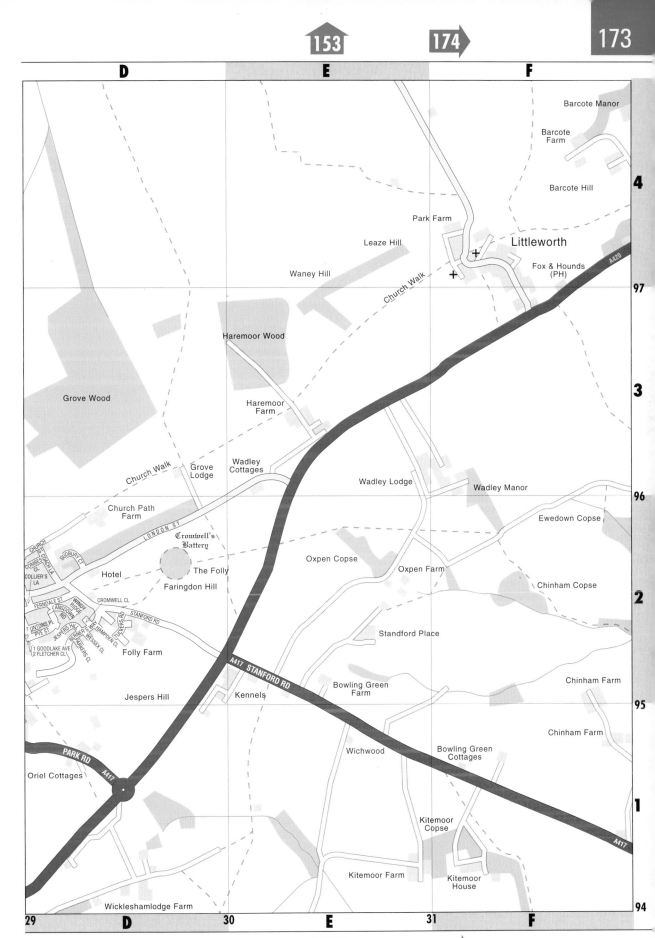

Barcote Manor

Barcote Farm

Barcote Hill

4

Park Farm

Leaze Hill

Littleworth

Waney Hill

Church Walk

Fox & Hounds (PH)

A420

97

Haremoor Wood

Grove Wood

3

Haremoor Farm

Church Walk

Grove Lodge

Wadley Cottages

Wadley Lodge

Wadley Manor

96

Church Path Farm

LONDON ST

Cromwell's Battery

Ewedown Copse

CHURCH ST
COMBES GL
COACH LA
COLLIER'S LA
SUDBURY CT

Hotel

The Folly

Faringdon Hill

Oxpen Copse

Oxpen Farm

Chinham Copse

2

FERNDALE ST
WINDY RIDGE
LANSDOWN RD
CROMWELL CL
STANFORD RD

Standford Place

UNTONS PL
PYE ST
JESPERS HL
BERNER'S WAY
HAMPDEN CL
WESSEX CL
TUCKERS RD
PADGERS CL

Folly Farm

1 GOODLAKE AVE
2 FLETCHER CL

Chinham Farm

Jespers Hill

A417 STANFORD RD

Kennels

Bowling Green Farm

95

Chinham Farm

PARK RD

Wichwood

Bowling Green Cottages

Oriel Cottages

A417

1

Kitemoor Copse

A417

Kitemoor Farm

Kitemoor House

Wickleshamlodge Farm

94

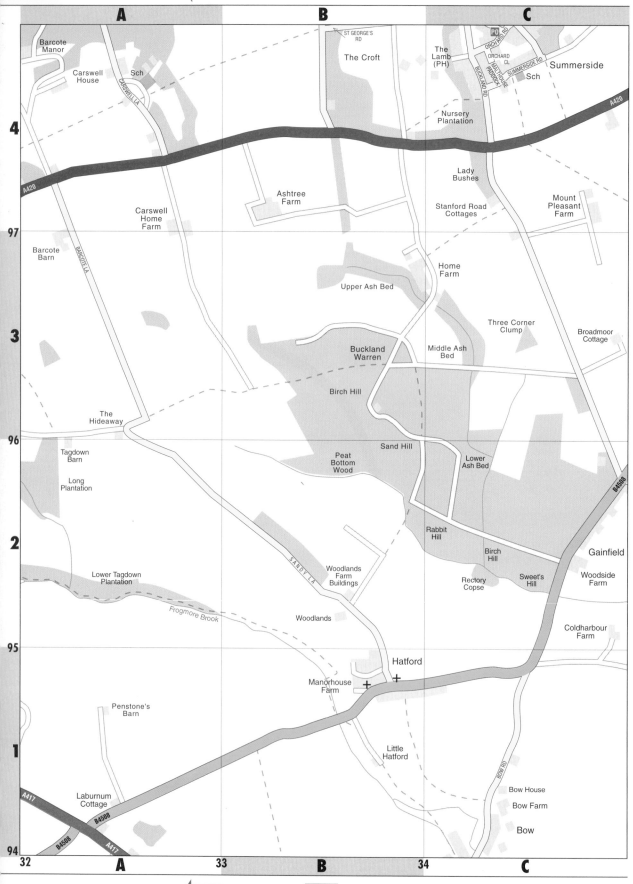

Barcote Manor
Carswell House
Sch
CARSWELL LA
Barcote Barn
BARCOTE LA
A420

St George's Rd
The Croft
The Lamb (PH)
PO
ORCHARD RD
ORCHARD CL
MALTHOUSE PADDOCK
BUCKLAND RD
SUMMERSIDE RD
Summerside
Sch
A420

Carswell Home Farm
Ashtree Farm
Nursery Plantation
Lady Bushes
Stanford Road Cottages
Mount Pleasant Farm

Home Farm
Upper Ash Bed
Three Corner Clump
Broadmoor Cottage

The Hideaway
Buckland Warren
Middle Ash Bed
Birch Hill

Tagdown Barn
Long Plantation
Peat Bottom Wood
Sand Hill
Lower Ash Bed
B4508

Lower Tagdown Plantation
SANDY LA
Woodlands Farm Buildings
Rabbit Hill
Birch Hill
Rectory Copse
Sweet's Hill
Gainfield
Woodside Farm

Frogmore Brook
Woodlands
Hatford
Coldharbour Farm

Manorhouse Farm
Penstone's Barn
Little Hatford
BOW RD

A417
Laburnum Cottage
B4508
Bow House
Bow Farm
Bow

B4508
A417

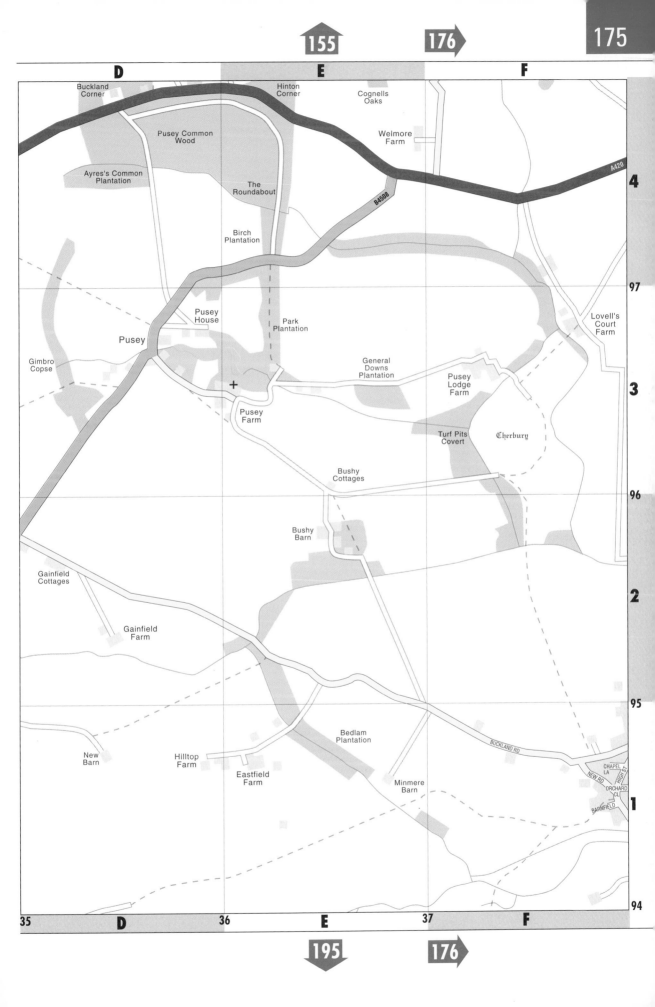

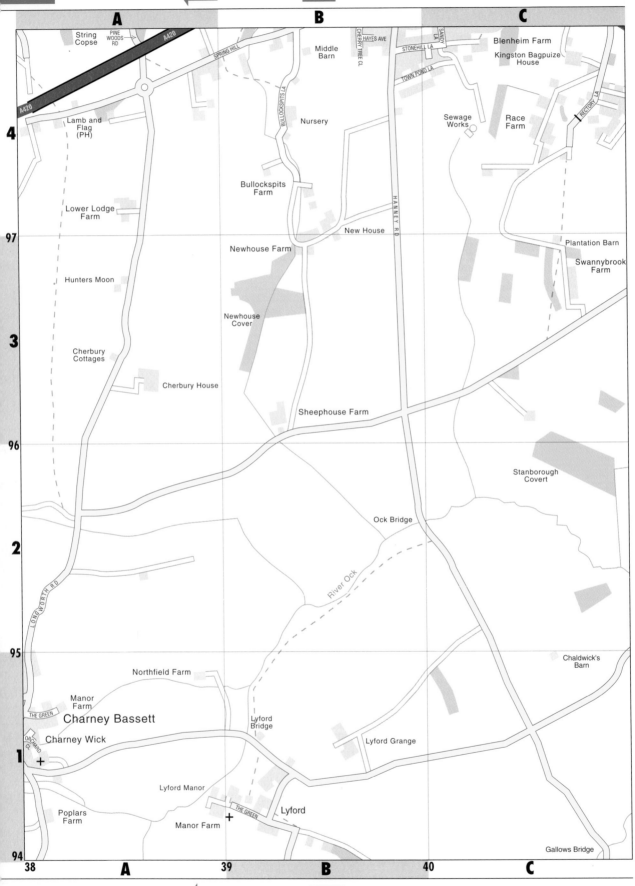

A B C

String
Copse
PINE
WOODS
RD
SPRING HILL
A420
A420
Middle
Barn
CHERRY TREE CL
HAYES AVE
STONEHILL LA
TOWN POND LA
SANDY
Blenheim Farm
Kingston Bagpuize
House

Lamb and
Flag
(PH)
Nursery
BULLOCKSPITS LA
Sewage
Works
Race
Farm
RECTORY LA

Lower Lodge
Farm
Bullockspits
Farm
New House
HANNEY RD
Plantation Barn
Swannybrook
Farm
Newhouse Farm

Hunters Moon

Newhouse
Cover

Cherbury
Cottages

Cherbury House

Sheephouse Farm

Stanborough
Covert

Ock Bridge

LONGWORTH RD

River Ock

Chaldwick's
Barn

Northfield Farm

Manor
Farm
THE GREEN
Charney Bassett
Lyford
Bridge
Lyford Grange

Charney Wick
ORCHARD CL
+

Lyford Manor
THE GREEN
+
Lyford
Poplars
Farm
Manor Farm

Gallows Bridge

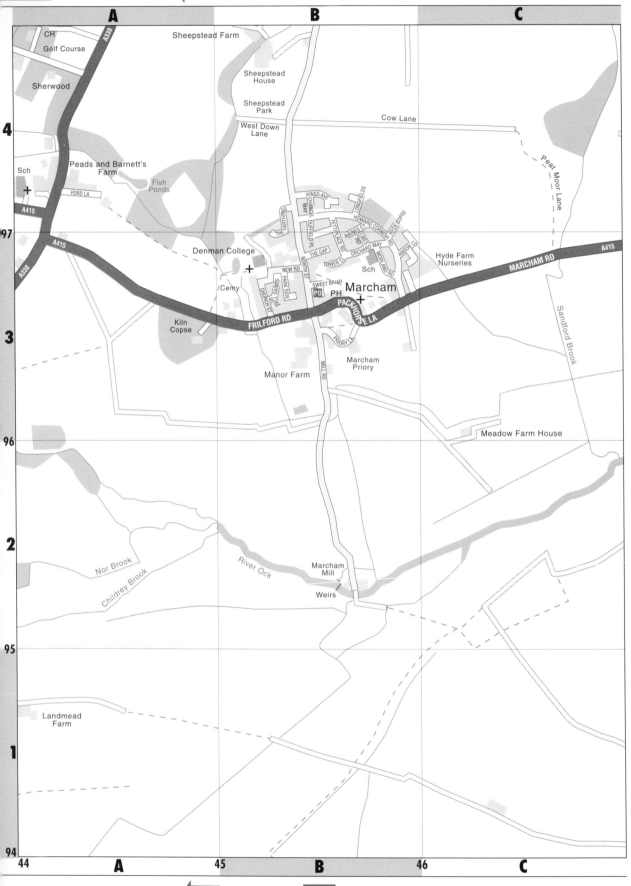

A   B   C

CH
Golf Course
Sherwood
Sheepstead Farm
Sheepstead House
Sheepstead Park
West Down Lane
Cow Lane

4

Peads and Barnett's Farm
Sch
Fish Ponds
FORD LA
A415
A338

97

A415
Denman College
Cemy
Kiln Copse
FRILFORD RD
NORTH ST
CHURCH ST
SALTYS LA
NEW RD
PARK SIDE
THE FAITHINGS
KINGS AVE
CHANCEL WAY
DUFFIELD PL
THE GAP
TOWER CL
ORCHARD WAY
FETTIPLACE RD
HAINES CL
CLIVES RD
HOWARD CORNISH RD
HYDE COPSE
ANSON CL
Sch
Marcham
PO
PH
SWEET BRIAR
PACKHORSE LA
MYRLAND RD
Hyde Farm Nurseries
MARCHAM RD
A415
Peat Moor Lane

3

Kiln Copse
PRIORY LA
MILL RD
Manor Farm
Marcham Priory
Sandford Brook

96

Meadow Farm House

2

Nor Brook
Childrey Brook
River Ock
Marcham Mill
Weirs

95

Landmead Farm

1

94

44   A   45   B   46   C

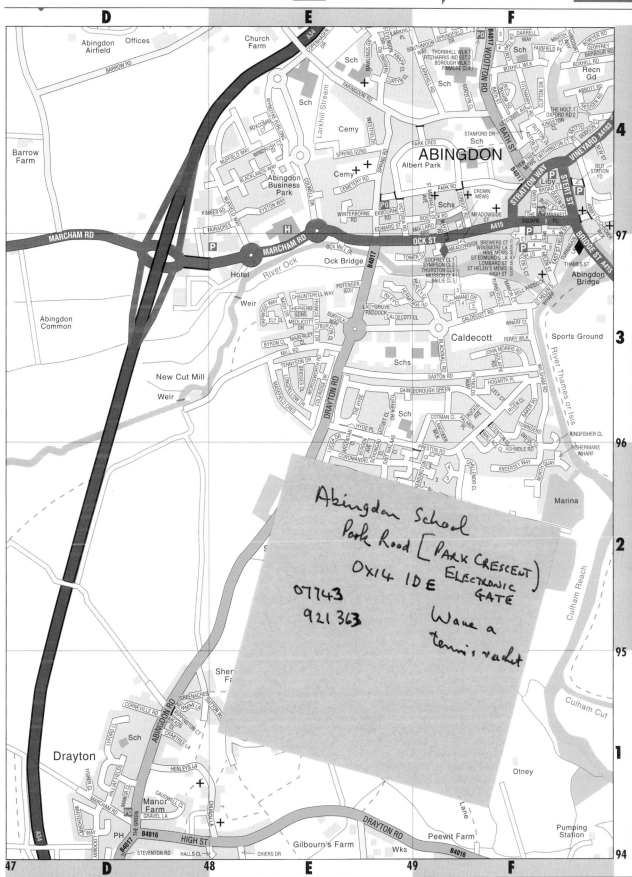

Abingdon School
Park Road [PARK CRESCENT]
ELECTRONIC
OX14 1DE GATE

07743
921 363
Wave a
tennis racket

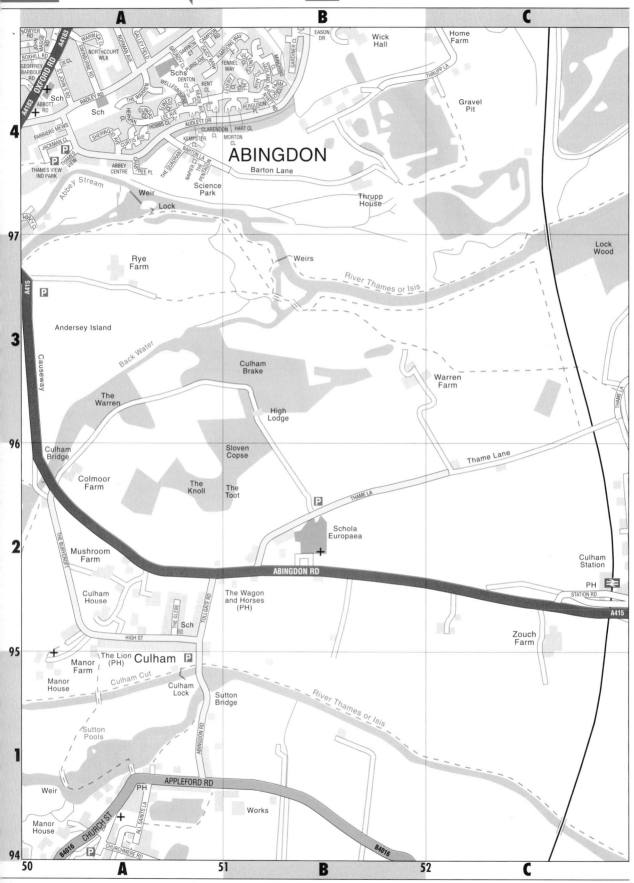

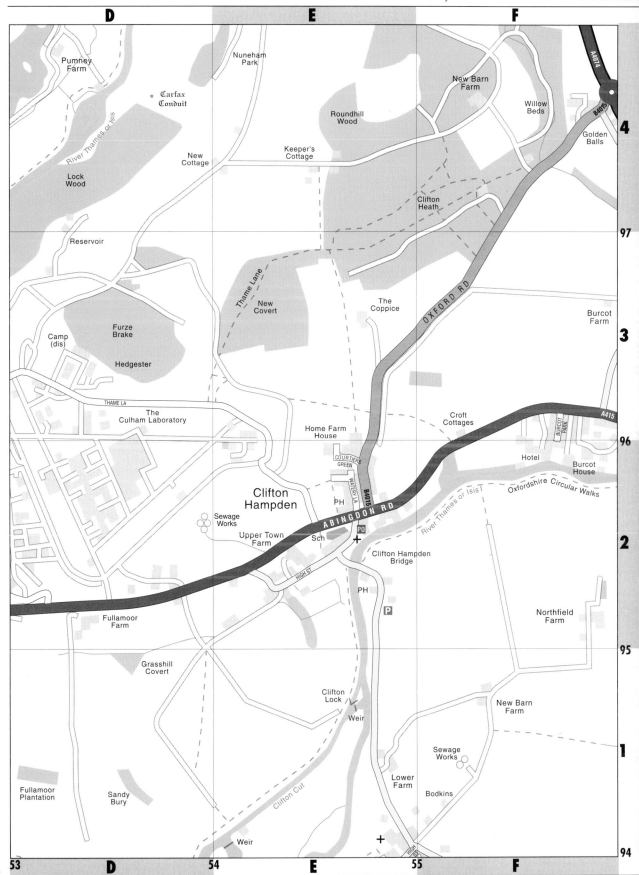

D
E
F

4

Pumney
Farm

Nuneham
Park

New Barn
Farm

Willow
Beds

A4074

B4015

Golden
Balls

Carfax
Conduit

Roundhill
Wood

Keeper's
Cottage

New
Cottage

River Thames or Isis

Clifton
Heath

97

Lock
Wood

Reservoir

Thame Lane

New
Covert

The
Coppice

OXFORD RD

Burcot
Farm

3

Camp
(dis)

Furze
Brake

Hedgester

Croft
Cottages

A415

96

THAME LA

The
Culham Laboratory

Home Farm
House

BURCOT PARK

Hotel

Burcot
House

COURTIERS
GREEN

Oxfordshire Circular Walks

Clifton
Hampden

PH

WATER LA

B4015

ABINGDON RD

River Thames or Isis

2

Sewage
Works

Upper Town
Farm

Sch

PO

Clifton Hampden
Bridge

Northfield
Farm

HIGH ST

PH

Fullamoor
Farm

P

95

Grasshill
Covert

Clifton
Lock

Weir

New Barn
Farm

1

Fullamoor
Plantation

Sandy
Bury

Clifton Cut

Weir

Lower
Farm

Bodkins

Sewage
Works

HIGH ST

94

A   B   C

Baldon Brook

B4015

B4015

Golden Balls

A4074

4

The Copse

97

Burcot Farm

TOWER RD

PRITCHARD CL

BARRINGTON CL

RUSSELL JACKSON CL

CRUTCH FURLONG

FANE DR

GLYME DR

CHERWELL RD

EVENLODE DR

LAY AVE

COLNE DR

WEST CROFT

COLWELL DR

GREEN FURLONG

OCK DR

Berinsfield

3

SHADWELL RD

WIMBLESTRAW RD

LEACH RD

WEY RD

BULLINGDON AVE

Schs

CHILTERN CL

LODEN AVE

Mount Farm

Dorchester Rd

Works

BERINSFIELD RDBT

A415

BALFOUR COTTS

ABINGDON RD

A415

WINDRUSH RD

KENNET CL

WIMBLE STRAW RD

96

Burcot

PH

LINNET CL

BURCOT LA

Wally Corner

DORCHESTER RD

Weir

2

Oxfordshire Circular Walks

River Thames or Isis

ABINGDON RD

DRAYTON RD

Queenford Farm

95

River Thame

THE MEWS

OXFORD RD

Queenford Bridge

PH

Bishop's Court

Cemy

DRAYTON RD

HERRINGCOTE

PAGE FURLONG

MARTIN S LA

1

Dorchester
ROMAN TOWN

JEMMETTS CL

CROWN LA

QUEENS ST

HIGH ST

Sch

QUEENS CL

MANOR FARM RD

KINGS CL

BEECHCROFT

MALTHOUSE

PO

WATLING LA

PH

Mus

Weir

Abbey Bridge

ROTTEN ROW

BRIDGE END

Overy Farm

Overy

A4074

94

56   A   57   B   58   C

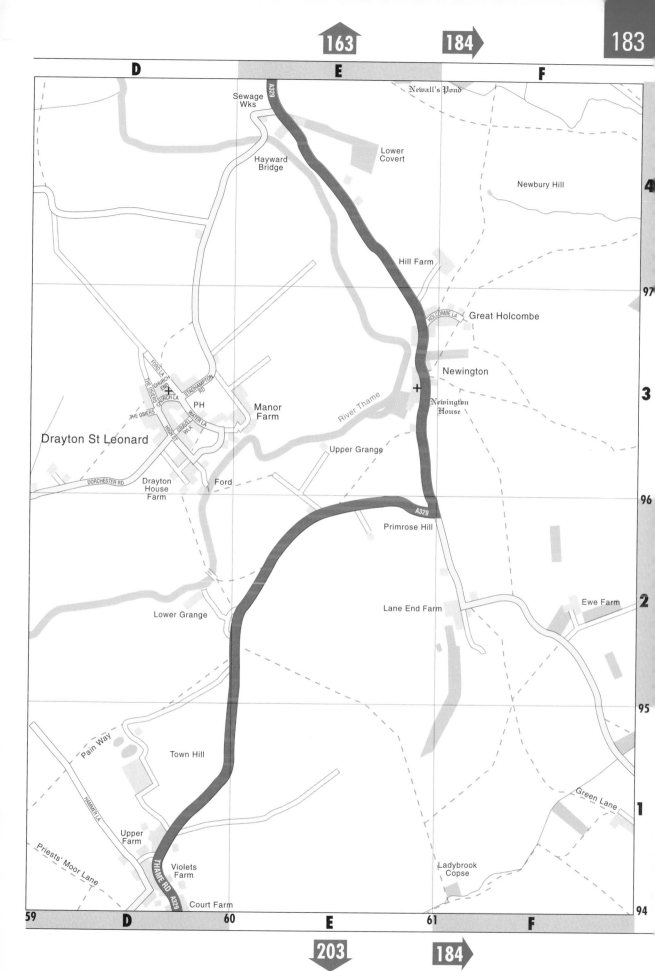

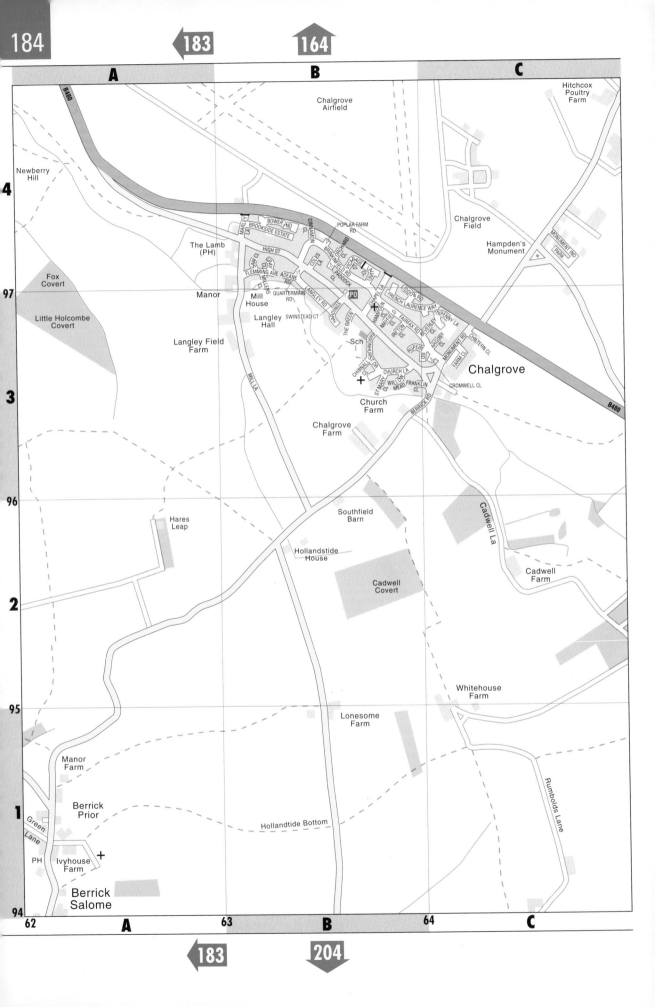

A **B** **C**

4

Newberry Hill

B480

Chalgrove Airfield

Hitchcox Poultry Farm

Chalgrove Field

Hampden's Monument

MONUMENT IND PARK

MARLEY LA
BOWER END
BROOKSIDE ESTATE
CINNAMON CL
POPLAR FARM RD

The Lamb (PH)

HIGH ST

Fox Covert

97

Little Holcombe Covert

Manor

Mill House

SWAN CL
GOWER CL
FLEMMING AVE
MILLERS
ADEANE RD
QUARTERMAIN RD
BRUNKFIELD RD
PADDOCK CL
SAGE CL
LAZAR
CHAPEL LA
FRENCH LAURENCE WAY
LODDON RD
DYPENNY LA

P0

Langley Hall

SWINSTEAD CT

Langley Field Farm

MILL LA

Sch

THE GREEN
HAMMONDS
BARNHOUSE CT
CHIBNALL CL
ST MARY CL
WILLOW MEAD
CHURCH LA
RUPERT RD
FRANKLIN CL
BERRICK RD
CROMWELL CL
FAIRFAX RD
HEVERLEY
IRETON CL
MAYFIELD
ARGOSY
MONUMENT RD
FARM CL
CHILTERN CL

Chalgrove

3

Church Farm

Chalgrove Farm

B480

96

Southfield Barn

Cadwell La

Hares Leap

Hollandstide House

Cadwell Farm

Cadwell Covert

2

Whitehouse Farm

95

Lonesome Farm

Manor Farm

Rumbolds Lane

1

Berrick Prior

Green Lane

PH

Ivyhouse Farm

Hollandtide Bottom

94

Berrick Salome

62 **A** 63 **B** 64 **C**

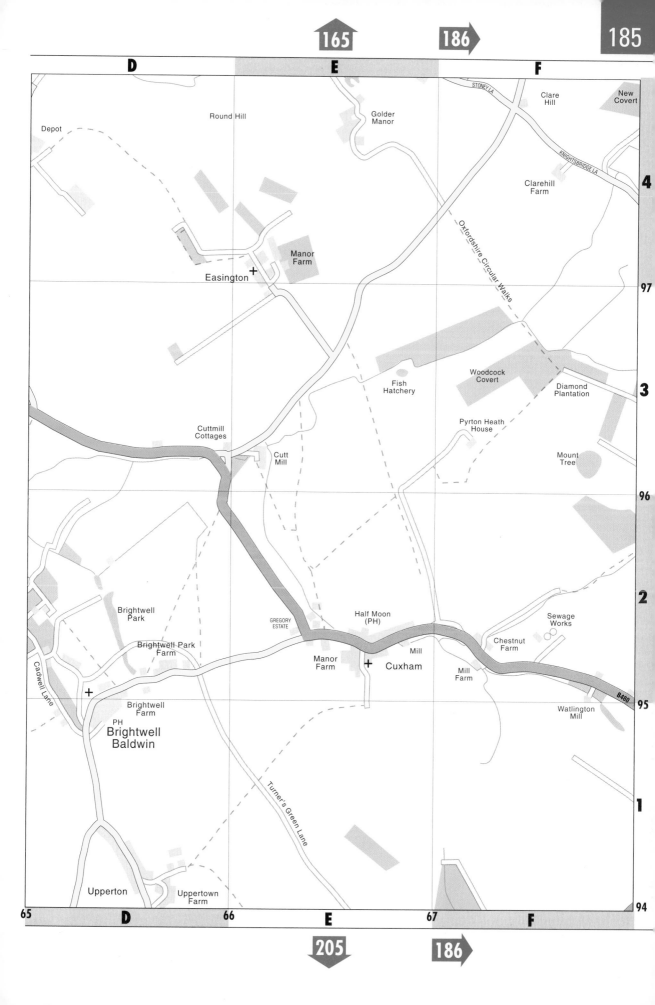

STONEY LA
Clare Hill
New Covert
Round Hill
Golder Manor
Depot
KNIGHTSBRIDGE LA
Clarehill Farm
4
Oxfordshire Circular Walks
Manor Farm
Easington +
97
Fish Hatchery
Woodcock Covert
Diamond Plantation
3
Cuttmill Cottages
Pyrton Heath House
Mount Tree
Cutt Mill
96
Brightwell Park
Half Moon (PH)
Sewage Works
2
GREGORY ESTATE
Chestnut Farm
Brightwell Park Farm
Manor Farm
Mill
Cuxham
Cadwell Lane
+
Mill Farm
B480
95
+
Brightwell Farm
Watlington Mill
PH
Brightwell Baldwin
Turner's Green Lane
1
Upperton
Uppertown Farm

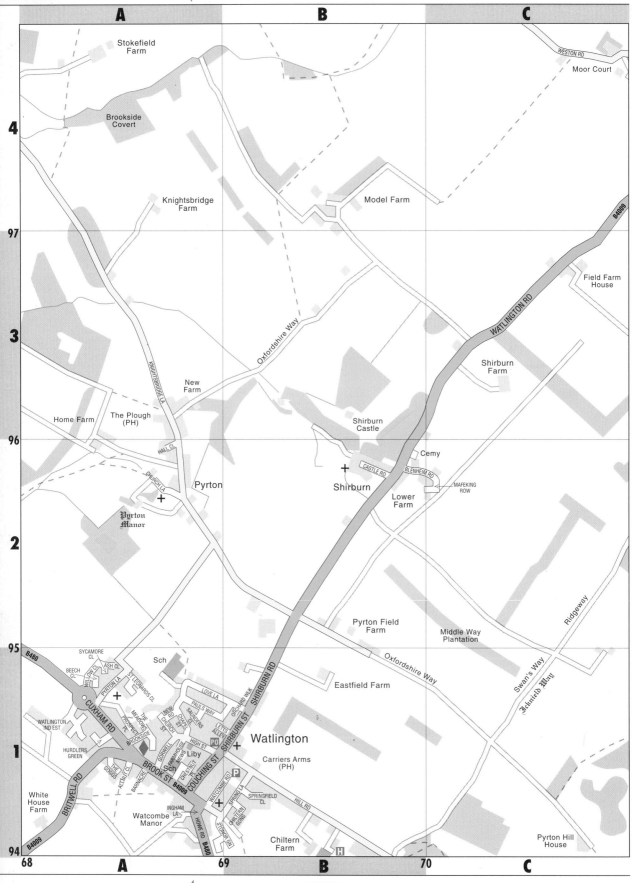

A B C

Stokefield
Farm

WESTON RD

Moor Court

Brookside
Covert

4

Knightsbridge
Farm

Model Farm

97

B4009

Field Farm
House

Oxfordshire Way

WATLINGTON RD

3

Shirburn
Farm

KNIGHTSBRIDGE LA

New
Farm

Home Farm

The Plough
(PH)

HALL CL

Shirburn
Castle

Cemy

96

CHURCH LA

Pyrton

+

Shirburn

CASTLE RD

BLENHEIM RD

MAFEKING
ROW

Lower
Farm

Pyrton
Manor

2

Ridgeway

Pyrton Field
Farm

Middle Way
Plantation

Swan's Way

Icknield Way

95

B480

Sch

Oxfordshire Way

Eastfield Farm

SYCAMORE
CL

BEECH
CL

ASH CL

WILLOW CL

PYRTON LA

ST LEONARDS CL

SHIRBURN RD

LOVE LA

ORCHARD WLK

SHIRBURN ST

PAUL'S WAY

SANDERS

CUXHAM RD

THE
MEADOWS

PROSPECT PL

NEW
RD

CHURCH
ST

CHAPEL
ST

LETTS
ALLEY

SPRING LA

WATLINGTON
IND EST

HIGH ST

PO

Watlington

1

HURDLERS
GREEN

BRITWELL RD

BROOK ST

GORWELL

SUMMERHOUSE
MEWS

CHESTNUT

Liby

Sch

COUCHING ST

P

Carriers Arms
(PH)

White
House
Farm

B4009

THE
GOGGS

AZLNUT CL

BARNACRE

B4009

WATCOMBE RD

SPRING LA

CHILTERN
GDNS

SPRINGFIELD
CL

HILL RD

Watcombe
Manor

INGHAM
LA

HOWE RD

STONOR GN

B480

Chiltern
Farm

H

Pyrton Hill
House

94

B4009

68 A 69 B 70 C

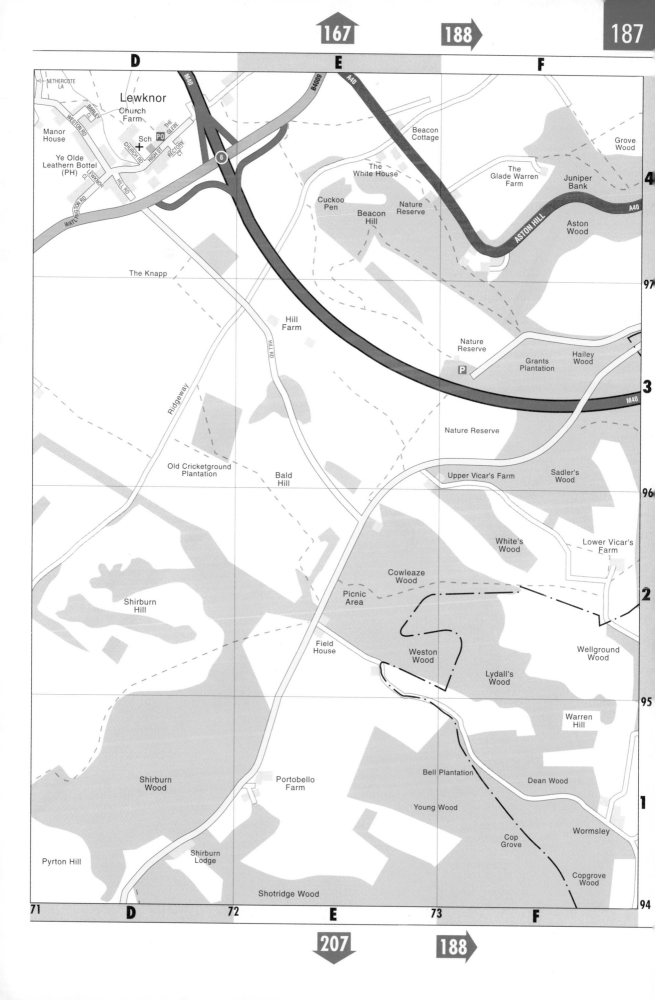

D
E
F

NETHERCOTE LA

Lewknor

Church
Farm

Manor
House

Ye Olde
Leathern Bottel
(PH)

WESTON RD
BARLEY CL
THE GLEBE
CHURCH RD
HIGH ST
RECTORY CT
HILL RD
LEWKNOR
WATLINGTON RD

Sch
PO
+

6

M40

B4009

A40

Beacon
Cottage

The
White House

The
Glade Warren
Farm

Grove
Wood

Cuckoo
Pen

Nature
Reserve

Juniper
Bank

4

ASTON HILL

Aston
Wood

A40

Beacon
Hill

The Knapp

97

Hill
Farm

Nature
Reserve

Grants
Plantation

Hailey
Wood

M40

Ridgeway

HILL RD

P

3

Old Cricketground
Plantation

Bald
Hill

Nature Reserve

Upper Vicar's Farm

Sadler's
Wood

96

White's
Wood

Lower Vicar's
Farm

Shirburn
Hill

Cowleaze
Wood

Picnic
Area

Weston
Wood

Lydall's
Wood

Wellground
Wood

2

Field
House

Warren
Hill

95

Shirburn
Wood

Portobello
Farm

Bell Plantation

Dean Wood

Young Wood

Wormsley

1

Pyrton Hill

Shirburn
Lodge

Cop
Grove

Copgrove
Wood

Shotridge Wood

71
D
72
E
73
F
94

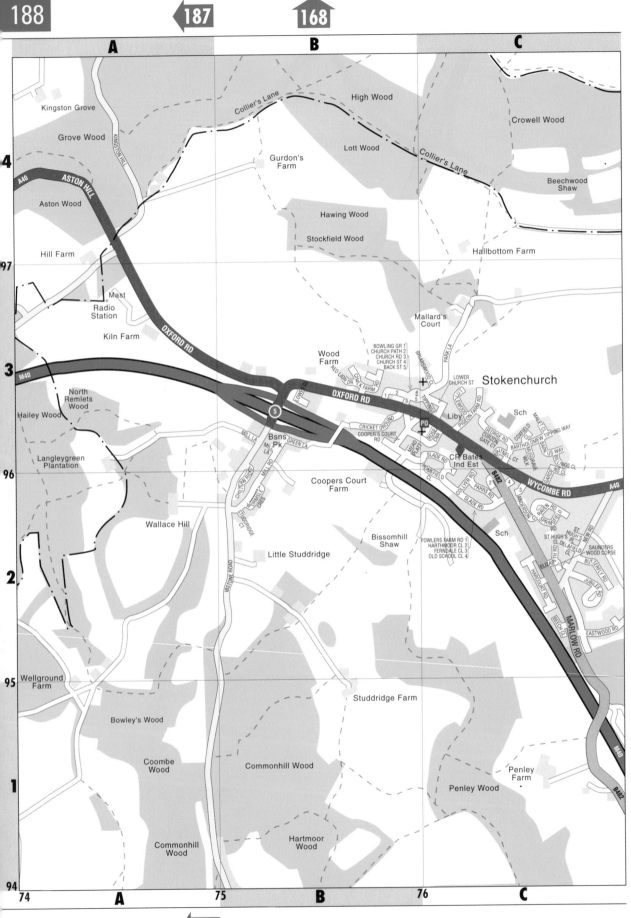

Map Labels

Column A

Kingston Grove

Grove Wood

Kingston Hill

A40 ASTON HILL

Aston Wood

Hill Farm

97

Mast

Radio Station

Kiln Farm

OXFORD RD

M40 3

North Remlets Wood

Hailey Wood

Langleygreen Plantation

96

Bsns Pk

MILL LA

GREEN LA

MILL RD

CHILTERN RD

SPANDLE CRES

STUDDRIDGE CT

UPSTONE ROAD

Wallace Hill

2

Wellground Farm

95

Bowley's Wood

Coombe Wood

1

Commonhill Wood

94

Column B

Collier's Lane

High Wood

Lott Wood

Collier's Lane

Gurdon's Farm

Hawing Wood

Stockfield Wood

Wood Farm

RED LION DR

CHALK FARM

TOWER CL

OXFORD RD

Cricket Ground

Cooper's Court Rd

MEAD PLAT

Coopers Court Farm

Little Studdridge

Bissomhill Shaw

Studdridge Farm

Commonhill Wood

Hartmoor Wood

Column C

Crowell Wood

Beechwood Shaw

Hallbottom Farm

Mallard's Court

PARK LA

BRIARSWOOD

BOWLING GR 1
CHURCH PATH 2
CHURCH RD 3
CHURCH ST 4
BACK ST 5

LOWER CHURCH ST

Stokenchurch

1 2 3 4 5

TIPPINGS

Liby

PIGEON FARM RD

Sch

GEORGE RD
CURZON GATE CT
MALET CT
COXFIELD
BARTHOLOMEW
MUSGRAVE

TIPPING WAY
US WAY
US BILLINGS CL

PO

CR Bates Ind Est

SLADE RD

HOMEFIELD CL

COLYER RD

PARRS RD

SLADE RD

B482

WYCOMBE RD A40

Sch

FOWLERS FARM RD 1
HARTHMOOR CL 2
FERNDALE CL 3
OLD SCHOOL CL 4

ANDERSON CL

SPRINGFIELD

ST HUGH'S PL
CL DELAFIELD CL

ST HUGH'S RD

SAUNDERS WOOD CORSE

ELIZABETH RD

HARCOURT RD

RAVEN RD

BUTTERFLY RD

JUBILEE RD

MARLOW RD

BEECH CL

EASTWOOD RD

M40

B482

Penley Farm

Penley Wood

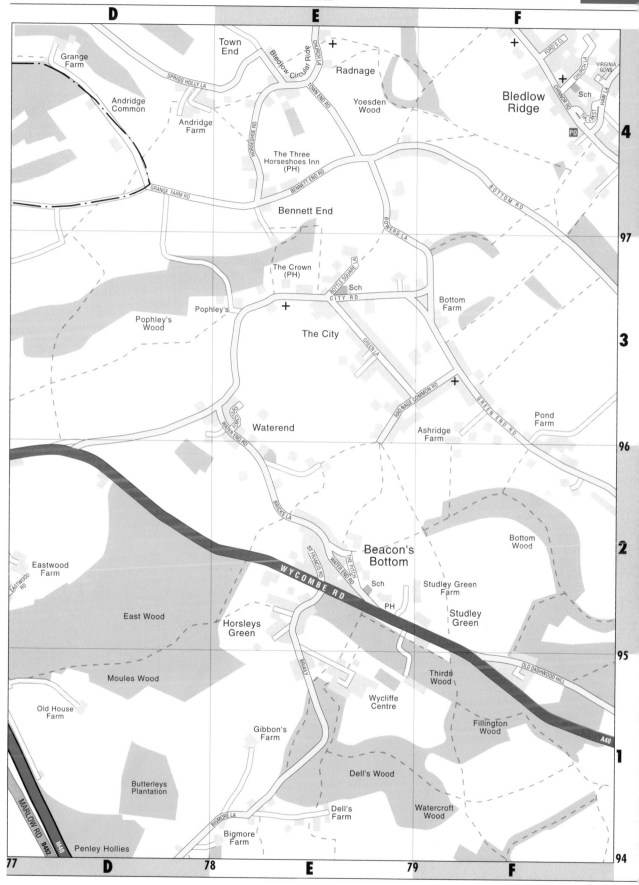

D **E** **F**

Grange Farm

Town End

Radnage

Yoesden Wood

Bledlow Ridge

SPRIGS HOLLY LA

Andridge Common

Andridge Farm

BLEDLOW CIRCULAR RIDE

TOWN END RD

CHURCH LA

FORD'S CL

CHURCH LA

VIRGINIA GDNS

CHINNOR RD

HAW LA

THE CREST

Sch

PO

4

The Three Horseshoes Inn (PH)

HORSESHOE RD

BENNETT END RD

Bennett End

GRANGE FARM RD

BOWERS LA

BOTTOM RD

97

The Crown (PH)

Pophley's

Pophley's Wood

BOTTLE SQUARE LA

Sch

CITY RD

The City

Bottom Farm

GREEN LA

RADNAGE COMMON RD

GREEN END RD

Ashridge Farm

Pond Farm

3

Waterend

BLEDLOW RD

WATER END RD

96

Eastwood Farm

EASTWOOD RD

East Wood

BRICKS LA

Beacon's Bottom

ST FRANCIS RD

WATER END RD

THE PITCH

Sch

PH

WYCOMBE RD

Studley Green Farm

Studley Green

Bottom Wood

2

Horsleys Green

Moules Wood

BRIARY

Wycliffe Centre

Thirds Wood

OLD DASHWOOD HILL

95

Old House Farm

Gibbon's Farm

Fillington Wood

A40

1

Butterleys Plantation

Dell's Wood

Dell's Farm

Watercroft Wood

MARLOW RD

B482

M40

Penley Hollies

BIGMORE LA

Bigmore Farm

77 **D** **78** **E** **79** **F** **94**

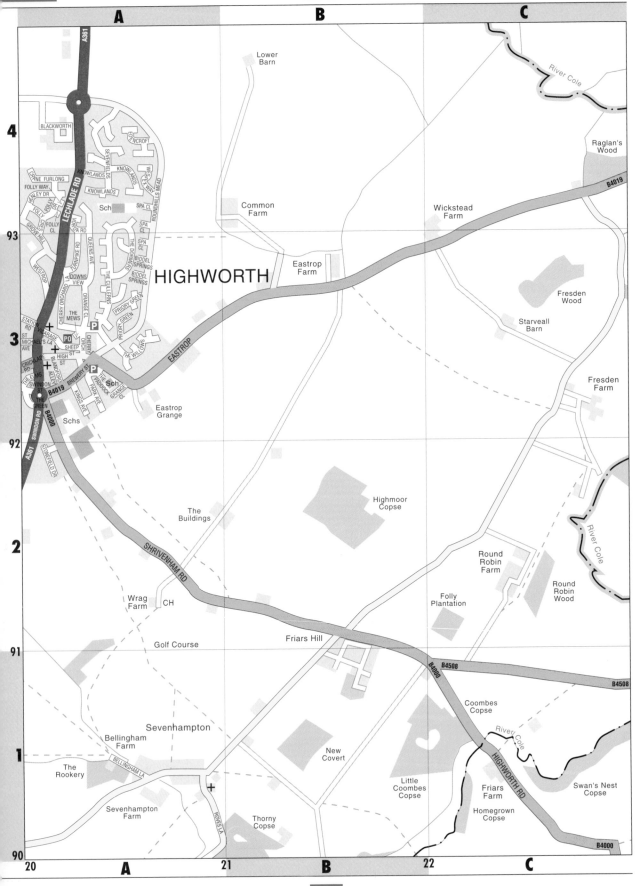

HIGHWORTH

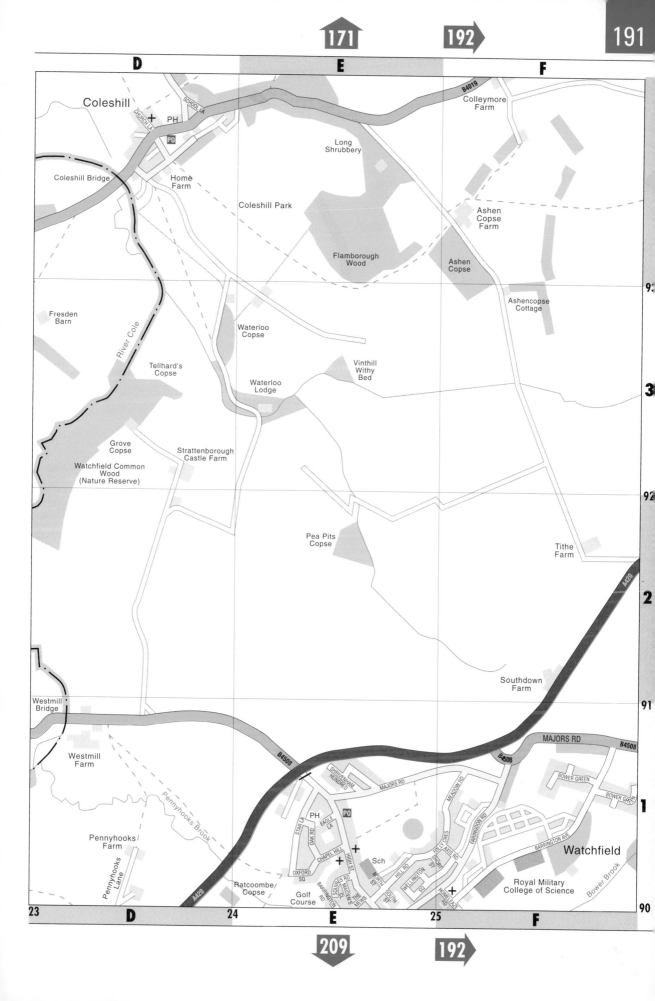

Coleshill

SCHOOL LA

CHURCH LA

PH

PO

B4019

Colleymore
Farm

Coleshill Bridge

Home
Farm

Long
Shrubbery

Coleshill Park

Ashen
Copse
Farm

Flamborough
Wood

Ashen
Copse

93

Ashencopse
Cottage

Fresden
Barn

River Cole

Waterloo
Copse

Vinthill
Withy
Bed

Tellhard's
Copse

3

Waterloo
Lodge

Grove
Copse

Strattenborough
Castle Farm

Watchfield Common
Wood
(Nature Reserve)

92

Pea Pits
Copse

Tithe
Farm

A420

2

Westmill
Bridge

Southdown
Farm

91

Westmill
Farm

MAJORS RD

B4508

B4508

Pennyhooks Brook

SHRIVENHAM
HUNDRED

MAJORS RD

MEADOW RD

BOWER GREEN

BOWER GREEN

Pennyhooks
Farm

PO

PH

STAR LA

EAGLE
LA

OAK RD

CHAPEL HILL

HIGH ST

Sch

FOLLY CRES

FARRINGTON RD

BARRINGTON AVE

1

Watchfield

Pennyhooks
Lane

OXFORD
SQ

BARRINGTON RD

COLLENS RD

MALDEN'S
THE
MEWS

NORTH
ST

HILL RD

SOUTH
ST

WELLINGTON
SQ

AXIS RD

SHORT ST

HOME CLOSE RD

Ratcoombe
Copse

Golf
Course

A420

Royal Military
College of Science

Bower Brook

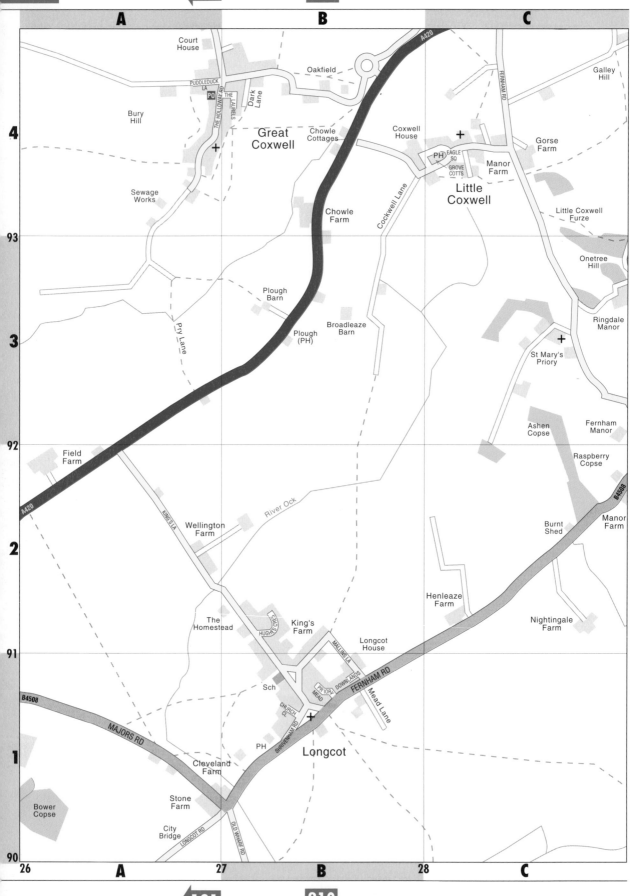

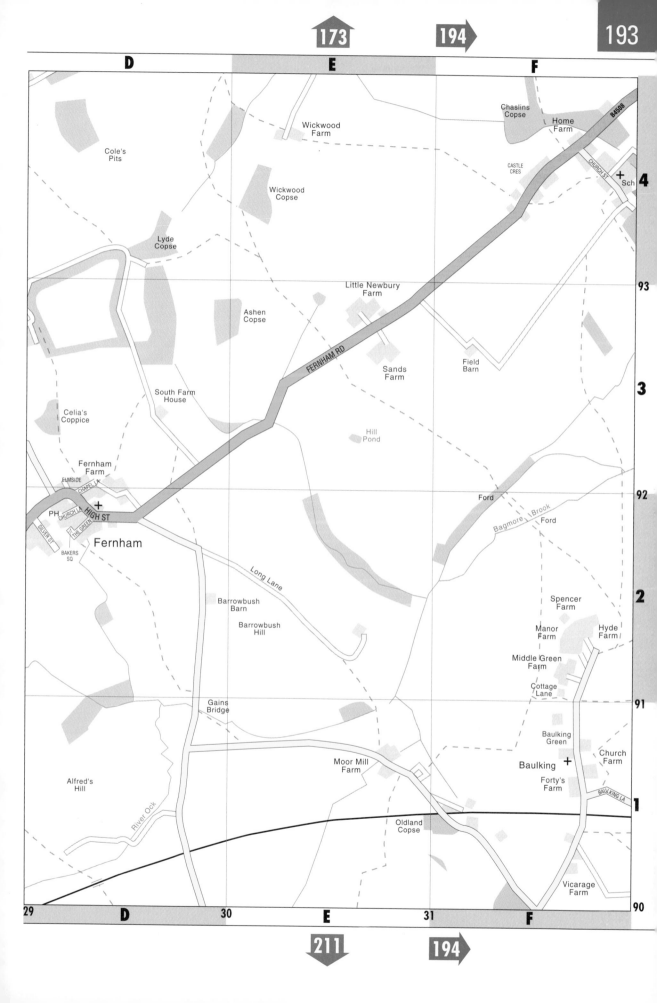

D E F

4

93

3

92

2

91

1

90

29 30 31

D E F

Cole's Pits

Wickwood Farm

Chaslins Copse

Home Farm

B4508

CASTLE CRES

CHURCH ST

Sch

Wickwood Copse

Lyde Copse

Little Newbury Farm

Ashen Copse

FERNHAM RD

Sands Farm

Field Barn

Celia's Coppice

South Farm House

Hill Pond

Ford

Fernham Farm

ELMSIDE

CHAPEL LA

Ford

Bagmore Brook

PH

CHURCH LA

HIGH ST

THE GREEN

SILVER ST

Fernham

BAKERS SQ

Long Lane

Spencer Farm

Barrowbush Barn

Manor Farm

Hyde Farm

Barrowbush Hill

Middle Green Farm

Cottage Lane

Gains Bridge

Baulking Green

Baulking

Church Farm

Alfred's Hill

Moor Mill Farm

Forty's Farm

BAULKING LA

River Ock

Oldland Copse

Vicarage Farm

B4508

A417 Quarry Barn

Shellingford

Upper Crale 1
Wordsworth Cl 2

Cottage Rd

Upper Gn

Bow Rd

Stanford House
Farm

Frogmore Brook

Chapel Rd

Frogmore La

7

2

Van Dieman's

Perry's
Rd

Joyce's
Rd

Glebe Rd

Tyrell Cl

Church Green

PO Anchor
Inn

Belcher's
Barn

**Stanford
in the Vale**

Horsecroft

Southdown

Sch

Shears La

Treadwells

The Way

Sch

Manor
Orbes

Hunters Field

Church Path

Warwick Cl

Kettle West

Dent La

High St

Marlborough La

Sch

Fishpond Copse
(Nature Reserve)

Ware Rd

White Horse
Business Park

Horse & Jockey
(PH)

Spencers Cl

Anvil Ct

Faringdon Rd

93

Rogues' Pit
Copse

Holywell Brook

Foxfield
Farm

Manor
Farm

Sewage
Works

Oak La

Park La

Mill
Farm

3

Rosey
Copse

River Ock

Sheepcroft
Farm

92

Baulking
Hill

Oldfield
Farm

Stutfield
Bridge

2

Works

A417

Green Close
Copse

Sheephouse
Leaze

Old Field
Meadow

91

Baulking La

Northfield
Farm

Stutfield Brook

Baulking Grange
Farm

1

Collier's
Barn

Collier's
Farm

Hale
Farm

Fox Covert

90

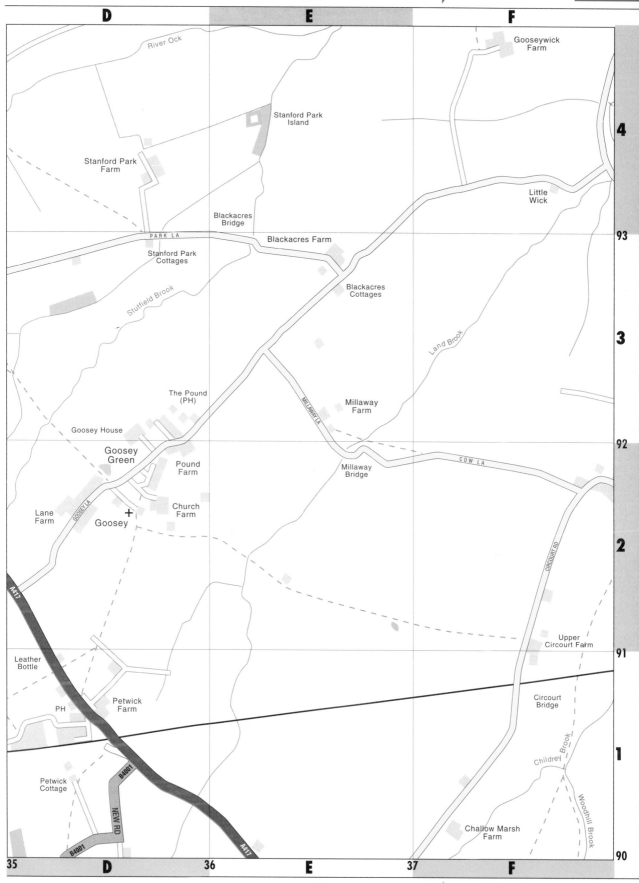

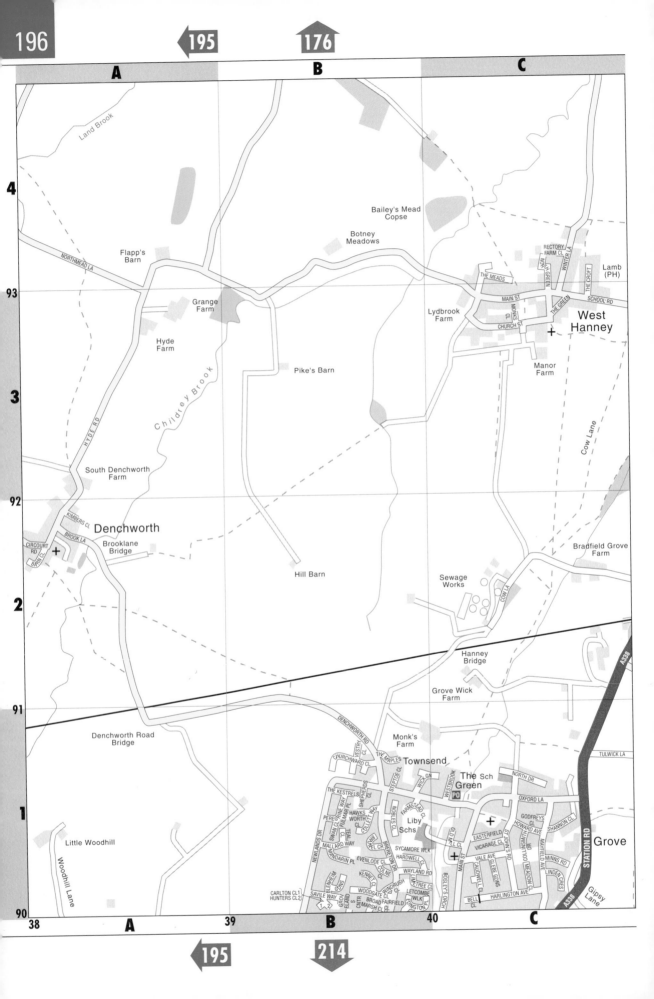

A   B   C

4

NORTHMEAD LA

Land Brook

Flapp's Barn

Bailey's Mead Copse

Botney Meadows

RECTORY FARM CL

WINTER LA

THE CROFT

Lamb (PH)

THE MEADS

NAG'S GREEN

93

Grange Farm

Hyde Farm

Pike's Barn

Lydbrook Farm

MAIN ST

MINNS CL

CHURCH ST

THE GREEN

SCHOOL RD

West Hanney

HYDE RD

Childrey Brook

3

Manor Farm

Cow Lane

South Denchworth Farm

92

KIMBERS CL

Denchworth

CIRCOURT RD

BARN CL

BROOK LA

Brooklane Bridge

Hill Barn

Sewage Works

COW LA

Bradfield Grove Farm

2

Hanney Bridge

Grove Wick Farm

A338

91

Denchworth Road Bridge

DENCHWORTH RD

Monk's Farm

Townsend

CHURCHWARD CL

WESTR... MAPLES

STEPTOE CL

WICK GN

WESTBROOK

The Sch Green
PO

NORTH DR

TULWICK LA

Little Woodhill

Woodhill Lane

THE KESTRELS

NEWLANDS DR

PEREGRINE WAY

SWAN CL

MALLARD WAY

MANDARIN PL

HAWKS WORTH

TEAL CL

COLLETT'S WAY

BREWER CT

NOBLES CL

HARDWELL CL

FARMSTEAD CL

SYCAMORE WLK

Liby Schs

ST JOHN'S RD

VICARAGE CL

GODFREYS CL

HOWARD AVE

OXFORD LA

SHANNON CL

MAYFIELD AVE

MINNS RD

LINDEN CRES

STATION RD

Grove

1

BLENHEIM

GRO... CONS

EVENLODE CL

COLNE

KENNET CL

WOODGATE CL

WINDRUSH

MARSH CL

WAYLAND RD

EASTERFIELD

VALE AVE

GLEBE GDNS

CALDWELL CL

HARLINGTON AVE

BELL...

BOSLEY'S ORCH

MEADOW CL

CARLTON CL1
HUNTERS CL2

SAVILE WAY

BROAD FAIRFIELD

LETCOMBE WLK

...INGTON

A338

Gipsy Lane

90

38   A   39   B   40   C

A　　　　　　　B　　　　　　　C

4

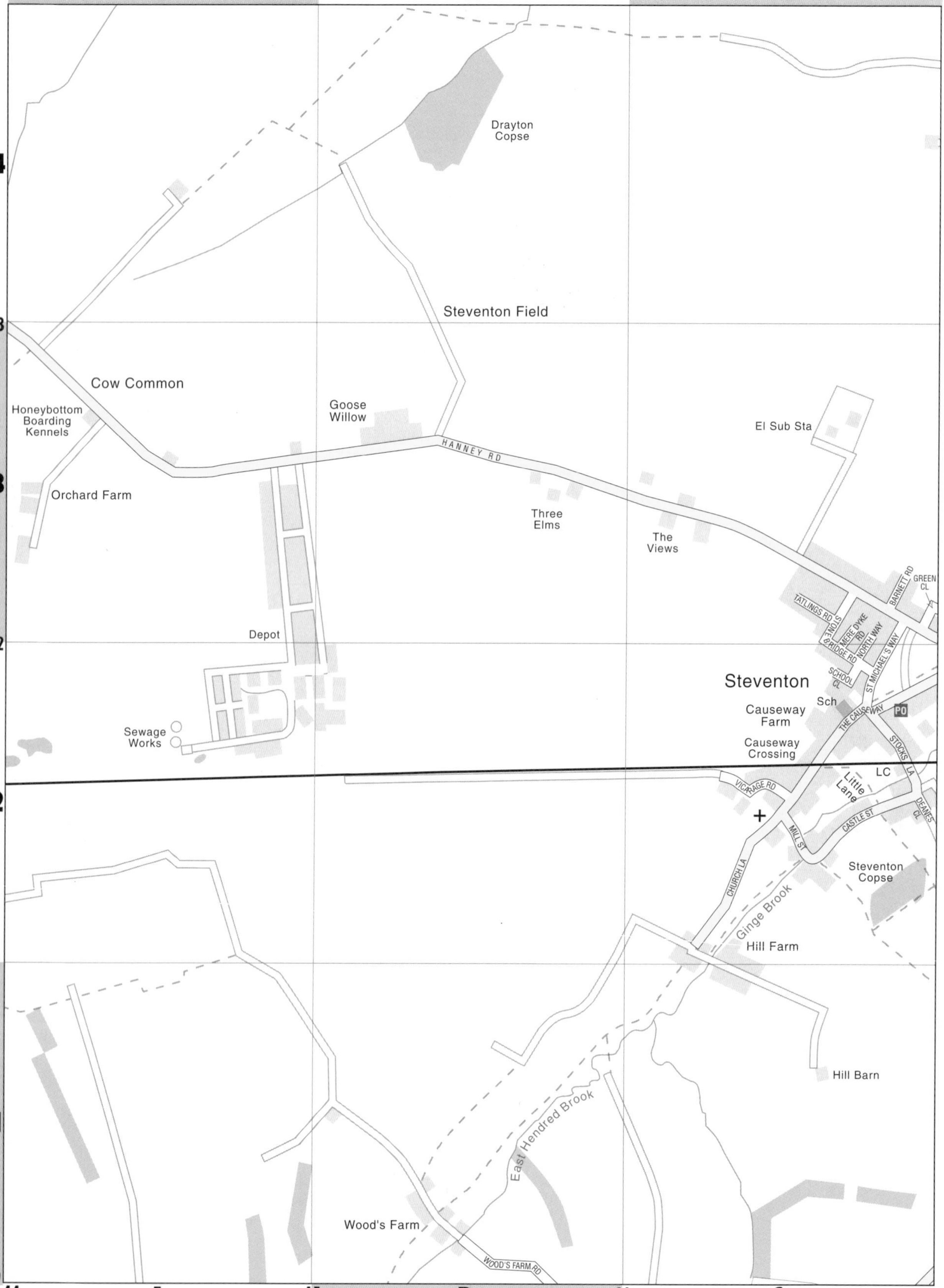

Drayton Copse

Steventon Field

93

Cow Common

Goose Willow

Honeybottom Boarding Kennels

El Sub Sta

HANNEY RD

Orchard Farm

3

Three Elms

The Views

GREEN CL

BARNETT RD

TATLINGS RD

S & RIDGE RD

WELL DYKE RD

NORTH WAY

ST MICHAEL'S WAY

Depot

92

Steventon

SCHOOL CL

Sch

PO

Causeway Farm

THE CAUSEWAY

STOCKS LA

Sewage Works

Causeway Crossing

LC

DEANS CL

2

VICARAGE RD

Little Lane

CASTLE ST

+

MILL ST

Steventon Copse

CHURCH LA

Ginge Brook

91

Hill Farm

Hill Barn

1

East Hendred Brook

Wood's Farm

WOOD'S FARM RD

90

44　　　　　A　　　　　45　　　　　B　　　　　46　　　　　C

199
180

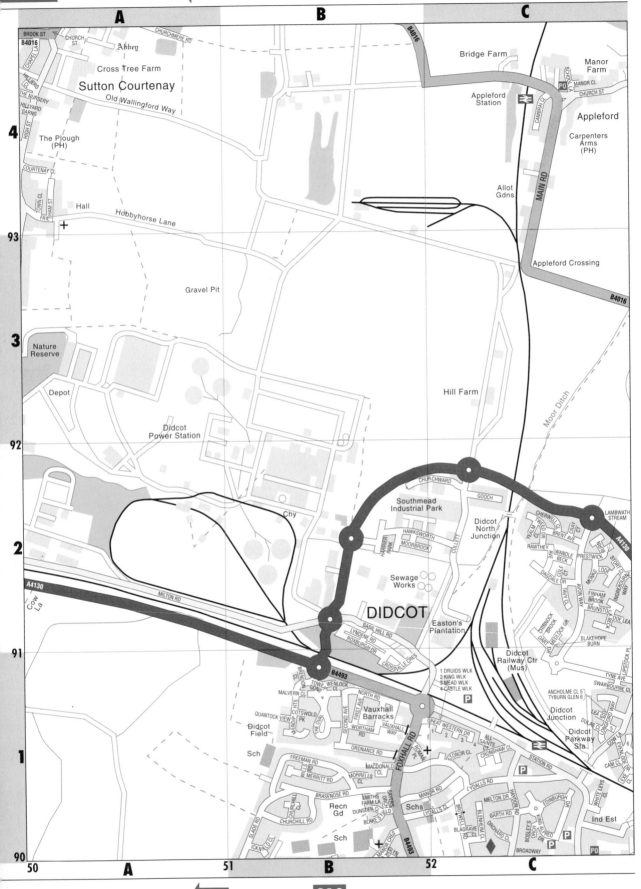

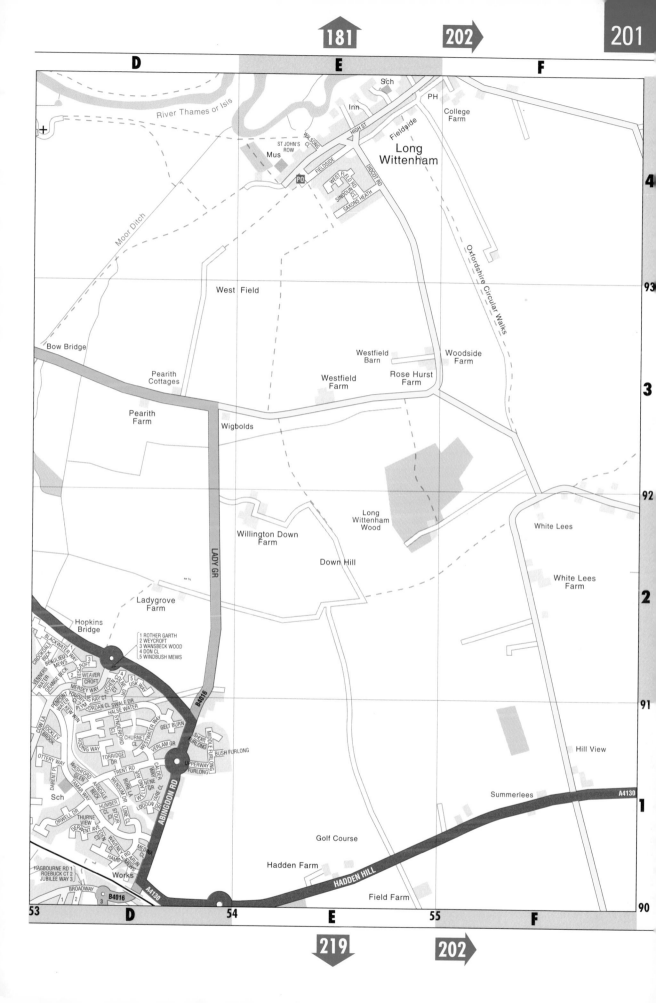

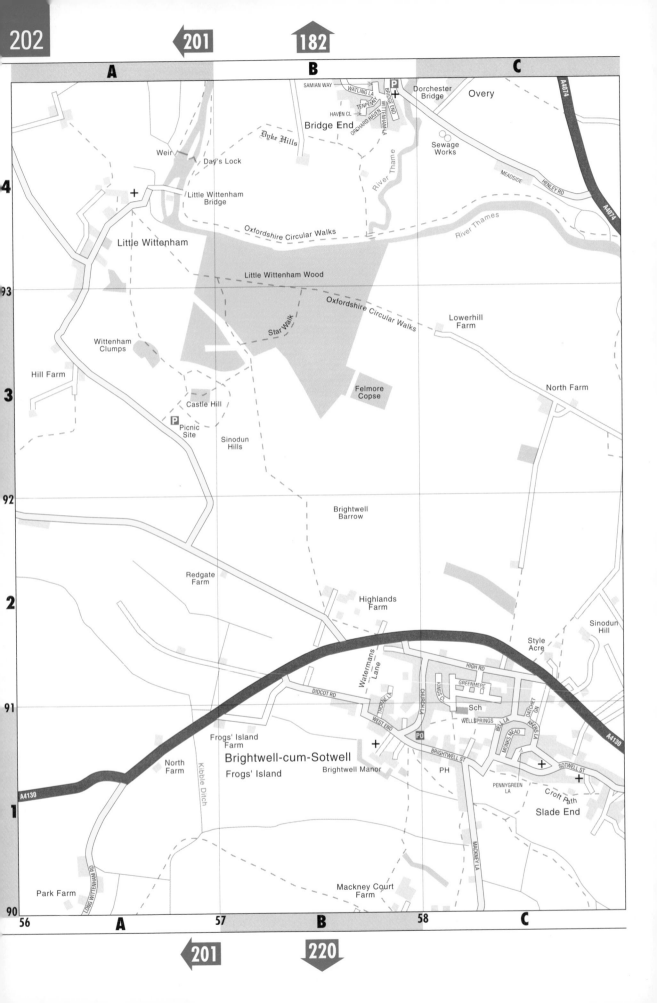

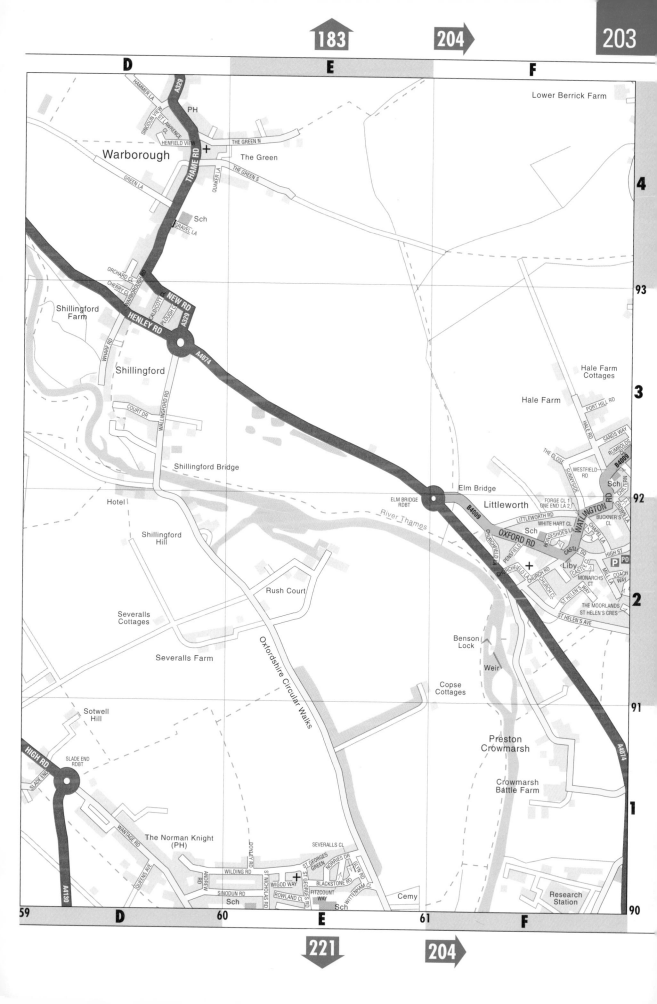

203
184

A **B** **C**

4

Parsonage Farm

Grace's Farm

WELLER CL

Hare Hall

Bunkers

Home Sweet Home (PH)

Scald Hill

Rumbolds Lane

CHAPEL LA

Roke

Rumbold's Copse

93

Roke Farm

The Horse and Harrow (PH)

Rokemarsh

THE SANDS

GROVE LA **B4009**

Port Hill House

BRACE LA

Tidmarsh Lane

3

B4009

WATLINGTON RD

COPPICE LA

NEWTON WAY

BLACKLANDS RD

GREEN CL

THE CEDARS

COTTESMORE LA

Windmill Farm

EYRES LA

Fifield Farm

Cottesmore Farm

Hyde Shaw

WESTFIELD RD

BROOK ST

PASSEY CRES

WYCHWOOD CL

92

OLD BARN CL

The Views

Shepherd's Hut (PH)

FIREBRASS HILL

CROWN SQ

OBSERVATORY LA

PADDOCK CL

Benson

Lower Farm

MARTYN'S WAY

CAT LA

BRITWELL RD

HAMPDEN WAY

CHAUCER CT

PO

1 CROWN LA
2 ALDRIDGE CL
3 THE MOORLANDS

Ewelme

2

ST HELEN'S CRES

OLD LONDON RD

ST HELEN'S AVE

Benson Airfield

Manor House

The Greyhound (PH)

WINGFIELD CL

HIGH ST

BURROWS HILL

PARSON'S LA

Church Farm

Sch

Fords Farm

CLAY LA

BELFAST RD

BLACKLEY CL

ANDOVER RD

SWIFT WAY

DEVON WAY

WHITCHURCH RD

CHIPMUNK RD

VIKING TERR

VALETTA RD

HERON RD

ARGOSY RD

91

ANSON RD

LANCASTER AVE

MOSQUITO LA

JAVELIN WAY

BLENHEIM PL

BATTLE RD

BARNETT WAY

CROSS AVE

BRYONY CL

Rabbits Hill

Cow Common

DAY'S LA

Sch

ALISTER TAYLOR AVE

GEOFFREY TUTTLE RD

ANTHONY HILL RD

FIELDEN RD

MCKEE SQ

FIELDEN CL

COCHRANE RD

BAKER AVE

BAKER CL

Swan's Way

1

BENSON LA

Sewage Wks

A4074

HUDLESTON AVE

BEGGARSBUSH HILL

The London Road (PH)

Mast

Gravel Pit

Marsh Wood

CLACK'S LA

90

62 **A** 63 **B** 64 **C**

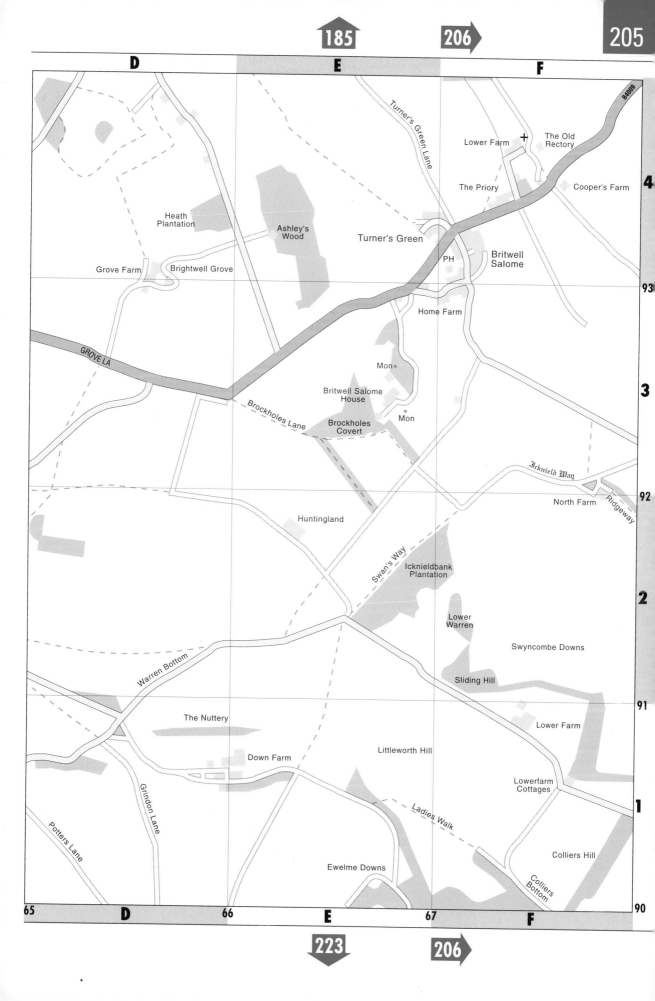

D
E
F

4

Turner's Green Lane

Lower Farm

The Old Rectory

The Priory

Cooper's Farm

Heath Plantation

Ashley's Wood

Turner's Green

PH

Britwell Salome

93

Grove Farm

Brightwell Grove

Home Farm

GROVE LA

Mon

Britwell Salome House

3

Brockholes Lane

Brockholes Covert

Mon

Icknield Way

92

North Farm

Ridgeway

Huntingland

Swan's Way

Icknieldbank Plantation

2

Lower Warren

Swyncombe Downs

Warren Bottom

Sliding Hill

91

The Nuttery

Lower Farm

Littleworth Hill

Down Farm

Lowerfarm Cottages

Grindon Lane

Ladies Walk

1

Potters Lane

Ewelme Downs

Colliers Hill

Colliers Bottom

65
D
66
E
67
F
90

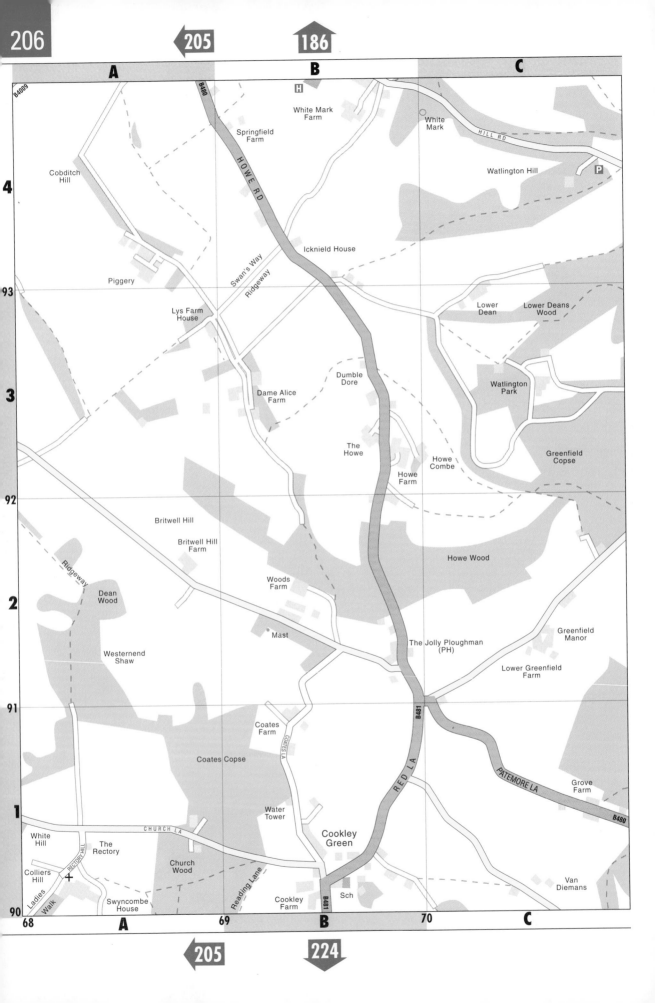

205
186

A   B   C

B4009

B480

H

White Mark Farm

White Mark

HILL RD

Springfield Farm

Watlington Hill

P

4

Cobditch Hill

HOWE RD

Icknield House

Swan's Way

Ridgeway

Lower Dean

Lower Deans Wood

93

Piggery

Lys Farm House

Dumble Dore

Watlington Park

3

Dame Alice Farm

The Howe

Howe Combe

Greenfield Copse

Howe Farm

92

Britwell Hill

Howe Wood

Britwell Hill Farm

Ridgeway

Woods Farm

Greenfield Manor

2

Dean Wood

Mast

The Jolly Ploughman (PH)

Lower Greenfield Farm

Westernend Shaw

91

Coates Farm

COATES LA

B481

PATEMORE LA

Coates Copse

RED LA

Grove Farm

B480

1

Water Tower

CHURCH LA

White Hill

Cookley Green

The Rectory

RECTORY HILL

Colliers Hill

Church Wood

Reading Lane

Van Diemans

Swyncombe House

Cookley Farm

B481

Sch

Ladies Walk

90

68   A   69   B   70   C

205
224

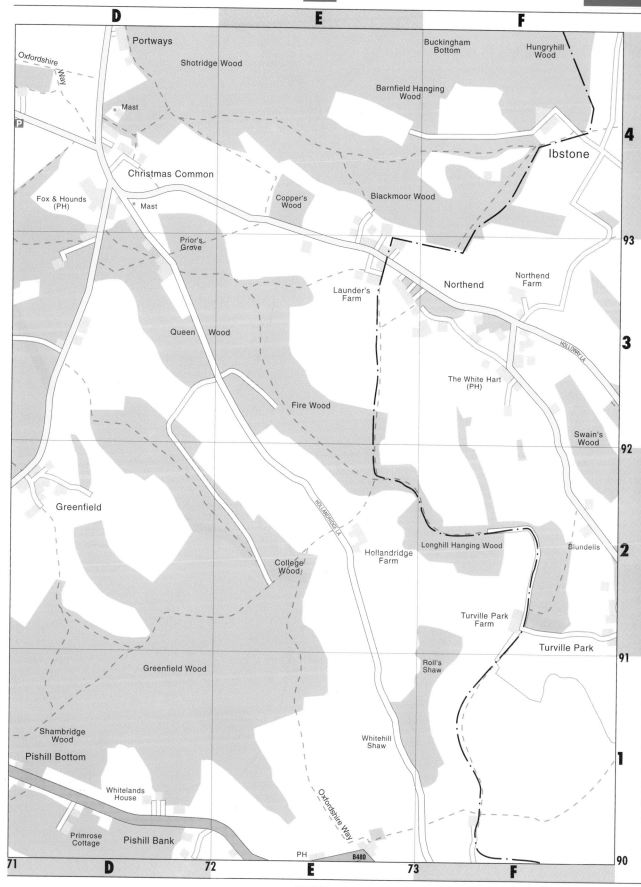

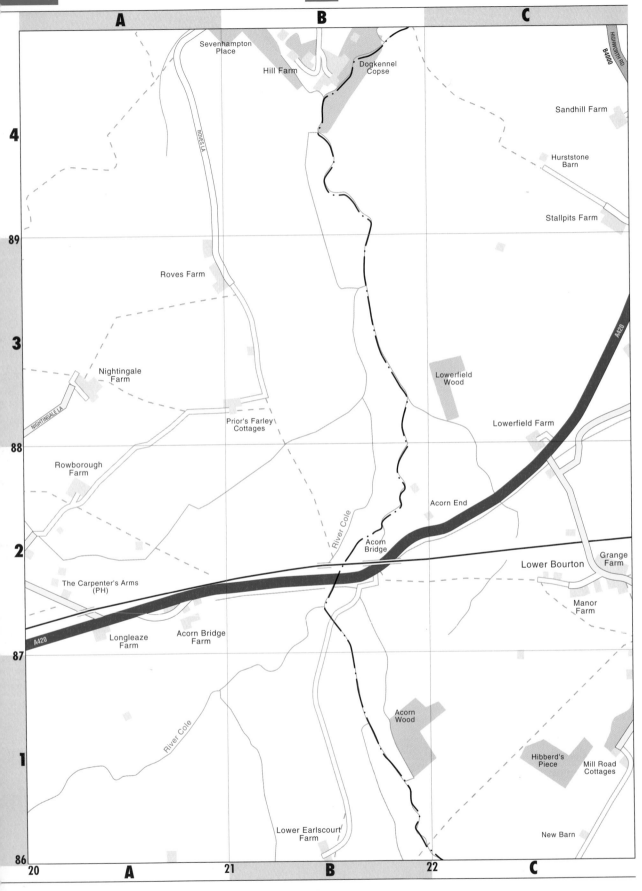

A   B   C

4

89

3

89

2

87

1

86

20   A   21   B   22   C

Sevenhampton Place
Hill Farm
Dogkennel Copse
Sandhill Farm
Hurststone Barn
Stallpits Farm
Roves Farm
ROVES LA
Nightingale Farm
NIGHTINGALE LA
Prior's Farley Cottages
Lowerfield Wood
Lowerfield Farm
Rowborough Farm
River Cole
Acorn End
Acorn Bridge
Lower Bourton
Grange Farm
The Carpenter's Arms (PH)
A420
Manor Farm
Longleaze Farm
Acorn Bridge Farm
River Cole
Acorn Wood
Hibberd's Piece
Mill Road Cottages
Lower Earlscourt Farm
New Barn
B4000
HIGHWORTH RD
A420

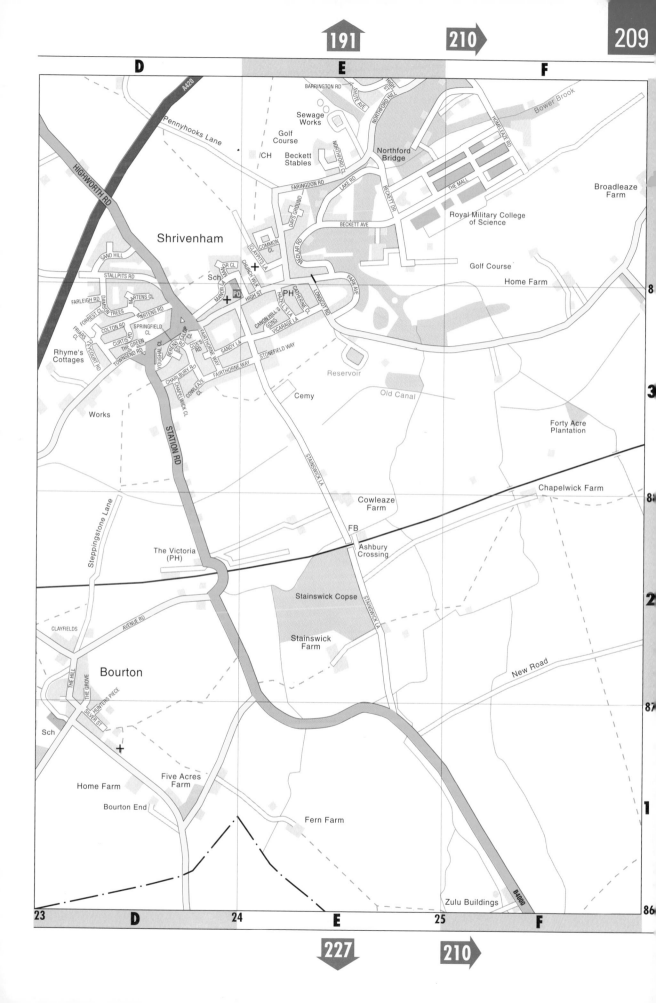

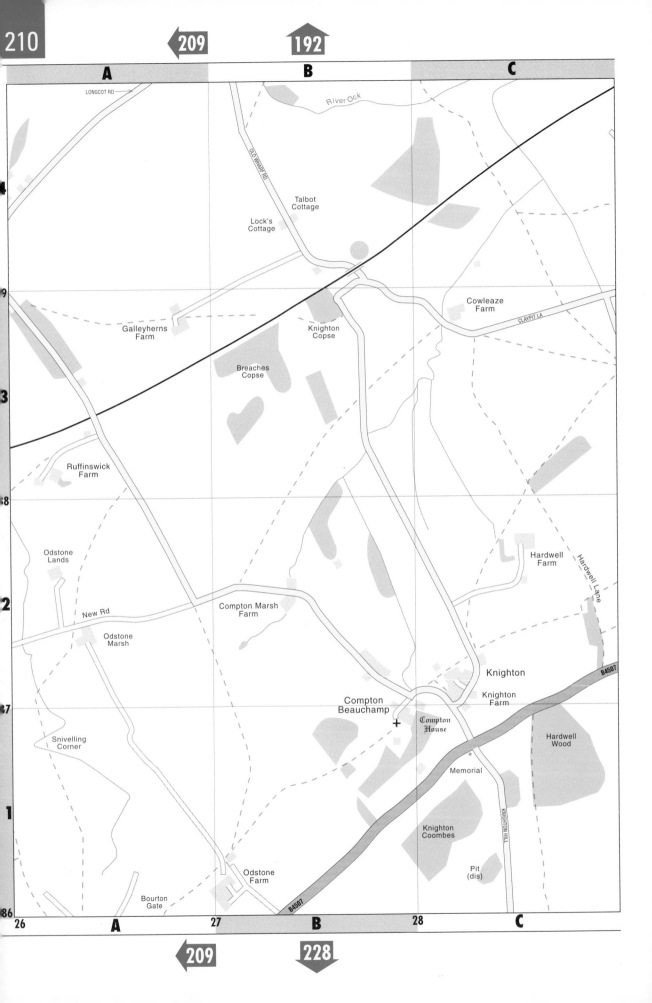

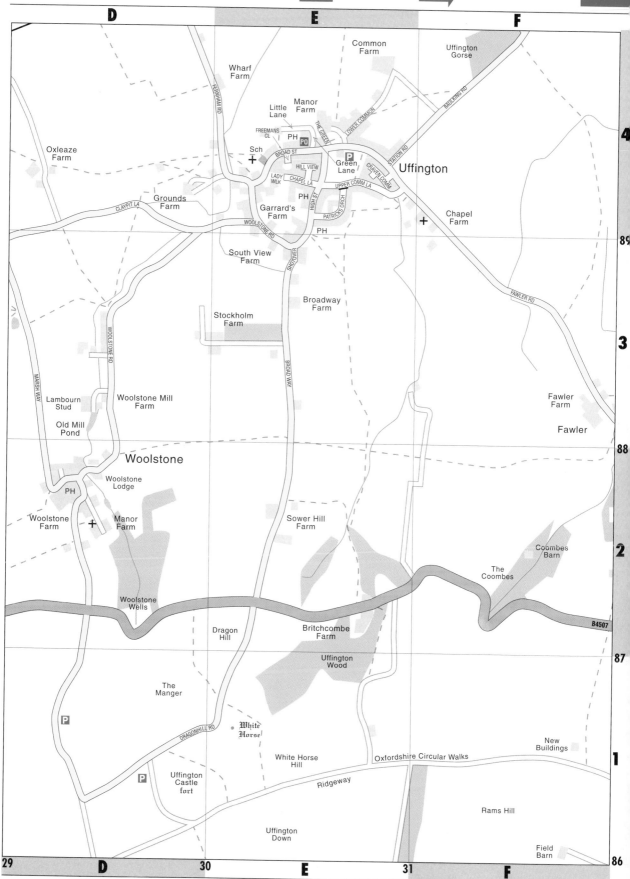

D

E

F

4

89

3

88

2

87

1

86

Common Farm

Wharf Farm

Uffington Gorse

BAULKING RD

Little Lane

Manor Farm

FREEMANS CL

PH

PO

THE GREEN

LOWER COMMON

STATION RD

Sch

BROAD ST

HILL VIEW

P

Green Lane

CRAVEN COMM

Uffington

Oxleaze Farm

FERNHAM RD

LADY WLK

CHAPEL LA

HIGH ST

PH

UPPER COMM LA

Grounds Farm

CLAYPIT LA

Garrard's Farm

PATRICKS ORCH

PH

Chapel Farm

WOOLSTONE RD

South View Farm

SHOTOVER

FAWLER RD

Broadway Farm

Stockholm Farm

BROAD WAY

Fawler Farm

WOOLSTONE RD

MARSH WAY

Lambourn Stud

Woolstone Mill Farm

Fawler

Old Mill Pond

Woolstone

88

PH

Woolstone Lodge

Woolstone Farm

Manor Farm

Sower Hill Farm

Coombes Barn

The Coombes

Woolstone Wells

B4507

Dragon Hill

Britchcombe Farm

Uffington Wood

The Manger

P

DRAGONHILL RD

White Horse

New Buildings

White Horse Hill

Oxfordshire Circular Walks

P

Uffington Castle fort

Ridgeway

Rams Hill

Uffington Down

Field Barn

29

D

30

E

31

F

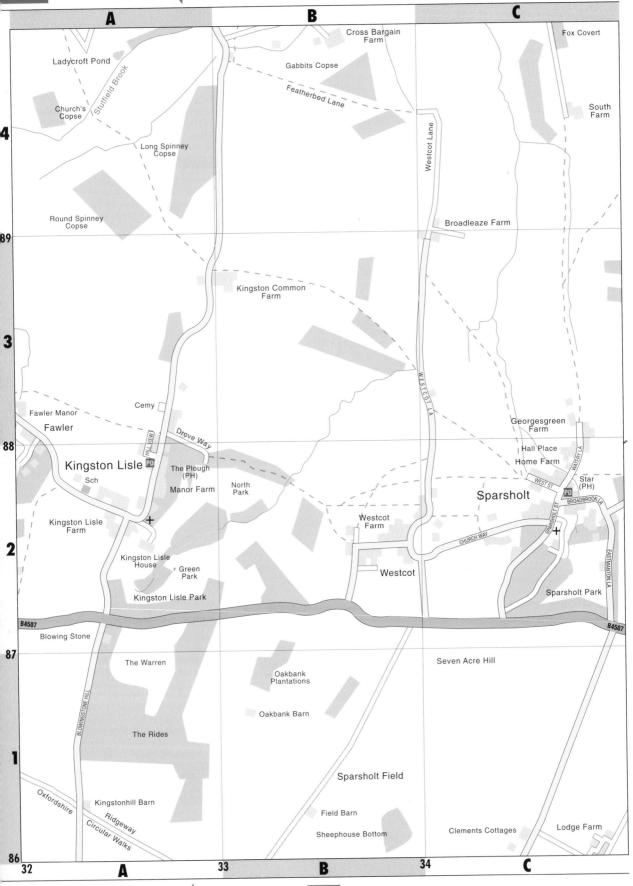

A   **B**   **C**

Ladycroft Pond

Cross Bargain Farm

Fox Covert

Gabbits Copse

Featherbed Lane

Church's Copse

Stutfield Brook

Westcot Lane

South Farm

4

Long Spinney Copse

Broadleaze Farm

Round Spinney Copse

89

Kingston Common Farm

WESTCOT LA

3

Fawler Manor

Fawler

Cemy

Drove Way

HILL VIEW

Georgesgreen Farm

Hall Place

Home Farm

88

Kingston Lisle

PO

Sch

The Plough (PH)

Manor Farm

North Park

Sparsholt

WEST ST

Star (PH)

PO

SPARSHOLT ST

BROADBROOK LA

WATERY LA

Kingston Lisle Farm

Westcot Farm

EASTMANTON LA

2

Kingston Lisle House

Green Park

Westcot

CHURCH WAY

Sparsholt Park

Kingston Lisle Park

B4507

B4507

Blowing Stone

87

The Warren

Seven Acre Hill

Oakbank Plantations

BLOWINGSTONE HILL

Oakbank Barn

The Rides

1

Sparsholt Field

Oxfordshire

Ridgeway

Circular Walks

Kingstonhill Barn

Field Barn

Sheephouse Bottom

Clements Cottages

Lodge Farm

86

32   **A**   **33**   **B**   **34**   **C**

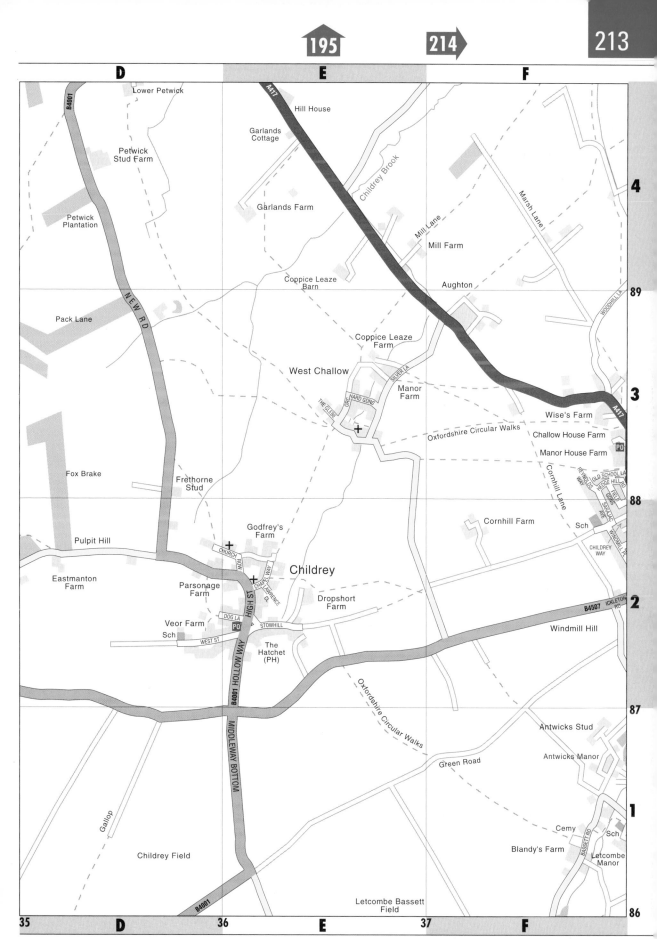

D
E
F

4
89
3
88
2
87
1
86

B4001

A417

Lower Petwick

Hill House

Garlands
Cottage

Petwick
Stud Farm

Childrey Brook

Garlands Farm

Mill Lane

Marsh Lane

Petwick
Plantation

Mill Farm

NEW RD

Coppice Leaze
Barn

Aughton

Woodhill La

Pack Lane

Coppice Leaze
Farm

West Challow

SILVER LA

Manor
Farm

A417

Wise's Farm

THE GLEBE

ORCHARD GDNS

Oxfordshire Circular Walks

Challow House Farm

PO

Manor House Farm

Fox Brake

Frethorne
Stud

Cornhill Lane

REYNOLDS WAY

OLD SCHOOL LA

HEDGE HILL RD

FELT

Sch

HEDGE HILL RD

SARUAC

AIRE

Pulpit Hill

Godfrey's
Farm

Cornhill Farm

Sch

CHILDREY
WAY

Eastmanton
Farm

CHURCH ROW

Childrey

WINDMILL PL

CHILDREY
WAY

Parsonage
Farm

CHAPEL WAY

LAWRENCE CL

Dropshort
Farm

B4507

ICKLETON RD

HIGH ST

Veor Farm

DOG LA

Windmill Hill

PO

Sch

WEST ST

STOWHILL

2

The
Hatchet
(PH)

Oxfordshire Circular Walks

B4001 HOLLOW WAY

87

Antwicks Stud

MIDDLEWAY BOTTOM

Green Road

Antwicks Manor

Gallop

1

Cemy

Sch

BASSETT RD

Childrey Field

Blandy's Farm

Letcombe
Manor

B4001

Letcombe Bassett
Field

86

35
D
36
E
37
F

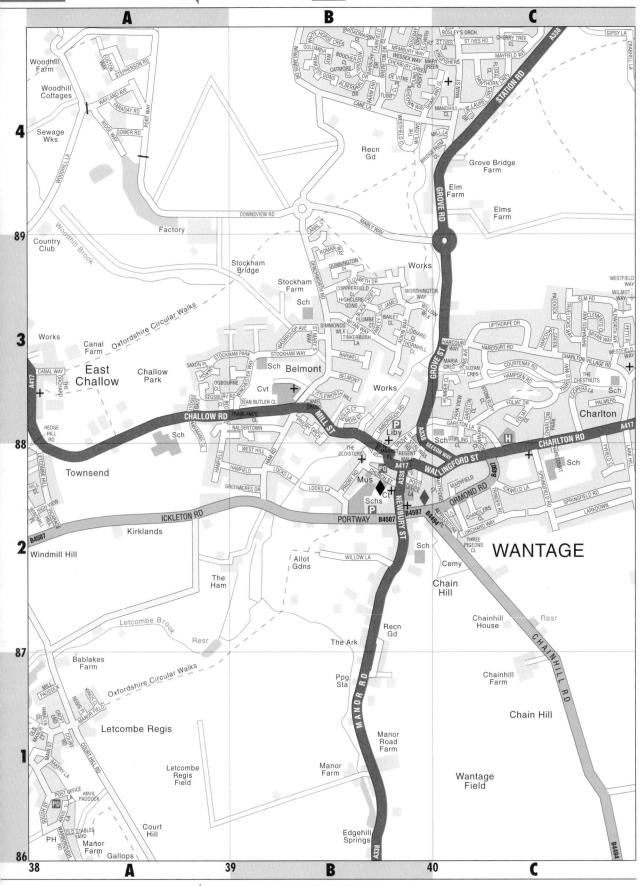

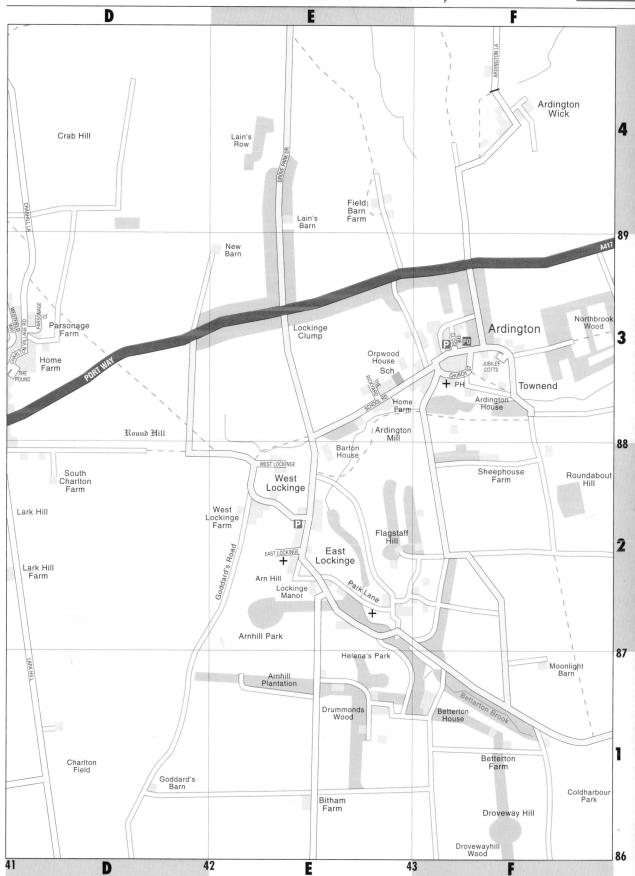

4

Crab Hill

Lain's
Row

Ardington
Wick

ARDINGTON LA

GROVE PARK DR

Lain's
Barn

Field
Barn
Farm

Northbrook
Wood

A417

89

New
Barn

CRABHILL LA

WESTFIELD WAY

OLD ICKNIELD WAY

PARSONAGE CL

Parsonage
Farm

Lockinge
Clump

Ardington

THE CLOSE
PO
P

CHARLTON

Home
Farm

THE
POUND

PORT WAY

Orpwood
House
Sch

THE RICKYARD

SCHOOL RD

Home
Farm

CHURCH ST

PH

JUBILEE
COTTS

Ardington
House

Townend

3

Round Hill

Ardington
Mill

88

South
Charlton
Farm

WEST LOCKINGE

West
Lockinge

Barton
House

Sheephouse
Farm

Roundabout
Hill

Lark Hill

West
Lockinge
Farm

P

Goddard's Road

Flagstaff
Hill

2

Lark Hill
Farm

EAST LOCKINGE

East
Lockinge

Arn Hill

Lockinge
Manor

Park Lane

LARK HILL

Arnhill Park

Helena's Park

Moonlight
Barn

87

Charlton
Field

Arnhill
Plantation

Betterton Brook

Drummonds
Wood

Betterton
House

Goddard's
Barn

Betterton
Farm

1

Bitham
Farm

Droveway Hill

Coldharbour
Park

Drovewayhill
Wood

86

215
198

A   B   C

4

Quab Hill

Quab Hill Farm

FEATHERBED LA

East Hendred Brook

Ludbridge Mill (disused)

Greensands

WOOD'S FARM RD

New Barn

Lud Bridge

A417

The Hare Inn

READING RD

Sheephouse Barn

ALLIN'S LA

SMITHS HOME FARM CL

RICKYARD CL

COULINGS CL

ORCHARD CL

WHITE RD

East Hendred

89

A417

THE GREENWAY

BANKSIDE

PO

MILL LA

ORCHARD LA

OLD RD

MILL LA

Recreation Ground

CHAPEL CL

CAT ST

ST HIGH

PO

Chapel

Eyston Arms (PH)

The Mill

Sewage Works

FORD LA

Hendred House

West Hendred

Sch

THE MILLHAM

Hall

MANOR LA

CHURCH ST

HORN LA

NEWBURY RD

ST MAIN

Sch

3

The Moors

Lockinge Brook

THE LYNCH

Hill Farm

COW Road

Lydebank Plantation

Red Barn

Goldbury Hill

Park Hill

88

Ginge Brook

Park Hill Row

Icknield

Aldfield Common

Pump House

Shadwell's Row

2

Black Mills Row

Parsonage Barn

Stileway Road

87

Lower Farm

Ellaway's Barn

TWENTIETH ST

West Ginge

Ginge House

East Ginge

Deer Park

1

Upper Farm

Ginge Manor

Downs Cottage

Stileway Road

Meashill Plantation

White Way

86

44   A   45   B   46   C

215
234

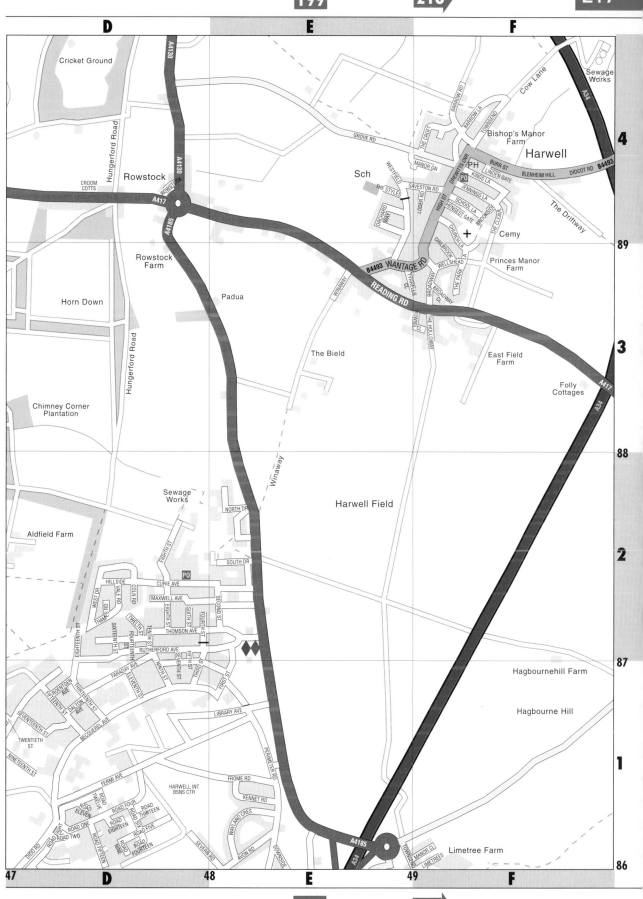

Cricket Ground

Sewage
Works

Cow Lane

Bishop's Manor
Farm

Harwell

GROVE RD

BARROW RD
BARROW LA
TOWNSEND
THE CROFT

MANOR GN

BURR ST
LINDEN GATE
BLENHEIM HILL
DIDCOT RD

PH
PO
KINGS LA

Sch

WESTFIELD
THE STYLES
GAVESTON RD
LODER RD
JENNINGS LA
HIGH ST
SCHOOL LA
HENGEST GATE
BROOKSIDE
THE CLEAVE

ORCHARD WAY

The Driftway

Croom
Cotts

Rowstock

A4130
ROWSTOCK
A417

A4185

A417
A34

B4493

89

Cemy
+
CHURCH LA
CHILBROOK

Princes Manor
Farm

Rowstock
Farm

B4493 WANTAGE RD
READING RD

WINAWAY

TYRRELLS CL
THE DOWNS
BROADWAY
BROADWAY CL
THE PARK
WELLSHEAD
THE HOLLOWAY

Padua

Horn Down

Hungerford Road

Chimney Corner
Plantation

The Bield

East Field
Farm

Folly
Cottages

Winaway

Harwell Field

3

88

Aldfield Farm

Sewage
Works

NORTH DR

EIGHTH ST
PO
SOUTH DR
SECOND ST

Hagbournehill Farm

Hagbourne Hill

2

87

HILLSIDE
WEST DR
VALE RD
COLN RD
CURIE AVE
MAXWELL AVE
EIGHTH ST
SIXTH ST
SECOND ST
CLUB
THAMES
SIXTEENTH ST
TWELFTH ST
FOURTEENTH ST
TENTH ST
THOMSON AVE
FOURTH ST
FIFTH ST

FARADAY AVE
ELEVENTH ST
NINTH ST
SEVENTH ST
RUTHERFORD AVE
FIFTH ST
QUINII ST
FIRST ST

EIGHTEENTH ST

ROENTGEN AVE
THIRTEENTH ST
DALTON AVE
FIFTEENTH ST

SEVENTEENTH ST

TWENTIETH ST

NINETEENTH ST

BECQUEREL AVE

LIBRARY AVE

FERMI AVE

PERIMETER RD

1

HARWELL INT
BSNS CTR

ROAD
TWELVE
ROAD
ELEVEN
ROAD EIGHT
ROAD ONE
ROAD TWO
ROAD FIFTEEN
ROAD
EIGHTEEN
ROAD
NINE
ROAD FOUR
ROAD THIRTEEN
ROAD FIVE
ROAD SIX
ROAD
FOURTEEN

DIDCOT RD

FROME RD
KENNET RD
WAYLAND CRES
SEVERN RD
AVON RD
DOWNSIDE

A4185
A34

TOWNSEND
MANOR CL
LIMETREES

Limetree Farm

86

A **B** **C**

OXFORD CRES
SLADE RD
PIXTON CL
SHERWOOD RD
WANTAGE RD
B4493
MANOR CRES
GLYN AVE
BROADWAY
ST PETER'S RD
ST ANDREW'S RD
VICARAGE RD
CHURCH ST
WESSEX RD
BOURNE ST
HIGH ST

Zulu Farm

DIDCOT RD

Alma Barn

ELBOURNE
BARLEY FLDS

COLLINGWOOD RD
DRAKE AVE
COLBORNE RD
NORREY'S RD
PARK RD
PARK RD
EDMONDS CT
PRIEST RD
FAIRACRES RD
SAMOR WAY

H

Ct Liby

PO

KYNASTON RD
LABURNUM GR

Cemy

Down Farm

WHEATFIELDS
MEADOW WAY
BRUNEL RD
MORREY'S CL
PARK CL

Edmunds Park

OATLAND RD
NEWLANDS AVE
CRAWN WRAYN
GLEBE RD
CLARENCE PL

Schs

THE CROFT
MERELAND RD
RICHMERE RD
RIDGEWAY RD
LYNDOUN RD

4

B4493

A34

GARDEN CL
PORTWAY

BOWNESS AVE
SOUTH PARK AVE
DOWNS AVE
TAVISTOCK AVE

Swimming Pool

ABBOTT RD
ABBOTT CL
ABBOTT RD

DIDCOT

ROYAL BERKSHIRE CT

BISHOPS ORCH

89

The Driftway

WARNER CRES
MORSE CL
EDWIN RD
LOYD RD
BARNES CL
BARNES RD
COXCROFT RD
QUEENSWAY
MOWBRAY RD

Sch
HARDINGS STRINGS

GREEN RD
GREEN CL

Playing Field

West Hagbourne Field

Coscote

East Hagbourne

WINDSOR CRES
LAKE RD
HARWOOD RD
WILCHER CL
NORTH CROFT

BAKERS LA

3

A417

Yew Tree Farm

UPPER CROSS LA 1
SHOE LA 2
Hall
MAIN RD

Sch
THE CROFT

PO
KINGSHOLME CL

Hakka's Brook

88

BROOK LA

MANOR CL
YORK RD
PO
FOXGLOVE LA
MAIN ST

Grove Farm

Manor Farm

Church Farm

Manor Farm

2

Pumping Station

Pumping Station

PH

West Hagbourne

NEWMANS CL

Common Barn

Common Lane

87

CHILTON RD

BEECHING CL
STATION RD
PROSPECT RD
FIELDSIDE
PO
POUND
PIDDINGTON
ORCHARD DR
CHURCH ST
STREAM RD

Owlscote Manor Farm

Frogalley Farm

Sewage Works

ALEXANDER CL
PH
HIGH ST

Upton

1

Lynch Way

Hollow Way

Upton Lodge

LONDON RD

WESTBROOK ST

Sch

86

A417

50 **A** **51** **B** **52** **C**

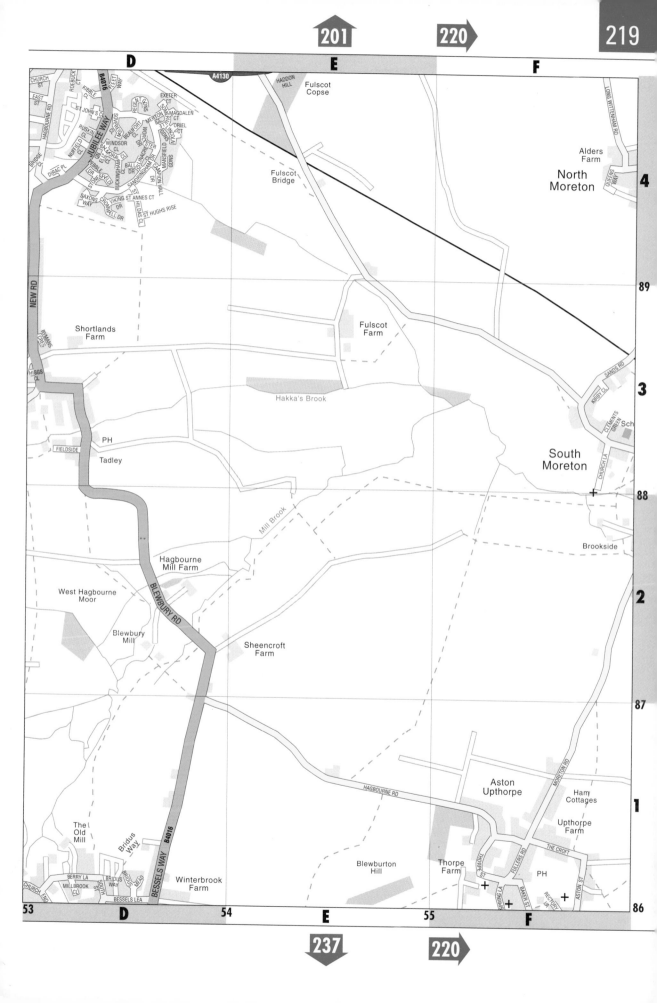

A **B** **C**

Mackney

MACKNEY LA

Sherwood
Farm

Kibble Ditch

4

ELM RD

LONG WITTENHAM RD

The Bear
(PH)

HIGH ST

BEAR LA

DUNSOMER HILL

89

Mill Brook

Glebe
Cottage

Hithercroft
Farm

3

HITHERCROFT

The Crown
(PH)

CROWN LA

PAPER MILL LA

Pumping
Station

MILL LA

88

Cholsey Hill

ANCHOR LA

Hillgreen
Farm

MORETON RD

The Manor

Sewage
Works

2

Poultry
Farm

Manor
Farm

CHURCH RD

87

GOLDFINCH LA

Red Lion
(PH)

The
Lees

Schs

MARYMEAD

WALLINGFORD RD

CROSS RD

PO

CHEQUERS PL

THE
FORTY

ILGES LA

Lees
Cottages

POUND LA

1

West
End

STATION RD

DROVESIDE RD

PATTENDOSTER LA

ANNE CL

L PL

COLLEGE CL

PANTERS

FAIR CL

QUEENS CL

KENNEDY CRES

WEST END

SANDY LA

BRICK

FORD CL

BROOK

CRESCENT WAY

HONEY LA

BUCK
THORN
LA

Pancroft
Farm

WESTFIELD
RD

KENTWOOD
CL

The
Elms

Cholsey
Station

PAPIST WAY

86

56 **A** 57 **B** 58 **C**

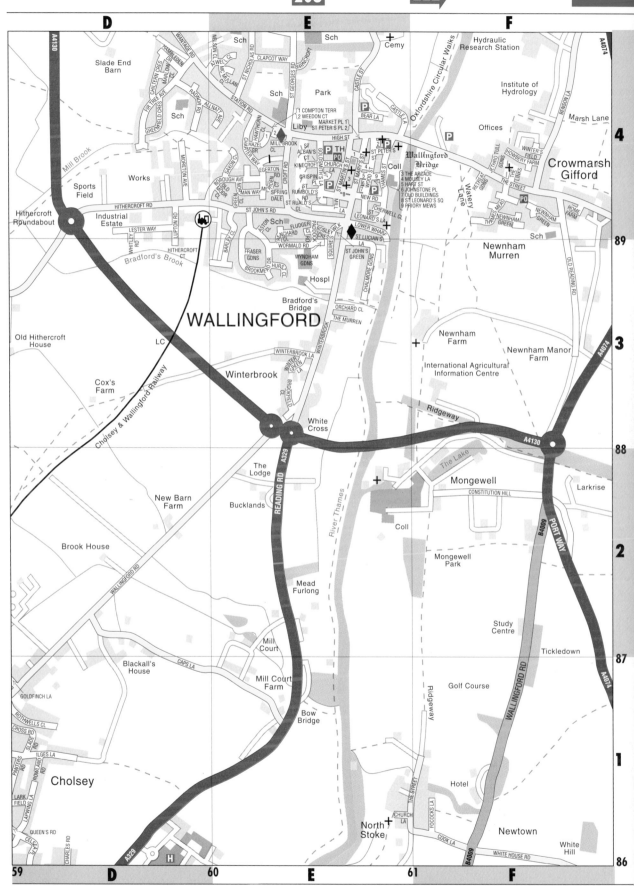

D
E
F

4

89

3

88

2

87

1

86

A4130

Slade End Barn

WANTAGE RD

Sch

NELSON CL

ST NICHOLAS RD

CLAPCOT WAY

Sch

BARNCROFT

ST GEORGES RD

Sch

Cemy

CASTLE ST

Oxfordshire Circular Walks

Hydraulic Research Station

A4074

CHILTERN AVE

HAMBLEDEN

MARLOW

FIR TREE AVE

GREENFIELD CRES

RADNOR CL

ALLNATT AVE

STATION RD

HAWTHORN CL

HAZEL CL

Sch

Park

CASTLE LA

BEAR LA

Institute of Hydrology

Marsh Lane

BENSON LA

Offices

HOWBERY FARM

WINTER'S FARM

4

CHATTER WAY

Liby

MILL BROOK CL

1 Compton Terr
2 Weedon Ct
Market Pl 1
St Peter's Pl 2

High St

ST PETER'S

Wallingford Bridge

P

P

Mill Brook

Works

SAXON CL

EGERTON RD

CROFT RD

ST ALBAN'S CT

KINECROFT

GOLDSMITHS LA

TH PO

ST MARTIN'S ST

ST PETER'S

Coll

JETHRO TULL GDNS

THE LINKS

THE STREET

Crowmarsh Gifford

PO

Sports Field

Hithercroft Roundabout

Industrial Estate

HITHERCROFT RD

LESTER WAY

WHITLEY RD

MORETON AVE

BOROUGH AVE

MAN WAY

PRYEN CL

GREEN CL

BARLEY CL

ST JOHN'S RD

GRISPIN PL

RUMBOLD'S LA

SPRING DALE

CHURCH LA

NEW RD

3 The Arcade
4 Mousey La
5 Hart St
6 Johnstone Pl
7 Old Buildings
8 St Leonard's Sq
9 Priory Mews

THAMES ST

CHERWELL CL

Watery Lane

RETREAT GDNS

THAMES MEAD

NEWNHAM GREEN

Newnham Green

HOME FARM

89

Bradford's Brook

CT

HITHERCROFT CT

LUPTON RD

ASTON CL

Sch

FLUDGER CL

BOSLEY CRES

SQUIRES WALK

ST RUALD'S

WORMALD RD

ST LEONARD'S LA

Lower Wharf

ST LUCIAN'S LA

Newnham Murren

OLD READING RD

Sch

FRASER GDNS

BROOKMEAD DR

HURST CL

WYNDHAM GDNS

Hospl

CHALMORE GDNS

ST JOHN'S GREEN

ORCHARD CL

WALLINGFORD

Bradford's Bridge

The Murren

Newnham Farm

Newnham Manor Farm

A4074

Old Hithercroft House

LC

WINTERBROOK LA

WINTERBROOK

BROOKMEAD

International Agricultural Information Centre

Ridgeway

3

Cholsey & Wallingford Railway

Winterbrook

Cox's Farm

White Cross

The Lodge

READING RD

A329

The Lake

A4130

88

New Barn Farm

Bucklands

River Thames

Mongewell

Larkrise

CONSTITUTION HILL

B4009

PORT WAY

Brook House

Coll

Mongewell Park

2

WALLINGFORD RD

CAPS LA

Mead Furlong

Study Centre

Tickledown

A4074

87

Blackall's House

GOLDFINCH LA

ROTHWELLS CL

CROSS RD

SLADE END

ILGES LA

Mill Court

Mill Court Farm

Ridgeway

Golf Course

WALLINGFORD RD

B4009

1

Cholsey

PANTERS RD

ROWLAND RD

LAPWING LA

LARK FIELD

QUEEN'S RD

CELE

CHARLES RD

Bow Bridge

THE STREET

Hotel

Newtown

White Hill

North Stoke

CHURCH LA

FOGOCKS LA

COOK LA

WHITE HOUSE RD

86

A329

H

239

222

59
60
61

D
E
F

221
204

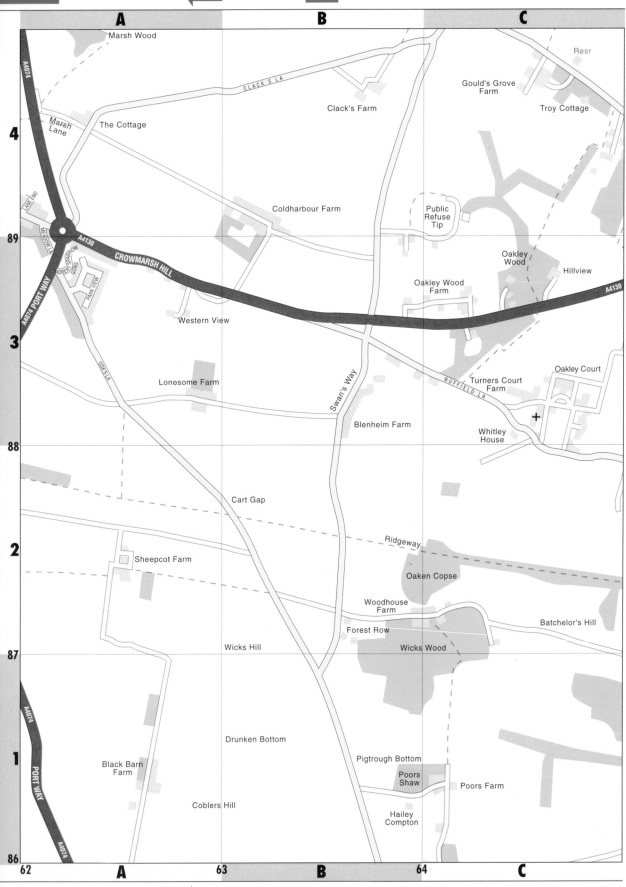

Marsh Wood

A4074

CLACK'S LA

Clack's Farm

Gould's Grove Farm

Resr

4 Marsh Lane

The Cottage

Troy Cottage

Coldharbour Farm

Public Refuse Tip

Oakley Wood

Hillview

LANE END

89

MEADOW LA

A4130

ROBERT SPARROW GDNS

CROWMARSH HILL

Oakley Wood Farm

A4130

PARK VIEW

Western View

3 A4074 PORT WAY

COX'S LA

Lonesome Farm

Swan's Way

NUFFIELD LA

Turners Court Farm

Oakley Court

Blenheim Farm

Whitley House

+

88

Cart Gap

Ridgeway

2

Sheepcot Farm

Oaken Copse

Batchelor's Hill

Woodhouse Farm

Forest Row

Wicks Wood

87 Wicks Hill

Drunken Bottom

Pigtrough Bottom

1 A4074

PORT WAY

Black Barn Farm

Poors Shaw

Poors Farm

Coblers Hill

Hailey Compton

A4074

86

62 **A** 63 **B** 64 **C**

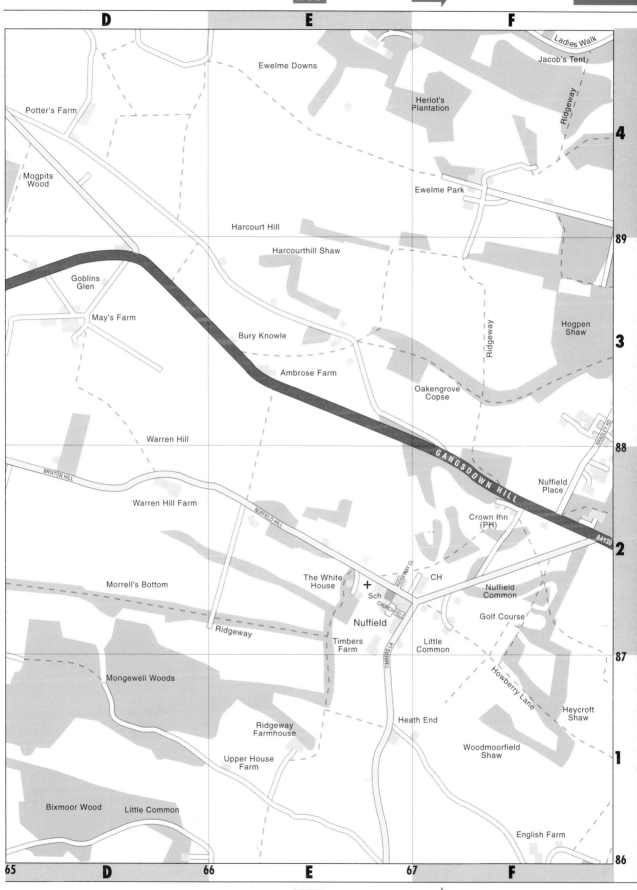

Ladies Walk
Jacob's Tent
Ewelme Downs
Heriot's Plantation
Ridgeway
Potter's Farm
Mogpits Wood
Ewelme Park
Harcourt Hill
Harcourthill Shaw
Goblins Glen
May's Farm
Bury Knowle
Ridgeway
Hogpen Shaw
Ambrose Farm
Oakengrove Copse
Warren Hill
GANGSDOWN HILL
Nuffield Place
BRIXTON HILL
Warren Hill Farm
NUFFIELD HILL
Crown Inn (PH)
A4130
Morrell's Bottom
The White House
Sch
CH
Nuffield Common
Golf Course
RIDGEWAY CL
Ridgeway
CHURCHFIELD
Nuffield
Timbers Farm
Little Common
Mongewell Woods
TIMBERS LA
Howbery Lane
Heycroft Shaw
Heath End
Ridgeway Farmhouse
Woodmoorfield Shaw
Upper House Farm
Bixmoor Wood
Little Common
English Farm
BRADLEY RD

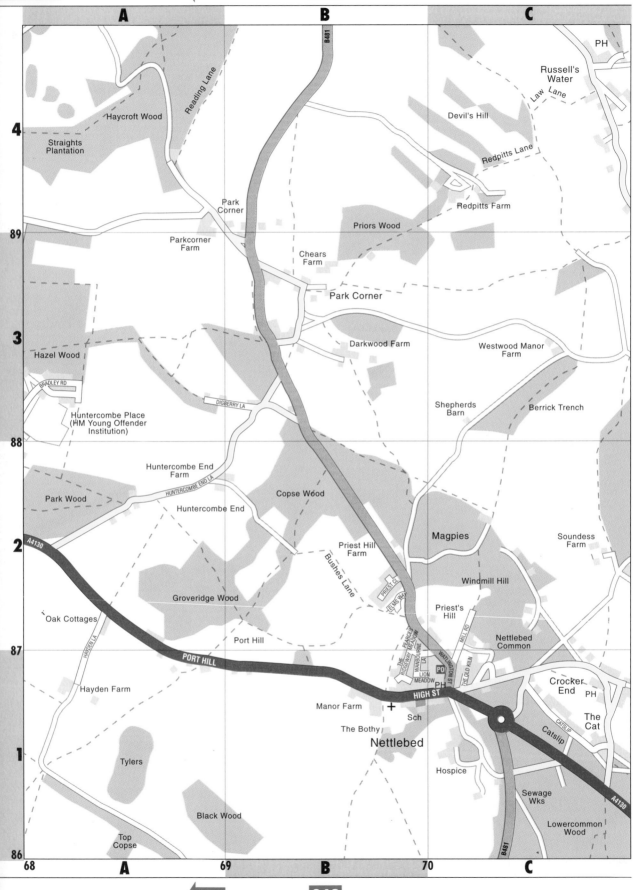

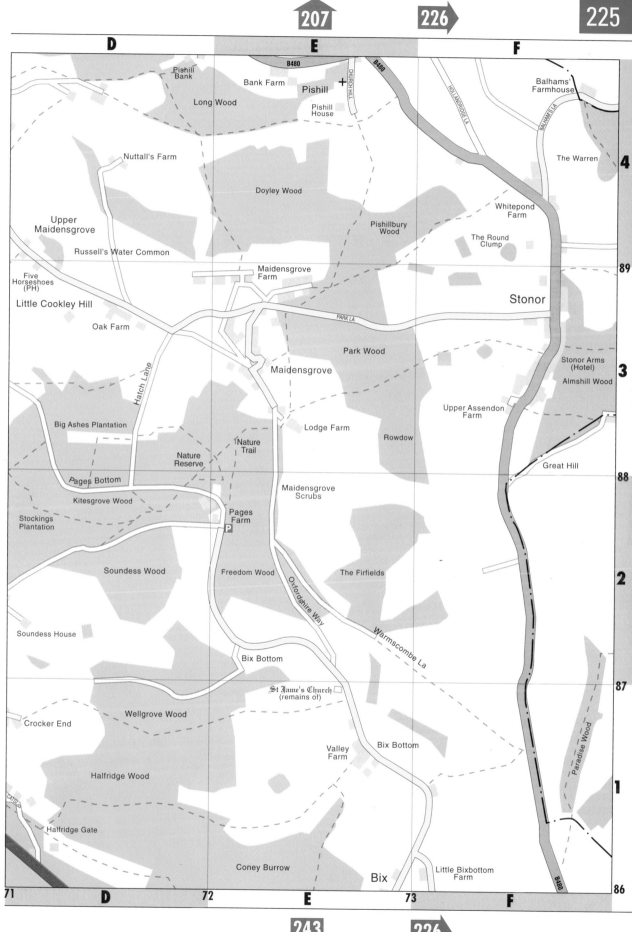

225

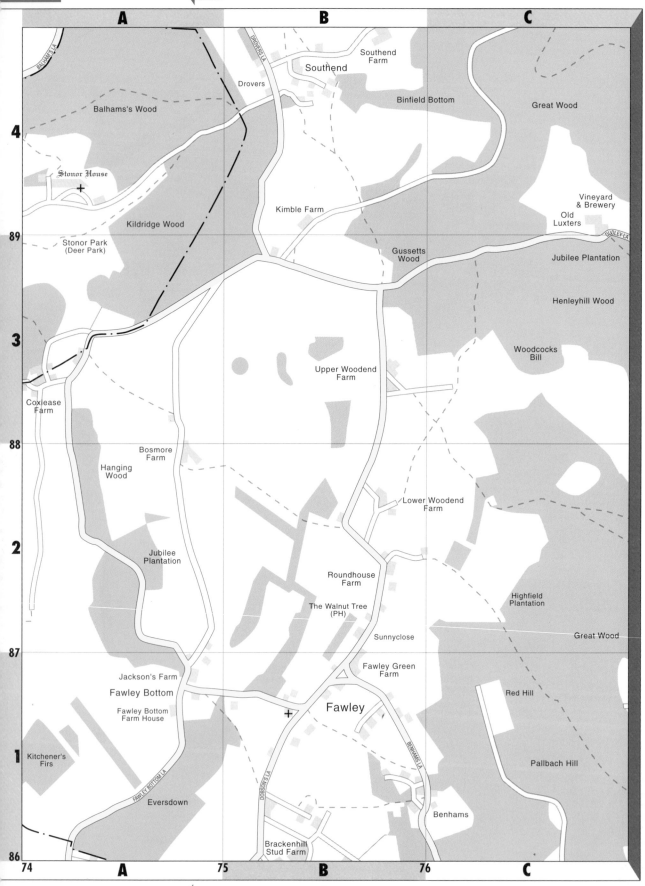

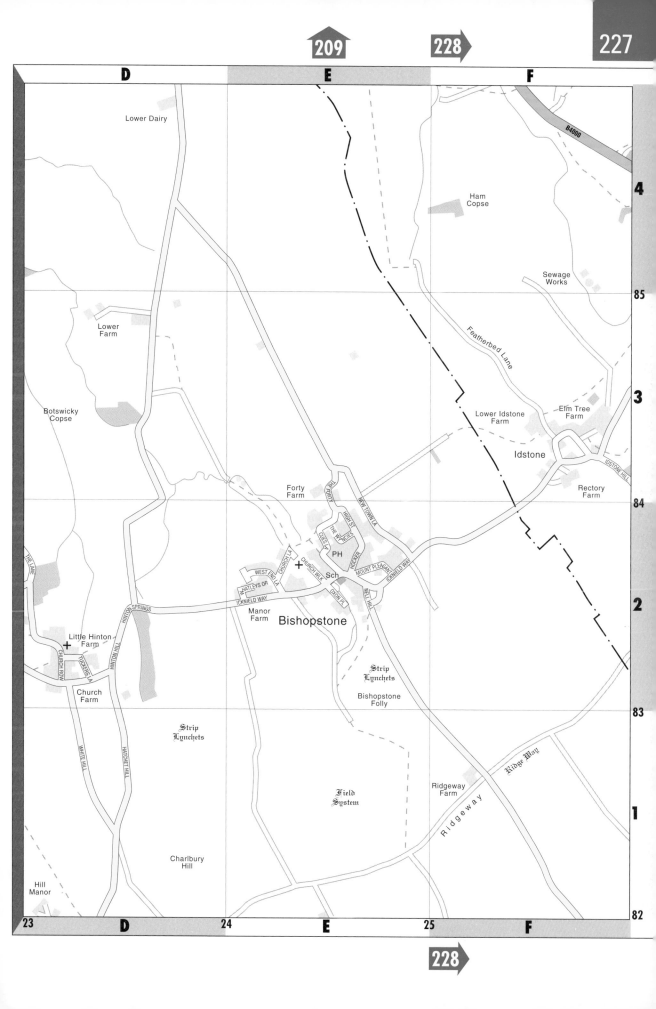

D E F

4

Lower Dairy

B4000

Ham Copse

Sewage Works

85

Lower Farm

Featherbed Lane

3

Botswicky Copse

Lower Idstone Farm

Elm Tree Farm

Idstone

IDSTONE HILL

Forty Farm

NEW TOWN LA

Rectory Farm

84

THE PORTY

HIGH ST

CUES LA

THE WYNCIES

HOOKER

PH

MOUNT PLEASANT WAY

WEST END LA

CHURCH LA

CHURCH WLK

Sch

OXON PL

ICKNIELD WAY

NELL HILL

THE LANE

HATLEYS OR

ICKNIELD WAY

HINTON SPRINGS

Manor Farm

Bishopstone

2

Little Hinton Farm

CHURCH ROW

TUCKERS LA

HINTON DOWN

Strip Lynchets

Church Farm

Bishopstone Folly

83

WHITE HILL

HATCHET HILL

Strip Lynchets

Ridgeway Farm

Ridge Way

Field System

Ridgeway

1

Charlbury Hill

Hill Manor

82

227
210

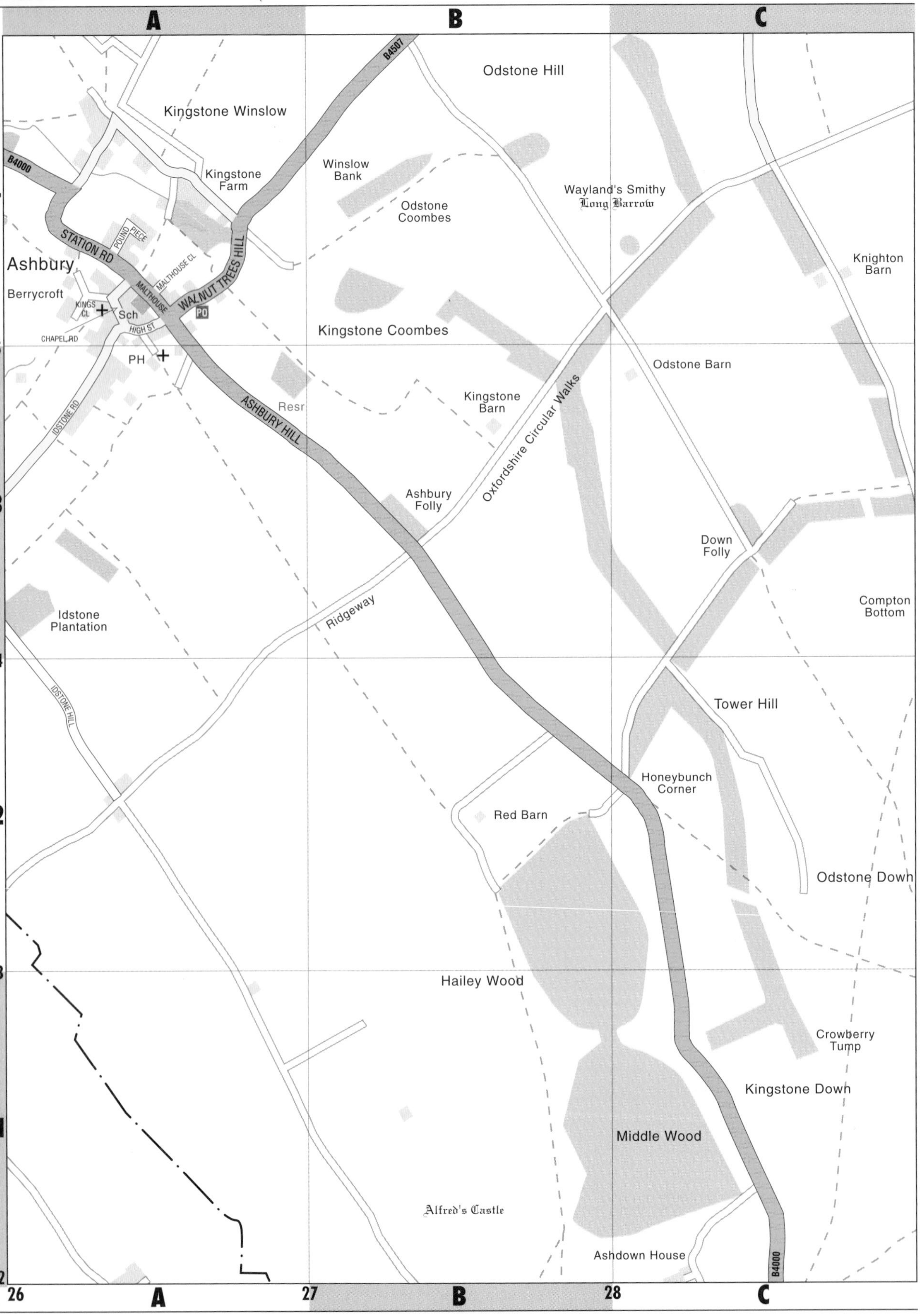

A
B
C
4
85
3
84
2
83
1
82
26
27
28
B4507
B4000
Odstone Hill
Kingstone Winslow
Kingstone Farm
Winslow Bank
Odstone Coombes
Wayland's Smithy
Long Barrow
Knighton Barn
Ashbury
Berrycroft
STATION RD
POUND PIECE
MALTHOUSE CL
MALTHOUSE
WALNUT TREES HILL
PO
KINGS CL
Sch
HIGH ST
CHAPEL RD
PH
Kingstone Coombes
Odstone Barn
Kingstone Barn
Resr
ASHBURY HILL
IDSTONE RD
Oxfordshire Circular Walks
Ashbury Folly
Down Folly
Compton Bottom
Ridgeway
Idstone Plantation
IDSTONE HILL
Tower Hill
Honeybunch Corner
Red Barn
Odstone Down
Hailey Wood
Crowberry Tump
Kingstone Down
Middle Wood
Alfred's Castle
Ashdown House
B4000

227
245

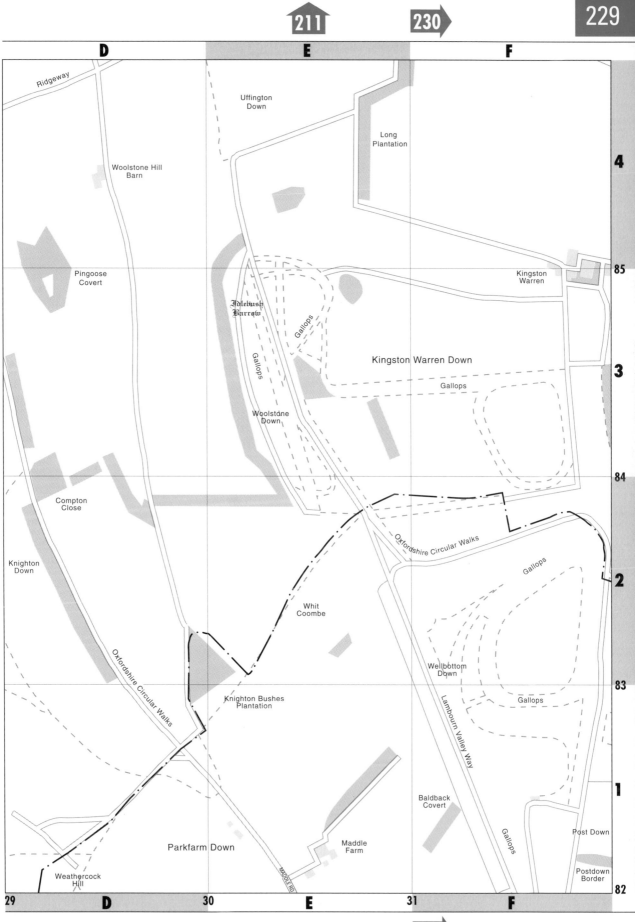

D
E
F

Ridgeway

Uffington
Down

Long
Plantation

4

Woolstone Hill
Barn

Kingston
Warren

85

Pingoose
Covert

Idlebush
Barrow

Gallops

Kingston Warren Down

Gallops

3

Gallops

Woolstone
Down

Gallops

84

Compton
Close

Oxfordshire Circular Walks

Gallops

Knighton
Down

2

Whit
Coombe

Wellbottom
Down

Oxfordshire Circular Walks

Gallops

83

Knighton Bushes
Plantation

Lambourn Valley Way

Baldback
Covert

1

Post Down

Gallops

Parkfarm Down

Maddle
Farm

Postdown
Border

MADDLE RD

Weathercock
Hill

82

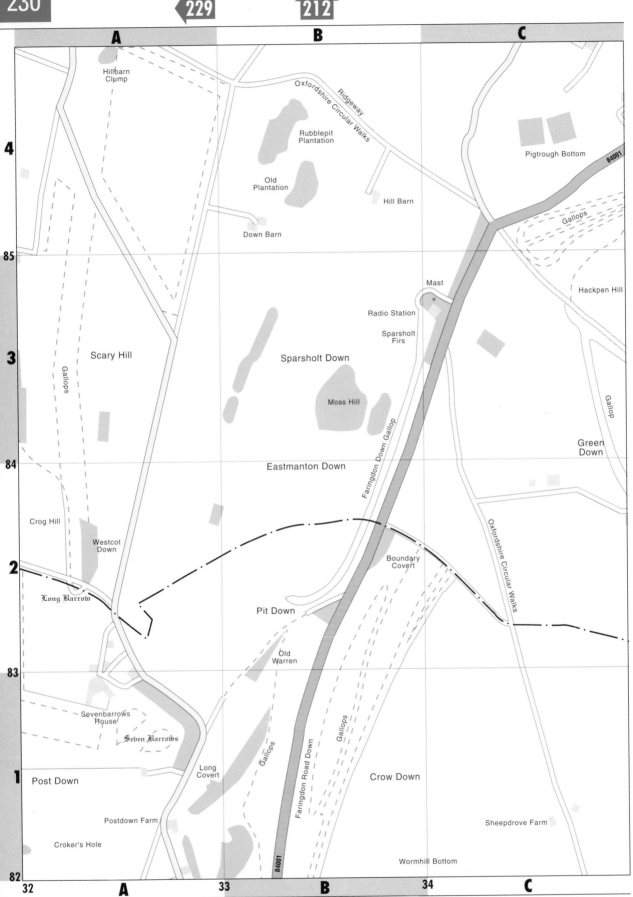

A B C

4

Hillbarn
Clump

Oxfordshire Circular Walks

Ridgeway

Rubblepit
Plantation

Old
Plantation

Pigtrough Bottom

B4001

Hill Barn

Down Barn

Gallops

85

Mast

Hackpen Hill

Radio Station

Sparsholt
Firs

3

Scary Hill

Sparsholt Down

Gallops

Moss Hill

Gallop

Green
Down

84

Eastmanton Down

Faringdon Down Gallop

Crog Hill

Oxfordshire Circular Walks

Westcot
Down

Boundary
Covert

2

Long Barrow

Pit Down

Old
Warren

83

Sevenbarrows
House

Seven Barrows

Gallops

Gallops

1

Post Down

Long
Covert

Faringdon Road Down

Crow Down

Postdown Farm

Sheepdrove Farm

Croker's Hole

B4001

Wormhill Bottom

82

32 A 33 B 34 C

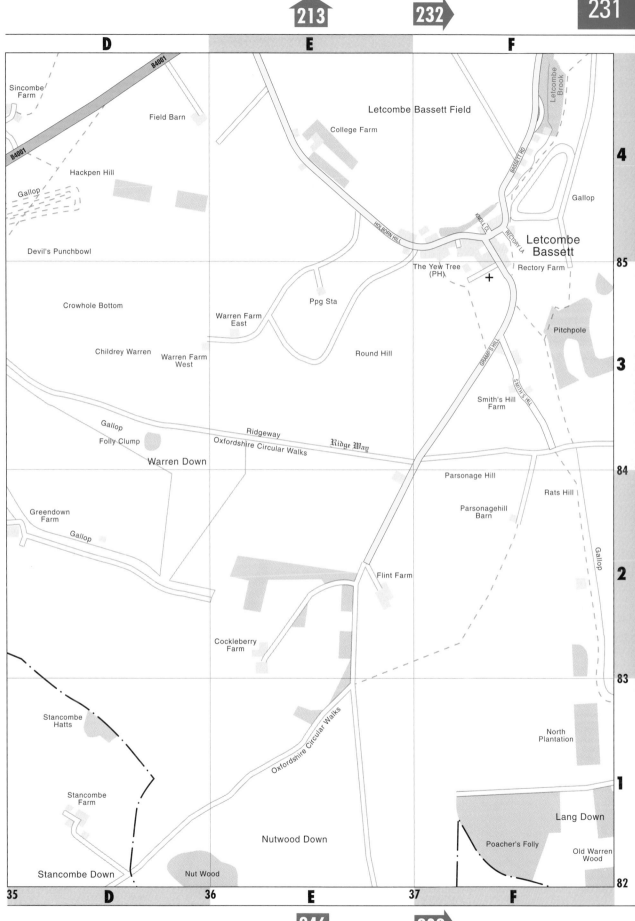

D

B4001

Sincombe Farm

Field Barn

4

Hackpen Hill

Gallop

B4001

Letcombe Bassett Field

College Farm

Letcombe Brook

BASSETT RD

Gallop

HOLBORN HILL

KNOLL CT

RECTORY LA

Letcombe Bassett

Devil's Punchbowl

The Yew Tree (PH)

+

Rectory Farm

85

Crowhole Bottom

Ppg Sta

Pitchpole

Warren Farm East

Round Hill

GRAMP'S HILL

SMITH'S HL

3

Childrey Warren

Warren Farm West

Smith's Hill Farm

Gallop

Ridgeway

Folly Clump

Oxfordshire Circular Walks

Ridge Way

Warren Down

Parsonage Hill

84

Greendown Farm

Rats Hill

Gallop

Parsonagehill Barn

Gallop

2

Flint Farm

Cockleberry Farm

83

Stancombe Hatts

North Plantation

Stancombe Farm

Oxfordshire Circular Walks

1

Lang Down

Stancombe Down

Nutwood Down

Poacher's Folly

Old Warren Wood

Nut Wood

82

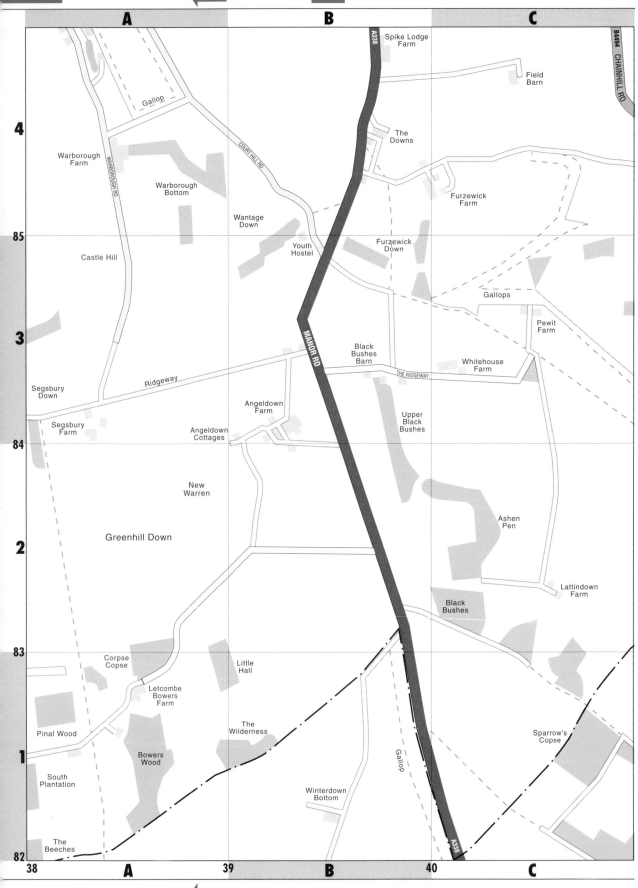

A338
Spike Lodge Farm
B4494 CHAINHILL RD
Field Barn
Gallop
4
The Downs
COURT HILL RD
Warborough Farm
WARBOROUGH RD
Warborough Bottom
Furzewick Farm
Wantage Down
85
Furzewick Down
Youth Hostel
Castle Hill
Gallops
Pewit Farm
3
MANOR RD
Black Bushes Barn
THE RIDGEWAY
Whitehouse Farm
Ridgeway
Segsbury Down
Angeldown Farm
Upper Black Bushes
Segsbury Farm
Angeldown Cottages
84
New Warren
Ashen Pen
2
Greenhill Down
Lattindown Farm
Black Bushes
83
Corpse Copse
Little Hall
Letcombe Bowers Farm
Sparrow's Copse
The Wilderness
Pinal Wood
1
Bowers Wood
Gallop
South Plantation
Winterdown Bottom
The Beeches
A338
82

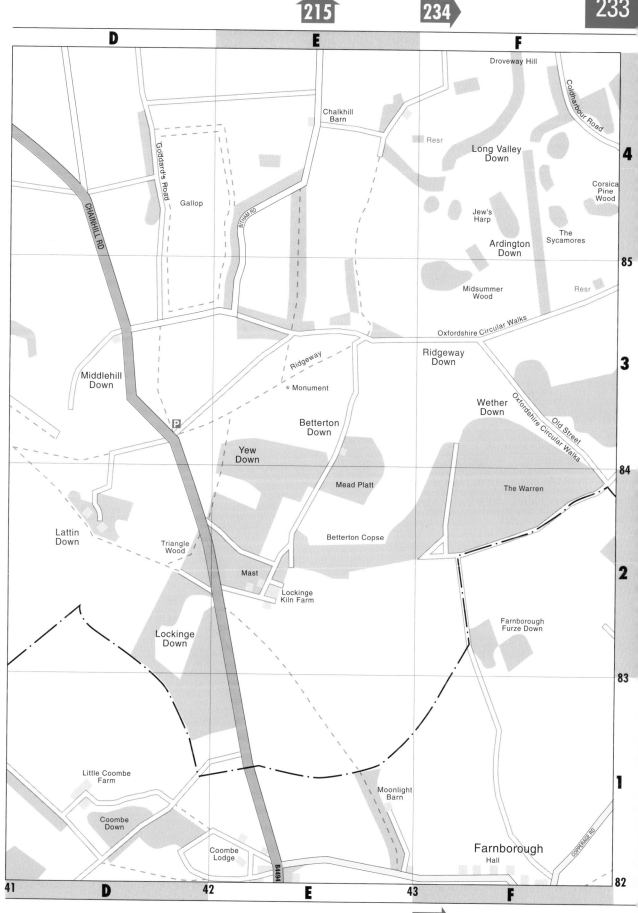

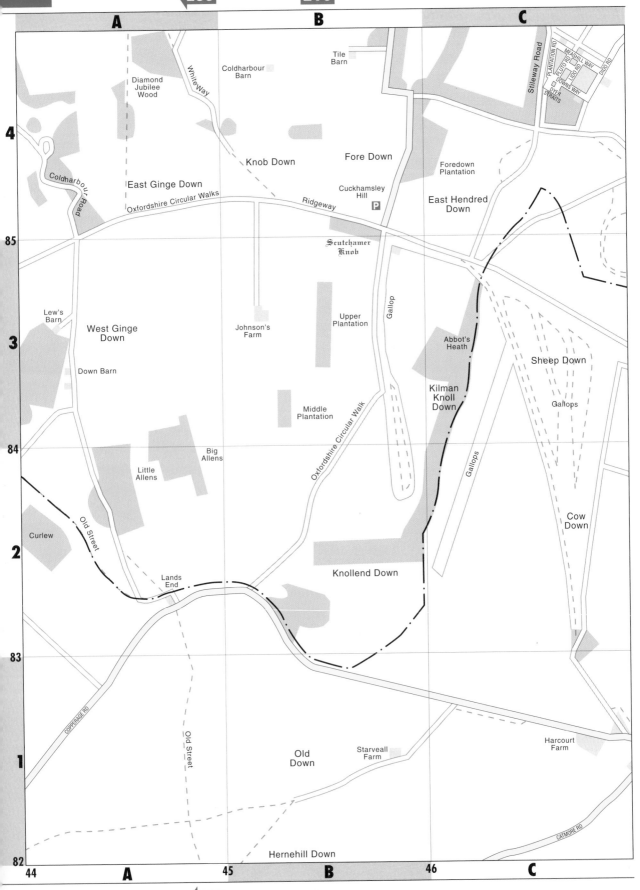

233

216

A   B   C

Stileway Road

PLANTATION RD
MEASHILL WAY
PLUTO RD
LIDO RD
DUDO RD
DOWN'S WAY
DYER STRAITS

Tile
Barn

4

Diamond
Jubilee
Wood

WhiteWay

Coldharbour
Barn

Knob Down

Fore Down

Foredown
Plantation

East Hendred
Down

Coldharbour Road

East Ginge Down

Oxfordshire Circular Walks

Ridgeway

Cuckhamsley
Hill
P

85

Scutchamer
Knob

Lew's
Barn

West Ginge
Down

Johnson's
Farm

Upper
Plantation

Gallop

Abbot's
Heath

Sheep Down

3

Down Barn

Kilman
Knoll
Down

Gallops

Middle
Plantation

Oxfordshire Circular Walk

84

Big
Allens

Little
Allens

Gallops

Cow
Down

Curlew

Old Street

2

Lands
End

Knollend Down

83

COPPERAGE RD

Old Street

1

Old
Down

Starveall
Farm

Harcourt
Farm

CATMORE RD

82

Hernehill Down

44   A   45   B   46   C

233

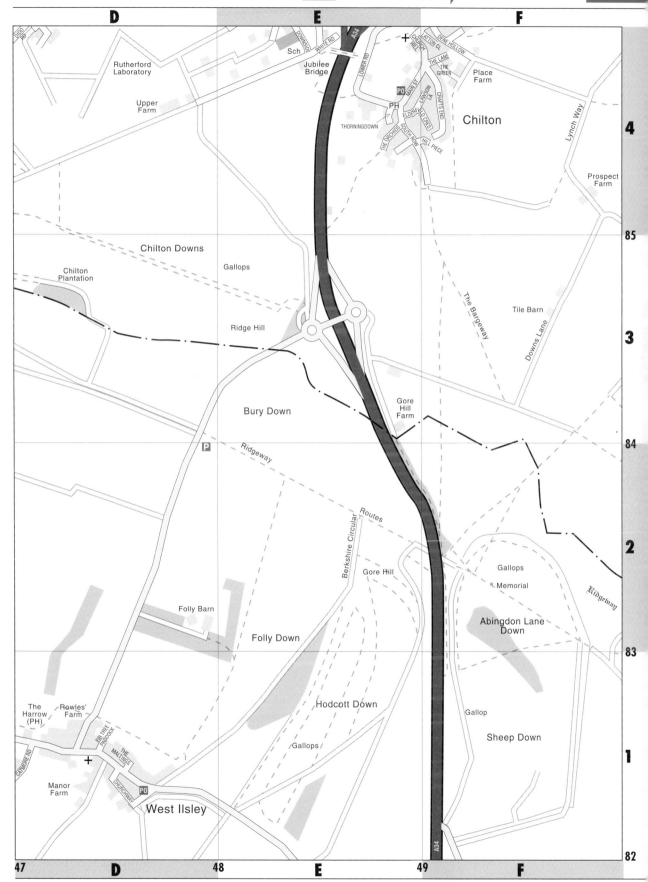

Rutherford
Laboratory

Upper
Farm

Sch

WHITE RD

DOWNSIDE

Jubilee
Bridge

LOWER RD

A34

DENE HOLLOW

LATTON CL

CHURCH HILL

THE LANE

THE GREEN

Place
Farm

PO

MAIN ST

PH

THORNINGDOWN

THE ORCHIDS

ELDERFIELD (CRES)

SOUTH ROW

LAWSON LA

CRAFT'S END

HILL PIECE

Chilton

Lynch Way

Prospect
Farm

Chilton Downs

Gallops

Chilton
Plantation

Ridge Hill

The Bargeway

Tile Barn

Downs Lane

Bury Down

Gore
Hill
Farm

P

Ridgeway

Berkshire Circular

Routes

Gore Hill

Gallops

Memorial

Ridgeway

Abingdon Lane
Down

Folly Barn

Folly Down

Hodcott Down

The
Harrow
(PH)

Rowles'
Farm

BIG TREE
PADDOCK

THE MALTINGS

CATMORE RD

Manor
Farm

CHURCHWAY

PO

Gallops

Gallops

Gallop

Sheep Down

West Ilsley

A34

4

85

3

84

2

83

1

82

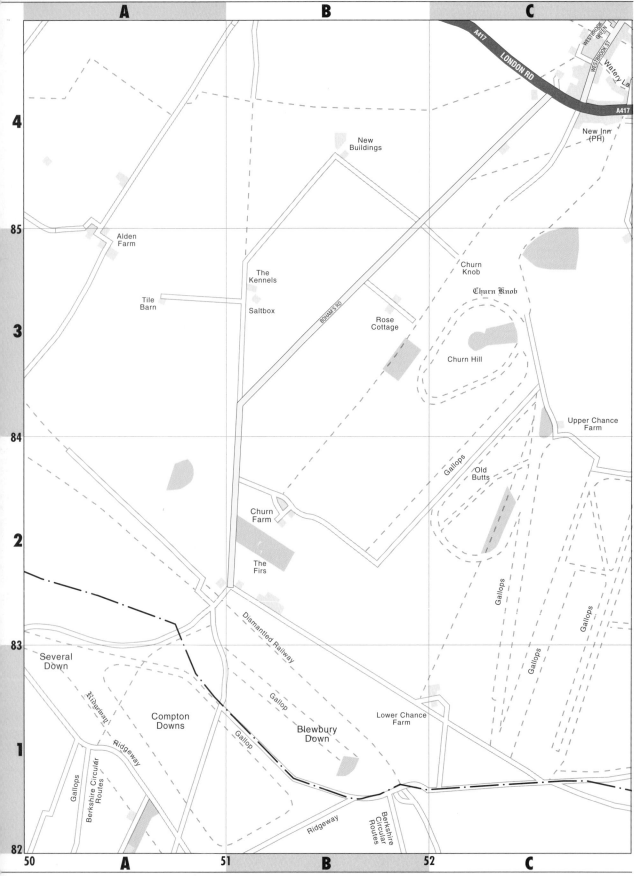

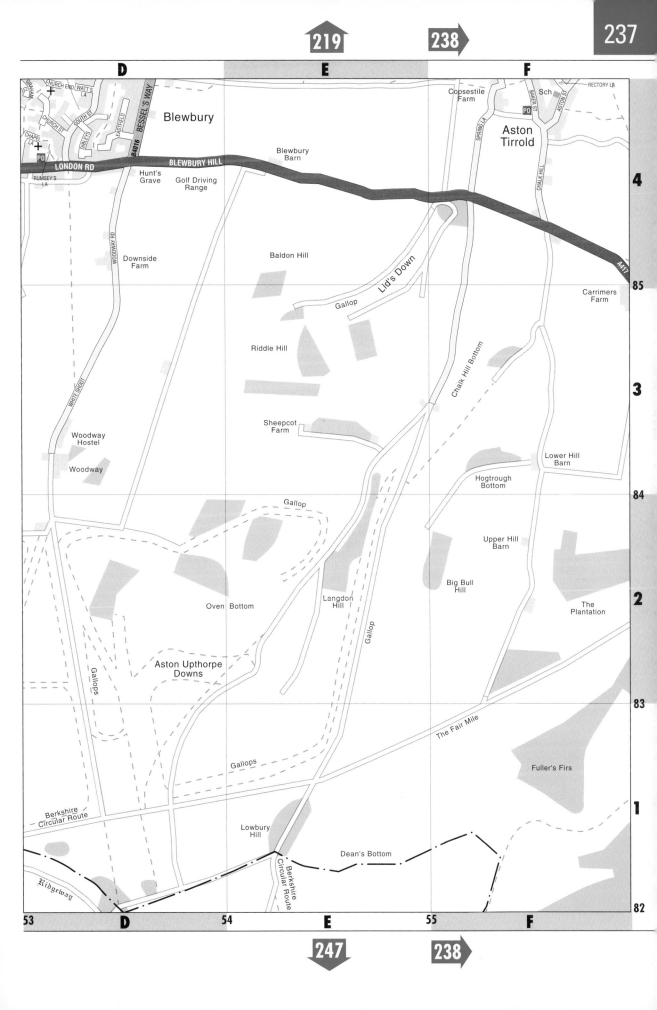

D
E
F

Blewbury

CHURCH END
WATT'S LA
BRANHAM CL
CHURCH ST
SOUTH ST
EASTFIELD
DIBLEYS
CHAPEL LA
PO
RUMSEY'S LA
LONDON RD
BESSEL'S WAY
B4016

BLEWBURY HILL

Copsestile Farm

RECTORY LA
Sch
BAKER ST
SPRING LA
ASTON ST
PO
Aston Tirrold
CHALK HILL

4

Hunt's Grave
Golf Driving Range

Blewbury Barn

Downside Farm

WOODWAY RD

Baldon Hill

Lid's Down

Gallop

A417

85

Carrimers Farm

WHITE SHOOT

Riddle Hill

Chalk Hill Bottom

3

Woodway Hostel

Woodway

Sheepcot Farm

Lower Hill Barn

Hogtrough Bottom

84

Gallop

Upper Hill Barn

Oven Bottom

Langdon Hill

Gallop

Big Bull Hill

The Plantation

2

Gallops

Aston Upthorpe Downs

83

The Fair Mile

Fuller's Firs

Gallops

Berkshire Circular Route

1

Lowbury Hill

Dean's Bottom

Berkshire Circular Route

Ridgeway

82

53
D
54
E
55
F

237
220

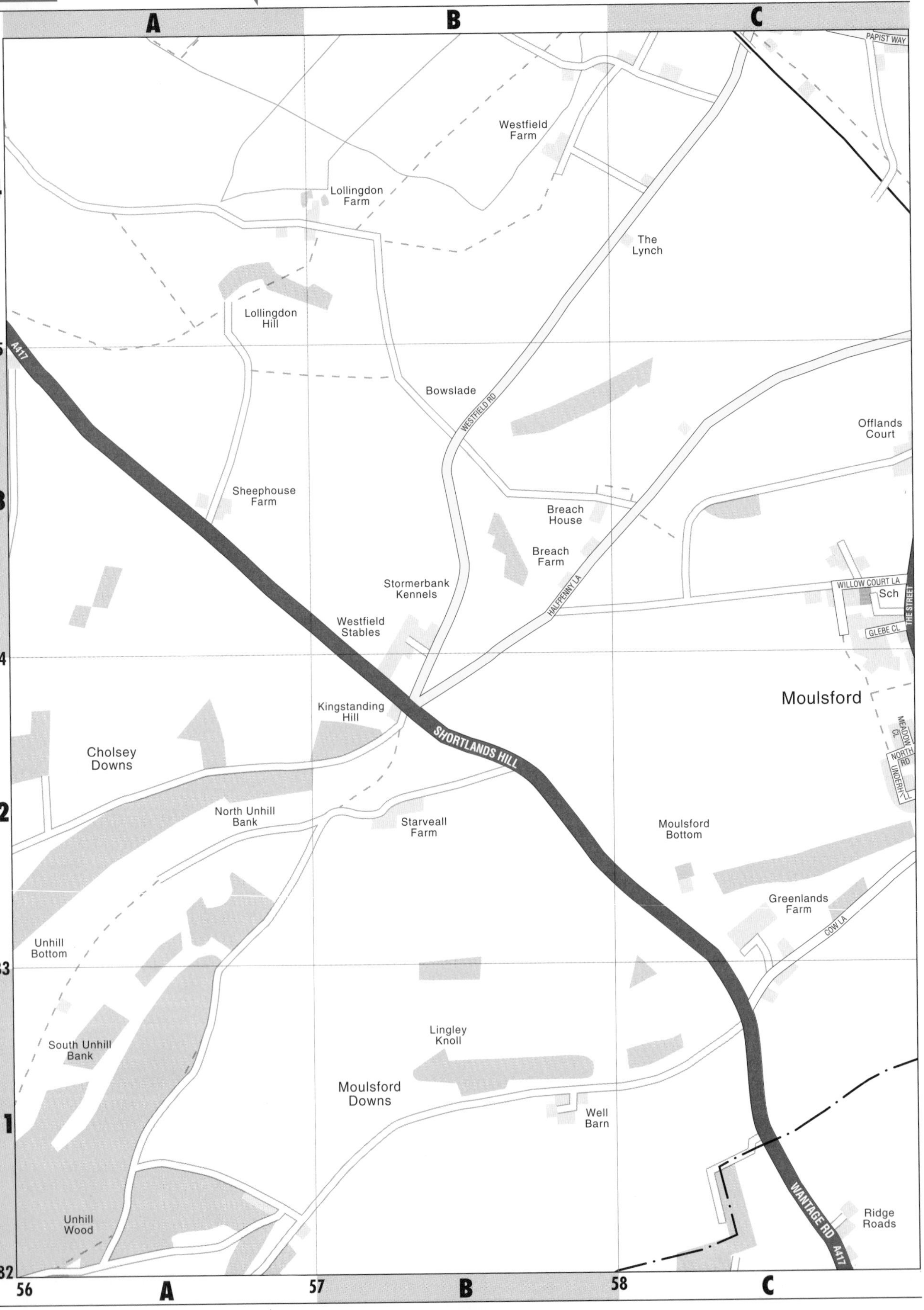

A **B** **C**

PAPIST WAY

Westfield
Farm

4

Lollingdon
Farm

The
Lynch

Lollingdon
Hill

85

A417

Bowslade

WESTFIELD RD

Offlands
Court

Sheephouse
Farm

3

Breach
House

Breach
Farm

HALFPENNY LA

Stormerbank
Kennels

WILLOW COURT LA

Sch

THE STREET

Westfield
Stables

GLEBE CL

84

Moulsford

Kingstanding
Hill

SHORTLANDS HILL

MEADOW CL

Cholsey
Downs

NORTH RD

UNDERHILL

2

North Unhill
Bank

Starveall
Farm

Moulsford
Bottom

Greenlands
Farm

COW LA

Unhill
Bottom

83

South Unhill
Bank

Lingley
Knoll

1

Moulsford
Downs

Well
Barn

WANTAGE RD

Unhill
Wood

Ridge
Roads

A417

82

56 **A** 57 **B** 58 **C**

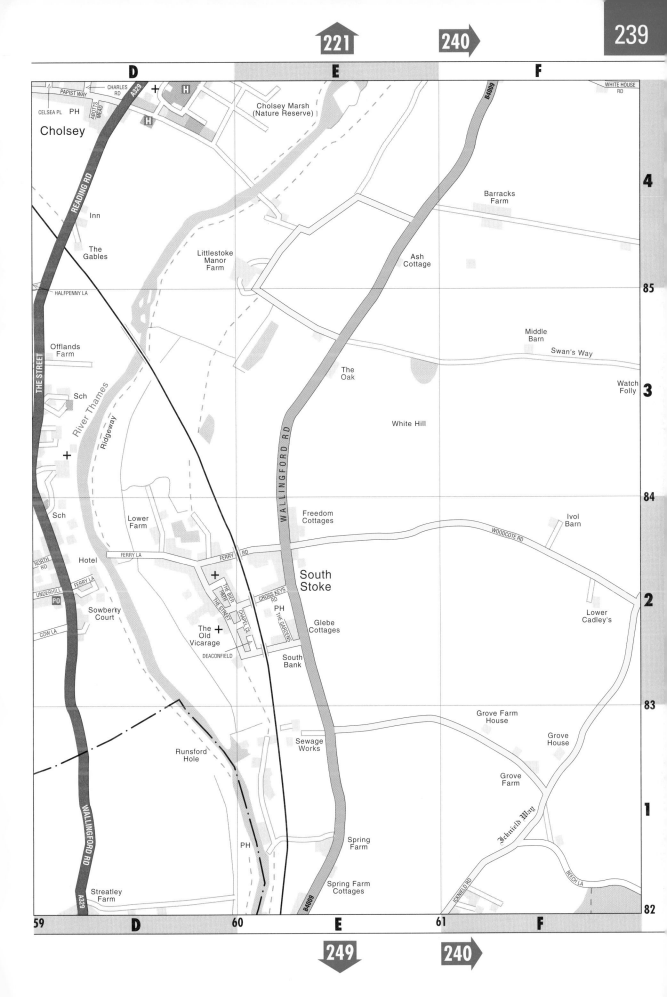

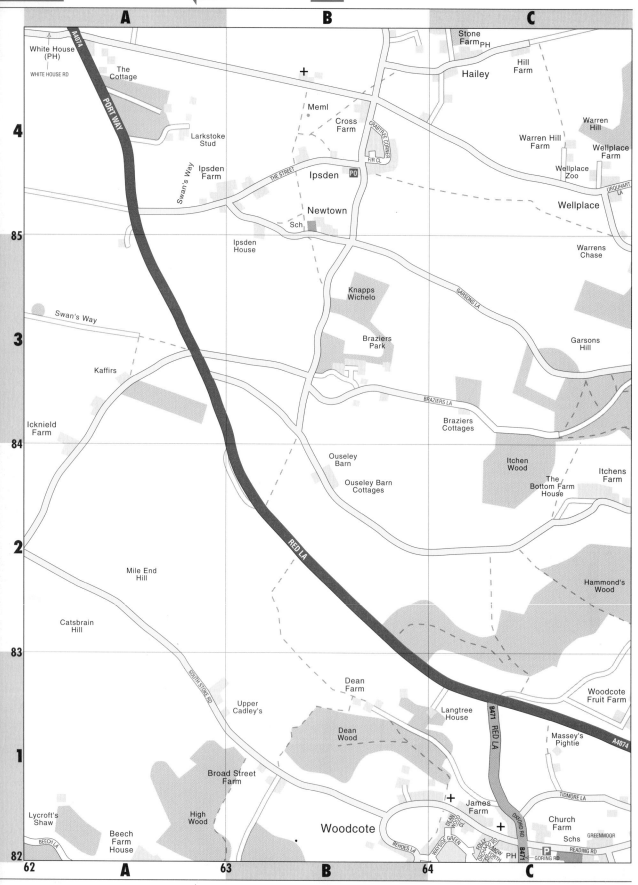

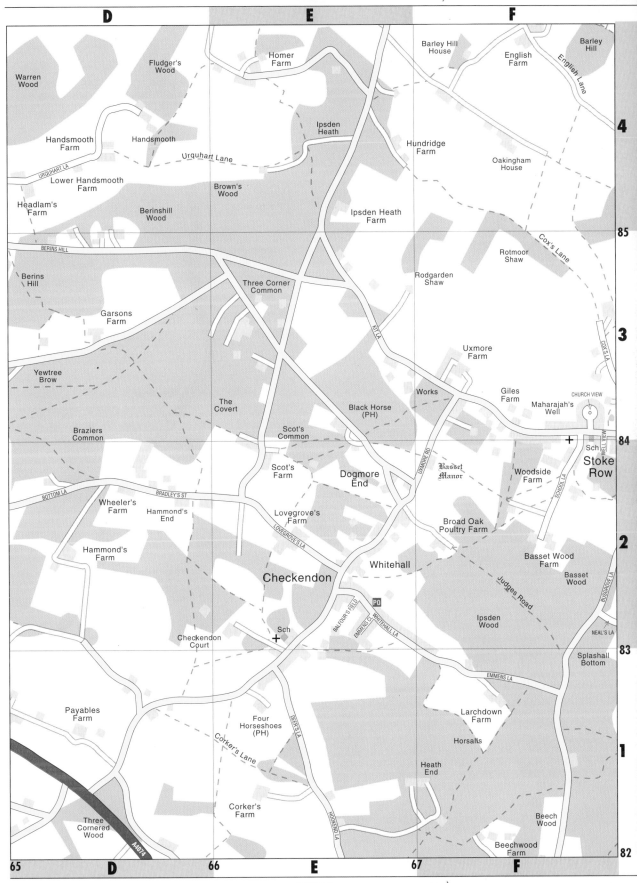

Warren Wood
Fludger's Wood
Homer Farm
Barley Hill House
English Farm
Barley Hill
English Lane

Handsmooth Farm
Handsmooth
Ipsden Heath
Hundridge Farm
Oakingham House

Urquhart Lane
URQUHART LA
Lower Handsmooth Farm
Brown's Wood

Headlam's Farm
Berinshill Wood
Ipsden Heath Farm
Cox's Lane

BERINS HILL
Rotmoor Shaw

Berins Hill
Three Corner Common
Rodgarden Shaw

Garsons Farm
KIT LA
Uxmore Farm
COX'S LA

Yewtree Brow
Works
Giles Farm
Maharajah's Well
CHURCH VIEW

The Covert
Black Horse (PH)
CHURCH VIEW

Scot's Common
Sch
Stoke Row

Braziers Common
Scot's Farm
Dogmore End
Basset Manor
Woodside Farm
SCHOOL LA

BOTTOM LA
BRADLEY'S ST
Wheeler's Farm
Hammond's End
Lovegrove's Farm
UXMORE RD
Broad Oak Poultry Farm

Hammond's Farm
LOVEGROVE'S LA
Whitehall
Basset Wood Farm
Basset Wood
BURGROVE LA

Checkendon
Judges Road
Ipsden Wood
NEAL'S LA

PO
Sch
Checkendon Court
BALFOUR'S FIELD
EMMENS CL
WHITEHALL LA
Splashall Bottom

83
EMMENS LA

Payables Farm
Four Horseshoes (PH)
DEER'S LA
Larchdown Farm
Horsalls

Corker's Lane
Heath End
Beech Wood

Three Cornered Wood
A4074
Corker's Farm
HOOKEND LA
Beechwood Farm

241
224

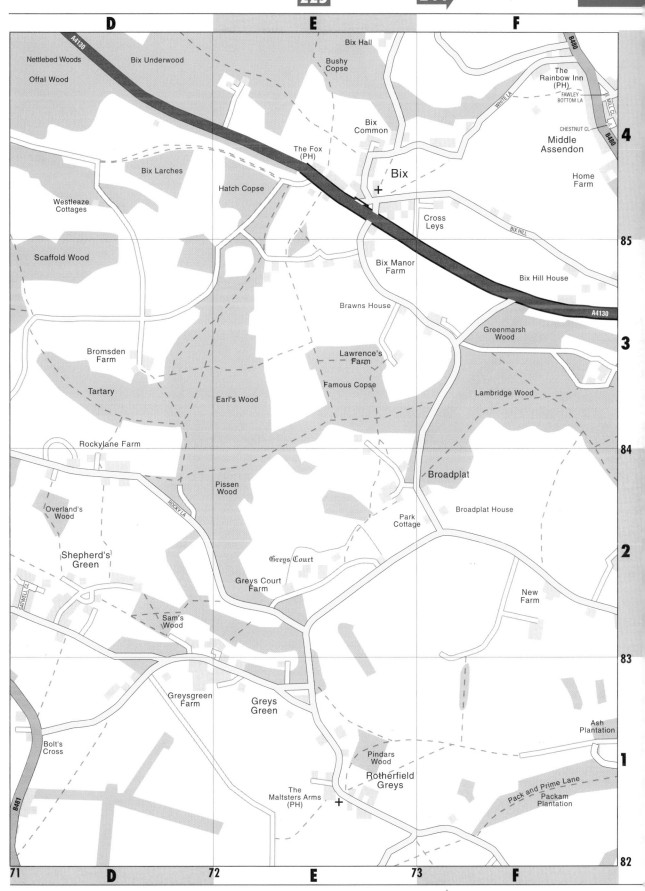

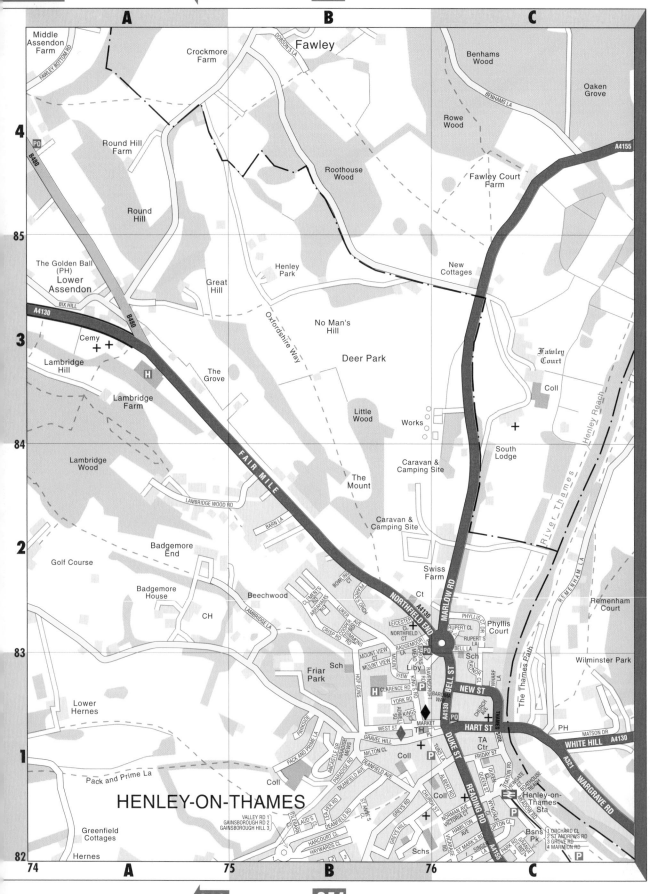

231

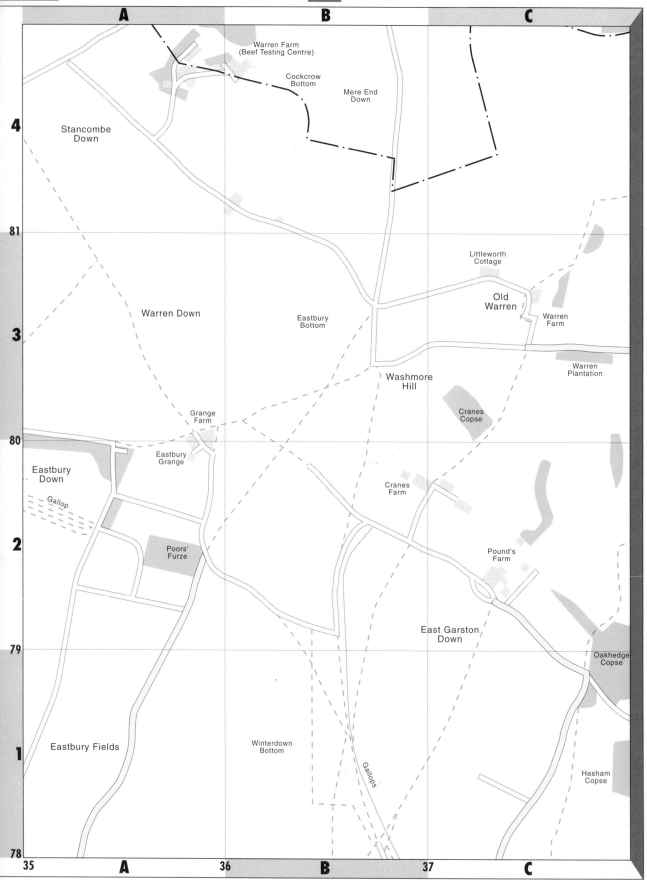

Warren Farm
(Beef Testing Centre)

Cockcrow
Bottom

Mere End
Down

Stancombe
Down

Littleworth
Cottage

Old
Warren

Warren
Farm

Warren Down

Eastbury
Bottom

Warren
Plantation

Washmore
Hill

Cranes
Copse

Grange
Farm

Eastbury
Grange

Eastbury
Down

Cranes
Farm

Gallop

Poors'
Furze

Pound's
Farm

East Garston
Down

Oakhedge
Copse

Eastbury Fields

Winterdown
Bottom

Gallops

Hasham
Copse

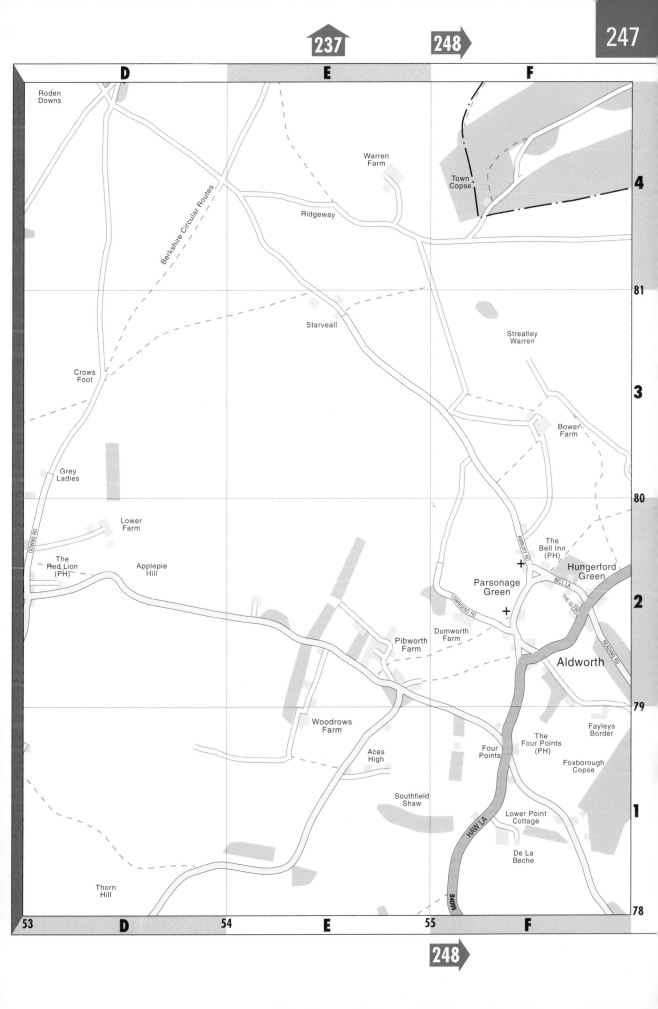

Roden
Downs

Warren
Farm

Town
Copse

4

Ridgeway

Berkshire Circular Routes

81

Starveall

Streatley
Warren

Crows
Foot

3

Bower
Farm

Grey
Ladies

80

Lower
Farm

DOWNS RD

The
Bell Inn
(PH)

AMBURY RD

Hungerford
Green

The
Red Lion
(PH)

Applepie
Hill

Parsonage
Green

BELL LA

THE GLEBE

2

TOWNSEND RD

Dumworth
Farm

Pibworth
Farm

Aldworth

READING RD

79

Woodrows
Farm

Fayleys
Border

Aces
High

Four
Points

The
Four Points
(PH)

Foxborough
Copse

Southfield
Shaw

HAW LA

Lower Point
Cottage

1

De La
Beche

Thorn
Hill

B4009

78

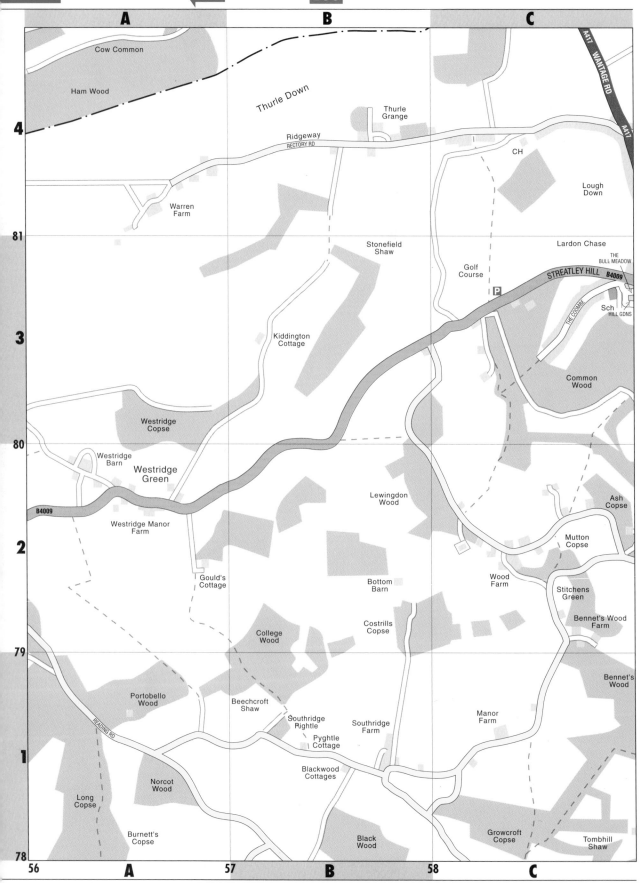

A   B   C

Cow Common

Ham Wood

Thurle Down

Thurle Grange

A417 WANTAGE RD

4

Ridgeway

RECTORY RD

CH

Lough Down

Warren Farm

81

Stonefield Shaw

Golf Course

Lardon Chase

THE BULL MEADOW

STREATLEY HILL B4009

P

Sch HILL GDNS

THE COOMBE

Kiddington Cottage

3

Common Wood

Westridge Copse

80

Westridge Barn

Westridge Green

Lewingdon Wood

Ash Copse

B4009

Mutton Copse

Westridge Manor Farm

Wood Farm

Stitchens Green

Gould's Cottage

2

Bottom Barn

Bennet's Wood Farm

College Wood

Costrills Copse

79

Bennet's Wood

Portobello Wood

Beechcroft Shaw

Southridge Pightle

Southridge Farm

Manor Farm

READING RD

Pyghtle Cottage

1

Blackwood Cottages

Norcot Wood

Long Copse

Growcroft Copse

Tombhill Shaw

Burnett's Copse

Black Wood

78

56   A   57   B   58   C

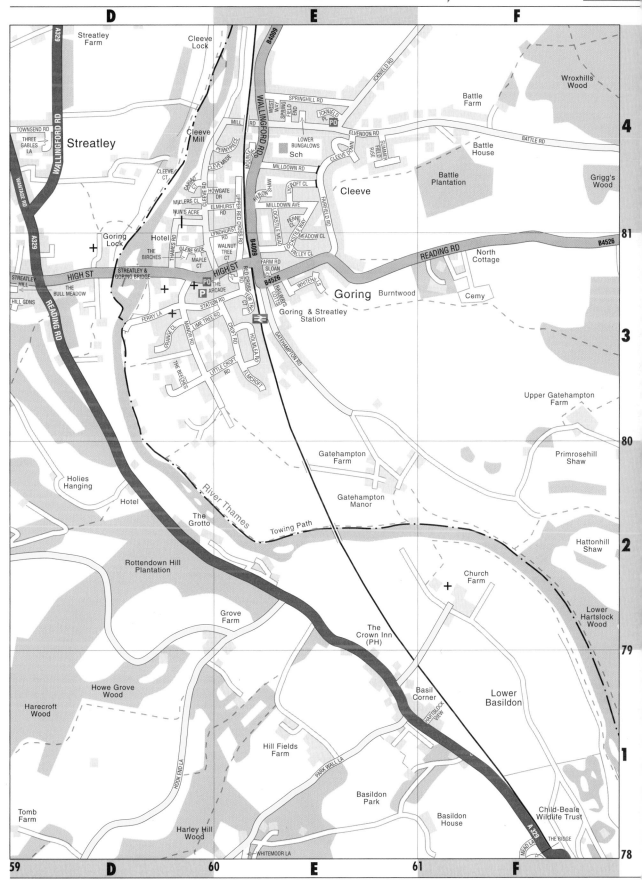

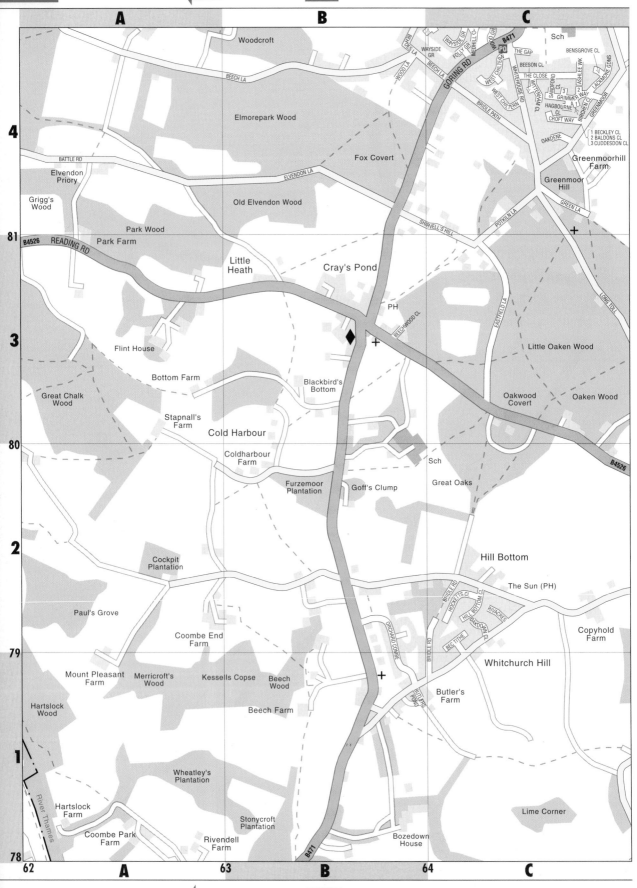

PH
Cocks Hill
Ward's Farm
Sch
Lower Farm
HOOK END LA
Ward Shaw
Rumerhedge Farm
Rumerhedge Wood
Ashlee Wood
Poultry Farm
Hook End Farm
Hook End
4
Lackmore Wood
Nippers Grove
The Oaks
81
College Wood or Abbot's Wood
Valentine Wood
Whitewood Heath
PARK LA
Parklane Shaw
Common Wood
B4526
3
LONG TOLL
Common Covert
Bensgrove Wood
Collegewood Farm
Kempwood Cottage
80
Newhouse Farm
Bensgrove Farm
The Hocket
Little College Wood
READING RD
Poultry Farm
Abbotsfield
Charity Farm
DEADMAN'S LA
Hawhill Wood
Highfield Shaw
HORSEPOND RD
A4074
Cane End House
2
Sch
H
+
Holme Copse
Nuney Green
Walk Shaw
Ladygrove Farm
Haw Farm
Nuney Copse
Goring Heath
Thicket Copse
Nuney Wood
PO
Withy Shaw
Querns
Gutteridge's Wood
79
Collinsend Common
King Charles's Head (PH)
Nuney Wood
Bown's Hill
Westholme Farm
Bunce's Lane
Collins End
Coxsetter's Wood
1
Holmes's Farm
Holly Copse
Whittles Farm
Cross Lanes
Path Hill
Pathhill Farm
Long Ground Plantation
Bottom Wood
Stirrups
The Baulk

A   B   C

Manor Farm

Park Farm

COLMORE LA

DIVE LA   STEVENS LA

Peppard Hill

Peppard Common

B481

WYFOLD LA

Wyfold Grange

CHILTERN RD

Sch

STOKE ROW RD

PEPPARD HILL

SPRINGWOOD LA

4

Rotherfield Peppard

81

GALLOWSTREE RD

Wyfold Wood

New Copse

Shiplake Bottom

SHIPLAKE BOTTOM CRES

GRAVEL HILL

BLOUNTS COURT RD

PRIORY COPSE

PEPPARD RD B481

CHURCHILL CRES

PO

Sch

OLD COPSE GDNS

CARLING RD

BEECH RISE

GRAVEL HILL

NEWFIELD RD

Sonning Common

WOODLANDS RD

HEDGE FLD

SEDGEWELL RD

JOSSY CL

HAZEL GDNS

WOOD LANE CL

INGLEWOOD CT

3

Withy Copse

WYFOLD RD

Common Farm

WOODSIDE LA

HEARNS LA

THE HAMLET

Gallowstree Common

Bishopswood Farm

LAMBOURNE RD

ORCHARD CL

BRIMAR CL

RUSSET CL

WALNUT CL

APPLETREE SMITH

GREEN LA

BASKERVILLE RD

V. SLEY

WYCHWOOD CL

WOOD LA

PO

PO

ORCHARD FIELD

HORSEPOND RD

The Crown & Anchor (PH)

ASHFORD AV

PAGES ORCH

CROWSLEY WAY

GROVE RD

Sch

80

READE'S LA

CHERITON PL

SEA RD

ELM CT

Coldnorton Wood

HAZELMOOR LA

Sch

ROWAN CL

WESTLEIGH DR

BIRCH CL

CH CL

Coldnorton Shaw

Oakridge Farm

WOOD LA

Sch

KIDMORE LA

KENNYLANDS RD

ILEX CL

2

Cane End Farm

GRAVEL LEAZE

Holly Tree Farm

New Inn (PH)

Kidmore End

PO

Sch

READING RD A4074

Curtis Farm

BUTLERS ORCH

COOPERS PIGHTLE

Cemy

Vines Farm

79

Madge Gray's Wood

Highland Wood

Stocking Shaw

CHALKHOUSE GREEN RD

GREEN DEAN HILL

Cross Farm

Kidmore House

1

Green Dean Wood

Hodmore Farm

Tankers Table Farm

MILL LA

Bardolph's Wood

TOKERS GREEN RD

DYSONS WOOD LANE

CHALKHOUSE GREEN LA

A4074

The Pack Horse (PH)

Dyson's Wood

TANNERS LA

KINNAIRD END RD

78

Hodmore Farm Cottage

SHEEPWAYS LA

Tinker's Green

68   A   69   B   70   C

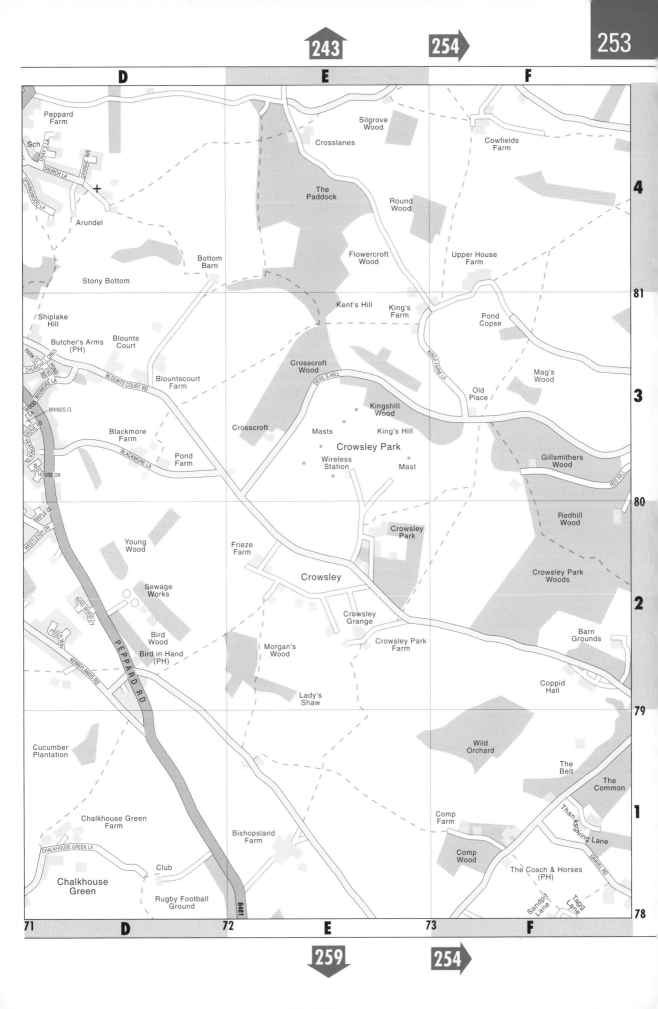

253
244

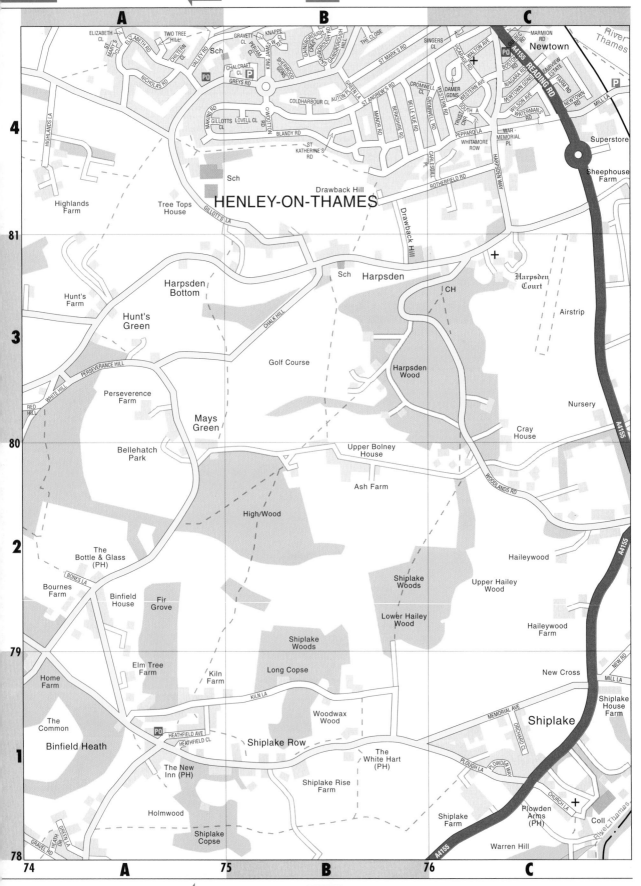

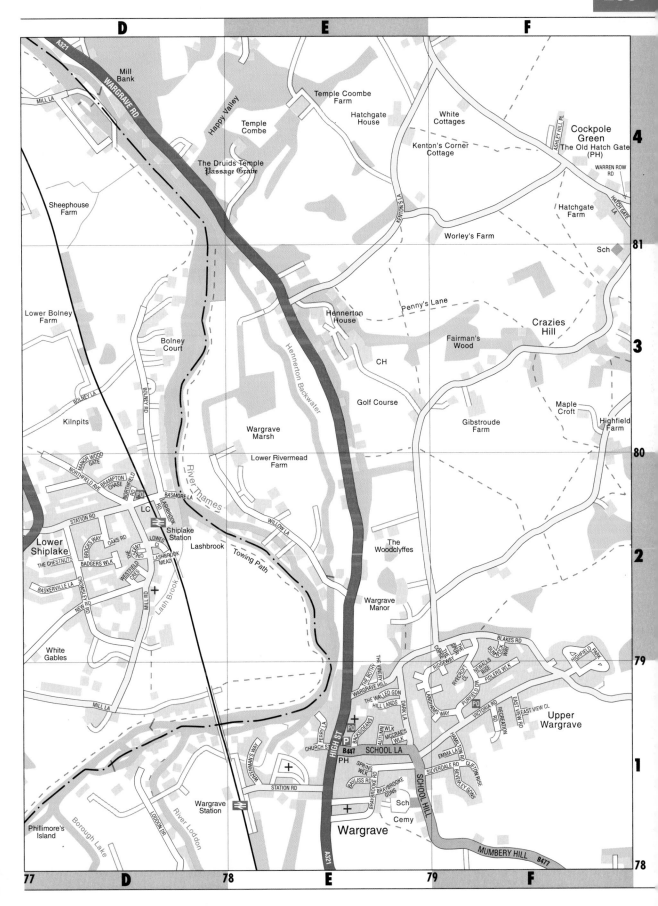

Mill Bank

MILL LA

A321

WARGRAVE RD

Happy Valley

Temple Combe Farm

Temple Coombe

Hatchgate House

White Cottages

Kenton's Corner Cottage

Cockpole Green

ASHLEY HILL PL

The Old Hatch Gate (PH)

WARREN ROW RD

4

The Druids Temple

Passage Grave

KENTON'S LA

Worley's Farm

Hatchgate Farm

HATCHGATE LA

Sch

81

Sheephouse Farm

Penny's Lane

Hennerton House

Crazies Hill

Lower Bolney Farm

Bolney Court

BOLNEY LA

Hennerton Backwater

CH

Fairman's Wood

3

BOLNEY RD

Golf Course

Gibstroude Farm

Maple Croft

Highfield Farm

Kilnpits

Wargrave Marsh

80

River Thames

Lower Rivermead Farm

MANOR WOOD GATE

NORTHFIELD AVE

BRAMPTON CHASE

NORTHFIELD RD

PO

BASMORE LA

LASHBROOK RD

LC

WILLOW LA

The Woodclyffes

STATION RD

Shiplake Station

Lashbrook

Towing Path

BROOKS WAY

OAKS RD

THE SPINT

LOWES CL

LASHBROOK MEAD

Lower Shiplake

THE CHESTNUTS

BADGERS WLK

WESTFIELD CRES

Wargrave Manor

BLAKES RD

Upper Wargrave

2

BASKERVILLE LA

CROWSLEY RD

MILL RD

Lash Brook

THE SPUR

DUNT AVE

AWN

HIGHFIELD PARK

White Gables

CORWEN RD

THE BOTH

RIDGEWAY

RYECROFT CL

NEWALLS RISE

FIDLERS WLK

PURFIELD DR

VICTORIA RD

EAST VIEW CL

79

MILL LA

Wargrave Hill

WARGRAVE HILL

THE WALLED GDN

HILL LANDS

DARK LA

LANGHAM'S WAY

PO

HAMILTON RD

CLIFTON RISE

RECREATION RD

EAST VIEW RD

RIVERMAN'S WAY

FERRY LA

CHURCH ST

HIGH ST

PO

P

BACKSIDEANS

AUTUMN WLK

McCRAE'S WLK

SCHOOL LA

EMMA LA

SILVERDALE RD

BEVERLEY GDNS

1

STATION RD

B447

PH

SPRING WLK

BAYLISS RD

BRAYBROOKE GDNS

BRAYBROOKE RD

Sch

SCHOOL HILL

Wargrave Station

River Loddon

Cemy

Phillimore's Island

Borough Lake

LODDON DR

A321

Wargrave

MUMBERY HILL

B477

78

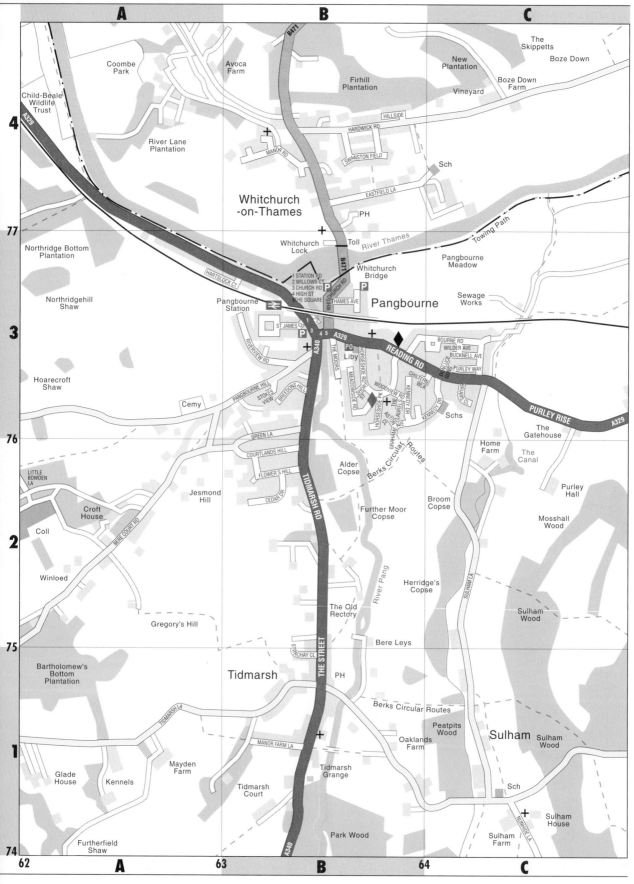

A   B   C

Coombe Park

Child-Beale Wildlife Trust

River Lane Plantation

Avoca Farm

Firhill Plantation

The Skippetts

Boze Down

New Plantation

Vineyard

Boze Down Farm

HILLSIDE

HARDWICK RD

SWANISTON FIELD

Sch

4

A329

MANOR RD

EASTFIELD LA

Whitchurch -on-Thames

Northridge Bottom Plantation

HARTSLOCK CT

PH

Whitchurch Lock

Toll

River Thames

Towing Path

77

B471

Whitchurch Bridge

Pangbourne Meadow

Northridgehill Shaw

1 STATION RD
2 WILLOWS CT
3 CHURCH RD
4 HIGH ST
5 THE SQUARE

Pangbourne Station

P

P

THAMES AVE

Pangbourne

Sewage Works

Hoarecroft Shaw

ST JAMES CT

P

A340

THE MOORS

PO
Liby

RIVERVIEW RD

BOURNE RD
WILDER AVE
BUCKNELL AVE

PURLEY WAY

READING RD

Cemy

Pangbourne Hill

STOKES VIEW

BREEDONS HILL

HORSESHOE RD

MEADOWSIDE RD

WOODVIEW RD

KENNEDY DR

CHILTERN WLK

DUVALS CL
GORSE
BRIARS CL

3

A329

Schs

PURLEY RISE

A329

Berks Circular Routes

GREEN LA

COURTLANDS HILL

FLOWER'S HILL

Alder Copse

Home Farm

The Gatehouse

The Canal

76

CEDAR DR

GRAHAME AVE
HORSESHOE PK
ASTON CL

Purley Hall

LITTLE BOWDEN LA

Jesmond Hill

Further Moor Copse

Broom Copse

Mosshall Wood

Croft House

Coll

BERE COURT RD

TIDMARSH RD

River Pang

Herridge's Copse

SULHAM LA

2

Winloed

Sulham Wood

Gregory's Hill

The Old Rectory

Bere Leys

75

Bartholomew's Bottom Plantation

STRACHAY CL

THE STREET

PH

Berks Circular Routes

Tidmarsh

Peatpits Wood

Oaklands Farm

Sulham

Sulham Wood

TIDMARSH LA

MANOR FARM LA

1

Glade House

Kennels

Mayden Farm

Tidmarsh Grange

Sch

A340

Tidmarsh Court

Park Wood

NUNHIDE LA

Sulham House

Furtherfield Shaw

Sulham Farm

74

62   A   63   B   64   C

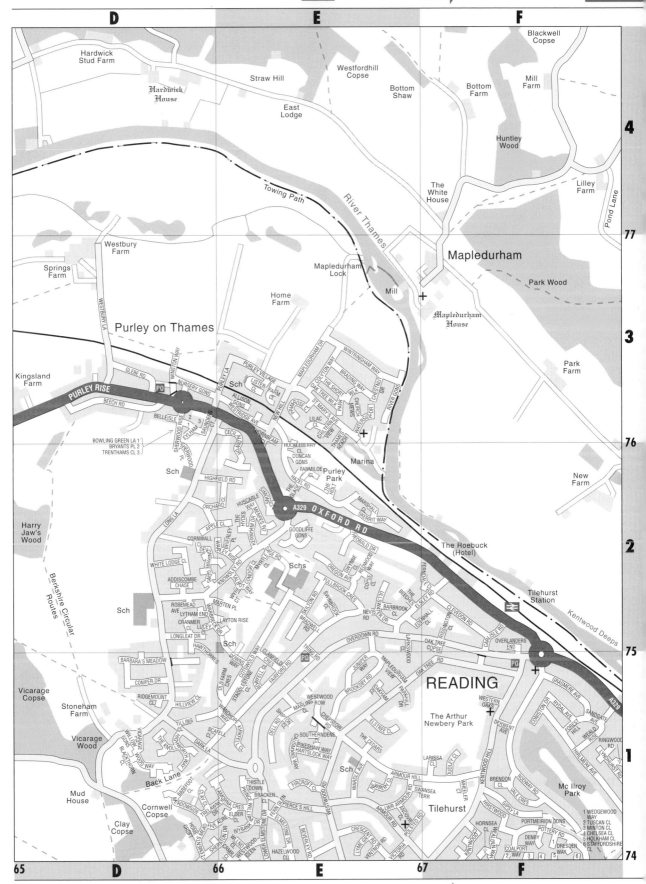

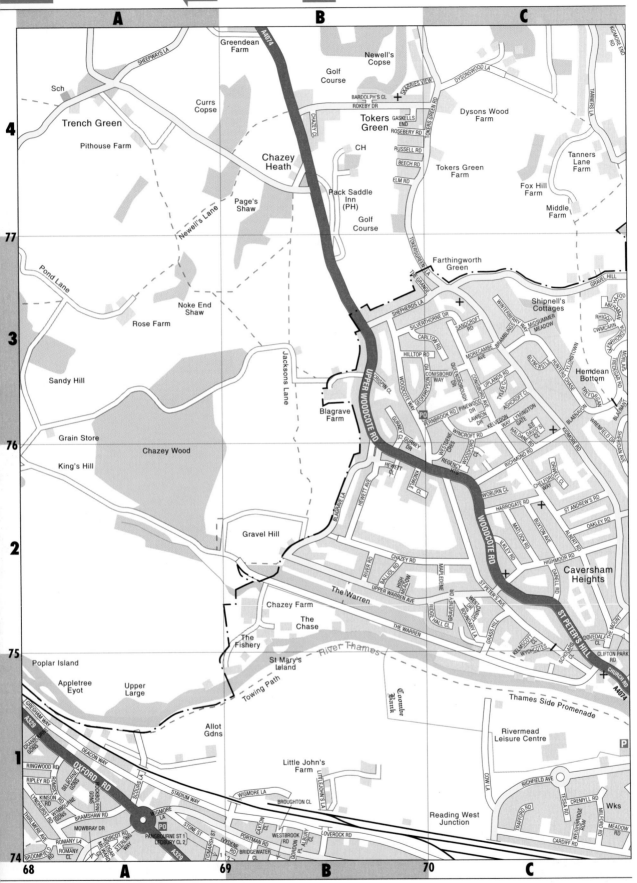

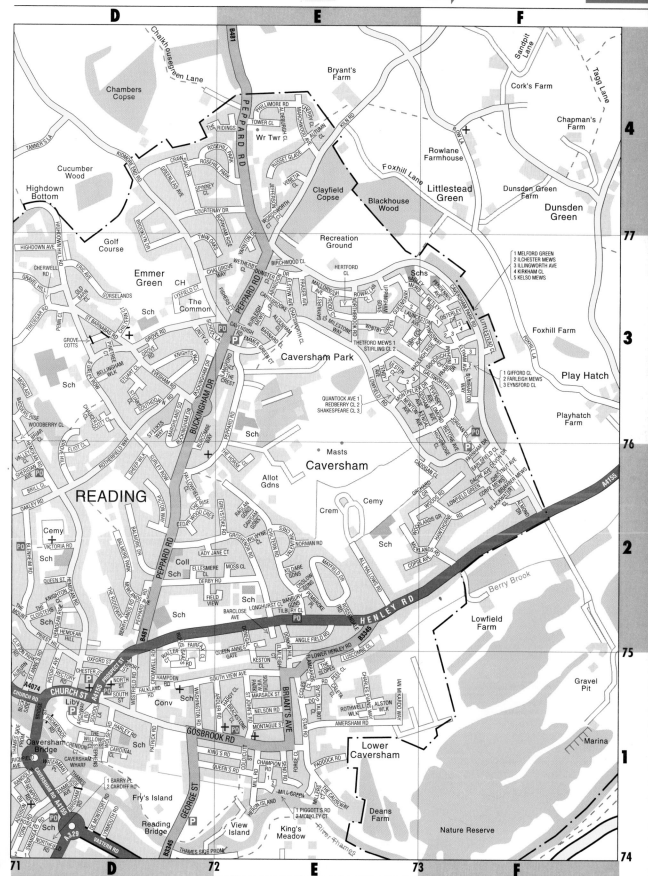

D E F

4

77

3

76

2

75

1

74

Chalkhousegreen Lane
B481

Chambers Copse

Cucumber Wood

Highdown Bottom

TANNER'S LA

HIGHDOWN AVE
HIGHDOWN HILL RD

CHERWELL RD
ERIC AVE
GRAVEL HILL

OLD BARN CL
GORSELANDS

TREDEGAR RD
PENN CL

ST BARNABAS RD

GROVE COTTS
PINE TREE RD
BELLINGHAM WLK
STUART CL
SOUTHDOWN
Sch

MORRIS CT
BADGERS RISE
WOODBERRY CL
BRIAR CL
VALLEY CL
HEMDEAN RD
SHERIDAN CL
BRILL CL

OAKLEY RD

Cemy
VICTORIA RD
PO
Sch

BLENHEIM RD
QUEEN ST
KNIGHTON RD
THE CLOISTERS
Sch
HEMDEAN HILL
PRIEST HILL

AUBURN RD
CLIFTON PARK RD
ST ANNES RD
PRIORY AVE

CHURCH ST
A4155
Liby

Caversham Bridge
RICHFIELD AVE
WATERMAN PL
THAMES SIDE

RANDOLPH RD
NEWPORT RD
YORK RD
SWANSEA RD
NORTHFIELD RD
PO
Sch
A 329
VASTERN RD

KIDMORE END RD

GREENLEAS AVE
SPINNEY CL
CRANMER
HAY DR
ROSEHILL PARK
ROSEHILL DR

COURTENAY DR
BROOKLYN DR
BURNHAM RISE

TWIN OAKS

PEPPARD RD

THE RIDINGS
PHILLIMORE RD
TOWER CL
ALDEBURGH CL
MARCHWOOD AVE
AUTUMN CL
CHERRY CL

Wr Twr
WORDSWORTH
JEFFERSON DR
VENETIA CL
RUSSET GLADE

Emmer Green
CH
The Common

CHALGROVE WAY
WETHERBY DR
FISHERS RD
LYEFIELD CT
BURLEIGH MEWS
CAVENDISH
EMMER GREEN CT
Sch
PO

BUCKINGHAM DR

GROVE RD
KNIGHTS WAY
CHAUCER CT
SCOTT CL
CHAUCER CT
EVESHAM RD
UNITY CL
LANGDON
THE CREST

ST LUKES WAY
MARSH LAND SQ
BURCOMBE WAY
PEPPARD RD

ELIOT CL
ROTHERFIELD WAY

Sch
THE HORSE

SHEEP WLK
SURLEY ROW
FALLOWFIELD CL

PICTON WAY
BALMORE DR
BALMORE PARK
NEWLANDS AVE

THE RISE
GREYSTOKE RD
CEDAR WOOD CRES

OAKLEY RD

B481

RUFUS ISAACS RD
WALLER CT
FAIRFAX RD
OXFORD ST
CHESTER ST
NORTH ST
SOUTH ST
PROSPECT ST
RECTORY RD
CROMWELL RD
WESTFIELD RD
WASHINGTON RD
FALKLAND

SHORT ST

PEPPARD RD

Coll
Sch
LADY JANE CT
ELLESMERE RD
MOSS CL
DERBY RD
FIELD VIEW
Sch
BARCLOSE AVE
LONGHURST CL

PRIORY AVE
HARLEY RD
Sch
ARCHWAY RD
SCHOOL RD
KIDMORE RD
PATRICK RD

THE WILLOWS
STEPHENS RD
CRENDON CT
Caversham Wharf
CARDINAL CL

GEORGE ST
B3345

KING'S RD

QUEEN'S RD

Reading Bridge
THAMES SIDE PROM

READING

Golf Course

GROVE RD

Caversham Park

Birchwood Cl

Hertford Cl

Clayfield Copse

Recreation Ground

Bryant's Farm

KILN RD

Foxhill Lane

Blackhouse Wood

Littlestead Green

Schs

MALLORY RD
NORTHBROOK RD
MILESTONE WAY
THETFORD MEWS 1
STIRLING CL 2

CHATSWORTH CL
CARISBROOKE
ALDERMAN RD
BARNARD CL
ELSTOW AVE
FRASER AVE
ISHTHWAY
ROWAN
WHITBY GREEN

ROWAN LA
QUEENS LA
LAUNCESTON AVE
KINGSWAY
GOODLIFFE
OSTERLEY DR

HADLEIGH RISE
MONTPELIER DR
PEVEREL DR
GALSWORTHY DR

NEWTON AVE
LOMOND AVE
KENDAL AVE
HIGHDOWN AVE
TESTONE AVE

Masts

Allot Gdns

QUANTOCK AVE 1
REDBERRY CL 2
SHAKESPEARE CL 3

Sch

RALAN GDNS
CAWSHAM GDNS
CAWSHAM GDNS
GROSVENOR RD
WILLWYNE CL
CHILTERN RD
VALENTINE CL
NORMAN RD

Caversham

Crem

Cemy

Sch

ORCHARD CL
CADOGAN CL
WOODS RD
WOODLANDS GR
LOWFIELD GREEN
HAWTHORNE
MACKLANDS
COPSE AVE

HENLEY RD
B3345

KILDARE GDNS
BANBURY CL
TILBURY CL
ANGLE FIELD RD
DONKIN HILL
BRIAR'S AVE

DONEGAL CL

Sch
PEMBROKE RD
MAYFIELD DR
ALL HALLOWS RD
PESSENDGE

Berry Brook

LUSCOMBE CL

Lowfield Farm

Gravel Pit

Marina

B Mews
ALMOND

A4155

EARLSFIELD DR
DACRE AVE
DEVON DR
CORFE MEWS
CHESTNUT AVE
BLACKWATER MEWS
BRADMEY MEWS

PO
Playhatch Farm

Foxhill Farm

FOXHILL LA
Play Hatch

Foxhill Farm

Littlestead Green

Rowlane Farmhouse

Cork's Farm

Chapman's Farm

Sandpit Lane

Tagg Lane

ROW LA

Dunsden Green Farm

Dunsden Green

ELTHAM AVE
LITTLESTEAD CL
DUMBARTON WAY
JORDAN CL
FARNHAM DR
TABITHA
PO

1 MELFORD GREEN
2 ILCHESTER MEWS
3 ILLINGWORTH AVE
4 KIRKHAM CL
5 KELSO MEWS

1 GIFFORD CL
2 FARLEIGH MEWS
3 EYNSFORD CL

1 BARRY PL
2 CARDIFF RD

Fry's Island

View Island

King's Meadow

Heron Island

1 PIGGOTT'S CL
2 MONKLEY CT

MILL GREEN
MILLERS RD
THE CAUSEWAY

Lower Caversham

Deans Farm

Nature Reserve

River Thames

GOSBROOK RD

SOUTH VIEW AVE
MARSACK ST
NELSON RD
MONTAGUE ST
KING'S RD
QUEEN'S RD
CHAMPION RD
MILL RD

SOUTH VIEW PARK
ST JOHN'S RD
STAR RD
SEND RD
FORBES RD
PADDOCK RD

EL MEADE
BRACKSTONE
YARDLY CL
HAMPDEN RD

Conv

KESTON CL
QUEEN ANNES GATE

AMERSHAM RD
ROTHWELL WLK
ALSTON WLK
IAN MIKARDO WAY
CHARLES EVANS WAY
TALBOT
CATA

LOWER HENLEY RD
THE SLOPES
FLAMBARDS
PEEL CL

CHURCH ST

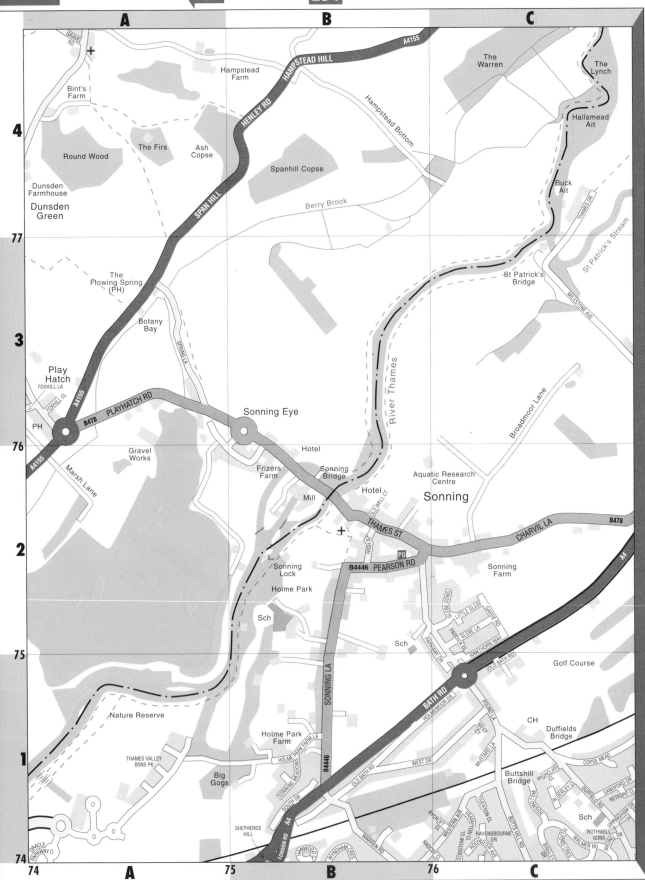

Street names are listed alphabetically and show the locality, the Postcode District, the page number and a reference to the square in which the name falls on the map page

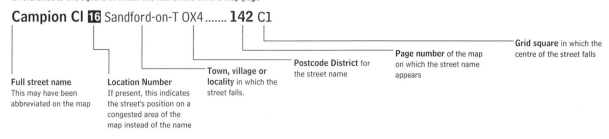

Campion Cl 16 Sandford-on-T OX4 .... 142 C1

Full street name
This may have been abbreviated on the map

Location Number
If present, this indicates the street's position on a congested area of the map instead of the name

Town, village or locality in which the street falls.

Postcode District for the street name

Page number of the map on which the street name appears

Grid square in which the centre of the street falls

Abbreviations used in the index

App **Approach**
Arc **Arcade**
Ave **Avenue**
Bvd **Boulevard**
Bldgs **Buildings**
Bsns Pk **Business Park**
Bsns Ctr **Business Centre**
Bglws **Bungalows**
Cswy **Causeway**
Ctr **Centre**
Cir **Circus**

Cl **Close**
Comm **Common**
Cnr **Corner**
Cotts **Cottages**
Ct **Court**
Ctyd **Courtyard**
Cres **Crescent**
Dr **Drive**
Dro **Drove**
E **East**
Emb **Embankment**

Ent **Enterprise**
Espl **Esplanade**
Est **Estate**
Gdns **Gardens**
Gn **Green**
Gr **Grove**
Hts **Heights**
Ho **House**
Ind Est **Industrial Estate**
Intc **Interchange**
Junc **Junction**

La **Lane**
N **North**
Orch **Orchard**
Par **Parade**
Pk **Park**
Pas **Passage**
Pl **Place**
Prec **Precinct**
Prom **Promenade**
Ret Pk **Retail Park**
Rd **Road**

Rdbt **Roundabout**
S **South**
Sq **Square**
Strs **Stairs**
Stps **Steps**
St **Street, Saint**
Terr **Terrace**
Trad Est **Trading Estate**
Wlk **Walk**
W **West**
Yd **Yard**

Town and village index

Church Cowley Rd OX4 ..... 142 A3
Church End
Blewbury OX11 ..... 219 D1
Croughton NN13 ..... 36 B4
Drayton St L OX10 ..... 183 D3
South Leigh OX8 ..... 119 E3
Standlake OX8 ..... 137 E2
Church Fields OX8 ..... 89 E4
Church Furlong OX15 ..... 20 B4
Church Green
Long Crendon HP18 ..... 129 E4
Stanford in the V SN7 ..... 194 C4
Witney OX8 ..... 118 A4
Church Hill Chilton OX11 ..... 235 E4
Great Haseley OX44 ..... 164 C4
LIttle Milton OX44 ..... 163 F3
Stonor RG9 ..... 225 E4
Tackley OX5 ..... 77 D3
Warmington OX17 ..... 3 D2
Church Hill Rd OX4 ..... 142 A2
Church La Adderbury OX17 ..... 23 D2
Aston Rowant OX9 ..... 167 E2
Banbury OX15, OX16, OX17 ..... 16 B3
Bicester OX6 ..... 65 F1
Bishopstone SN6 ..... 227 E2
Bledington OX7 ..... 54 B1
Bledlow Ridge HP14 ..... 189 F4
Bledlow Ridge HP14 ..... 189 E4
Brackley NN13 ..... 24 B1
Brightwell-cum-S OX10 ..... 202 C2
Burford OX18 ..... 100 C3
Cassington OX8 ..... 107 E1
Chacombe OX17 ..... 10 C2
Chalgrove OX44 ..... 184 B3
Charlbury OX7 ..... 73 D2
Charlton-on-O OX5 ..... 95 D2
Chinnor OX9 ..... 168 B3
Chipping Norton OX7 ..... 42 C2
Coleshill SN6 ..... 191 D4
Croughton NN13 ..... 36 B4
Crowmarsh G OX10 ..... 221 E1
Drayton OX14 ..... 179 E1
Drayton St L OX10 ..... 183 D3
Ewelme RG9 ..... 206 A1
Fernham SN7 ..... 193 D2
Fringford OX6 ..... 52 B4
Fulbrook OX18 ..... 100 C3
Hailey OX8 ..... 104 A3
Hampton Poyle OX5 ..... 93 D2
Hanwell OX17 ..... 8 C2
Harwell OX11 ..... 217 F4
Hornton OX15 ..... 7 E3
Horton-cum-S OX33 ..... 112 A3
Islip OX5 ..... 93 F1
Kirtlington OX5 ..... 78 A2
Langford GL7 ..... 132 B1
Longworth OX13 ..... 156 A2
Lower Heyford OX6 ..... 62 B3
Ludgershall HP18 ..... 98 B4
Marston OX3 ..... 123 F3
Middle Barton OX7 ..... 61 D4
Middleton Cheney OX17 ..... 10 C1
Milcombe OX15 ..... 21 D1
Mixbury OX6 ..... 38 C4
Mollington OX17 ..... 4 A2
Rotherfield Peppard RG9 ..... 253 D4
Shilton OX18 ..... 115 D3
Shiplake RG9 ..... 254 C1
South Moreton OX11 ..... 219 F3
Steventon OX13 ..... 198 C2
Towersey OX9 ..... 148 C4
Wallingford OX10 ..... 221 E4
Watlington OX9 ..... 186 A2
Wendlebury OX6 ..... 80 A2
Weston-on-the-G OX6 ..... 79 D1
Witney OX8 ..... 118 B4
Yarnton OX5 ..... 108 A2
Church Meadow OX7 ..... 70 A1
Church Mews RG8 ..... 257 E3
Church Mill Cl OX8 ..... 137 E2
Church Path
Stanford in the V SN7 ..... 194 C4
Stokenchurch HP14 ..... 188 B3
Church Pl GL56 ..... 54 A4
Church Rd Appleton OX13 ..... 158 A4
Ardley OX6 ..... 50 B2
Benson OX10 ..... 203 F2
Brackley NN13 ..... 24 A4
Caversham RG4 ..... 259 D1
Chadlington OX7 ..... 57 E1
Chinnor OX9 ..... 168 B3
Cholsey OX10 ..... 220 C2
Great Milton OX44 ..... 145 D1
Hinton Waldrist SN7 ..... 155 F1
Horspath OX33 ..... 143 E3
Ickford HP18 ..... 127 F2
Lewknor OX9 ..... 187 D4
Long Hanborough OX8 ..... 106 B4
Lower Odington GL56 ..... 54 A4
Milton-u-W OX7 ..... 70 A1
North Leigh OX8 ..... 105 D4
Pangbourne RG8 ..... 256 B3
Radley OX14 ..... 160 C2
Sandford-on-T OX4 ..... 161 D4
Stokenchurch HP14 ..... 188 B3
Thame OX9 ..... 129 F1
Weston-on-the-G OX6 ..... 79 D1
Wheatley OX33 ..... 144 A4
Church Rise OX7 ..... 88 B3
Church Row
Bishopstone SN6 ..... 227 D2
Childrey OX12 ..... 213 E2
Church Sq OX5 ..... 93 F1
Church St Ardington OX12 ..... 215 F3
Bampton OX18 ..... 134 C2
Barford St M OX15 ..... 32 C3
Beckley OX3 ..... 111 D2
Bicester OX6 ..... 65 F1
Church St continued
Bladon OX20 ..... 91 D1
Bledington OX7 ..... 54 B1
Blewbury OX11 ..... 237 D4
Bloxham OX15 ..... 21 E2
Bodicote OX15 ..... 22 C4
Caversham RG4 ..... 259 D1
Charlbury OX7 ..... 73 D2
Chipping Norton OX7 ..... 42 C2
Deddington OX15 ..... 33 F2
Didcot OX11 ..... 218 C4
Ducklington OX8 ..... 118 A2
East Hendred OX12 ..... 216 B3
Eynsham OX8 ..... 120 C4
Faringdon SN7 ..... 172 C2
Fifield OX7 ..... 69 D1
Henley-on-T RG9 ..... 244 B1
Idbury OX7 ..... 69 D2
Kidlington OX5 ..... 92 C1
Kingham OX7 ..... 55 D2
Marcham OX13 ..... 178 B3
Marsh Gibbon OX6 ..... 67 F2
Shellingford SN7 ..... 193 F4
Shipton-u-W OX7 ..... 85 E4
Stokenchurch HP14 ..... 188 B3
Stonesfield OX8 ..... 89 E4
Sutton Courtenay OX14 ..... 180 A1
Upper Heyford OX6 ..... 48 C3
Upton OX11 ..... 218 B1
Wantage OX12 ..... 214 B2
Wargrave RG10 ..... 255 E1
Watlington OX9 ..... 186 A1
West Hanney OX12 ..... 196 C3
Wootton OX20 ..... 75 F2
Wroxton OX15 ..... 15 D4
Church View
Ascott-u-W OX7 ..... 71 E1
Bampton OX18 ..... 134 C2
Banbury OX16 ..... 16 A2
Brackley NN13 ..... 24 A4
Carterton OX18 ..... 115 F1
Charlton-on-O OX5 ..... 95 D3
Freeland OX8 ..... 106 A3
Stoke Row RG9 ..... 241 F3
Church View Rd OX8 ..... 117 F4
Church Way
N Hinksey Vill OX2 ..... 122 B1
Oxford OX4 ..... 141 F2
Sparsholt OX12 ..... 212 C2
Church Wlk Banbury OX16 ..... 16 B3
Bishopstone SN6 ..... 227 E2
Combe OX8 ..... 90 A2
Oxford OX2 ..... 123 D2
Shipton-u-W OX7 ..... 70 B1
Shrivenham SN6 ..... 209 E4
Upper Heyford OX6 ..... 62 C4
Churchfield RG9 ..... 223 E2
Churchfield La OX10 ..... 203 F2
Churchill Cl Didcot OX11 ..... 200 B1
Woodstock OX20 ..... 91 D3
Churchill Cres OX9 ..... 148 A4
Churchill Dr OX3 ..... 124 B1
Churchill Gate OX20 ..... 91 E3
Churchill Pl OX2 ..... 122 C4
Churchill Rd Bicester OX6 ..... 65 F2
Chipping Norton OX7 ..... 42 B1
Didcot OX11 ..... 200 B1
Kidlington OX5 ..... 108 C4
Kingham OX7 ..... 55 D4
Churchill Way OX8 ..... 106 A4
Churchlea OX17 ..... 4 A2
Churchmere Rd OX14 ..... 180 A1
Churchward OX11 ..... 200 C2
Churchward Cl OX12 ..... 196 B1
Churchway RG20 ..... 235 D1
Chure The OX5 ..... 95 D2
Churnet Cl OX11 ..... 201 D1
Cinnaminta Rd OX3 ..... 142 C4
Cinnamon Cl OX44 ..... 184 B4
Circourt Rd OX12 ..... 195 F2
Circular Rd OX6 ..... 81 D3
Circus St OX4 ..... 141 F4
City Rd HP14 ..... 189 E3
Clack's La Benson OX10 ..... 222 B4
Crowmarsh G OX10 ..... 222 B4
Clanfield Cres RG31 ..... 257 E1
Clapcot Way OX10 ..... 221 E4
Clare Terr OX18 ..... 115 E1
Clarence Pl OX11 ..... 218 C4
Clarence Rd RG9 ..... 244 B1
Clarendon Cl OX14 ..... 180 A4
Clarendon Dr OX9 ..... 130 A1
Clarks La CV36 ..... 28 A3
Clarkston Rd OX18 ..... 115 E1
Clay Bank OX15 ..... 30 A4
Clay Cl RG31 ..... 257 D1
Clay La OX10 ..... 204 B1
Claydon Rd OX17 ..... 4 C2
Clayfields SN6 ..... 209 D2
Claymond Rd OX3 ..... 124 C2
Claypit La SN7 ..... 211 D4
Claypits La SN6 ..... 209 E4
Clays Cl OX3 ..... 124 A3
Cleave The OX11 ..... 217 F4
Cleavers OX9 ..... 168 A3
Cleavers Sq OX4 ..... 142 C1
Cleeve Down RG8 ..... 249 E4
Cleeve Rd RG8 ..... 249 D4
Cleeves Ave OX7 ..... 42 C3
Cleeves Cnr OX7 ..... 42 C3
Clematis Pl OX4 ..... 142 C1
Clements Cl OX12 ..... 214 C3
Clements Green OX11 ..... 219 F3
Clements La OX6 ..... 67 F1
Clements Mead RG31 ..... 257 D1
Clements Rd RG9 ..... 244 B2
Clerkenwell Cotts HP17 ..... 130 C3
Cleve Ct RG8 ..... 249 D4
Clevedon Rd RG31 ..... 257 F2
Cleveland Cl OX5 ..... 109 D4
Cleveland Dr OX4 ..... 142 B3
Clevelands OX14 ..... 160 A1
Cleveley Rd OX7 ..... 58 C3
Clevemede RG8 ..... 249 E4
Cleycourt Rd SN6 ..... 209 D3
Clifden Rd HP18 ..... 127 E3
Clifford Pl OX2 ..... 122 B4
Clifton Dr OX14 ..... 179 F4
Clifton Rd OX15 ..... 34 B2
Clifton Rise RG10 ..... 255 F1
Clinton Cl OX4 ..... 141 F2
Clive Rd OX4 ..... 142 B3
Clock Tower SN7 ..... 172 C1
Cloisters The
Caversham RG4 ..... 259 D2
Wantage OX12 ..... 214 B2
Close The Ardington OX12 ..... 215 F3
Benson OX10 ..... 203 F3
Chipping Warden OX17 ..... 5 F3
Epwell OX15 ..... 13 D3
Great Bourton OX17 ..... 9 E4
Henley-on-T RG9 ..... 254 B4
Lechlade GL7 ..... 150 B3
Stanton Harcourt OX8 ..... 138 A4
Woodcote RG8 ..... 250 C4
Closes The OX5 ..... 92 C1
Clover Cl OX2 ..... 140 A3
Clover Pl Eynsham OX8 ..... 120 B4
Oxford OX4 ..... 142 C1
Coach La SN7 ..... 173 D2
Coach Way OX10 ..... 203 F2
Coalport Way RG30 ..... 257 F1
Coates La RG9 ..... 206 B1
Cobden Cres OX1 ..... 141 E4
Cochrane Rd OX10 ..... 204 B1
Cockcroft Rd OX11 ..... 218 C4
Cockington Green OX16 ..... 16 C4
Cockpit Cl OX20 ..... 91 D3
Cocks La OX33 ..... 125 E4
Cockshoot Cl OX8 ..... 89 E4
Cogges Hill Rd OX8 ..... 118 B4
Coghill OX5 ..... 93 D4
Coker Cl OX6 ..... 65 F1
Colborne Rd OX11 ..... 218 B4
Coldharbour Cl RG9 ..... 254 B4
Coldicutt St RG4 ..... 259 E1
Cole Ct OX11 ..... 200 C2
Colegrave Rd OX15 ..... 21 F3
Colegrove Down OX2 ..... 140 A3
Colemans Hill OX3 ..... 124 C2
Coleridge Cl Bicester OX6 ..... 65 D2
Oxford OX4 ..... 142 B3
Coleridge Dr OX14 ..... 179 E3
Colerne Rd OX18 ..... 115 F2
Coles La OX44 ..... 184 B4
Colesbourne Rd OX15 ..... 21 E2
Collcutt Cl OX33 ..... 143 E4
College Cl Cholsey OX10 ..... 220 C1
Holton OX33 ..... 126 B1
College Farm OX7 ..... 57 D1
College Farm Cl OX5 ..... 94 C2
College La Oxford OX4 ..... 123 E1
Oxford, Littlemore OX4 ..... 142 A1
College The OX18 ..... 101 F2
College Way OX33 ..... 143 D3
Collett OX11 ..... 200 C2
Collett Way OX12 ..... 196 B1
Colley Wood OX1 ..... 141 F1
Collice St OX5 ..... 109 F4
Collier's La SN7 ..... 173 D2
Collingwood Cl OX14 ..... 159 F1
Collingwood Rd OX11 ..... 218 B4
Collins St OX4 ..... 141 F4
Collinsmith Dr OX12 ..... 196 C1
Collinsons Row OX7 ..... 73 D2
Collinwood Cl OX3 ..... 124 C2
Collinwood Rd OX3 ..... 124 C2
Collyer Rd HP14 ..... 188 C2
Colmore La RG9 ..... 252 C4
Coln Rd OX11 ..... 217 D2
Colne Cl Bicester OX6 ..... 65 E1
Grove OX12 ..... 196 B1
Colne Dr Berinsfield OX10 ..... 182 B3
Didcot OX11 ..... 201 D2
Colony Rd OX15 ..... 19 D4
Colterne Cl OX3 ..... 124 A3
Coltman Ave HP18 ..... 129 E3
Colton Rd SN6 ..... 209 D3
Coltsfoot Sq 5 OX4 ..... 142 C1
Columbia Way OX12 ..... 214 B4
Columbine Gdns OX4 ..... 143 D1
Colvile Cl OX18 ..... 134 C2
Colwell Dr Abingdon OX14 ..... 179 E4
Oxford OX3 ..... 125 D2
Witney OX8 ..... 117 F3
Colwell Rd OX10 ..... 182 B3
Colyton Way RG8 ..... 257 E3
Combe Gate OX8 ..... 90 A2
Combe Rd Oxford OX2 ..... 123 D1
Stonesfield OX8 ..... 89 E4
Combes Cl SN7 ..... 173 D2
Combewell OX44 ..... 143 E1
Comfrey Rd OX4 ..... 142 C2
Common Cl
North Leigh OX8 ..... 105 D3
Shrivenham SN6 ..... 209 E4
Common La OX7 ..... 42 B1
Common Rd Beckley OX3 ..... 110 C2
North Leigh OX8 ..... 105 D3
Compass Cl OX4 ..... 142 B2
Compton Ave RG31 ..... 257 D3
Compton Ct CV36 ..... 27 F4
Compton Dr OX14 ..... 160 A1
Compton Rd OX16 ..... 16 B3
Compton Terr OX10 ..... 221 E4
Condor Cl RG31 ..... 257 E2
Conduit Hill Rise OX9 ..... 147 F4
Conduit Rd OX14 ..... 179 F4
Conifer Cl OX2 ..... 140 B4
Conifer Dr Bicester OX6 ..... 65 F3
Reading RG31 ..... 257 D1
Conifer Rise OX16 ..... 9 D1
Conigre OX9 ..... 168 A3
Conisboro Ave RG4 ..... 258 C3
Conisboro Way RG4 ..... 258 C3
Coniston Ave OX3 ..... 124 A2
Coniston Dr RG30 ..... 257 F1
Connolly Dr OX18 ..... 115 E2
Constable's Croft OX6 ..... 96 C4
Constitution Hill OX10 ..... 221 F2
Conway Dr OX16 ..... 15 F3
Conway Rd OX13 ..... 159 E1
Conyger Cl OX5 ..... 93 F1
Cook La OX10 ..... 221 F1
Cook's Hill OX15 ..... 14 A3
Cooks La OX7 ..... 41 F3
Coolidge Cl OX3 ..... 124 B1
Coombe Hill Cres OX9 ..... 147 F4
Coombe The RG8 ..... 248 C3
Coombes Cl OX7 ..... 85 E4
Cooper Cl OX7 ..... 42 C2
Cooper Pl OX3 ..... 124 C2
Cooper Rd RG9 ..... 244 B2
Cooper's Court Rd HP14 ..... 188 B3
Coopers Gate OX16 ..... 16 B4
Coopers Gn OX6 ..... 65 F3
Coopers La OX12 ..... 214 C3
Coopers Pightle RG4 ..... 252 B2
Cope Cl OX2 ..... 140 B4
Cope Rd OX16 ..... 16 B3
Copenhagen Dr OX13 ..... 159 E1
Copperage Rd OX11 ..... 234 A1
Coppice Cl OX16 ..... 16 C2
Coppock Cl OX3 ..... 124 C1
Coppperfield Cl OX12 ..... 214 B3
Copse Ave RG4 ..... 259 F2
Copse Cl RG31 ..... 257 E2
Copse La OX3 ..... 124 A3
Copse Mead RG5 ..... 260 C1
Copse The Abingdon OX14 ..... 160 B1
Wargrave RG10 ..... 255 F2
Copson La OX44 ..... 163 E1
Copthorne Rd OX5 ..... 108 C4
Corbett Rd OX18 ..... 115 E1
Cordrey Green OX4 ..... 141 F2
Corfe Mews RG4 ..... 259 F2
Coriander Way 4 OX4 ..... 142 C1
Corn Avill Cl OX14 ..... 160 B1
Corn Bar OX8 ..... 117 F4
Corn St OX8 ..... 118 A4
Corndell Gdns OX8 ..... 118 A4
Corneville Rd OX14 ..... 179 D1
Cornfield Cl OX8 ..... 117 F4
Cornish Rd OX7 ..... 42 B1
Cornmarket
Faringdon SN7 ..... 172 C2
Thame OX9 ..... 147 F4
Cornmarket St OX1 ..... 123 E1
Cornwall Cl RG31 ..... 257 D2
Cornwallis Cl OX4 ..... 142 A3
Cornwallis Rd OX4 ..... 142 A3
Coromandel OX14 ..... 179 E2
Corunna Cres OX4 ..... 142 C3
Cosford Gdns OX6 ..... 66 A2
Costar Cl OX4 ..... 142 B1
Cot's Gn OX5 ..... 92 B1
Cote Rd OX18 ..... 135 F2
Cothill Rd OX13 ..... 158 C2
Cotman Cl OX14 ..... 179 F3
Cotmore Cl OX9 ..... 148 A4
Cotmore Gdns OX9 ..... 148 A4
Cotshill Gdns OX7 ..... 42 C2
Cotswold Cl
Minster Lovell OX8 ..... 102 C1
Sibford Ferris OX15 ..... 19 D4
Cotswold Cnr OX7 ..... 29 D2
Cotswold Cres
Chipping Norton OX7 ..... 42 C1
Marston OX3 ..... 123 F3
Cotswold Cres Bglws OX7 ..... 42 C1
Cotswold Meadow OX8 ..... 117 E4
Cotswold Pk OX11 ..... 200 B1
Cotswold Rd OX2 ..... 140 A3
Cotswold Terr OX7 ..... 42 C1
Cotswold View OX7 ..... 73 D2
Cotswold Way
Carterton OX18 ..... 115 E2
Reading RG31 ..... 257 E1
Cottage Rd SN7 ..... 194 B4
Cottages The GL7 ..... 114 A3
Cottesmore La OX10 ..... 204 B3
Cottesmore Rd OX4 ..... 142 A2
Cotton Grass Cl OX4 ..... 142 C1
Couching St OX9 ..... 186 A1
Coulings Cl OX12 ..... 216 B4
Council Houses OX7 ..... 45 E4
County Rd NN13 ..... 24 A3
County Trading Est OX4 ..... 142 C2
County View OX15 ..... 34 B2
Coupland Rd OX13 ..... 159 D3
Court Cl Kidlington OX5 ..... 108 B4
Shipton-u-W OX7 ..... 85 E4
Warmington OX17 ..... 3 D2
Court Close Rd OX9 ..... 148 C4
Court Dr OX10 ..... 203 D3
Court Farm Rd OX4 ..... 141 F2
Court Hill Rd OX12 ..... 214 A1
Court Place Gdns OX4 ..... 141 F2
Court Rd OX12 ..... 214 A1
Court The OX14 ..... 159 F1
Courtenay Cl OX14 ..... 200 A4
Courtenay Dr RG4 ..... 259 D4
Courtenay Rd OX12 ..... 214 C3
Courtfield Rd OX33 ..... 125 E4
Courthouse HP18 ..... 129 E4
Courtiers Green OX14 ..... 181 E2
Courtington La OX15 ..... 21 E3
Courtland Rd OX4 ..... 142 A2
Courtlands Hill RG8 ..... 256 B2
Courtlands Rd OX7 ..... 85 E4
Courts Gdns OX8 ..... 118 B4
Covent Cl OX14 ..... 160 A2
Coverley Rd OX3 ..... 142 B4
Covert The OX20 ..... 91 E3
Cow La Denchworth OX12 ..... 195 F2
Didcot OX11 ..... 201 D1
Grove OX12 ..... 196 C2
Kennington OX1 ..... 141 F1
Longworth OX13 ..... 156 B2
Moulsford OX10 ..... 238 C2
Reading RG1 ..... 258 C1
Steeple Aston OX6 ..... 62 A4
Cowell Pl OX8 ..... 118 A4
Cowleaze OX9 ..... 168 A3
Cowleaze Cl SN6 ..... 209 D3
Cowley Junc OX4 ..... 142 C2
Cowley Pl OX4 ..... 141 F4
Cowley Rd Oxford OX4 ..... 142 A2
Oxford, Littlemore OX4 ..... 142 A4
Cowper Cl OX6 ..... 65 D2
Cox La OX7 ..... 42 A1
Cox's Alley OX3 ..... 124 C2
Cox's La
Crowmarsh G OX10 ..... 222 A3
Stoke Row RG9 ..... 241 F3
Cox's Rd SN6 ..... 209 D3
Coxfield Cl HP14 ..... 188 C3
Coxmoor Cl OX7 ..... 54 C2
Coxwell Gdns SN7 ..... 172 C2
Coxwell Hall Mews SN7 ..... 172 C1
Coxwell Rd SN7 ..... 172 C1
Coxwell St SN7 ..... 172 C2
Cozens La OX7 ..... 54 C2
CR Bates Ind Est HP14 ..... 188 C3
Crabhill La OX12 ..... 215 D4
Crabtree Cnr OX10 ..... 240 B4
Crabtree La OX14 ..... 179 D1
Crabtree Pl OX14 ..... 180 A4
Crabtree Rd
Haddenham HP17 ..... 130 C3
N Hinksey Vill OX2 ..... 140 B4
Crafts End OX11 ..... 235 F4
Cranbourne Gdns RG30 ..... 258 A1
Cranbrook Ct OX8 ..... 118 A3
Cranbrook Dr OX1 ..... 160 C4
Crane Furlong SN6 ..... 190 A4
Cranesbill Way OX4 ..... 142 C1
Cranham St OX2 ..... 123 D2
Cranham Terr OX2 ..... 123 D2
Cranleigh Cl OX16 ..... 16 A2
Cranley Rd OX3 ..... 124 C2
Cranmer Cl RG31 ..... 257 D2
Cranmer Rd OX4 ..... 142 C3
Cranwell Ave OX18 ..... 115 F1
Cratlands Cl OX44 ..... 163 E1
Craufurd Rd OX4 ..... 142 C3
Craven Comm SN7 ..... 211 E4
Craven Way OX11 ..... 218 C4
Crawborough Rd OX7 ..... 73 E2
Crawley Rd OX8 ..... 104 A1
Crawshay Dr RG4 ..... 259 D4
Cray Ct OX11 ..... 200 C2
Creampot Cl OX17 ..... 4 C1
Creampot Cres OX17 ..... 4 C1
Creampot La OX17 ..... 4 C1
Crecy Wlk OX20 ..... 91 E3
Cremyll Rd RG1 ..... 258 C1
Crescent Cl OX4 ..... 142 B3
Crescent Rd Oxford OX4 ..... 142 B3
Reading RG31 ..... 257 E1
Crescent The
Adderbury OX17 ..... 23 D3
Bicester OX6 ..... 65 E2
Carterton OX18 ..... 133 E4
Sandford-on-T OX4 ..... 161 E4
Shiplake RG9 ..... 255 D2
Steeple Aston OX6 ..... 62 A4
Witney OX8 ..... 104 B1
Crescent Way OX10 ..... 220 C1
Cress Hill Pl OX3 ..... 124 C2
Crest The
Bledlow Ridge HP14 ..... 189 F4
Caversham RG4 ..... 259 E3
Crick Rd OX2 ..... 123 E2
Cricket Ground HP14 ..... 188 B3
Cricket Rd OX4 ..... 142 A3
Cricklade Rd SN6 ..... 190 A3
Cripley Pl OX2 ..... 123 D1
Cripley Rd OX2 ..... 123 D1
Crisp Rd RG9 ..... 244 B2
Crispin Cl RG4 ..... 258 B3
Crispin Pl OX10 ..... 221 E4
Croasdell Cl OX14 ..... 179 F2
Crockwell Cl OX6 ..... 65 F1
Crockwell St CV36 ..... 27 F4
Croft Ave OX5 ..... 108 C4
Croft Cl Merton OX6 ..... 95 E4
Oxford OX3 ..... 123 F2
Thame OX9 ..... 148 A4
Croft Ctyd HP17 ..... 130 C3
Croft End OX12 ..... 214 A1
Croft La OX17 ..... 23 D2
Croft Rd Goring RG8 ..... 249 E3
Oxford OX3 ..... 123 F2
Thame OX9 ..... 148 A4
Wallingford OX10 ..... 221 E4
Croft The
Aston Tirrold OX11 ..... 219 F1
Didcot OX11 ..... 218 C4

High St
Abingdon OX13, OX14 179 F4
Adderbury OX17 23 D2
Ascott-u-W OX7 71 E1
Ashbury SN6 228 A4
Aston OX18 135 E2
Aston Rowant OX9 167 F2
Bampton OX18 134 C2
Banbury OX15, OX16, OX17 16 B3
Barford St M OX15 32 C3
Benson OX10 203 F2
Bishopstone SN6 227 E2
Bloxham OX15 21 F3
Bodicote OX15 22 B4
Burford OX18 100 C3
Chalgrove OX44 184 B4
Charlton-on-O OX5 95 D2
Charney Bassett OX12 175 F1
Childrey OX12 213 E2
Chinnor OX9 168 B4
Chipping Norton OX7 42 C2
Clifton Hampden OX14 181 E2
Cropredy OX17 4 C1
Croughton NN13 36 B4
Cuddesdon OX44 144 A1
Culham OX14 180 A2
Cumnor OX2 139 E3
Deddington OX15 33 F2
Didcot OX11 218 C4
Dorchester OX10 182 B1
Drayton OX14 179 D1
Drayton St L OX10 183 D3
East Hendred OX12 216 C3
Ewelme OX10 204 C2
Eynsham OX8 120 C4
Fernham SN7 193 D2
Fifield OX7 69 D1
Finstock OX7 88 A3
Goring RG8 249 E3
Great Rollright OX7 29 D2
Haddenham HP17 130 C3
Harwell OX11 217 F4
Highworth SN6 190 A3
Hinton Waldrist SN7 155 F1
Hook Norton OX15 30 A4
Islip OX5 93 F1
Lechlade GL7 150 B2
Lewknor OX9 187 D4
Long Crendon HP18 129 E3
Long Wittenham OX14 201 E4
Ludgershall HP18 98 A4
Middleton Cheney OX17 17 F4
Milton (Abingdon) OX14 199 E3
Milton-u-W OX7 70 A1
Nettlebed RG9 224 B1
North Moreton OX11 220 A4
Oxford OX1 123 E1
Pangbourne RG8 256 B3
Ramsden OX7 88 A2
Ratley OX15 2 A2
Shipton-u-W OX7 85 E4
Shrivenham SN6 209 E3
Shutford OX15 14 A3
Sonning RG4 260 B2
Souldern OX6 35 F2
South Newington OX15 31 F4
Standlake OX8 137 E2
Stanford in the V SN7 194 C4
Steventon OX13 199 D2
Stonesfield OX8 89 E4
Streatley RG8 249 D3
Sutton Courtenay OX14 200 A4
Tetsworth OX9 166 A4
Thame OX9 129 F1
Uffington SN7 211 E4
Upper Heyford OX6 48 C1
Upton OX11 218 B1
Wallingford OX10 221 E4
Wargrave RG10 255 E1
Watchfield SN6 191 E1
Watlington OX9 186 A1
Wheatley OX33 144 A4
Whitchurch RG8 256 B4
Witney OX8 118 A4
Woodstock OX20 91 D3
Wootton OX20 75 F2
High View OX12 214 A2
Highbridge Cl RG4 259 F2
Highclere Gdns
Banbury OX16 15 F3
Wantage OX12 214 B3
Highdown Ave RG4 259 F4
Highdown Hill Rd
Caversham RG4 259 D4
Mapledurham RG4 259 D4
Highfield HP18 129 E4
Highfield Ave OX3 124 B1
Highfield Cl OX9 147 E4
Highfield Park RG10 255 F1
Highfield Rd RG31 257 E2
Highlands OX16 9 D1
Highlands La RG9 254 A4
Highmoor Rd RG4 258 C2
Hightown Gdns OX16 16 B2
Hightown Leyes OX16 16 B2
Hightown Rd OX16 16 B2
Highworth Pl OX8 118 A4
Highworth Rd
Faringdon SN7 172 C1
Shrivenham SN6 209 D4
Highworth Way RG31 257 D1
Hill Bottom Cl RG8 250 C2
Hill Cl Charlbury OX7 73 E2
Chipping Norton OX7 42 C1
East Challow OX12 214 A2
Hill Cres OX7 88 B3
Hill Farm Ct OX9 168 B3
Hill Farm La OX6 47 E3
Hill Gdns RG8 249 D3
Hill La OX18 152 B4
Hill Lands RG10 255 E1
Hill Piece OX11 235 F4
Hill Rd Chinnor OX9 168 B3
Lewknor OX9 187 D4
Lewknor OX9 187 E3
Watchfield SN6 191 E1
Watlington OX9 206 C4
Hill Rise
Great Rollright OX7 29 D2
Horspath OX33 143 E3
Woodstock OX20 91 D4
Hill The Aynho OX17 35 E4
Bourton SN6 209 D2
Burford OX18 100 C2
Garsington OX44 143 F1
Hill Top La OX9 168 C2
Hill Top Rd OX4 142 A4
Hill View Carterton OX18 115 E2
Kingston Lisle OX12 212 A2
Oxford OX3 125 D2
Uffington SN7 211 E4
Hill View Cres OX16 16 A4
Hill View La OX13 159 D4
Hillary Dr OX11 218 C4
Hillary Way OX33 144 B4
Hillcraft Rd OX33 125 E4
Hilliat Fields OX14 179 D1
Hilliers Cl OX14 200 A4
Hillsborough Cl OX4 142 A2
Hillsborough Rd OX4 142 A2
Hillside Harwell OX11 217 D2
Whitchurch RG8 256 B4
Hillside Cl Banbury OX16 16 C2
Upper Arncott OX6 96 C4
Hillside Rd OX7 46 C1
Hilltop HP18 129 E3
Hilltop Gdns OX5 93 F1
Hilltop Rd RG4 258 B3
Hillview Cl RG31 257 D1
Hillview Rd Abingdon OX14 159 F1
Oxford OX2 123 D1
Hillwerke OX9 168 B3
Hilly Lawn Ct OX7 42 C2
Hillyard Barns OX14 200 A4
Hilton Rd OX16 16 A3
Hinksey Hill OX1 141 D2
Hinksey Hill Intc OX1 141 E2
Hinton Hill SN6 227 D2
Hinton Rd
Hinton Waldrist OX13 156 A2
Longworth OX13 156 A2
Hinton Springs SN6 227 D2
Hirstwood RG30 257 F1
Hiskins OX12 214 A3
Hitchman Dr OX7 42 C2
Hithercroft Cholsey OX10 220 B3
South Moreton OX11 220 B3
Hithercroft Ct OX10 221 D3
Hithercroft Rd OX10 221 D4
Hive Mews OX14 179 F3
Hixet Wood OX7 73 D2
HM Prison (Bullingdon)
OX6 97 D3
Hobbs Cl OX14 180 A4
Hobby Ct OX4 142 C1
Hobson Rd OX2 123 D4
Hocker Bench SN6 227 E2
Hocketts Cl RG8 250 C2
Hockmore St OX4 142 B2
Hodge Ct OX1 141 E4
Hodgson Cl OX6 49 F4
Hogarth Pl OX14 179 F3
Hogg End Bloxham OX15 21 F2
Chipping Warden OX17 5 F3
Holborn Hill OX12 231 E4
Holcombe La OX10 183 E3
Holford Rd OX8 117 F4
Holis Cl OX8 118 B4
Holkham Cl RG30 257 F1
Holland Cl OX9 168 B4
Holland Pl OX3 142 C4
Holland Rd OX14 160 A1
Hollandridge La RG9 207 E2
Hollands Rise OX!7 23 F2
Holley Cres OX3 124 C2
Holliers Cl Sydenham OX9 167 E4
Thame OX9 147 F4
Holliers Cres OX7 60 C4
Hollington HP18 129 D4
Hollow Furlong OX8 107 E1
Hollow Way Aynho OX17 35 E4
Childrey OX12 213 E2
Oxford OX3, OX4 142 B3
Holloway Hill OX15 12 A1
Holloway La
Compton Wynyates OX15 12 A1
Ibstone RG9 207 F3
Holloway Rd OX33 144 A4
Holloway Rd The SN7 192 A4
Holloway The
Harwell OX11 217 F3
Mollington OX17 4 A2
Holly Cl Bicester OX6 65 F3
Kidlington OX5 108 C4
Rotherfield Peppard RG9 242 C3
Hollybush Rd
Carterton OX18 115 E1
Hook Norton OX15 30 A4
Hollybush Row OX1 123 D1
Holm Sq OX6 65 F3
Holm Way OX6 65 F3
Holme Park Farm La RG4 260 B1
Holmemoor Dr RG4 260 C1
Holmlea Rd RG8 249 E3
Holoway Rd OX8 118 A4
Holt The Abingdon OX14 179 F4
Mollington OX17 3 F2
Purley on T RG8 257 E2
Holt Weer Cl OX2 109 D1
Holyoake Rd OX3 124 B2
Holyrood Cl RG4 259 E3
Holywell Cl OX14 160 B1
Holywell St OX1 123 E1
Home Cl Carterton OX18 115 E1
Cutteslowe OX2 122 B4
Kidlington OX5 92 C1
Wootton (Oxford) OX13 159 D3
Home Croft RG31 257 D1
Home Farm OX10 221 F4
Home Farm Cl
Ambrosden OX6 81 E2
East Hendred OX12 216 B4
Shipton-u-W OX7 85 E4
Home Farm Ct OX17 23 D2
Homefield Cl HP14 188 C2
Homeleaze Rd SN6 209 F4
Homestall Cl OX2 122 A1
Homestead Cres OX6 63 D4
Homestead Rd OX16 16 C1
Homestead The
Bladon OX20 91 E2
Kidlington OX5 108 B4
Thame OX9 129 F1
Hone Ct OX7 73 D2
Honey La OX10 220 C1
Honeybottom La OX13 159 D3
Honeyham Cl OX18 116 B2
Honeysuckle Cl OX6 65 F3
Honeysuckle Gr OX4 143 D1
Honor Cl OX5 108 C4
Hook End La RG8 249 D1
Hook Norton Rd OX15 19 D4
Hookend La RG8 251 E4
Hooks Cl GL7 132 C1
Hop Gdns RG9 244 B1
Hopcraft Cl OX6 96 C4
Hopcraft La OX15 33 F2
Hopkins Ct OX4 142 B3
Hopton Rd OX9 130 A1
Horley Path Rd OX15 8 A1
Horn Hill OX15 32 C3
Horn Hill Rd OX17 22 C2
Horn La Adlestrop OX12 40 A3
East Hendred OX12 216 B3
Hornbeam Cl Banbury OX16 16 A3
Purley on T RG8 257 E3
Hornbeam Dr OX4 143 D1
Horne OX6 66 A4
Hornbeam Rd OX6 65 F3
Hornsea Cl RG30 257 F1
Hornton Hollow OX15 21 E2
Horse Cl The RG4 259 E2
Horse Close Cotts OX44 164 B4
Horse Fair
Banbury OX15, OX16 16 B3
Chipping Norton OX7 42 C2
Deddington OX15 33 F2
Horse Shoe La OX20 72 A4
Horsecroft SN7 194 C4
Horseman Cl OX3 124 A3
Horsemere La OX8 107 E1
Horsepond Rd RG4 252 A3
Horseshoe La OX20 75 F2
Horseshoe Park RG8 256 B3
Horseshoe Rd
Bledlow Ridge HP14 189 E4
Pangbourne RG8 256 B3
Horseshoes La OX10 203 F2
Horsham Cl OX16 8 C1
Horspath Driftway OX3 142 C4
Horspath Rd OX4 142 C3
Horton Ave OX9 148 A4
Horton Cl OX9 148 A4
Horton La OX15 21 D1
Horton View OX16 16 B2
Horwood Cl OX3 124 B2
Hosker Cl OX3 125 D2
Hound Cl OX14 160 B1
Howard Ave OX12 196 C1
Howard Cornish Rd OX13 178 B4
Howard Rd OX16 16 C3
Howard St OX4 142 A3
Howbery Farm OX10 221 F4
Howe Cl OX33 144 A4
Howe Rd OX9 206 B4
Howes La OX6 65 D2
Howgate Dr RG8 249 E4
Howland Rd OX9 148 A3
Hoyle Cl OX8 104 A2
Huckleberry Cl RG8 257 E2
Hudleston Ave OX10 204 B1
Hudson St Bicester OX6 65 E2
Deddington OX15 33 F2
Hugh Allen Cres OX3 123 F2
Hughes Cl OX7 73 E1
Hughes Cres SN7 192 B2
Humber Cl Didcot OX11 201 D1
Wantage OX12 214 C3
Humber St OX15 21 F2
Humber Wlk OX16 15 F4
Humfrey Rd OX3 124 C2
Humphries Cl OX18 115 F2
Hundred Acre Cl OX4 142 C4
Hunsdon Rd OX4 142 A2
Hunt Cl OX6 65 F1
Hunt Rd OX9 148 A4
Hunt's Cl OX8 89 E4
Hunter Cl Abingdon OX14 160 A2
Oxford OX4 142 C3
Huntercombe End La
RG9 224 A2
Hunters Chase RG4 258 C3
Hunters Cl OX12 196 B1
Hunters Field SN7 194 C4
Hunters Piece SN6 209 D1
Hunters Point OX9 168 B3
Hunts Cl OX18 100 C2
Hurdeswell OX8 90 A1
Hurdlers Green OX9 186 A1
Hurst Cl OX10 221 E3
Hurst La Cumnor OX2 140 A3
Freeland OX8 106 A4
Hurst Rise Rd OX2 140 B4
Hurst St OX4 141 F4
Huscarle Way RG31 257 E2
Hutchcomb Rd OX2 140 B4
Hutchcombe Farm Cl
OX2 140 B4
Huxley Cl Bicester OX6 65 E2
Wootton (Oxford) OX13 159 D3
Hyacinth Wlk OX4 161 F4
Hyde Copse OX13 178 B4
Hyde Gr OX15 21 E2
Hyde Pl OX14 179 E3
Hyde Rd OX12 196 A3
Hyde The OX14 179 E3
Hydes The RG31 257 E2
Hydrangea Wlk OX16 9 D1
Hythe Bridge St OX1 123 D1

Ian Mikardo Way RG4 259 E1
Ibstone Ave RG4 259 F3
Ibstone Rd HP14 188 B2
Ickford Rd
Shabbington HP18 128 B1
Tiddington OX9 145 F4
Worminghall HP18 127 F3
Ickleton Rd
East Challow OX12 214 A2
Wantage OX12 214 A2
Icknield Cl
Aston Rowant OX9 168 A2
Didcot OX11 200 B1
Icknield La OX12 214 C2
Icknield Pl RG8 249 E4
Icknield Rd RG8 249 E4
Icknield Way SN6 227 E2
Idbury Cl OX8 117 E4
Idstone Hill SN6 228 A2
Idstone Rd SN6 228 A3
Iffley Rd OX4 141 F4
Iffley Turn OX4 142 A3
Ilchester Mews RG4 259 F3
Ilex Cl RG4 252 C2
Ilges La OX10 221 D1
Ilkley Rd RG4 258 C2
Illingworth Ave RG4 259 F3
Ilsley Cl RG4 252 C3
Imperial Ct RG9 244 C1
Independent Bsns Pk
HP14 188 B3
Ingham La OX9 186 A1
Ingle Cl OX3 124 A2
Inglewood Cl RG4 252 C3
Ingrebourne Way OX11 200 C2
Inkerman Cl OX14 159 E1
Innsworth Rd OX18 115 F2
Inott Furze OX3 142 B4
Insall Rd OX7 42 C2
Ireton Cl OX44 184 B3
Ireton Ct OX9 129 F1
Iron Down Hill
Barford St M OX15 32 B2
South Newington OX15 31 F2
Ironstone Hollow OX15 30 B4
Ironstones OX16 16 A4
Isis Ave OX6 65 D1
Isis Bsns Ctr OX4 142 C3
Isis Cl Abingdon OX14 160 B1
Long Hanborough OX8 106 A4
Islip Rd Bletchingdon OX5 93 D4
Cutteslowe OX2 123 D4
Islsley Rd OX3 124 C2
Itchen Ct OX11 201 D2
Ivatt Wlk OX16 16 C4
Ivy La Mollington OX17 4 A2
Oxford OX3 124 B2
Ivybank RG31 257 E1
Ivydene Rd RG30 258 B1

Jack Argent Cl OX4 142 C1
Jack Straw's La OX3 124 A2
Jackdaw La OX4 141 F4
Jackies La OX33 144 B4
Jackman Cl OX14 180 A4
Jackson Cl OX18 115 E1
Jackson Dr OX1 141 F1
Jackson Rd Bledington OX7 54 B1
Cutteslowe OX2 109 D1
Jacobs Cl OX8 104 A1
Jacobs Yd OX7 60 C4
James Ct OX18 152 C4
James St OX4 141 F4
James Wolfe Rd OX4 142 C4
Jane Seaman Ct OX4 143 D1
Japonica Cl OX6 65 F3
Japonica Wlk OX16 9 D1
Jarn Way OX1 140 B1
Jarvis La OX6 66 A1
Jasmine Cl OX4 142 C2
Jasmine Pl OX6 65 F3
Javelin Way OX10 204 B2
Jay Cl OX6 81 D4
Jaynes Cl OX16 16 B1
Jefferson Cl RG4 259 E4
Jefferson Way OX9 148 A4
Jeffersons Piece OX7 73 E3
Jemmetts Cl OX10 182 B1
Jennings La OX11 217 F4
Jericho St OX2 123 D2
Jerome Way OX5 92 B3
Jersey Dr OX16 9 D1
Jersey Rd OX4 142 A2
Jervis Cl OX7 60 C4
Jespers Hill SN7 173 D2
Jesse's La HP18 129 E3
Jessops Cl OX3 123 F3
Jethro Tull Gdns OX10 221 F4
Jeune St OX4 141 F4
Joan Lawrence Pl OX3 124 C1
John Buchan Rd OX3 124 A3
John Garne Way OX3 124 A1
John Lopes Rd OX8 120 C4
John Mason Rd OX14 180 A4
John Morris Rd OX14 179 F3
John Piers La OX1 141 E3
John Snow Pl OX3 124 C2
John Towle Cl OX1 141 E3
Johnson Cl OX44 143 E1
Johnston's Way OX7 42 C1
Johnstone Pl OX10 221 E4
Jordan Cl Caversham RG4 259 F3
Didcot OX11 201 D1
Jordan Hill OX2 109 D1
Josey Cl RG4 252 C3
Jourdain Rd OX4 142 C2
Jowett Wlk OX1 123 E1
Joyce's Rd SN7 194 B4
Jubilee Cl OX6 62 A4
Jubilee Cotts OX12 215 F3
Jubilee Ct OX16 16 B3
Jubilee Rd HP14 188 C2
Jubilee Way OX11 219 D4
Jubillee La OX7 85 D4
Judd's Cl OX8 118 B4
Judges Cl OX5 108 C4
Junction Rd Banbury OX16 16 C3
Churchill OX7 55 F2
Oxford OX4 142 B3
Juniper Cl OX16 9 D1
Juniper Dr OX4 142 C1
Juniper Gdns OX6 65 F3
Juniper Way RG31 257 E1
Juxon St OX2 123 D2

Kames Cl OX4 142 A3
Katchside OX14 199 F3
Katherine's Wlk GL7 150 B2
Keats Cl OX6 65 D2
Keats Rd OX16 16 A2
Keble Cl GL7 150 B3
Keble Rd Bicester OX6 65 F2
Oxford OX1 123 E2
Kedleston Rise OX16 16 C1
Keene Cl OX4 161 D4
Keens La OX9 168 B3
Keeys Cl OX6 50 B2
Kelburne Rd OX4 142 A2
Kelham Hall Dr OX33 144 A4
Kelly's Rd OX33 143 F4
Kelmscott Cl RG4 258 C2
Kelso Mews RG4 259 F3
Kelvedon Way RG4 258 C3
Kemps Rd OX17 23 D3
Kempson Cres OX4 142 A1
Kempster Cl OX14 180 A4
Kendal Ave RG4 259 F3
Kendal Cres OX2 109 D1
Kendal Piece OX7 73 E2
Kenhill Rd OX15 6 B1
Kenilworth Ave OX4 142 A4
Kenilworth Rd OX2 139 F2
Kenilworth Way OX16 15 F3
Kenley Ave OX18 115 F2
Kennedy Cl OX4 142 C4
Kennedy Cres OX10 220 C1
Kennedy Dr RG8 256 C3
Kennedy Rd OX6 65 E1
Kennel La
Chipping Norton OX7 42 A1
Steventon OX13 199 D3
Kennet Cl Berinsfield OX10 182 B2
Bicester OX6 65 E1
Grove OX12 196 B1
Kennet Rd Abingdon OX14 160 A1
Harwell OX11 217 E1
Kennett Rd OX3 124 B1
Kennington Rd
Kennington OX1 141 F1
Kennington OX1 160 C3
Radley OX14 160 C3
Kennington Rdbt OX1 141 F2
Kennylands Rd RG4 253 D2
Kensington Cl
Abingdon OX14 179 F2
Kings Sutton OX17 23 F3
Kent Cl Abingdon OX14 180 A4
Oxford OX4 142 C2
Kentons La RG10 255 E4
Kentwood Cl
Cholsey OX10 220 C1
Reading RG30 257 F1
Kentwood Hill RG31 257 F1
Kenville Rd OX1 141 F1
Kernham Dr RG31 257 E2
Kerry Cl OX16 9 D1
Kersington Cres OX4 142 B2
Kerwood Cl OX20 91 D4
Keston Cl RG4 259 E1
Kestrel Cl OX18 115 E2
Kestrel Cres OX4 142 B1
Kestrel Pl OX4 142 B1
Kestrel Way OX6 81 D4
Kestrels The OX12 196 B1
Ketchmere Cl HP18 129 E3
Kew Win OX11 201 D1
Keydale Rd OX33 143 F4

Lyn – Mol 271

Lyneham Rd Bicester OX6 ..... 66 A2
Milton-u-W OX7 ..... 70 A2
Lynges Cl OX14 ..... 160 A1
Lynmouth Rd Didcot OX11 .. 218 C4
Reading RG1 ..... 259 D1
Lynn Cl OX3 ..... 123 F2
Lynt Rd SN6 ..... 170 A3
Lynton La OX8 ..... 107 E1
Lyon Cl OX14 ..... 160 A1
Lysander Cl OX6 ..... 66 A2
Lytham End RG31 ..... 257 D2
Lytton Rd OX4 ..... 142 A3

Maberley Cl OX14 ..... 179 E3
Mably Way OX12 ..... 214 B4
Macaulay Cl OX6 ..... 65 E2
Macdonald Cl OX11 ..... 200 B1
Mackenzie Cl OX6 ..... 65 E2
Mackley Cl OX15 ..... 33 F2
Macray Rd OX8 ..... 118 A2
Mafeking Row OX9 ..... 186 C2
Magdalen Cl OX6 ..... 65 F2
Magdalen Ct OX11 ..... 219 D4
Magdalen Pl OX18 ..... 115 E1
Magdalen Rd OX4 ..... 142 A4
Magdalen St OX1 ..... 123 E1
Magnolia Cl OX5 ..... 108 C4
Magnolias The
Banbury OX16 ..... 9 D1
Bicester OX6 ..... 65 F3
Magpie La OX1 ..... 123 E1
Maidcroft Rd OX4 ..... 142 B3
Maiden's Cl SN6 ..... 191 E1
Maidley Cl OX8 ..... 104 B1
Main Ave OX4 ..... 161 E4
Main Rd Broughton OX15 ..... 15 E1
Curbridge OX8 ..... 117 E3
East Hagbourne OX11 ..... 218 C3
Fyfield OX13 ..... 157 E1
Long Hanborough OX8 ..... 90 B1
Middleton Cheney OX17 ..... 17 F4
Sutton Courtenay OX14 ..... 200 C4
West Hanney OX12 ..... 196 C3
Main St Adlestrop OX12 ..... 40 B2
Bledington OX7 ..... 54 B1
Chilton OX11 ..... 235 E4
Duns Tew OX6 ..... 47 E3
East Hanney OX12 ..... 197 D3
Finstock OX7 ..... 88 C4
Fringford OX6 ..... 52 B3
Grove OX12 ..... 196 C1
Hanwell OX17 ..... 8 C2
Hethe OX6 ..... 52 A4
Letcombe Bassett OX12 ..... 214 A1
Mollington OX17 ..... 4 A2
North Newington OX15 ..... 15 D2
Over Norton OX7 ..... 42 C3
Shalstone MK18 ..... 25 F3
Sibford Gower OX15 ..... 19 D4
Sibford Gower OX15 ..... 19 D4
Tadmarton OX15 ..... 20 B4
Turweston NN13 ..... 24 B4
West Hagbourne OX11 ..... 218 B2
Westbury NN13 ..... 25 D2
Wroxton OX15 ..... 15 D4
Majors Rd SN6 ..... 191 F1
Makins Rd RG9 ..... 254 B4
Malet Cl HP14 ..... 188 C3
Malford Rd OX3 ..... 124 C2
Mall The SN6 ..... 209 F4
Mallard Cl OX4 ..... 142 B1
Mallard Way OX12 ..... 196 B1
Mallins La SN7 ..... 192 B2
Mallory Ave RG4 ..... 259 E3
Maltfield Rd OX3 ..... 124 A3
Malthouse SN6 ..... 228 A4
Malthouse Cl SN6 ..... 228 A4
Malthouse La
Bodicote OX15 ..... 22 B4
Dorchester OX10 ..... 182 B1
Long Compton CV36 ..... 27 F3
Shutford OX15 ..... 14 A3
Malthouse Paddock SN7 .. 174 C4
Maltings Ct OX15 ..... 21 E2
Maltings The RG20 ..... 235 D1
Maltsters OX8 ..... 89 E4
Malvern Cl Banbury OX16 ..... 16 B1
Didcot OX11 ..... 200 B1
Malyns Cl OX9 ..... 168 B4
Mandarin Pl OX12 ..... 196 B1
Mandeville Cl OX14 ..... 160 A1
Mandhill Cl OX12 ..... 214 C4
Manning Cl OX15 ..... 21 F1
Mannings Cl OX15 ..... 19 D4
Manor Cl Aston OX18 ..... 135 F1
Cassington OX8 ..... 107 E1
Drayton OX14 ..... 179 D1
Great Bourton OX17 ..... 9 E4
Shrivenham SN6 ..... 209 D4
Sutton Courtenay OX14 ..... 200 C4
West Hagbourne OX11 ..... 218 B2
Manor Cres Didcot OX11 ..... 200 B1
Standlake OX8 ..... 137 E2
Stanford in the V SN7 ..... 194 C4
Manor Ct Abingdon OX14 ..... 179 F3
Banbury OX16 ..... 16 C4
Chadlington OX7 ..... 57 E1
Manor Dr OX33 ..... 143 E3
Manor Farm Cl
Kingham OX7 ..... 54 C3
Merton OX6 ..... 95 E4
Manor Farm Ct OX20 ..... 75 F2
Manor Farm La RG8 ..... 256 B1
Manor Farm Rd
Dorchester OX10 ..... 182 B1
Horspath OX33 ..... 143 E3
Manor Field OX12 ..... 214 A1
Manor Gn OX11 ..... 217 F4
Manor Gr OX1 ..... 160 C4
Manor La Clanfield OX18 ..... 152 C4
East Hendred OX12 ..... 216 A3
Shrivenham SN6 ..... 209 D3
Manor Orch OX15 ..... 8 A2
Manor Park OX17 ..... 1 B1
Manor Pl OX1 ..... 123 F1
Manor Rd Adderbury OX17 ..... 22 C2
Banbury OX16, OX17 ..... 16 C4
Bladon OX20 ..... 91 D1
Brize Norton OX18 ..... 116 A2
Carterton OX18 ..... 115 E3
Chinnor OX9 ..... 149 D3
Didcot OX11 ..... 200 B1
Ducklington OX8 ..... 118 A2
Fringford OX6 ..... 52 B4
Goring RG8 ..... 249 D3
Great Bourton OX17 ..... 9 E4
Henley-on-T RG9 ..... 254 B4
Middle Barton OX7 ..... 46 B1
Oxford OX1 ..... 123 F1
South Hinksey OX1 ..... 141 D3
Wantage OX12 ..... 232 B3
Whitchurch RG8 ..... 256 B4
Witney OX8 ..... 118 B4
Woodstock OX20 ..... 91 D4
Manor Way OX5 ..... 92 C1
Manor Wood Gate RG9 ..... 255 D2
Manorsfield Rd OX6 ..... 65 F1
Mansell Cl OX8 ..... 106 B3
Mansfield Gdns OX11 ..... 219 D4
Mansfield Rd OX1 ..... 123 E1
Mansion Hill OX17 ..... 17 F4
Mansmoor Rd OX5 ..... 94 C4
Manston Cl OX6 ..... 66 A2
Manzel Rd OX6 ..... 66 A3
Maple Ave OX5 ..... 108 C4
Maple Cl Banbury OX16 ..... 16 C1
N Hinksey Vill OX2 ..... 140 B4
Sonning Common RG4 ..... 253 D2
Maple Ct Goring RG8 ..... 249 D3
Kidlington OX5 ..... 108 C4
Maple Rd Bicester OX6 ..... 65 F1
Faringdon SN7 ..... 172 C2
Thame OX9 ..... 147 E4
Maple Way OX7 ..... 71 D1
Maple Well OX8 ..... 89 E4
Mapledene RG4 ..... 258 C2
Mapledurham Dr RG8 ..... 257 E3
Mapledurham View RG31 .. 257 E1
Maples The
Carterton OX18 ..... 115 E1
Grove OX12 ..... 196 B1
March Rd OX17 ..... 3 E2
Marcham Rd
Abingdon OX13, OX14 ..... 179 D4
Drayton OX14 ..... 179 D1
Marcham OX13 ..... 179 D4
Marchwood Ave RG4 ..... 259 E4
Margaret Cl Banbury OX16 ..... 16 A3
Bicester OX6 ..... 65 E2
Margaret Rd
Adderbury OX17 ..... 23 D3
Oxford OX3 ..... 124 C1
Maria Cres OX12 ..... 214 C3
Marie Cl OX6 ..... 67 F4
Marigold Cl 10 OX4 ..... 142 C1
Marines Dr SN7 ..... 172 C1
Marjoram Cl OX4 ..... 143 D1
Mark Rd OX3 ..... 124 C1
Market End Way OX6 ..... 65 E2
Market Pl Abingdon OX14 ..... 179 F4
Banbury OX15, OX16 ..... 16 B3
Deddington OX15 ..... 33 F2
Faringdon SN7 ..... 172 C2
Henley-on-T RG9 ..... 244 B1
Lechlade GL7 ..... 150 B2
Wallingford OX10 ..... 221 E4
Wantage OX12 ..... 214 B2
Woodstock OX20 ..... 91 D3
Market Sq Bicester OX6 ..... 65 F1
Witney OX8 ..... 118 A4
Market St Charlbury OX7 ..... 73 D2
Chipping Norton OX7 ..... 42 C2
Oxford OX1 ..... 123 E1
Woodstock OX20 ..... 91 D3
Marlborough Ave OX5 ..... 92 B1
Marlborough Cl
Carterton OX18 ..... 115 F1
Eynsham OX8 ..... 120 C4
Faringdon SN7 ..... 172 C2
Kidlington OX5 ..... 92 B1
Kings Sutton OX17 ..... 23 F3
Oxford OX4 ..... 142 A1
Marlborough Cr
Long Hanborough OX8 ..... 106 A4
Woodstock OX20 ..... 91 D4
Marlborough Ct OX2 ..... 122 C1
Marlborough Dr OX8 ..... 107 E1
Marlborough Gdns SN7 ..... 172 C1
Marlborough La
Stanford in the V SN7 ..... 194 C4
Witney OX8 ..... 118 A4
Marlborough Pl
Banbury OX16 ..... 16 B3
Charlbury OX7 ..... 73 D2
Eynsham OX8 ..... 120 C4
Faringdon SN7 ..... 172 C1
Marlborough Rd
Banbury OX16 ..... 16 B3
Chipping Norton OX7 ..... 42 C2
Oxford OX1 ..... 141 E4
Marlborough St SN7 ..... 172 C2
Marley Ind Est OX16 ..... 16 B4
Marley La OX44 ..... 184 B4
Marley Way OX16 ..... 16 B4
Marling Cl RG31 ..... 257 E1
Marlow Cl OX10 ..... 221 D4
Marlow Rd
Beacon's Bottom HP14 ..... 189 D1
Henley-on-T RG9 ..... 244 C2
Marlowe Cl OX16 ..... 15 F3
Marmion Rd RG9 ..... 254 C4
Marriott Cl OX2 ..... 109 D1
Marriotts Cl HP17 ..... 130 C3
Marriotts La HP17 ..... 130 C3
Marriotts Way HP17 ..... 130 C3
Marsack St RG4 ..... 259 E1
Marsh Cl OX5 ..... 108 B3
Marsh Ct OX14 ..... 179 F4
Marsh End OX9 ..... 147 D1
Marsh La Clanfield OX18 ..... 152 C4
Fyfield OX13 ..... 157 D2
Marston OX3 ..... 124 A3
Marsh Rd Oxford OX4 ..... 142 B3
Shabbington HP18 ..... 128 B2
Marsh Way SN7 ..... 211 D3
Marshall Cl
Chipping Norton OX7 ..... 42 C1
Reading RG8 ..... 257 E2
Marshall Cres OX7 ..... 46 C1
Marshall Rd OX4 ..... 142 B3
Marshalls Cl OX15 ..... 6 B1
Marshland Sq RG4 ..... 259 D3
Marston Ferry Rd
Cutteslowe OX2 ..... 123 E3
Marston OX2 ..... 123 E3
Marston Rd
Oxford OX3, OX4 ..... 123 F2
Thame OX9 ..... 130 A1
Marston St OX4 ..... 141 F4
Marten Gate OX16 ..... 16 B2
Marten Pl RG31 ..... 257 D2
Martens Cl SN6 ..... 209 D3
Martens Rd SN6 ..... 209 D3
Martin Cl OX6 ..... 80 C4
Martin's La OX10 ..... 182 B1
Martyn's Way OX10 ..... 204 C2
Maryfield OX12 ..... 214 C2
Marygreen OX12 ..... 214 B4
Marylands Green OX44 ..... 162 B1
Marymead OX10 ..... 220 C1
Mascall Ave OX3 ..... 142 C4
Mascord Cl OX16 ..... 16 A3
Mascord Rd OX16 ..... 16 A3
Masefield Cl OX6 ..... 65 E2
Masefield Cres OX14 ..... 179 E3
Masefield Rd OX16 ..... 16 A2
Masons' Rd OX3 ..... 124 C1
Massey Cl OX3 ..... 124 B1
Mather Rd OX3 ..... 124 C2
Mathews Way OX13 ..... 159 D3
Matlock Rd RG4 ..... 258 C2
Matson Dr RG9 ..... 244 C1
Mattock Way OX14 ..... 160 A2
Mattock's Cl OX3 ..... 124 B1
Maud Cl OX6 ..... 65 E2
Maule Cl OX15 ..... 21 F1
Maunds The OX15 ..... 33 F2
Mavor Cl OX20 ..... 91 D4
Mawles La OX7 ..... 85 E4
Maxwell Ave OX11 ..... 217 D2
May's Cl OX6 ..... 49 F4
Mayfair Rd OX4 ..... 142 A2
Mayfield Ave OX12 ..... 196 C1
Mayfield Cl
Carterton OX18 ..... 115 E1
Chalgrove OX44 ..... 184 B3
Mayfield Dr RG4 ..... 259 E2
Mayfield Rd Banbury OX16 ..... 16 B1
Cumnor OX2 ..... 121 D1
Cutteslowe OX2 ..... 123 D4
Mayott's Rd OX14 ..... 179 F4
McCraes Wlk RG10 ..... 255 E1
McKee Sq OX10 ..... 204 B1
McMullan Cl OX10 ..... 221 E4
Mead La RG8 ..... 249 F1
Mead Platt HP14 ..... 188 B3
Mead Rd OX15 ..... 32 C4
Mead The OX17 ..... 3 F2
Mead Way OX5 ..... 92 C1
Mead Wlk OX11 ..... 200 C1
Meaden Hill OX3 ..... 124 A3
Meadow Bank SN7 ..... 172 C2
Meadow Cl Cumnor OX2 ..... 121 D2
Goring RG8 ..... 249 E3
Grove OX12 ..... 196 C1
Moulsford OX10 ..... 238 C2
Shipton-u-W OX7 ..... 70 B1
Meadow La
Crowmarsh G OX10 ..... 222 A3
Fulbrook OX18 ..... 100 C3
Oxford OX4 ..... 141 F3
Shipton-u-W OX7 ..... 70 B1
Meadow Prospect OX2 ..... 122 B4
Meadow Rd Chinnor OX9 ..... 168 B3
Henley-on-T RG9 ..... 244 C1
Reading RG1 ..... 258 C1
Watchfield SN6 ..... 191 F1
Meadow View
Adderbury OX17 ..... 23 D2
Banbury OX16, OX17 ..... 16 C2
Kidlington OX5 ..... 92 C1
Long Crendon HP18 ..... 129 F2
Wendlebury OX6 ..... 79 F2
Witney OX8 ..... 118 B4
Meadow View Rd OX1 ..... 160 C4
Meadow Way Didcot OX11 .. 218 B4
Faringdon SN7 ..... 172 C1
Kingham OX7 ..... 54 C2
Thame OX9 ..... 129 F1
Yarnton OX5 ..... 108 B3
Meadow Wlk OX20 ..... 91 E3
Meadowbank Cl
Ascott-u-W OX7 ..... 71 D1
Long Crendon HP18 ..... 129 E4
Meadows The OX9 ..... 186 A1
Meadowside
Abingdon OX14 ..... 179 F3
Reading RG31 ..... 257 D1
Meadowside Ct OX14 ..... 179 F4
Meadowside Rd RG8 ..... 256 B3
Meads Cl OX14 ..... 179 D1
Meads The OX12 ..... 196 C4
Meadside OX10 ..... 202 C4
Meashill Way OX11 ..... 234 C4
Medcroft Rd OX5 ..... 77 D3
Medhill Cl RG8 ..... 250 C4
Medina Cl OX11 ..... 201 D1
Medina Gdns OX6 ..... 65 D1
Medlar Rd SN6 ..... 209 E4
Medlicott Dr OX14 ..... 179 E3
Medlock Gr OX11 ..... 200 C2
Medway OX12 ..... 197 D3
Medway Cl OX13 ..... 159 E2
Medway Rd OX13 ..... 159 E2
Melbourne Cl OX16 ..... 16 C2
Melford Green RG4 ..... 259 F3
Melton Dr OX11 ..... 200 C1
Melville Cl OX6 ..... 65 D1
Membury Way OX12 ..... 214 B4
Memorial Ave RG9 ..... 254 C1
Mendip Hts OX11 ..... 200 B1
Menmarsh Rd HP18 ..... 127 F3
Menpes Rd RG31 ..... 257 E2
Mercury Cl OX18 ..... 134 C2
Mercury Rd OX4 ..... 143 D1
Mere Dyke Rd OX13 ..... 198 C3
Mere Rd Cutteslowe OX2 ..... 122 C4
Finmere MK18 ..... 39 E3
Meredith Cl OX6 ..... 65 E2
Mereland Rd OX11 ..... 218 C4
Merewood Ave OX3 ..... 125 D2
Merganser Dr OX6 ..... 81 D4
Meriden Ct OX10 ..... 221 E4
Merlin Cl OX18 ..... 115 E2
Merlin Rd Abingdon OX14 ... 159 D1
Oxford OX4 ..... 142 C1
Merlin Way OX6 ..... 81 D4
Merritt Rd OX11 ..... 200 B1
Merrivale's La OX15 ..... 21 F2
Merrymouth Rd OX7 ..... 69 D1
Mersey Way OX11 ..... 201 D2
Merton Cl Didcot OX11 ..... 219 D4
Eynsham OX8 ..... 120 B4
Merton Rd OX6 ..... 81 E2
Merton St Banbury OX16 ..... 16 C3
Oxford OX1 ..... 123 E1
Merton Way OX5 ..... 108 A3
Merton Wlk OX6 ..... 65 F2
Metcalf Cl OX15 ..... 179 F2
Metcalfe Cl OX15 ..... 15 E4
Meteor Cl OX6 ..... 66 A2
Mewburn Rd OX16 ..... 16 A3
Mews The Highworth SN6 ... 190 A3
Watchfield SN6 ..... 191 E1
Micklands Rd RG4 ..... 259 F2
Mickle Way OX33 ..... 125 F2
Middle Aston La
North Aston OX6 ..... 48 A3
Steeple Aston OX6 ..... 48 A3
Middle Furlong OX11 ..... 201 D1
Middle Hill OX15 ..... 30 A4
Middle La Shotteswell OX17 ..... 8 B4
Wroxton OX15 ..... 14 B4
Middle Rd OX18 ..... 99 D3
Middle Row OX7 ..... 42 C2
Middle St OX5 ..... 93 F1
Middle Way Chinnor OX9 ..... 168 A3
Cutteslowe OX2 ..... 123 D4
Islip OX5 ..... 93 F1
Middleton Rd
Banbury OX16, OX17 ..... 16 C4
Bucknell OX6 ..... 64 C4
Chacombe OX17 ..... 10 C2
Middleton Stoney Rd
OX6 ..... 65 E1
Middleway Bottom OX12 ... 213 E1
Middleway Rd OX12 ..... 213 E1
Midget Cl OX14 ..... 179 E3
Midsummer Meadow
RG4 ..... 258 C3
Midway OX17 ..... 11 D1
Miles Dr OX12 ..... 214 C4
Milestone Ave RG4 ..... 260 C3
Milestone Rd OX18 ..... 115 E1
Milestone Way RG4 ..... 259 E3
Mileway Gdns OX3 ..... 124 B1
Milford Rd Reading RG1 ..... 258 C1
Wootton OX20 ..... 76 A2
Milking La OX8 ..... 104 A2
Mill Cl Bix RG9 ..... 243 F4
Chadlington OX7 ..... 57 D1
Charlton-on-O OX5 ..... 95 D3
Deddington OX15 ..... 33 F2
Mill End OX5 ..... 93 D1
Mill Green Bampton OX18 ... 134 C1
Caversham RG4 ..... 259 E1
Mill Green Cl OX18 ..... 134 C1
Mill La Adderbury OX17 ..... 23 D2
Alvescot OX18 ..... 133 E3
Banbury OX15, OX16, OX17 ... 16 B3
Benson OX10 ..... 203 F2
Black Bourton OX18 ..... 133 F3
Brackley NN13 ..... 24 A3
Chalgrove OX44 ..... 184 B3
Chinnor OX9 ..... 168 A4
Chipping Warden OX17 ..... 5 F3
Clanfield OX18 ..... 152 C4
Croughton NN13 ..... 36 B4
Drayton (Banbury) OX15 ..... 15 E4
East Hendred OX12 ..... 216 A3
East Hendred OX12 ..... 216 B3
Great Haseley OX44 ..... 164 B4
Mill La continued
Grove OX12 ..... 214 C4
Haddenham HP17 ..... 130 A2
Henley-on-T RG9 ..... 254 C4
Horton-cum-S OX33 ..... 112 A3
Kidmore End RG4 ..... 252 B1
Kings Sutton OX17 ..... 23 F2
Kirtlington OX5 ..... 77 F2
Lechlade GL7 ..... 150 C2
Lower Heyford OX6 ..... 62 B3
Marston OX3 ..... 123 F4
Middle Barton OX7 ..... 60 C4
Milton (Abingdon) OX14 ..... 199 E3
Oxford
OX3, OX33, OX4, OX44 ..... 141 F2
Shiplake RG9 ..... 255 D1
South Moreton OX11 ..... 220 A3
Stokenchurch HP14 ..... 188 B3
Sutton Courtenay OX14 ..... 199 F4
Upper Arncott OX6 ..... 96 C4
Upper Heyford OX6 ..... 48 C1
Wallingford OX10 ..... 221 E4
Westbury NN13 ..... 25 D2
Weston-on-the-G OX6 ..... 79 D1
Wootton OX20 ..... 75 F2
Mill Orch OX12 ..... 197 D3
Mill Paddock
Abingdon OX14 ..... 179 F3
Letcombe Bassett OX12 ..... 214 A1
Mill Rd
Abingdon OX13, OX14 ..... 179 E3
Caversham RG4 ..... 259 E1
Cutteslowe OX2 ..... 122 B4
Goring RG8 ..... 249 E4
Marcham OX13 ..... 178 B3
Nettlebed RG9 ..... 224 C2
Shiplake RG9 ..... 255 D2
Stokenchurch HP14 ..... 188 B3
Stratton Audley OX6 ..... 52 C1
Mill St Eynsham OX8 ..... 120 C4
Islip OX5 ..... 109 F4
Kidlington OX5 ..... 92 C1
Oxford OX2, OX33 ..... 123 D1
Stanton St John OX33 ..... 125 F4
Steventon OX13 ..... 198 C2
Wantage OX12 ..... 214 B3
Witney OX8 ..... 104 A1
Mill St Mews OX8 ..... 120 C4
Millaway La OX12 ..... 195 E3
Millbank OX2 ..... 141 D4
Millbrook Cl
Blewbury OX11 ..... 219 D1
Wallingford OX10 ..... 221 E4
Milldown Ave RG8 ..... 249 E4
Milldown Rd RG8 ..... 249 E4
Miller Rd Banbury OX16 ..... 16 A3
Wheatley OX33 ..... 144 B4
Miller's Acre OX2 ..... 109 D1
Millers Cl Chalgrove OX44 ..... 184 B4
Goring RG8 ..... 249 D4
Millers La OX15 ..... 7 E4
Millers Turn OX9 ..... 168 A3
Millfield Ave OX6 ..... 67 F2
Millfield Cl OX6 ..... 67 F2
Millham The OX12 ..... 216 A3
Millmoor Cres OX8 ..... 120 C4
Mills La OX15 ..... 15 D4
Millstream Ct OX2 ..... 122 B4
Millview OX7 ..... 42 C1
Millway Cl OX2 ..... 122 C4
Millway La OX13 ..... 157 F3
Millwood End OX8 ..... 90 A1
Millwood Vale OX8 ..... 90 A1
Millwright Cl OX16 ..... 16 A3
Milne Pl OX3 ..... 124 A3
Milton Cl Bicester OX6 ..... 65 E2
Henley-on-T RG9 ..... 244 B1
Milton Cres OX33 ..... 125 F2
Milton La OX13 ..... 199 D3
Milton Manor Dr OX44 ..... 163 F3
Milton Park OX14 ..... 199 E2
Milton Rd Bloxham OX15 ..... 21 F2
Milton (Banbury) OX15 ..... 22 B1
Oxford OX4, OX44 ..... 142 A3
Shipton-u-W OX7 ..... 70 B1
Sutton Courtenay OX14 ..... 199 F3
Sutton Courtenay OX14 ..... 200 A2
Milton St OX16 ..... 16 B3
Milvery Way OX4 ..... 142 A2
Minchery Farm Cotts
OX4 ..... 142 B1
Minchery Rd OX4 ..... 142 B1
Minchins Cl OX14 ..... 180 B4
Minnow La OX18 ..... 99 E3
Minns Ind Est OX2 ..... 122 B1
Minns Rd OX12 ..... 196 C1
Minster Rd
Brize Norton OX18 ..... 116 A3
Oxford OX4 ..... 142 A4
Minster Riding OX8 ..... 102 C2
Minton Cl RG30 ..... 257 F1
Minty Cl OX18 ..... 115 E1
Mirfield Rd OX8 ..... 117 F4
Mistletoe Gn OX4 ..... 142 C1
Mitchell Cl Thame OX9 ..... 147 F4
Wootton (Oxford) OX13 ..... 159 D4
Moat Cl OX18 ..... 116 A2
Moat La OX6 ..... 67 F1
Moat The OX7 ..... 54 C3
Moat's Cres OX9 ..... 148 A4
Mobbs La OX15 ..... 30 A4
Moberly Cl OX4 ..... 141 F4
Moir Ct OX12 ..... 214 B3
Mold Cres OX16 ..... 16 A3
Mole Pl 15 OX4 ..... 142 C1

Mollington La OX17 ... 3 D2
Molyneux Dr OX15 ... 22 C4
Monarchs Ct OX10 ... 203 F2
Monique Ct OX16 ... 9 D1
Monks Cl
Dorchester OX10 ... 182 C1
Oxford OX4 ... 142 B1
West Hanney OX12 ... 196 C3
Monks Lode OX11 ... 200 C2
Monks Mead OX10 ... 202 C1
Monmouth Rd OX1 ... 141 E3
Mons Way OX14 ... 159 E1
Montabaur Rd NN13 ... 24 A4
Montagu Rd OX2 ... 140 B4
Montague St RG4 ... 259 E1
Montgomery Rd OX6 ... 66 A4
Montpelier Dr RG4 ... 259 E3
Montrose Way OX9 ... 148 A4
Monument Ind Park
OX44 ... 184 C4
Monument Rd OX44 ... 184 C3
Monument St OX16 ... 16 B3
Moody Rd OX3 ... 123 F2
Moor Ave OX8 ... 104 A1
Moor La OX15 ... 31 F4
Moor Pond Cl OX6 ... 65 F1
Moorbank OX4 ... 142 C2
Moorbrook OX11 ... 200 B2
Moorend La Thame OX9 ... 129 F1
Thame OX9 ... 130 A1
Moorfield Ct OX16 ... 16 C3
Moorgate GL7 ... 150 A2
Moorhen Wlk OX4 ... 142 C1
Moorland Rd OX8 ... 117 F4
Moorlands Cl OX8 ... 103 F1
Moorlands The
Benson OX10 ... 204 A2
Kidlington OX5 ... 92 C1
Moors Cl OX8 ... 118 A3
Moors Drive The OX17 ... 17 F4
Moors The Kidlington OX5 ... 92 B1
Pangbourne RG8 ... 256 B3
Morecambe Ave RG4 ... 258 C3
Moreton Ave OX10 ... 221 D4
Moreton La Northmoor OX8 156 C4
Thame OX9 ... 147 F4
Moreton Rd
Aston Tirrold OX11 ... 219 F1
Cutteslowe OX2 ... 123 D3
Morgan Cl OX16 ... 15 F4
Morlais RG4 ... 259 D3
Morland Cl OX33 ... 144 A4
Morland Rd OX13 ... 178 B3
Morlands OX12 ... 197 D4
Morrell Ave OX4 ... 142 A4
Morrell Cl OX5 ... 108 B4
Morrell Cres OX4 ... 142 A1
Morrells Cl OX11 ... 200 B1
Morris Cres OX4 ... 142 A3
Morris Dr OX16 ... 15 F4
Morse Rd OX11 ... 218 B3
Mortimer Dr OX3 ... 123 F2
Mortimer Rd OX4 ... 141 F2
Morton Ave OX5 ... 108 C4
Morton Cl Abingdon OX14 ... 180 B4
Kidlington OX5 ... 108 C4
Morton King Cl HP18 ... 128 B2
Mosquito La OX10 ... 204 B1
Moss Cl RG4 ... 259 E2
Motte The OX14 ... 179 F4
Mount Owen Rd OX18 ... 135 D2
Mount Pl OX2 ... 123 D1
Mount Pleasant
Bishopstone SN6 ... 227 E2
Lechlade GL7 ... 150 B2
Mount St OX2 ... 123 D1
Mount The
Caversham RG4 ... 258 C2
Tetsworth OX9 ... 166 A4
Mount View RG9 ... 244 B1
Mount View Ct RG9 ... 244 B1
Mountfield RG8 ... 249 E4
Mountfield Rd OX8 ... 117 F4
Mousey La OX10 ... 221 E4
Mowbray Dr
RG1 & RG30 & RG31 ... 258 A1
Mowbray Rd OX11 ... 218 C3
Mowforth Cl RG8 ... 240 C1
Mulberries The OX12 ... 197 D3
Mulberry Dr Bicester OX6 ... 65 F3
Wheatley OX33 ... 144 A4
Mulcaster Ave OX5 ... 108 C4
Mullard Way OX14 ... 179 F4
Mumbery Hill RG10 ... 255 F1
Murcott Rd OX6 ... 96 B3
Murdock Cl OX15 ... 33 F2
Murdock Rd OX6 ... 66 A1
Murren The OX10 ... 221 E3
Museum Rd OX1 ... 123 E1
Musgrave Rd OX9 ... 168 B4
Musgrave Wlk HP14 ... 188 C3
Mustard La RG4 ... 260 C1
Myrtle Cl
Long Hanborough OX8 ... 90 A1
Reading RG31 ... 257 E2

Naldertown OX12 ... 214 B3
Napier Ct OX14 ... 180 A4
Napier Rd OX4 ... 142 B3
Nappins Cl HP18 ... 129 E3
Naseby Cl OX9 ... 130 A1
Nash Dr OX14 ... 179 E3
Nash La OX8 ... 106 A4
Neal's La RG9 ... 242 A1
Needlemakers HP18 ... 129 E4
Neithrop Ave OX16 ... 16 A4
Neithrop Cl OX16 ... 16 A4
Nell Hill SN6 ... 227 E2
Nelson Cl OX10 ... 221 E4
Nelson Rd RG4 ... 259 E1
Nelson St Oxford OX2 ... 123 D1
Thame OX9 ... 147 F4
Nene Gr OX11 ... 201 D1
Nene Rd OX13 ... 159 E1
Nether Cl NN13 ... 24 A4
Netheravon Cl OX18 ... 115 F1
Nethercote La OX9 ... 167 D1
Nethercote Rd OX5 ... 77 E3
Netherton La OX13 ... 157 E2
Netherton Rd OX13 ... 157 F3
Netherwoods Rd OX3 ... 124 C1
Netherworton Rd OX15 ... 32 C3
Netley Cl RG4 ... 259 F3
Netting St OX15 ... 30 A4
Nettlebed Mead OX4 ... 142 C1
Nettleton Dr OX6 ... 63 E4
Neunkirchen Way OX6 ... 81 D4
Neville Way SN7 ... 194 C4
Nevis Rd RG31 ... 257 E2
New Cotts HP18 ... 129 E3
New Cross Rd OX3 ... 124 C2
New High St OX3 ... 124 B1
New Hill RG8 ... 257 E3
New Inn Hall St OX1 ... 123 E1
New Inn Rd OX3 ... 111 D1
New Pond La OX5 ... 95 D3
New Rd Adderbury OX17 ... 22 C2
Bampton OX18 ... 134 C2
Banbury OX15, OX16, OX17 ... 16 B3
Bledington OX7 ... 54 B1
Bletchingdon OX5 ... 93 D4
Charney Bassett OX12 ... 175 F1
Childrey OX12 ... 213 D3
East Hagbourne OX11 ... 219 D3
Great Tew OX7 ... 45 E3
Hailey OX8 ... 104 A3
Kingham OX7 ... 54 C2
Long Hanborough OX8 ... 90 A1
Marcham OX13 ... 178 B3
Oxford OX1, OX3 ... 123 D1
Radley OX14 ... 160 C1
Ratley OX15 ... 2 A2
Shiplake RG9 ... 255 D2
Shotteswell OX17 ... 8 B4
Stokenchurch HP14 ... 188 C2
Wallingford OX10 ... 221 E4
Warborough OX10 ... 203 D3
Watlington OX9 ... 186 A1
Woodstock OX20 ... 91 D3
Wootton OX20 ... 75 E4
New Row OX6 ... 64 C4
New St Abingdon OX14 ... 179 F4
Bicester OX6 ... 65 F2
Chipping Norton OX7 ... 42 C2
Deddington OX15 ... 33 F2
Henley-on-T RG9 ... 244 C1
New Town La SN6 ... 227 E2
New Yatt La OX8 ... 104 C4
New Yatt Rd Hailey OX8 ... 104 B2
Witney OX8 ... 104 B2
Newalls Rise RG10 ... 255 F1
Newbery Cl RG31 ... 257 E1
Newbold Cl OX16 ... 16 C2
Newbury Rd OX12 ... 216 C3
Newbury St OX12 ... 214 B2
Newcombe Cl OX15 ... 21 D1
Newells Cl OX44 ... 163 E1
Newfield Rd RG4 ... 252 C3
Newgate Rd OX6 ... 95 F3
Newington Rd OX44 ... 163 E1
Newland OX8 ... 104 B1
Newland Cl OX8 ... 120 C4
Newland Pl OX16 ... 16 B3
Newland Rd OX16 ... 16 B3
Newland St OX8 ... 120 C4
Newlands Ave
Caversham RG4 ... 259 D2
Didcot OX11 ... 218 C4
Newlands Dr OX12 ... 196 B1
Newlands La RG9 ... 242 A3
Newlands Mill OX8 ... 104 B1
Newlin Cl OX4 ... 141 F2
Newman Ct Curbridge OX8 . 103 E1
Oxford OX4 ... 123 F1
Newman La OX14 ... 179 D1
Newman Rd OX4 ... 142 A2
Newmans Cl OX11 ... 218 B2
Newmill La OX8 ... 103 F1
Newnham Green OX10 ... 221 F4
Newnhamhill Bottom
RG9 ... 242 A3
Newport Cl OX5 ... 108 B4
Newport Rd RG1 ... 259 D1
Newton Ave RG4 ... 259 E3
Newton Rd OX1 ... 141 E4
Newton Way OX10 ... 204 A3
Newtown Gdns RG9 ... 254 C4
Newtown Rd RG9 ... 254 C4
Niagara Rd RG9 ... 254 C4
Nicholas Ave OX3 ... 123 F2
Nicholas Rd RG9 ... 254 A4
Nicholson Rd OX3 ... 123 F2
Nightingale Ave OX4 ... 142 C1
Nightingale La SN6 ... 208 A3
Nightingale Pl OX6 ... 81 D4
Nine Acres Cl OX7 ... 73 D2
Nine Acres La OX7 ... 73 D2
Nineteenth St OX11 ... 217 D1
Ninety Cut Hill OX18 ... 102 A2
Ninth Ave OX3 ... 142 C4
Ninth St OX11 ... 217 D1
Nixon Rd OX4 ... 141 F3
Nizewell Head OX6 ... 62 A4
Nobles Cl Grove OX12 ... 196 B1
N Hinksey Vill OX2 ... 140 A4
Nobles La OX2 ... 140 A4
Nor Brook Cl OX14 ... 160 B1
Norcot Rd RG30 ... 258 A1
Norfolk Cl OX14 ... 160 C1
Norfolk St OX1 ... 141 E4
Norham Gdns OX2 ... 123 E2
Norham Rd OX2 ... 123 E2
Norman Ave
Abingdon OX14 ... 160 A1
Henley-on-T RG9 ... 244 C1
Norman Rd RG4 ... 259 E2
Norman Smith Rd
13 OX4 ... 142 C1
Norman Way OX10 ... 221 E4
Normandy Cres OX4 ... 142 C3
Norreys Ave OX1 ... 141 E3
Norreys Cl OX11 ... 218 B4
Norreys Rd Cumnor OX2 ... 139 F3
Didcot OX11 ... 218 B4
Norries Dr OX10 ... 203 E1
Norris Cl Abingdon OX14 ... 160 B1
Adderbury OX17 ... 22 C1
Norris Rd OX6 ... 96 C4
North Aston Rd OX6 ... 47 E3
North Ave OX14 ... 160 A1
North Bar Pl OX16 ... 16 B3
North Bar St OX16 ... 16 B3
North Cl OX9 ... 145 F4
North Croft OX11 ... 218 C3
North Dr Grove OX12 ... 196 C1
Harwell OX11 ... 217 E2
North Green OX12 ... 196 C4
North Hill HP18 ... 98 A1
North Hinksey La OX2 ... 140 C4
North Hinksey Village
OX2 ... 140 C4
North La OX6 ... 79 D1
North Leigh Bsns Pk OX8 .. 105 E4
North Manor Estate The
OX44 ... 143 F1
North Mill Rd OX9 ... 149 F3
North Parade Ave OX2 ... 123 E2
North Pl OX3 ... 124 B2
North Quay OX14 ... 179 F2
North Rd Didcot OX11 ... 200 B1
Moulsford OX10 ... 238 C2
North Side OX6 ... 48 A1
North St Aston OX18 ... 135 F2
Banbury OX16 ... 16 C4
Bicester OX6 ... 65 F1
Caversham RG4 ... 259 D1
Fritwell OX6 ... 49 F4
Islip OX5 ... 93 F1
Marcham OX13 ... 178 B3
Middle Barton OX7 ... 60 C4
Oxford OX2 ... 123 D1
Thame OX9 ... 129 F1
Watchfield SN6 ... 191 E1
North Way Cutteslowe OX2 . 109 D1
Oxford OX3 ... 124 C2
Steventon OX13 ... 198 C2
Northampton Rd OX1 ... 141 E3
Northbrook Rd RG4 ... 259 E3
Northcourt La OX14 ... 160 A1
Northcourt Rd OX14 ... 159 F1
Northcourt Wlk OX14 ... 180 A4
Northern By-pass Rd
Cutteslowe OX2 ... 108 C1
Marston OX3 ... 124 B3
Oxford OX3 ... 124 B3
Northfield Ave RG9 ... 255 D2
Northfield Cl OX4 ... 142 B1
Northfield Ct RG9 ... 244 B2
Northfield End RG9 ... 244 B2
Northfield Rd
Abingdon OX14 ... 160 A2
Oxford OX3 ... 124 C2
Reading RG1 ... 259 D1
Shiplake RG9 ... 255 D2
Northford Cl SN6 ... 209 E4
Northford Hill SN6 ... 209 E4
Northmead La OX12 ... 196 A4
Northmoor Rd OX2 ... 123 E3
Northolt Rd OX18 ... 115 F2
Northwood Cres OX18 ... 115 F2
Northwood Rd OX8 ... 103 E1
Norton Cl OX3 ... 124 B1
Norton Pk OX7 ... 42 C2
Norton Rd OX18 ... 115 F2
Norwood Ave OX13 ... 156 C1
Nottwood La RG9 ... 242 A3
Nowell Rd OX4 ... 141 F2
Nuffield Cl Bicester OX6 ... 65 F2
Didcot OX11 ... 219 D4
Nuffield Dr OX16 ... 16 A4
Nuffield Hill RG9 ... 223 E2
Nuffield La OX10 ... 222 C3
Nuffield Rd OX3 ... 124 C1
Nuffield Way OX14 ... 179 E4
Nuneham Sq OX14 ... 179 F4
Nunhide La RG8 ... 256 C1
Nunnery Cl OX4 ... 142 B1
Nuns Acre RG8 ... 249 D4
Nurseries Rd OX5 ... 108 B4
Nursery Cl OX3 ... 124 B1
Nursery Dr OX16 ... 16 B4
Nursery Gdns RG8 ... 257 D3
Nursery La OX16 ... 16 B4
Nursery Rd OX8 ... 105 E4
Nursery The OX14 ... 200 A4
Nuthatch Cl OX4 ... 142 C1
Nyatt Rd OX14 ... 180 B4

O'Connors Rd OX8 ... 102 C1
Oak Ave OX14 ... 160 C3
Oak Cl OX6 ... 65 F2
Oak Dr OX5 ... 92 C1
Oak End Way OX9 ... 168 B3
Oak Farm Cl OX9 ... 166 A4
Oak La Ambrosden OX6 ... 81 E2
Stanford in the V SN7 ... 194 C3
Oak Rd SN6 ... 191 E1
Oak St GL7 ... 150 B2
Oak Tree Copse RG31 ... 257 F2
Oak Tree Rd RG31 ... 257 E1
Oak Tree Wlk RG8 ... 257 E3
Oakdene RG8 ... 250 C4
Oakdown Cl RG8 ... 250 C2
Oakey Cl OX18 ... 133 E3
Oakfield Rd OX18 ... 115 E1
Oakfields Ind Est OX8 ... 120 B3
Oakham Cl RG31 ... 257 E1
Oakham Rd GL56 ... 27 D1
Oakland Cl OX8 ... 105 F4
Oakland Rd OX16 ... 16 B1
Oakley La OX9 ... 168 A3
Oakley Rd
Caversham RG4 ... 258 C2
Chinnor OX9 ... 168 B3
Oaks Rd RG9 ... 255 D2
Oaksmere OX13 ... 158 A3
Oakthorpe Pl OX2 ... 123 D3
Oakthorpe Rd OX2 ... 123 D3
Oasis Park OX8 ... 120 B3
Oatland Rd OX11 ... 218 C4
Oatlands Rd OX2 ... 122 C1
Observatory Cl OX10 ... 204 A2
Observatory St OX2 ... 123 D2
Ock Dr OX10 ... 182 B3
Ock Mill Cl OX14 ... 179 E3
Ock St OX14 ... 179 F3
Ockley Brook OX11 ... 201 D1
Octavian Way NN13 ... 24 A4
Oddley La HP27 ... 169 E4
Odiham Ave RG4 ... 259 F3
Odiham Cl OX18 ... 115 F2
Offas Cl OX10 ... 204 A3
Ogbourne Cl OX12 ... 214 A3
Old Arncott Rd OX6 ... 81 E2
Old Barn Cl Benson OX10 ... 204 A2
Caversham RG4 ... 259 D3
Old Bath Rd RG4 ... 260 B1
Old Bridge Rd OX15 ... 21 F2
Old Buildings OX10 ... 221 E4
Old Burford Rd OX7 ... 54 B1
Old Chapel Cl OX5 ... 92 C1
Old Coachyard The OX8 ... 104 A1
Old Copse Gdns RG4 ... 252 C3
Old Croft Cl OX9 ... 167 F2
Old Dashwood Hill HP14 ... 189 F1
Old Farm Cl
Abingdon OX14 ... 180 B4
Worminghall HP18 ... 127 E3
Old Farm Cres RG31 ... 257 E1
Old Field OX44 ... 164 A4
Old Forge Cl OX7 ... 54 B1
Old Forge Rd OX7 ... 29 D2
Old George Yd OX18 ... 100 C3
Old Glebe OX15 ... 20 B4
Old Greyfriars St OX1 ... 141 E4
Old Grimsbury Rd OX16 ... 16 C4
Old High St OX3 ... 124 B2
Old Kiln The RG9 ... 224 C1
Old London Rd
Benson OX10 ... 204 A2
Tiddington OX9 ... 145 F2
Wheatley OX33 ... 144 B4
Old Maltings The OX9 ... 129 F1
Old Manor Ct OX12 ... 214 A1
Old Marston Rd OX3 ... 123 F2
Old Mill Cl OX12 ... 196 C1
Old Moor OX14 ... 199 E3
Old Moor Cl OX10 ... 221 E4
Old Nursery View OX1 ... 141 E2
Old Orchard OX9 ... 149 F1
Old Parr Cl OX16 ... 16 B3
Old Parr Rd OX16 ... 16 B3
Old Place Yd OX6 ... 65 F1
Old Plough Wlk OX15 ... 33 D2
Old Pound The OX13 ... 159 D3
Old Rd East Hendred OX12 ... 216 C3
Great Tew OX7 ... 45 E4
Oxford OX3, OX33 ... 124 C1
Ratley OX15 ... 2 A2
Wheatley OX33 ... 143 F4
Old Reading Rd OX10 ... 221 F3
Old Rectory Ct OX6 ... 80 A2
Old Sawmills Rd SN7 ... 172 C1
Old School Cl Bicester OX6 ... 65 F4
Stokenchurch HP14 ... 188 C2
Old School End OX15 ... 30 A4
Old School La OX12 ... 213 F3
Old Stables The OX3 ... 124 B2
Old Stables Yard OX12 ... 214 A1
Old Station Yd OX14 ... 179 F4
Old Town NN13 ... 24 A4
Old Wharf Rd SN7 ... 210 B4
Old Windmill Way HP18 ... 129 E4
Old Witney Rd OX8 ... 120 B4
Oliver Rd OX4 ... 142 C3
One End La OX10 ... 203 F2
Onslow Dr OX9 ... 130 A1
Onslow Gdns RG4 ... 259 E2
Oracle Parkway RG4 ... 260 A1
Orange Cl SN6 ... 190 A3
Orchard Ave RG4 ... 252 C3
Orchard Cl Abingdon OX14 ... 160 A1
Banbury OX15, OX16 ... 16 A3
Bucknell SN7 ... 174 C4
Cassington OX8 ... 107 E1
Chalgrove OX44 ... 184 B4
Charney Bassett OX12 ... 175 F1
Cholsey OX10 ... 221 E3
Combe OX8 ... 90 A2
Orchard Cl continued
Didcot OX11 ... 200 C1
East Hanney OX12 ... 197 D3
East Hendred OX12 ... 216 C4
Eynsham OX8 ... 120 C4
Henley-on-T RG9 ... 244 C1
Lechlade GL7 ... 150 B2
Purley on T RG31 ... 257 E2
Salford OX7 ... 41 F2
Shiplake RG9 ... 254 C1
Thame OX9 ... 148 A4
Upton OX11 ... 218 B1
Warborough OX10 ... 203 D4
Wheatley OX33 ... 144 A4
Orchard Combe RG8 ... 250 B2
Orchard Field RG4 ... 252 B3
Orchard Field La OX20 ... 91 E2
Orchard Gdns OX12 ... 213 E3
Orchard Gr Bloxham OX15 ... 21 E2
Caversham RG4 ... 259 F2
Orchard Ground OX7 ... 69 E1
Orchard Haven OX10 ... 202 B4
Orchard Hill SN7 ... 172 C2
Orchard La Cropredy OX17 ... 4 C1
East Hendred OX12 ... 216 B3
Upper Heyford OX6 ... 62 C4
Wootton (Oxford) OX1 ... 140 B1
Orchard Piece OX17 ... 4 A2
Orchard Pl NN13 ... 25 D2
Orchard Rd Ardley OX6 ... 50 A2
Buckland SN7 ... 174 C4
Hook Norton OX15 ... 30 A4
N Hinksey Vill OX2 ... 140 A4
Orchard Rise OX6 ... 79 F4
Orchard Row OX18 ... 100 C3
Orchard The
Appleton OX13 ... 158 A4
East Challow OX12 ... 214 A3
Merton OX6 ... 95 E4
Orchard View OX17 ... 4 C1
Orchard Way
Banbury OX16, OX17 ... 16 A3
Bicester OX6 ... 65 E2
Chinnor OX9 ... 168 B3
Harwell OX11 ... 217 E4
Kidlington OX5 ... 108 C4
Kingham OX7 ... 54 C2
Marcham OX13 ... 178 B3
Middle Barton OX7 ... 46 C1
Oxford OX4 ... 142 B2
Wantage OX12 ... 214 C2
Witney OX8 ... 118 A4
Orchard Wlk OX9 ... 186 B1
Orchids The OX11 ... 235 E4
Ordnance Rd OX11 ... 200 B1
Oregon Ave RG31 ... 257 E2
Oriel Ct OX11 ... 219 D4
Oriel Sq OX1 ... 123 E1
Oriel St OX1 ... 123 E1
Oriel Way OX6 ... 65 F2
Orkney Pl OX8 ... 117 F4
Ormond Rd Thame OX9 ... 130 A1
Wantage OX12 ... 214 C2
Orpwood Way OX14 ... 179 E3
Orwell Cl RG4 ... 258 C2
Orwell Dr OX11 ... 201 D1
Osberton Rd OX2 ... 123 D4
Osborne Cl Bicester OX6 ... 65 E1
Cutteslowe OX2 ... 122 C4
Kidlington OX5 ... 108 B4
Osiers The OX10 ... 183 D3
Osler Rd OX3 ... 124 B2
Osney Cl OX15 ... 30 A4
Osney La OX1 ... 123 D1
Osney Mead OX2 ... 141 D4
Osprey Cl OX6 ... 81 D4
Osterley Dr RG4 ... 259 F3
Osterley Gr OX16 ... 16 A2
Oswestry Rd OX1 ... 141 E3
Otmoor La Beckley OX3 ... 111 D2
Charlton-on-O OX5 ... 95 D2
Otters Reach OX1 ... 141 F1
Ottery Way OX11 ... 201 D1
Otwell Cl OX14 ... 160 A1
Ouseley Cl OX3 ... 123 F2
Outram Rd OX4 ... 142 A3
Oval The Bicester OX6 ... 65 E2
Didcot OX11 ... 200 B1
Oxford OX4 ... 142 A2
Over Norton Rd OX7 ... 42 C2
Overbrooke Gdns OX4 ... 143 D1
Overdale Cl OX3 ... 124 C2
Overdown Rd RG31 ... 257 E1
Overlanders End RG31 ... 257 F2
Overmead OX14 ... 179 F2
Overmead Green OX4 ... 142 C1
Overstrand Cl OX6 ... 66 A2
Overthorpe Rd OX16 ... 16 C3
Overton Dr OX9 ... 130 A1
Owlington Cl OX2 ... 122 B1
Ox Cl OX14 ... 180 A4
Oxen Piece OX44 ... 145 E1
Oxeye Ct OX4 ... 161 F4
Oxford Bsns Pk N OX4 ... 142 B3
Oxford Bsns Pk S OX4 ... 142 B2
Oxford Cl OX5 ... 77 F2
Oxford Cres OX11 ... 218 B4
Oxford Hill OX8 ... 118 B4
Oxford La OX12 ... 196 C1
Oxford Rd
Abingdon OX13, OX14 ... 160 A3
Adderbury OX17 ... 23 D2
Banbury OX15, OX16, OX17 ... 16 B2
Benson OX10 ... 203 F2
Bicester OX6 ... 80 B4
Bletchingdon OX5 ... 93 D4
Burford OX18 ... 100 C2
Clifton Hampden OX14 ... 181 F3

Sarajac Ave OX12 ... 213 F2
Sarsden Cl OX7 ... 57 D1
Sarum Cl OX18 ... 115 F2
Satin La OX15 ... 33 F2
Satwell Cl RG9 ... 243 D2
Saunders Cl OX9 ... 186 A1
Saunders Ct RG8 ... 257 D3
Saunders Rd OX4 ... 142 A3
Saunders Wood Copse
HP14 ... 188 C2
Savile Rd OX1 ... 123 E1
Savile Way OX12 ... 196 B1
Saw Cl OX44 ... 184 B4
Sawpit Rd OX4 ... 142 C2
Sawpits La GL56 ... 40 A1
Saxel Cl OX18 ... 135 F2
Saxifrage Sq OX4 ... 142 C1
Saxon Cl OX10 ... 221 E4
Saxon Pl OX12 ... 214 A3
Saxon Way Oxford OX3 ... 124 A2
Witney OX8 ... 118 A4
Saxons Heath OX14 ... 201 E4
Saxons Way OX11 ... 219 D4
Saxton Rd OX14 ... 179 F3
Sayers Orch OX11 ... 200 B1
Scafell Cl RG31 ... 257 E1
Scampton Cl OX6 ... 66 A2
Schilling St OX6 ... 63 D4
Schofield Ave OX8 ... 104 A2
Schofield Gdns OX8 ... 104 A2
Schofields Way OX15 ... 21 F3
Scholar Pl OX2 ... 140 B4
Scholars Acre OX18 ... 115 E2
Scholars Cl RG4 ... 258 C2
Schongau Cl OX14 ... 179 E2
School Cl Ickford HP18 ... 128 A2
Long Compton CV36 ... 27 F3
Longworth OX13 ... 156 B2
Steventon OX13 ... 198 C2
School End OX17 ... 35 E4
School Hill
Minster Lovell OX8 ... 102 C2
Mollington OX17 ... 3 F2
Wargrave RG10 ... 255 E1
School La
Aston Rowant OX9 ... 167 F2
Banbury OX15, OX16, OX17 ... 16 B3
Black Bourton OX18 ... 133 F3
Caversham RG4 ... 259 D1
Caversham, The Common
RG4 ... 259 D3
Chilson OX7 ... 71 F3
Coleshill SN6 ... 191 D4
Great Bourton OX17 ... 9 E4
Harwell OX11 ... 217 F4
Kingston Bagpuize OX13 ... 156 C1
Middleton Stoney OX6 ... 64 A2
Milton (Abingdon) OX14 ... 199 E2
Milton (Abingdon) OX14 ... 199 E3
Minster Lovell OX8 ... 102 C2
North Newington OX15 ... 15 E2
Shabbington HP18 ... 128 B2
Stadhampton OX44 ... 163 E1
Stoke Row RG9 ... 241 F2
Sutton Courtenay OX14 ... 200 C4
Upper Heyford OX6 ... 62 C4
Wargrave RG10 ... 255 E1
Warmington OX17 ... 3 D2
School Paddock OX6 ... 64 C4
School Pl OX1 ... 141 E3
School Rd
Ardington OX12 ... 215 E3
Finstock OX7 ... 88 B3
Kidlington OX5 ... 92 C1
West Hanney OX12 ... 196 C3
School View OX16 ... 16 C3
School Yd OX44 ... 163 E1
Schooler's La OX12 ... 40 B2
Scotland End OX15 ... 30 A4
Scotsgrove Cotts HP17 ... 130 A2
Scott Cl Bicester OX6 ... 65 E2
Caversham RG4 ... 259 D3
Kidlington OX5 ... 108 B4
Scott Rd OX2 ... 123 D4
Scotts Cnr NN13 ... 25 D2
Scotts La OX6 ... 67 F1
Scours La RG30 ... 258 A1
Scruton Cl OX3 ... 124 C2
Seacourt Rd OX2 ... 122 B1
Sealham Rd OX8 ... 118 A2
Second Ave OX11 ... 200 B1
Second St Croughton NN13 ... 36 C3
Harwell OX11 ... 217 E2
Sedgefield Cl RG4 ... 252 C3
Sedgemoor Dr OX9 ... 130 A1
Sedgewell Rd RG4 ... 252 C3
Seelscheid Way OX6 ... 81 D4
Seeson Way OX12 ... 214 C2
Sefton Pl OX15 ... 22 C4
Sefton Rd OX3 ... 124 C2
Segsbury Rd OX12 ... 214 A3
Selborne Gdns RG30 ... 258 A1
Sellwood Dr OX18 ... 115 F2
Sellwood Rd OX14 ... 159 F1
Selwyn Cres OX14 ... 160 C1
Send Rd RG4 ... 259 E1
Sermon Cl OX3 ... 124 C1
Seven Acres
Long Crendon HP18 ... 129 D4
Thame OX9 ... 148 A4
Sevenfields SN6 ... 190 A4
Seventeenth St OX11 ... 217 D1
Seventh Ave OX33 ... 142 C4
Seventh St OX11 ... 217 D2
Severalls Cl OX10 ... 203 E1
Severn Cl OX6 ... 65 D2
Severn Rd Abingdon OX13 ... 159 E1
Harwell OX11 ... 217 D1
Sewell Cl OX14 ... 160 B1
Sewell's La OX9 ... 167 F4
Shackleton Cl OX6 ... 66 A2
Shades The OX16 ... 16 B3
Shadwell Rd OX10 ... 182 B3
Shaftesbury Rd OX3 ... 124 C3
Shakespeare Cl RG4 ... 259 E3
Shakespeare Dr OX6 ... 65 E2
Shakespeare Rd OX8 ... 120 B4
Shannon Cl OX12 ... 196 C1
Shannon Rd OX6 ... 65 D1
Sharland Cl OX12 ... 214 C4
Sharman Beer Ct OX9 ... 147 F4
Shaw Cl OX6 ... 65 E2
Shaw's Copse OX14 ... 160 C1
Sheards La SN7 ... 194 C4
Shearings The OX15 ... 30 A4
Shearwater Dr OX6 ... 81 D4
Sheen Cl OX6 ... 65 F3
Sheep St Bicester OX6 ... 65 F1
Burford OX18 ... 100 C3
Charlbury OX7 ... 73 D2
Highworth SN6 ... 190 A3
Sheep Wlk RG4 ... 259 D2
Sheepwash La OX13 ... 199 D3
Sheepway Ct OX4 ... 142 A2
Sheepways La RG4 ... 258 A4
Sheerstock HP17 ... 130 C3
Sheldon Rd HP18 ... 128 A2
Sheldon Way OX4 ... 142 B2
Shelford Pl OX3 ... 124 B1
Shelley Cl Abingdon OX14 ... 160 A1
Banbury OX16 ... 16 A2
Bicester OX6 ... 65 E2
Oxford OX3 ... 124 C1
Shelley Rd OX4 ... 142 A3
Shepard Way OX7 ... 42 C2
Shepherd Gdns OX14 ... 179 E3
Shepherds Cl Grove OX12 ... 196 B1
Weston-on-the-G OX6 ... 79 D1
Shepherds Hill
Sandford-on-T OX4 ... 142 C1
Woodstock RG5 ... 260 B1
Shepherds La RG4 ... 258 B3
Sheraton Dr RG31 ... 257 E1
Sherborne St GL7 ... 150 B2
Sherbourne Rd OX8 ... 117 E4
Sheridan Ave RG4 ... 259 D2
Sheriff's Dr OX2 ... 122 C4
Sherwood Ave OX14 ... 180 A4
Sherwood Cl OX6 ... 66 B1
Sherwood Gdns RG9 ... 254 B4
Sherwood Pl RG8 ... 257 D2
Sherwood Rd OX11 ... 218 B4
Sherwood Rise RG8 ... 257 D3
Shifford La OX8 ... 137 E1
Shilbrook Manor OX18 ... 133 F2
Shillbrook Ave OX18 ... 115 E3
Shilldeane Dr OX18 ... 115 E2
Shilton Rd Burford OX18 ... 100 C2
Carterton OX18 ... 115 E2
Ship St OX1 ... 123 E1
Shiplake Bottom RG4 ... 252 C3
Shipston Rd CV36 ... 27 F4
Shipton Cl RG31 ... 257 E1
Shipton Rd Ascott-u-W OX7 ... 71 D1
Shipton-u-W OX7 ... 70 A1
Woodstock OX20 ... 91 E3
Shirburn Rd OX9 ... 186 B1
Shirburn St OX9 ... 186 B1
Shirelake Cl OX1 ... 141 E4
Shires Rd NN13 ... 24 A3
Shirvell's Hill RG8 ... 250 C4
Shoe La
East Hagbourne OX11 ... 218 C3
Oxford OX1 ... 123 E1
Shooters Hill RG8 ... 256 A3
Short Furlong OX11 ... 201 D1
Short St Caversham RG4 ... 259 D1
Pangbourne RG8 ... 256 B3
Watchfield SN6 ... 191 E1
Short The RG8 ... 257 E3
Shortlands Hill OX10 ... 238 B2
Shotover SN7 ... 211 E3
Shrieves Cl OX14 ... 160 A1
Shrivenham Hundred
SN6 ... 191 E1
Shrivenham Rd
Highworth SN6 ... 190 A2
Longcot SN7 ... 192 B1
Shute Ave SN6 ... 209 E4
Shutford Rd
North Newington OX15 ... 15 D2
Tadmarton OX15 ... 20 C4
Sibford Rd
Hook Norton OX15 ... 30 A4
Shutford OX15 ... 13 F2
Sideleigh Rd OX15 ... 22 C4
Sidings Rd OX7 ... 55 F3
Sidney St OX4 ... 141 F4
Signet End OX18 ... 100 C2
Silkdale Cl OX4 ... 142 B3
Silver Birches OX33 ... 125 F4
Silver La OX12 ... 213 E3
Silver Rd OX4 ... 142 A4
Silver St Bourton SN6 ... 209 D1
Chacombe OX17 ... 10 C2
Fernham SN7 ... 193 D2
Tetsworth OX9 ... 166 A4
Wroxton OX15 ... 15 D4
Silverdale Rd RG10 ... 255 F1
Silvermead HP18 ... 127 E3
Silverthorne Dr RG4 ... 258 C3
Simmonds Wlk OX12 ... 214 B3
Simmons Rd RG9 ... 244 B2
Simmons Way OX9 ... 129 F1
Simon's Cl OX33 ... 144 A4
Simons Cl RG31 ... 257 E2
Simons La OX7 ... 85 E4
Simpsons Way OX1 ... 160 C4
Sinclair Ave OX16 ... 16 A4
Sinclair Dr OX16 ... 16 A4
Singer La RG9 ... 244 C1
Singers Cl RG9 ... 254 C4
Sinnels Field OX7 ... 85 F4
Sinodun Cl OX14 ... 201 E4
Sinodun Rd Didcot OX11 ... 218 C4
Wallingford OX10 ... 203 E1
Sinodun View OX10 ... 203 D4
Sint Niklaas Cl OX14 ... 179 E2
Sir Georges La OX17 ... 23 D2
Siskin Rd GL54 ... 68 A3
Sixpenny La OX44 ... 184 C3
Sixteenth St OX11 ... 217 D2
Sixth St Croughton NN13 ... 36 C4
Harwell OX11 ... 217 D2
Skarries View RG4 ... 258 B4
Skene Cl OX3 ... 124 B1
Skerrit Way RG8 ... 257 E2
Skilton Rd RG31 ... 257 E2
Skimmingdish La OX6 ... 65 F3
Skimmingdish Rd OX6 ... 66 A2
Skinner Rd OX6 ... 66 B1
Skippett La OX7 ... 88 A2
Skippon Way OX9 ... 129 F1
Skittle Alley OX17 ... 35 E4
Slade Cl OX3 ... 124 B1
Slade End OX10 ... 203 D1
Slade End Rdbt OX10 ... 203 D1
Slade Rd Cholsey OX10 ... 221 D1
Didcot OX11 ... 200 B1
Stokenchurch HP14 ... 188 C2
Slade The Charlbury OX7 ... 73 E2
Oxford OX3 ... 142 C4
Slave Hill HP17 ... 130 C3
Slaymaker Cl OX3 ... 124 C1
Sloan Ct RG8 ... 249 E3
Slopes The RG4 ... 259 E1
Small Ho OX15 ... 19 E4
Smith Barry Cres GL54 ... 68 A2
Smith Barry Rd GL54 ... 68 A2
Smith Cl RG4 ... 252 C3
Smith's Cl OX18 ... 135 F1
Smiths Farm La OX11 ... 200 B1
Smiths Hill OX12 ... 231 F3
Smiths Rickyard OX12 ... 216 B4
Snakehill La OX15 ... 33 D2
Snipe Rd GL54 ... 68 A2
Snowdon Mede OX3 ... 124 A2
Snows La OX33 ... 125 E4
Snowshill Dr OX8 ... 103 E1
Snowsill Dr OX8 ... 117 E4
Snowswick La SN7 ... 170 C3
Snuff La OX17 ... 8 B4
Snuggs La OX12 ... 197 D4
Soden Rd OX6 ... 63 E4
Solters Cl HP18 ... 98 B4
Somerton Rd Ardley OX6 ... 50 A2
North Aston OX6 ... 48 A4
Upper Heyford OX6 ... 48 C1
Somerville OX11 ... 219 D4
Somerville Ct OX17 ... 23 E2
Somerville Dr OX6 ... 65 F2
Songers Cl OX2 ... 140 A4
Sonning La RG4 ... 260 B1
Sonning Meadows RG4 ... 260 B1
Soot La OX17 ... 3 D2
Sopwith Rd GL54 ... 68 A3
Sorrel Rd OX4 ... 143 D1
Sotwell St OX10 ... 202 C1
South Ave Abingdon OX14 ... 159 F1
Henley-on-T RG9 ... 254 C4
Kidlington OX5 ... 108 C3
South Bar St OX16 ... 16 B3
South Cl OX5 ... 108 C3
South Dr Harwell OX11 ... 217 E2
Sonning RG4 ... 260 B1
South End
Great Rollright OX7 ... 29 D2
Haddenham HP17 ... 130 C3
South Gate Ct GL54 ... 68 A2
South Hills HP18 ... 98 A1
South Leigh Rd OX8 ... 119 D4
South Mere OX18 ... 116 B2
South Newington Rd
Barford St M OX15 ... 32 B3
Bloxham OX15 ... 21 D1
South Par OX2 ... 123 D4
South Park Ave OX11 ... 218 B4
South Parks Rd OX1 ... 123 E1
South Rd RG9 ... 242 A1
South Row OX11 ... 235 E4
South Side OX6 ... 62 A4
South St Banbury OX16 ... 16 C4
Blewbury OX11 ... 237 D4
Caversham RG4 ... 259 D1
Letcombe Bassett OX12 ... 214 A1
Lower Heyford OX6 ... 63 D3
Middle Barton OX7 ... 60 C4
Oxford OX2 ... 141 D4
Watchfield SN6 ... 191 E1
South Stoke Rd RG8 ... 240 A1
South View OX17 ... 9 E4
South View Ave RG4 ... 259 E1
South View Park RG4 ... 259 E1
Southam Rd
Banbury OX16, OX17 ... 9 E2
Cropredy OX17 ... 4 A2
Great Bourton OX17 ... 9 E2
Mollington OX17 ... 4 A2
Southampton St SN7 ... 172 C2
Southby Cl OX13 ... 158 A4
Southcroft OX3 ... 123 F3
Southdale Rd OX2 ... 123 D4
Southdown Ct SN7 ... 194 C4
Southdown Rd RG4 ... 259 D3
Southend OX44 ... 162 C4
Southern By-pass Rd
Kennington OX1 ... 141 E2
N Hinksey Vill OX2 ... 140 C4
Oxford OX1 ... 141 F2
South Hinksey OX1 ... 141 D2
Southern Rd OX9 ... 147 F4
Southerndene Cl RG31 ... 257 E1
Southfield Dr OX14 ... 199 F4
Southfield La OX6 ... 49 F4
Southfield Park OX4 ... 142 A4
Southfield Rd OX4 ... 142 A4
Southlands OX18 ... 135 F1
Southlawn OX8 ... 117 F4
Southmoor Pl OX2 ... 123 D2
Southmoor Rd OX2 ... 123 D2
Southmoor Way OX14 ... 179 F4
Southrop Rd OX15 ... 30 A3
Southwold OX6 ... 65 F3
Southwood Rd OX8 ... 103 E1
Sovereign Cl OX11 ... 219 D4
Spa Cl SN6 ... 190 A4
Span Hill RG4 ... 260 B4
Spareacre La OX8 ... 120 C4
Sparrow Way OX4 ... 142 C1
Sparsey Pl OX2 ... 109 D1
Sparsholt St OX12 ... 212 C2
Spears The OX5 ... 108 A3
Speedwell St OX1 ... 141 E4
Spencer Ave OX5 ... 108 A3
Spencer Cres OX4 ... 142 A2
Spencers Cl SN7 ... 194 B4
Spenlove Cl OX14 ... 159 F1
Spenser Cl OX6 ... 65 E2
Spey Rd OX13 ... 159 E2
Speyside Cl OX18 ... 115 E3
Spier's La OX6 ... 67 F1
Spindleberry Cl OX4 ... 142 C1
Spindlers OX5 ... 92 C1
Spindleside OX6 ... 65 F3
Spinney Cl RG4 ... 259 D4
Spinney Dr OX16 ... 16 C2
Spinney Field OX4 ... 142 C1
Spinney The
Abingdon OX14 ... 159 E1
Launton OX6 ... 66 B1
Lechlade GL7 ... 150 B2
Spinneys Cl OX14 ... 160 C2
Spinneys The OX7 ... 58 C3
Spitfire Cl OX6 ... 66 A2
Spooner Cl OX3 ... 124 C2
Sprigs Holly La HP14 ... 189 D4
Spring Cl OX8 ... 118 A4
Spring Copse OX1 ... 141 E2
Spring Farm OX6 ... 47 E3
Spring Gdns OX14 ... 179 E4
Spring Hill OX13 ... 176 B4
Spring Hill Rd OX5 ... 107 F4
Spring La
Aston Tirrold OX11 ... 237 F4
Caversham RG4 ... 260 A3
Great Bourton OX17 ... 9 E3
Horspath OX33 ... 143 E4
Idbury OX7 ... 69 D2
Oxford OX3, OX33, OX4 ... 142 B1
Oxford,Headington Quarry
OX3, OX33, OX4 ... 124 C1
Watlington OX9 ... 186 B1
Spring Path OX9 ... 147 F4
Spring Pl OX7 ... 42 C1
Spring Rd OX14 ... 179 E4
Spring St OX7 ... 42 C2
Spring Wlk RG10 ... 255 E1
Springdale OX10 ... 221 E4
Springfield OX17 ... 8 C2
Springfield Ave OX16 ... 16 B2
Springfield Cl
Shrivenham SN6 ... 209 D3
Watlington OX9 ... 186 B1
Springfield Dr OX14 ... 179 F4
Springfield End RG8 ... 249 E4
Springfield Gdns OX9 ... 168 B4
Springfield Oval OX8 ... 103 F1
Springfield Park OX8 ... 103 F1
Springfield Rd
Bicester OX6 ... 65 F4
Kidlington OX5 ... 108 C4
N Hinksey Vill OX2 ... 140 B4
Stokenchurch HP14 ... 188 C2
Wantage OX12 ... 214 C2
Springhill Rd RG8 ... 249 E4
Springs The OX8 ... 118 A4
Springwell Hill OX5 ... 78 A1
Springwood La RG9 ... 253 D4
Spruce Dr OX6 ... 65 F3
Spruce Gdns OX4 ... 161 F4
Spruce Rd OX5 ... 108 C4
Spur The RG10 ... 255 F2
Square Firs OX8 ... 90 A3
Square The
Abingdon OX13, OX14 ... 179 F4
Aston OX18 ... 135 F2
Aynho OX17 ... 35 E4
Ducklington OX8 ... 118 A2
Eynsham OX8 ... 120 C4
Kings Sutton OX17 ... 23 F3
Long Crendon HP18 ... 129 E3
Longworth OX13 ... 156 A2
N Hinksey Vill OX2 ... 122 B1
Pangbourne RG8 ... 256 B3
Swalcliffe OX15 ... 19 F4
Squire's Wlk OX10 ... 221 E3
Squires Cl OX18 ... 116 B2
Squires Rd SN6 ... 191 E1
Squitchey La OX2 ... 123 D4
Stable Cl MK18 ... 39 E4
Stable Rd OX6 ... 65 F2
Staddlestone Cl RG31 ... 257 E1
Stadhampton Rd
Drayton St L OX10 ... 183 D3
LIttle Milton OX44 ... 163 F3
Stadium Way RG30 ... 258 A1
Staffordshire Cl RG30 ... 257 F1
Stainer Pl OX3 ... 123 F2
Stainfield Rd OX3 ... 124 A3
Stainswick La SN6 ... 209 E2
Stallpits Rd SN6 ... 209 D4
Stanbridge Cl OX16 ... 16 A3
Standlake Rd
Ducklington OX8 ... 118 B2
Northmoor OX8 ... 138 A1
Stanford Dr OX14 ... 179 F4
Stanford Rd SN7 ... 173 D2
Stanier Pl OX16 ... 16 C4
Stanley Cl OX2 ... 140 B4
Stanley Rd OX4 ... 141 F4
Stanmore Cres OX18 ... 115 F2
Stansfeld Pl OX3 ... 124 C1
Stansfield Cl OX3 ... 124 C1
Stanton Cl OX8 ... 117 F4
Stanton Harcourt Rd
South Leigh OX8 ... 119 E3
Witney OX8 ... 118 B4
Stanton Rd
Forest Hill OX33 ... 125 F2
N Hinksey Vill OX2 ... 140 C3
Stanville Rd OX2 ... 140 A4
Stanway Cl OX8 ... 103 E1
Stanway Rd OX3 ... 125 D2
Stanwell Cl OX17 ... 11 D1
Stanwell Dr OX17 ... 11 D1
Stanwell Lea OX17 ... 11 D1
Stanwell Rd OX17 ... 9 E4
Stapleton Rd OX3 ... 124 B1
Star La SN6 ... 191 E1
Star Rd RG4 ... 259 E1
Starina Croft OX16 ... 9 D1
Starnham Rd OX8 ... 118 A2
Starwort Path OX4 ... 142 C1
Station App Bicester OX6 ... 65 F1
Kidlington OX5 ... 92 B1
Station Field Ind Est OX5 ... 92 B1
Station La OX8 ... 118 A3
Station Rd Ardley OX6 ... 50 B2
Ashbury SN6 ... 228 A4
Aynho OX17 ... 35 D3
Bampton OX18 ... 134 C3
Black Bourton OX18 ... 133 F3
Blackthorn OX6 ... 82 A2
Bletchingdon OX5 ... 93 D4
Brize Norton OX18 ... 116 B2
Chinnor OX9 ... 168 B3
Chipping Norton OX7 ... 42 B1
Cholsey OX10 ... 220 C1
Churchill OX7 ... 54 C2
Cropredy OX17 ... 4 C1
Culham OX14 ... 180 C2
Didcot OX11 ... 200 C1
Eynsham OX8 ... 120 C4
Faringdon SN7 ... 172 C2
Goring RG8 ... 249 E3
Grove OX12 ... 214 C4
Haddenham HP17 ... 130 C3
Henley-on-T RG9 ... 244 C1
Highworth SN6 ... 190 A3
Hook Norton OX15 ... 30 B4
Kingham OX7 ... 54 C2
Launton OX6 ... 66 C2
Lechlade GL7 ... 150 B3
Lower Heyford OX6 ... 62 B3
Marsh Gibbon OX6 ... 67 F2
Pangbourne RG8 ... 256 B3
Shiplake RG9 ... 255 D2
Shipton-u-W OX7 ... 70 C1
Shrivenham SN6 ... 209 D3
South Leigh OX8 ... 119 E3
Uffington SN7 ... 211 E4
Upton OX11 ... 218 B1
Wallingford OX10 ... 221 E4
Wargrave RG10 ... 255 E1
Wheatley OX33 ... 144 A4
Station Yard Ind Est OX17 ... 23 D1
Station Yd Steventon OX13 ... 199 D2
Thame OX9 ... 148 A4
Staunton Rd OX3 ... 124 A2
Staverton Rd OX2 ... 123 D3
Steady's La OX8 ... 138 A4
Steep Rise OX3 ... 124 B3
Steeple Cl OX15 ... 21 F2
Steepness Hill OX15 ... 32 C2
Stenton Cl OX14 ... 179 F3
Stephen Rd OX3 ... 124 B2
Stephenson Rd OX12 ... 214 A4
Steptoe Cl OX12 ... 196 B1
Sterling Cl Bicester OX6 ... 66 A2
Kidlington OX5 ... 108 C4
Sterling Rd OX5 ... 108 C4
Sterling Road App OX5 ... 92 C1
Sterling Way RG30 ... 258 A1
Stert Rd OX9 ... 167 F2
Stert St OX14 ... 179 F4
Stevens La RG9 ... 252 B4
Stevenson Cl OX6 ... 65 E2
Stevenson Dr OX14 ... 179 E4
Steventon Rd
Drayton OX14 ... 199 D4
East Hanney OX12 ... 197 F4
Stewart St OX1 ... 141 E3
Stile Rd OX3 ... 124 B2
Stimpsons Cl OX2 ... 122 A1
Stirling Cl Carterton OX18 ... 115 E2
Caversham RG4 ... 259 E3
Wantage OX12 ... 214 C3

NG NH NJ NK
NM NN NO NP
NR NS NT NU
NX NY NZ
SC SD SE TA
SH SJ SK TF TG
SM SN SO SP TL TM
SR SS ST SU TQ TR
SW SX SY SZ TV

Any feature in this atlas can be given a unique reference to help you find the same feature on other Ordnance Survey maps of the area, or to help someone else locate you if they do not have a Street Atlas.

The grid squares in this atlas match the Ordnance Survey National Grid and are at 1 kilometre intervals. The small figures at the bottom and sides of every other grid line are the National Grid kilometre values (**00** to **99** km) and are repeated across the country every 100 km (see left).

To give a unique National Grid reference you need to locate where in the country you are. The country is divided into 100 km squares with each square given a unique two-letter reference. Use the administrative map to determine in which 100 km square a particular page of this atlas falls.

The bold letters and numbers between each grid line (**A** to **F**, **1** to **4**) are for use within a specific Street Atlas only, and when used with the page number, are a convenient way of referencing these grid squares.

Example The railway bridge over DARLEY GREEN RD in grid square A1

Step 1: Identify the two-letter reference, in this example the page is in **SP**

Step 2: Identify the 1 km square in which the railway bridge falls. Use the figures in the southwest corner of this square: Eastings **17**, Northings **74**. This gives a unique reference: **SP 17 74**, accurate to 1 km.

Step 3: To give a more precise reference accurate to 100 m you need to estimate how many tenths along and how many tenths up this 1 km square the feature is. This makes the bridge about **8** tenths along and about **1** tenth up from the southwest corner.

This gives a unique reference: **SP 178 741**, accurate to 100 m.

Eastings (read from left to right along the bottom) come before Northings (read from bottom to top). If you have trouble remembering say to yourself "Along the hall, THEN up the stairs"!

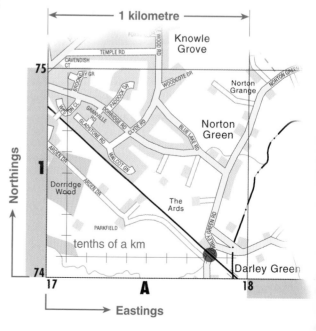

Ordnance Survey

Updated annually

MOTORING ATLAS
Britain

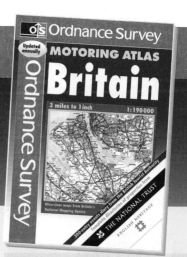

The best-selling *OS Motoring Atlas Britain* uses unrivalled and up-to-date mapping from the Ordnance Survey digital database. The exceptionally clear mapping is at a large scale of 3 miles to 1 inch (Orkney/Shetland Islands at 5 miles to 1 inch).

A special feature of the atlas is its wealth of tourist and leisure information. It contains comprehensive directories, including descriptions and location details, of the properties of the National Trust in England and Wales, the National Trust for Scotland, English Heritage and Historic Scotland. There is also a useful diary of British Tourist Authority Events listing more than 300 days out around Britain during the year.

Available from all good bookshops or direct from the publisher:
Tel: 01933 443863

The atlas includes:

◆ **112 pages of fully updated mapping**
◆ **45 city and town plans**
◆ **8 extra-detailed city approach maps**
◆ **route-planning maps**
◆ **restricted motorway junctions**
◆ **local radio information**
◆ **distances chart**
◆ **county boundaries map**
◆ **multi-language legend**

Street Atlases from Philip's

Philip's publish an extensive range of regional and local street atlases which are ideal for motoring, business and leisure use. They are widely used by the emergency services and local authorities throughout Britain.

Key features include:

◆ Superb county-wide mapping at an extra-large scale of 3½ inches to 1 mile, or 2½ inches to 1 mile in pocket editions

◆ Complete urban and rural coverage, detailing every named street in town and country

◆ Each atlas available in three handy formats – hardback, spiral, pocket paperback

'The mapping is very clear... great in scope and value'
★★★★ **BEST BUY**   **AUTO EXPRESS**

How to order

The Philip's range of street atlases is available from good retailers or directly from the publisher by phoning 01933 443863